Lonely Planet

Cyprus

Kyrenia (Girne) & the North
p160

Famagusta (Mağusa) & the Karpas (Kırpaşa) Peninsula
p179

North Nicosia (Lefkoşa)
p148

Larnaka & the East
p104

Troödos Mountains
p63

Nicosia (Lefkosia)
p126

Pafos & the West
p82

Lemesos & the South
p46

THIS EDITION WRITTEN AND RESEARCHED BY

Josephine Quintero

Jessica Lee

Contents

TURKISH PASTRIES, NORTH
NICOSIA (LEFKOŞA; P148)

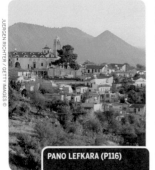

PANO LEFKARA (P116)

NEIL FARRIN / GETTY IMAGES ©

JUERGEN RICHTER / GETTY IMAGES ©

Contents

AGIOS GEORGIOS BEACH,
AKAMAS HEIGHTS (P95)

Welcome to Cyprus

Cyprus is far more than a lazy beach-time resort; the island is multilayered, like its history, with a compelling culture, lifestyle and landscape, overseen by warm, hospitable people.

Crossing the Line

Experiencing Cyprus' intrinsically different Greek and Turkish societies is increasingly easy, with seven access points linking the Greek Cypriot and Turkish Cypriot sides, including two pedestrian crossings in Nicosia (Lefkosia). There is something evocatively appealing about dipping into two very different cultures so effortlessly. Even if you only have time to visit the respective capitals, Nicosia or North Nicosia (Lefkoşa), be sure to cross the line, then complete your experience by sampling the local cuisine, visiting the museums and shopping for that one-off souvenir to impress the folks back home.

The Great Outdoors

The landscape and overall mild climate mean that outside is where it's at – and where you should be. First, there are the beaches, from the wild and windswept to the family friendly and packed. Every conceivable water sport is also on offer, from scuba diving the watery depths to skimming the surface on a kiteboard or windsurfer. And if you tire of all that blue, just head to the interior where pine-clad mountains, sweeping valleys and densely planted vineyards offer hiking, biking, wine tasting tours and, yes, even winter skiing.

A Sense of the Past

The story of Cyprus' tumultuous past is told through historic sites, Roman ruins, multifaceted museums and dusty urban streets. This sense of living history is highlighted most vividly in Pafos, with extraordinary archaeological sites like the Tombs of the Kings, which sprawls like an ancient theme park next to a pack-in-the-punters tourist resort. Digging into the island's past has unearthed fascinating relics, including neolithic dwellings, Bronze Age and Phoenician tombs, and exquisite Roman mosaics, while, on the streets, keep your eyes peeled for Venetian walls, Byzantine castles and churches, Roman monasteries and Islamic mosques.

A Culinary Feast

Meze is a delicious way to acquaint yourself with the local cuisine, tantalising the taste buds with small dishes ranging from creamy hummus to spicy grilled sausage, and everything in between. Heavily influenced by Turkish, Greek and Middle Eastern cuisine, Cypriot food includes some culinary stars unique to the island, including haloumi (helimi in Turkish), and the kebabs are also in a league of their own. The desserts are irresistible, flavoured with almonds, rose water and pistachios and ranging from creamy rice puddings to gloriously sticky baklava.

Why I Love Cyprus

By Josephine Quintero, Author

I have been visiting Cyprus for decades so the most uplifting experience for me, today, is the hassle-free stroll across the border and, more importantly, what it symbolises regarding the peace process. I love the earthy raw energy on both sides of the capital and the traditional character and culture that can seem watered down in the resorts. Visiting the mountain villages is another highlight, as is stumbling across a simple stone-clad Byzantine church with medieval icons and mesmerising friezes. And don't even get me started on the food...!

For more about our authors, see p280

Above: Pafos Castle (Kato Pafos; p87)

Cyprus

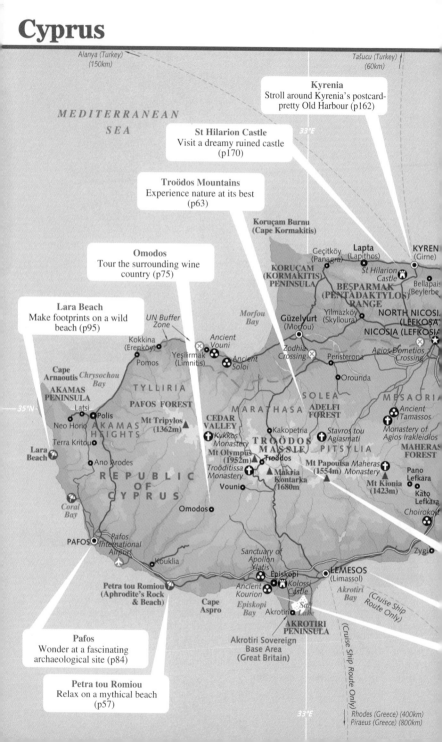

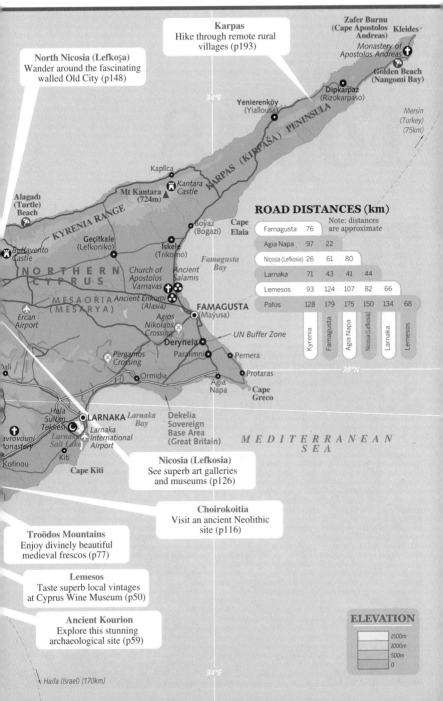

Cyprus'
Top 18

Kyrenia's Old Harbour

1 With the romantic silhouette of the mountains providing the backdrop, the slow pace of modern life in Northern Cyprus doesn't get any more idyllic than sitting by Kyrenia's U-shaped Old Harbour (p163). Its charming elevated buildings and well-kept storehouses once stockpiled tonnes of raw carob, then considered 'black gold' by the locals. Now these edifices house fashionably chic cafes and restaurants, where you can sit for hours with a Cypriot coffee or experience the nargileh (water pipes) as Turkish gulets (traditional wooden ships) bob sporadically, moored around the landing and castle.

Pafos Archaeological Site

2 One of the island's most mesmerising archaeological sites (p84) is located in the southerly resort of Pafos. A vast, sprawling site, the ancient city dates back to the late 4th century BC and what you see now is believed to be only a modest part of what remains to be excavated. Highlights include the intricate and colourful Roman floor mosaics at the heart of the original complex, first unearthed by a farmer ploughing his field in 1962. Pafos has been awarded joint European Capital of Culture in 2017, a well-deserved accolade for this extraordinary Cypriot resort.

NEIL FARRIN / GETTY IMAGES ©

STELLA / GETTY IMAGES ©

Meze

3 Once sampled, never forgotten: meze is a delicious and sociable way to enjoy a wide variety of foods and flavours. In general you should expect around 30 small dishes, starting with familiar favourites such as hummus, tzatziki, taramasalata and vegetables prepared with lashings of garlic, lemon and olive oil. Next to arrive is the wide range of traditional fish and meat dishes, like calamari (squid) and *sheftalia* (grilled sausage). It all adds up to a lot of food, so *siga, siga* (slowly, slowly) does it. A longtime favourite place to sample meze is at Zanettos Taverna (p137) in Nicosia (Lefkosia).

Hiking in the Troödos

4 These mountains (p63) offer an expanse of flora, fauna and geology across a range of pine forests, waterfalls, rocky crags and babbling brooks. The massif and summit of Mt Olympus, at an altitude of 1952m, provide spectacular views of the southern coastline and a welcome respite from the summer heat, with cool, fresh air you can inhale until your airways sing. Ramblers, campers, flower spotters and birdwatchers alike will be absorbed by the ridges, peaks and valleys that make up the lushest and most diverse hiking and nature trails on the island.

North Nicosia's Old City

5 Crossing the Green Line from Nicosia (Lefkosia) into North Nicosia (Lefkoşa; p148), the Turkish north of the city, is an extraordinary experience. Extending from smart Ledra St, old-fashioned shops selling faded jeans and frilly shirts are flanked by kebab kiosks, coffee shops and sweet stalls, counters piled high with fresh halvah. Visit the extraordinary mosque, tranquil hammam and various museums, or just wander the streets, staying until the evening, when the minarets' crescent moons are silhouetted against a backdrop of twinkling stars. Above: Büyük Han (p150)

Wine Villages Around Omodos

6 The far-reaching vineyards of the *kraso-horia* (wine villages; p76) dominate Omodos' surrounding slopes. Navigating this region, where every house was once said to have its own winemaking tools, is an adventure that requires discipline and good use of the spittoon. Boutique wineries now number over 50 here, spread across six or seven traditional villages, with a vast array of wines and grapes for the connoisseur's choice. The most famous indigenous varieties derive from the *mavro* (dark-red grape) and *xynisteri* (white grape) vines, along with another 10 varieties.

Lara Beach

7 Akamas Heights is an area largely unburdened by development, and access to Lara Beach (p95) is via a rough road, backed by desert-like scrubland, tinged with dark ochre and studded with gorse, bushy pines and seasonal wildflowers. This beach is widely considered to be the Republic's most spectacular and, thankfully, remains relatively untouched by tourism. Cupped by limestone rocks, the sand is soft and powdery and the sea is warm and calm. It's a magical place at sunset. Tread carefully though – this is prime turtle-hatching ground.

Luxurious Hammam Baths

8 Hammams can be found around the island and range from the luxurious to standard neighbourhood bathhouses. The Omeriye Hammam (p135) Turkish baths stand in the centre of the Nicosia (Lefkosia) Old City and date from the 16th century, sporting a stylish design: all glossy marble, subtle scents and flickering candles. Omeriye offers a choice of massage, body scrubs and hot-stone treatments and there is a small *teteria* (tea shop) for sipping aromatic teas served in traditional gold rim glasses.

Ancient City of Salamis

9 The once-proud beacon of Hellenic civilisation and culture on the island, Salamis (p188) was the most famous and grandiose of the ancient city kingdoms. Since antiquity, with its succession of kings dedicated to expanding the Athenian empire, the city saw great wealth and suffering like no other. Today you can roam the expansive site taking in the ruins of grand statues, porticoes, gymnasiums, pools, baths, courtyards, the agora (gathering place) and even what is left of the formerly prominent temple of Zeus.

Windsurfing

10 Imagine soaring across the surface of the Mediterranean, part surfing, part sailing, with nothing in front of you but the clear blue sea. The eastern coast of the island, with its numerous soft, sandy beaches, inlets and coves, provides every kind of wind and wave condition a water-sports junkie could want. Once you've conquered wind-god Aeolus' lighter blows, you can upgrade to kitesurfing as well, and see about getting some real air! Good places to take to the waves are at the beaches around Larnaka (p114), including Cape Kiti and Perivolia.

Petra tou Romiou

11 Also known as Aphrodite's Rock and Beach, this is possibly the most famous and mythical beach (p57) in Cyprus and it's certainly one of its most unusual and impressive. It's said that waves break over Aphrodite's Rock to form a pillar of foam with an almost human shape. For the best shot to impress your Facebook friends, head to the strategically positioned tourist pavilion at sunset. During the day, the sea here is delightfully cool and fresh and the beach is perfect for a picnic.

Cyprus Wine Museum

12 Taking a winery tour is becoming an increasingly attractive proposition for tourists here, as Cypriot winemaking continues to improve and expand. A trip to the wine museum (p50) in Lemesos is a good way for novices to be introduced to the history, methods and, most importantly, the taste of leading local wines. The tour includes several options, mainly depending on how much tasting you want to do. There's also a short film that explains how the island's wine trade has developed over time. Cheers!

Neolithic Site of Choirokoitia

13 This Unesco World Heritage Site (p116) is one of the most important and best-preserved prehistoric settlements in the Mediterranean. It dates to around 7000 BC and offers an incredible insight into the lives and living conditions of some of the first Cypriots. Visitors can wander the ruins of the cylindrical flat-roofed huts, which sit on a protected hillside within the boundaries of an ancient wall. Using original methods, archaeologists have also helped construct five replica huts on-site, which further enliven the experience.

Troödos Byzantine Churches

14 The proliferation of well-maintained 8th- to 12th-century churches nestled into the mountainside amaze with their vivid, timeless frescos by skilled painters. Oppression during Lusignan rule led Orthodox Cypriots, clergy and artisans to withdraw to the Troödos ranges, and these churches and chapels (p72) are the result of their dedication. Ten of them appear on the Unesco World Heritage Site List, truly crowning Cyprus as the 'island of the saints'. Above: Fresco in Panagia tou Araka (p80)

GAVIN NEWMAN / ALAMY ©

Diving

15 Presenting perfectly warmed waters with outstanding visibility and a range of marine life, underwater caves, reefs and shoals, the island has picturesque diving habitats covered. Should you tire of this bounty, the island offers multiple shipwrecks for you to explore, thanks to silted ruins, old shallow ports and bad navigating. They're capped off by one of the world's top 10 wreck dives, the *Zenobia* (p37), which foundered off the eastern coast of Larnaka Bay in 1980. Above: the wreck of the *Zenobia*

Pide & Lahmacun

16 In North Cyprus, half the fun of *pide* and *lahmacun* is watching how they're made. The dough bases are kneaded over and over and then topped with cheese and infused with garlic. *Pide* have their edges folded, while *lahmacun,* the flatter version, is usually topped with tender little pieces of beef and seasoned with lemon juice for contrast. The Turkish 'pizza makers' then dexterously slide them into the coal ovens using 1.2m peels. Fifteen minutes later, out they come, piping hot and perfectly browned. Served on wooden tables with white tablecloths, they're a humble, mouthwatering delight.

Ancient Kourion

17 Founded in neolithic times and gloriously perched on a hillside overlooking the sea, Ancient Kourion (p59) flourished under the Mycenaeans, Ptolemies, Romans and, later, the Christians. This is the most spectacular of the South's archaeological sites, including some well-preserved and fascinating mosaics, an early Christian basilica and a breathtaking amphitheatre that still hosts opera under the stars. After exploring the site, consider a dip in the sea at nearby Kourion Beach, where you can also find ruins of a port basilica dating from around the 6th century.

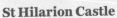

St Hilarion Castle

18 Legend has it that this dreamy fortress (p170) was the inspiration for the spectacularly animated palace of the wicked queen in Walt Disney's *Snow White*. Its ruins now form a jagged outline across the rocky landscape, exuding the Gothic charm of the Lusignan court that once convened here during the summer. The castle's precipitous staircases and overrun gardens and paths form an arduous climb to its tower. From here, though, the spectacular views across the sea to the Anatolian coast only add to its magical quality.

STEVE ALLEN / GETTY IMAGES ©

18

Need to Know

For more information, see Survival Guide (p247)

Currency
Republic of Cyprus:
euro (€)
Northern Cyprus:
Turkish lira (TL)

Language
Republic of Cyprus:
Cypriot Greek, English
Northern Cyprus:
Turkish

Visas
Generally no restrictions
for stays up to three
months in the Republic
and in Northern Cyprus.

Money
ATMs widely available.
Credit cards accepted in
most hotels, restaurants
and larger shops.

Mobile Phones
Pay-as-you-go mobiles
with credit available
from €25. Local SIM
cards are easily found
and can be used in
European and Australian
mobile phones.

Time
Eastern European Time
(GMT/UTC plus two
hours).

When to Go

Karpas (Kırpaşa) Peninsula
GO Mar–Jun

Kyrenia (Girne)
GO Mar–Jun, Sep–Oct

Nicosia (Lefkosia)
GO Mar–Jun, Sep–Nov

Troödos Mountains
GO Apr–Jun, Sep–Oct

Pafos
GO Mar–Jun, Sep–Oct

Dry climate
Warm to hot summers, mild winters

High Season (Jul–Aug, public holidays)

➡ Accommodation books out; prices increase by up to 30%.

➡ Beach resorts are crowded, especially with families.

➡ Marked increase in local tourism.

➡ Temperatures can reach up to 40°C.

Shoulder (Mar–Jun & Sep–Oct)

➡ Ideal time to travel; pleasant weather and fewer crowds.

➡ Perfect for outdoor activities, particularly hiking and cycling in the Troödos.

➡ April and May are a dazzle of wildflowers inland.

Low Season (Nov–Feb)

➡ Skiing in the Troödos.

➡ Can be wet and cool or pleasantly mild.

➡ Some hotels and restaurants in the main resorts are closed.

Useful Websites

Lonely Planet (www.lonely planet.com/cyprus) Destination information, hotel bookings, traveller forum and more.

Cypnet (www.cypnet.com) Information on history, accommodation, restaurants and more.

Cyprus Tourism Organisation (www.visitcyprus.org.cy) Official website of the Republic's CTO; useful for general tourist information.

Go North Cyprus (www.go northcyprus.com) Handy for finding flights, hotels and package holidays online.

Important Numbers

Republic of Cyprus country code	357
Northern Cyprus country code	90 392
International access code	00
Ambulance	199, 112
Police	155

Exchange Rates

Republic of Cyprus

Australia	A$1	€0.66
Canada	C$1	€0.65
Japan	¥100	€0.70
New Zealand	NZ$1	€0.62
UK	£1	€1.21
US	US$1	€0.72

Northern Cyprus

Australia	A$1	TL2.02
Canada	C$1	TL1.98
Japan	¥100	TL2.06
New Zealand	NZ$1	TL1.79
UK	£1	TL3.55
US	US$1	TL2.16

For current exchange rates see www.xe.com.

Daily Costs

Budget:
Less than €60

➡ Budget hotel room with shared bathroom: €25–35

➡ Excellent markets and supermarkets for self-caterers

➡ Check out museums with free entrance, plus free tourist-office-organised walks

Midrange:
€60–120

➡ Double room in midrange hotel: €60

➡ Three-course meal in decent restaurant: €25, plus wine

➡ Top museums, galleries and sights: average €5

Top End:
Over €120

➡ Top-end hotel room: €120

➡ Fine dining for lunch and dinner: €110

➡ Car rental from €3 per day

Opening Hours

These hours are for high season only and tend to decrease outside that time. They apply to both the North and South of the country, unless otherwise specified, and should be used only as a general guide.

Banks The Republic: 8.30am-12.30pm Mon-Fri; some also open 3.15-4.45pm Mon. Northern Cyprus: 8am-noon and 2-5pm Mon-Fri, 8am-noon Sat and Sun

Entertainment 9pm-3am Thu-Sun

Restaurants 11am-2pm and 7.30-11pm daily

Shops 9am-7pm Mon-Fri, closing 2pm Wed, 9am-2pm Sat

Tourist offices 8.30am-2.30pm and 3-6.30pm Mon-Fri, 8.30am-2.30pm Sat and Sun

Arriving in Cyprus

Larnaka airport Up to seven daily buses run from 6.20am to 9pm (5.45pm in winter). Taxis cost €15 to €20 and take around 10 minutes.

Pafos airport Two daily buses run from the airport at 7.30am and 6.30pm. Taxis cost €25 and take around 20 minutes.

Ercan airport Only flights originating in Turkey land here. Regular shuttle buses run between the airport and Kyrenia, North Nicosia (Lefkoşa) and Famagusta.

Getting Around

Cyprus is small enough to get around easily. Roads are good and well signposted, and traffic, overall, moves smoothly. Public transport is limited to buses and service taxis (stretch taxis that run on predetermined routes). There is no train network and no domestic air services in either the North or South.

Driving in Cyprus

First, and most important: drive defensively. Cyprus has one of the highest accident rates in Europe, often due to reckless driving. In the Republic of Cyprus *autopistas* (motorways) connect the airport to major resorts and towns, while secondary roads are normally well surfaced. If you are exploring the more mountainous interior around the Troödos, consider a car of at least 1600cc horsepower for smooth handling of those steep, windy roads; they are generally among the island's most scenic as well. Aside from the coastal resorts and main cities, street parking is usually easy to find. If you're planning to rent a car in high season, book well in advance. And don't forget, you drive on the left in Cyprus.

For much more on **getting around**, see p258

PLAN YOUR TRIP NEED TO KNOW

What's New

Kings Avenue Mall, Pafos

The largest shopping centre in Cyprus opened in November 2013 with close to 200 shops, restaurants and cafes, plus a multiscreen cinema. (p92)

Budget Accommodation, Kyrenia

Kyrenia now offers two dormitory options for budget travellers: both Cyprus Dorms and Nostalgia hotel provide clean dorm accommodation for €12 per night. (p211)

New Marina on the Karpas Peninsula

Yenierenköy's multimillion-dollar Karpaz Gate Marina is now open for yachties who want to berth in the Karpas. (p195)

Coastal Path, Pafos

A pretty, recently completed coastal path extends for some 5km around the headland from Pafos Castle en route to Coral Bay. (p89)

Plateia Eleftherias, Nicosia (Lefkosia)

This famous square flanking Nicosia's historic Venetian walls is planned to encompass walkways and a welcome green space right in the urban centre. (p142)

Craft Beer Brewery, Tsada

Craft beers have finally reached Cyprus with the opening of Aphrodite's Rock Brewery in Tsada (Pafos) in 2013. You can taste samples of all their brews, as well as take a brewery tour. (p89)

AG Leventis Gallery, Nicosia

This important new art museum includes paintings from Old Masters such as Murillo, El Greco and Gainsborough, as well as Impressionist greats like Monet, Renoir and Sisley. There is also a significant collection of works by Greek and Cypriot artists. (p133)

Cyprus Walking Festival

In 2014 the first annual Cyprus Walking Festival ran from March to early April. Organised by the Cyprus Tourism Organisation, guided walks take place in the Pafos, Agia Napa, Nicosia and Troödos areas throughout the month with transportation provided. (p23)

Cyprus Wildlife Ecology

This new tour company run by two eco-biologists specialises in birdwatching trips and other sustainable tourism tours. (p164)

New Capital Cafe Zone, Nicosia

A buzzing cafe scene has evolved across the Plateia Faneromenis in Nicosia's Old City, with numerous cafes and coffee shops sprawled across this lovely square encouraged by purposefully lower rents. (p138)

For more recommendations and reviews, see lonelyplanet.com/cyprus

If You Like...

Archaeology

The wealth of ancient sites in Cyprus makes it one of the most rewarding destinations for archaeology and history enthusiasts.

Ancient Salamis The island's most famous site, with impressive Roman monuments including a stunning ancient theatre. (p188)

Pafos Archaeological Site These remains of an ancient 4th-century-BC city are mesmerising. (p84)

Tombs of the Kings Explore these evocative and well-preserved underground tombs and chambers. (p84)

Ancient Kourion Kourion's magnificent neolithic amphitheatre still hosts concerts under the stars. (p59)

Hrysopolitissa Basilica & St Paul's Pillar A large and fascinating site that encompasses foundations of a 4th-century basilica and more. (p86)

Beaches

Deciding on a beach depends on how you want your sand-between-the-toes day out...

Lara Beach The Republic's most spectacular beach, cupped by limestone rocks, with golden, powdery and pristine sand. (p95)

Petra tou Romiou Also known as Aphrodite's Rock & Beach, this is Cyprus' most famous stretch of sand. (p57)

Golden Beach (Nangomi Bay) The longest beach on the island with miles of sand, curving dunes and feral donkeys grazing. (p193)

Fig Tree Bay Located in Protaras, this beach is great for swimming and snorkelling, plus it has excellent facilities for families. (p125)

Arts & Crafts

Traditional craftwork thrives here. Look for superb embroidery, carved backgammon sets and intricate basketry.

Cyprus Handicrafts Centre A reliable one-stop souvenir-shopping choice in Nicosia (Lefkosia). (p142)

Chrysaliniotissa Crafts Centre Several art and crafts studios surround a central courtyard here. (p133)

Büyük Han Shop in a traditional Ottoman-style inn with enticing craft workshops in North Nicosia (Lefkoşa). (p150)

Lefkara Full of dinky shops where you can browse for lace and local foodie treats. (p116)

Wine

The island's winemaking tradition goes back to antiquity.

Republic wine routes Pick up the local Republic of Cyprus tourist information booklet outlining six wine routes.

Lemesos Wine Festival This annual festival provides a suitably merry atmosphere for tasting the local tipple. (p51)

Around Omodos Explore the wine villages that surround Omodos on the southwest flank of the Troödos Mountains. (p76)

Cyprus Wine Museum The place to come if you fancy tasting (and learning about) the local tipple. (p50)

Being Pampered

And who doesn't want to be? Having your partner rub suncream on your back is a start but not quite in the same indulgence league as a having a chocolate massage in candlelight.

Ayii Anargyri Natural Healing Spa Resort This gorgeous spa hotel has fabulous facilities and treatments, and offers various spa packages for non-guests. (p206)

Büyük Hammam This traditional Turkish bath in North Nicosia offers a choice of luxurious treatments and massages. (p155)

Aphrodite Boat Charters & Fishing Offers leisure cruises for up to 12 people taking in idyllic isolated bays along the stunning Kyrienia coastline. (p165)

Cyprus Yacht Charters Contact these pros if you want to seriously splash out on a private yacht with captain and crew.

Annabelle Super-luxurious accommodation in Pafos; some rooms have private plunge pools. Or come here for the classic English tea. (p205)

Tantalising the Taste Buds

Cyprus is home to some delicious dishes that reflect Greek, Turkish and Middle Eastern influences. (p32)

Fruit juices Don't pass up an opportunity to try a freshly squeezed fruit juice at a juice bar.

Full kebabs Set the benchmark with this speciality of the North.

Pizza The Cypriot version is *pide*, topped with spicy meat or fish with melted cheese. Delicious!

Seafood meze A delicious way to taste tantalising morsels of everything from red mullet to prawns and octopus.

Haloumi (in Greek; helimi in Turkish) Made from goat or ewe's milk and delicious when fried and grilled. Make room in your hand luggage!

Loukoumi Known as Turkish delight in the West; try it with pistachios and almonds.

Top: Street dining
Bottom: Traditional loom weaving

Month by Month

January

Weather-wise January is generally mild, but the Troödos Mountains can be snow-capped so remember to pack your skis. Tourism is down and some resort-based restaurants and hotels are closed.

✈️ Agia Napa Cultural Winter

Enjoy free concerts, recitals and dance performances every Thursday at 8pm at the Agia Napa Municipal Conference Hall (www.agianapa.org.cy).

February

The weather is mild, so good for cycling and hiking the trails (although it can be wet). It's also fiesta time with the high-octane annual carnival.

✈️ Lemesos Carnival

Fancy-dress parades, festive floats and carafe loads of partying on the streets; the Lemesos Carnival (www.limassolmunicipal.com.cy/carnival) is a fabulous family-geared celebration.

✈️ Children's Carnival Parade

Held three days after the start of the Lemesos Carnival, the little ones have their chance to get into fancy dress and parade along the Lemesos seafront.

✈️ Green Monday

The first day of Lent is marked throughout the South by Greek Cypriots taking the day off and flocking to the countryside for a meat-free picnic, an unusual feast for an island of carnivores.

March

Enjoy wildflowers, particularly orchids, with more than 32 endemic varieties. Birdwatching, hiking and the occasional sunbed on the sand make this a good month for a springtime break.

✈️ Nicosia International Documentary Film Festival

View the cherry-picked international documentaries at this excellent festival (www.filmfestival.com.cy), which is great for getting a perspective on Cypriot issues.

🏃 Cyprus Walking Festival

Geared towards all levels of fitness with specially created trails, complete with signposting, the Cyprus Walking Festival (www.visitcyprus.com) kicked off in 2014 and offers a variety of walking tours in the Akamas, Famagusta and Troödos regions. Transport is provided free of charge.

April

The temperature can be perfect but expect crowds and a hike in flight and accommodation prices; it's school-holiday time during the Easter break.

✈️ Easter Parades

Chocolate eggs take a back basket here during

Easter week, when there are solemn parades with religious floats adorned with elaborate floral decorations, culminating in a spectacular firework show. This is the most important religious festival for Greek Cypriots.

May

A great month to visit with plenty of towel space on the sand, an average temperature of 26°C and warmer evenings for dining alfresco.

☆ Bellapais Music Festival

Centred on Bellapais Abbey, the Bellapais Music Festival (www.bellapaisfestival.com) starts waving the baton on 21 May with concerts and recitals.

June

The weather is a delight with an average of 11 hours of sunshine daily. Book accommodation well ahead: it's the start of the serious summer hols.

🏃 Classic Cars

Grab the tweed cap and don the shades – in early June the Aphrodite Classic Car Rally (www.fipa-cyprus.org.cy) takes place,

covering 300km across the island.

🎊 Kataklysmos Festival

Particularly appropriate for this sunny time of year, *kataklysmos* (meaning 'deluge' in Greek) is a traditional celebration of Noah and his escape from the flood. Rather the opposite takes place, however, with good-humoured water fights and water-based activities in Larnaka.

🎊 Güzelyurt Orange Festival

Running since 1977, this festival, which takes place at the end of the month, brims with local food, drinks, song and dance, as well as various tournaments for junior Güzelyurtians. This is one of the richest agricultural areas in North Cyprus.

July

The mercury is rising but the average temperature in the southern resorts is still a tolerable 32°C. This is the best month for music lovers, with several world-class festivals.

🎊 International Famagusta Art & Culture Festival

The North's biggest festival is the International

Famagusta Art & Culture Festival (www.magusa.org/festival) with music, theatre and arts in Famagusta's Othello's Tower and town square, and at Ancient Salamis during the last week of the month.

August

This is the month you use your umbrella – for shade: the sun is at its hottest, though it still rarely sizzles above 35°C. This is the peak of the tourist season; expect crowded beaches and higher prices.

🎊 Village Festivals

August is a popular month for village festivals. Keep an eye out for posters and ask at the local tourist offices. These annual fiestas have a real carnival atmosphere with live music, traditional dance and plenty of food and drink.

🎊 Mehmetcik Grape Festival

Wine and food feasting in this small village on the Karpas (Kırpaşa) Peninsula. Join in the King and Queen of Grape contest and have a whirl at the folk dancing.

🎊 Lemesos Documentary Festival

The Lemesos Documentary Festival (www.filmfestival.com.cy) is a great little festival for film lovers, with the latest documentaries and a chance at a masterclass with a guest director.

RAMADAN

The most important Muslim celebration of the year sees some locals in the North fasting. Eid, the last day of Ramadan, is a time for food and festivities. Ramadan dates vary each year, depending on the Islamic calendar.

September

This is still a hot and hectic month. Escape the clamour of the coastal resorts by heading inland to the Troödos Mountains for wine tasting, picnicking or gentle autumnal strolls.

🍷 Lemesos Wine Festival

Locals and tourists alike celebrate the Lemesos Wine Festival (www.limassolmu nicipal.com.cy/wine) in the Municipal Gardens with plenty of sniffing, swirling, spitting – and tasting.

🎭 Pafos Aphrodite Festival

Opera performances are staged under the stars at Pafos Castle during the Pafos Aphrodite Festival (www.pafc.com.cy).

October

Enjoy autumn golds and reds in the leafy Troödos

with temperatures hovering around 27°C – perfect for striding out...

🎭 Kyrenia Olive Festival

Held in Kyrenia and nearby Zeytinlik, this festival has folkloric dancing, shadow theatre and other eclectic performances. You can taste olives and even help plant the trees.

🎭 Lefkosia Film Festival

Can't make Cannes? Then check out the Lefkosia Film Festival (http://cyiff.cine artfestival.eu) at the end of the month with its free screenings from international directors.

November

Expect a mix of weather, including clear summer days. It's a quiet month for annual festivities and many hotels and restaurants pull down their shutters for the winter break.

🏃 Cyprus International 4-Day Challenge

The annual Cyprus Inter-national 4-Day Challenge (www.cypruschallenge. com) has four running rac-es, ranging from novice to marathon level, with routes set around the stunning Akamas Peninsula.

December

A month for family reunions, with Cypriots returning home to celebrate the festive season. The weather is changeable but, overall, mild with the occasional beach day – though the sea is very cold!

🎭 New Year's Eve

Fireworks and music into the night around Plateia Eleftherias in Nicosia (Lefkosia) and in other towns around the island.

Plan Your Trip
Itineraries

MEDITERRANEAN SEA

Morfou Bay

Nicosia (Lefkosia)

Famagusta Bay

Akamas Peninsula

Lara Beach

CYPRUS

Troödos Mountains

Larnaka

Coral Bay

Pafos

Lemesos

Choirokoitia

Petra tou Romiou

Ancient Kourion

Akrotiri Bay

2 WEEKS Top Spots in the Republic of Cyprus

This itinerary takes in the highlights of the Republic with a range that encompasses beaches, shopping, archaeological sites, forested mountains and the urban chic of the big city.

Fly into **Larnaka** and dip your feet into the Mediterranean at the local beaches before exploring the town, visiting the superb Pierides Archaeological Foundation, checking out the crafts sold from workshops in the former Turkish quarter, and enjoying a fine seafood meze at a beachside restau-rant. Day three, head for **Nicosia (Lefkosia)**, to spend a couple of days getting to know the historical centre with its museums, shops and traditional restaurants. Don't miss the city's latest art gallery, the fine AG Leventis, just outside the Venetian walls, and be sure to kick back with a frothy frappé at one of the cool new coffee shops on the Plateia Faneromenis, off Ledra St. If you want a further break from pounding the streets, consider a soothing massage at the hammam (Turkish baths). On day five, head to the hills and the shady green mountainous **Troödos** to trek, cycle, stroll, explore the tavernas or admire the

Tombs of the Kings (p84), Pafos

exquisite Byzantine churches with their vividly colourful friezes and icons.

Stop off at neolithic **Choirokoitia** as you roll down to **Lemesos**. Spend a couple of nights enjoying the varied sights and superb restaurants of the island's second city and consider taking a walking tour, organised by the tourist office, to acquaint yourself with the historic centre and main sights. Next day, visit nearby **Ancient Kourion**, a spectacular archaeological site perched on a hillside with sweeping sea views. Then head for the surf yourself and take a dip at the mythical **Petra tou Romiou** (Aphrodite's Rock & Beach).

On day 11, head to **Pafos**, with its mosaics, mysterious Tombs of the Kings and plentiful shops, restaurants and bars. Stay overnight and enjoy a long cool cocktail sitting at a beachfront bar enjoying the people-watching, the sunset and the unabashed summer-in-the-sun atmosphere of this popular holiday resort. The next day, escape the coastal crowds and base yourself in traditional agrotourism accommodation on the **Akamas Peninsula**, near some of the loveliest stretches of sand in the South, such as **Lara Beach**. Fly home from Larnaka or Pafos.

From Karpas to Akamas: Spanning the Peninsulas

10 DAYS

This itinerary travels from Cyprus' north to the south and includes an evocative journey to both peninsulas, home to some of the best beaches on the island (as well as those famous turtles).

From Larnaka airport head for the **Karpas (Kırpaşa) Peninsula**, a place that will linger in your memory for years to come. This 'tail end' of the island has stunning beaches, deserted and clean, with soft, golden sand. Turtles hatch at **Golden Beach (Nangomi Bay)**, where there's an official turtle-hatching program, and wild donkeys roam the endless fields. Spend at least two days here, including visiting the eco village at **Büyükkonuk** and climbing **Kantara Castle**.

Head back to the South via **Ancient Salamis**, the North's most impressive archaeological site. Dip into the sea at the adjacent beach before lunching at one of nearby **Famagusta's** atmospheric restaurants in the heart of the walled city. Move on and stay overnight in **Larnaka** to absorb its workaday bustle and fill your hand luggage with crafts bought direct from the workshops in the atmospheric former Turkish district. Spend the next day exploring the city, not forgetting the fascinating salt lake, a magnet for migrant birds, including flamingos. The next day, hightail it to **Lemesos** with its stylish and compact old town that's home to some of the most sophisticated dining choices on the island. Stay overnight and make an early start to the **Troödos Mountains** to work off all those calories with some scenic striding out. After a night or two in bucolic surroundings, continue on the nature trail to **Cedar Valley**, taking a soul-searching culture break at the **Kykkos Monastery** en route.

Stop at pretty **Fyti** for a meal at the central taverna; pick up some souvenir stitchery and stay at one of the nearby agrotourism accommodation options, surrounded by greenery and birdsong. Continue by stopping at traditional villages, like Simou, Drouseia and **Ineia**, from where you can drive westwards to **Lara Beach**, the South's best beach and, like the Karpas beaches, a turtle-hatching zone. You are now on the **Akamas Peninsula**, ideal for trekking and exploring the region's rural life, as well as swimming at some wonderfully wild and windswept beaches.

Top: Troödos Mountains (p63)
Bottom: Townhouse in Lemesos (Limassol; p48)

Essential Northern Cyprus

1 WEEK

Discover the highlights of Northern Cyprus with this tightly packed journey that encompasses picturesque harbours, wild countryside and scenic beaches, as well as extraordinary buildings, monuments and ruins, and an earthy and compelling urban scene.

Fly into Ercan and make your first stop **Kyrenia**; this is the Mediterranean as it used to be – a picturesque stone harbour, ending at a looming Byzantine castle. Splash out and stay at a waterfront hotel for two (or even three) nights. Before moving on, consider getting up close and personal with the natural beauty of the region by hiking part of the spectacular Kyrenia Mountain Trail. Alternatively, if you feel like something a mite more leisurely, consider taking a cruise on a Turkish gulet (traditional wooden ship) or just flopping on one of the unspoiled sandy beaches surrounding the town. For the best overview of your environs, head for **Bellapais (Beylerbeyi)**, home to a lovely Augustinian monastery with endless views of the surrounding mountains. Stay overnight, then backtrack to Kyrenia, via the fairytale **St Hilarion Castle**, not forgetting to climb the tower from where, on a clear day, you can spy the Taurus Mountains, 100km away in Turkey. Back on earth, set forth towards the northwest coast, stopping at pretty **Lapta (Lapithos)**, with its green leafy lanes and traditional charm. Stop at windswept **Horse Shoe Beach** for some superb fresh seafood at the beachside restaurant. History buffs can make a detour southwest to visit the fascinating ancient city kingdoms of Ancient Vouni and Ancient Soloi; otherwise, hit the road to **North Nicosia (Lefkoşa)**. Take in highlights like the Büyük Han and Selimiye Mosque then, time permitting, enjoy a rejuvenating massage at the Büyük Hammam and a leisurely lunch at one of the excellent restaurants (or a quick bite at an irresistible kebab stand). Continue to evocative **Famagusta** with its Venetian walls, looming and ruined Gothic buildings and Cyprus' best-preserved Lusignan monument, the magnificent Lala Mustafa Paşa mosque. From here take a drive to the most beautiful part of the island, the **Karpas (Kırpaşa) Peninsula**. Enjoy the beaches and stay in one of the rustically charming rural hotels on the peninsula before returning to Ercan, via Ancient Salamis, for your flight home.

Top: Bellapais Abbey (p171)
Bottom: Kyrenia Harbour (p163)

LATITUDESTOCK - TTL / GETTY IMAGES ©

DOUG PEARSON / GETTY IMAGES ©

PLAN YOUR TRIP ITINERARIES

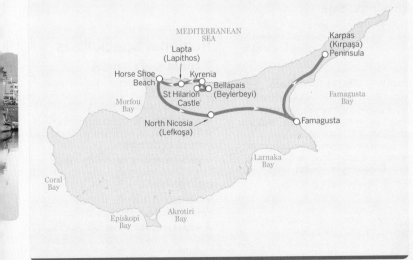

Plan Your Trip
Eat & Drink Like a Local

One of the best things about Cyprus is its varied and flavoursome cuisine. Cypriots love their food and take it very seriously. Celebrations and family get-togethers are rarely without an army of little plates crowding the long tables: the ubiquitous and irresistible meze.

The Year in Food

Spring (Feb-Apr)

A good season for warming *kleftiko* (oven-baked lamb), while mid-spring sees the emergence of wild fennel and asparagus, as well as *koupepia* (meat and fish wrapped in young vine leaves). During Lent, traditional fare includes *spanakopita* (spinach and egg wrapped in filo pastry); the main dish at Easter is *souvla* (barbecued meat), along with *flaounes* (savoury cakes) made with cheese, eggs, spices and herbs.

Summer (Jul-Sep)

Figs, mangoes, peaches, pears, plums: there's plenty of fresh fruit around, and in September, the Lemesos Wine Festival is an appropriate toast to autumn.

Autumn & Winter (Oct-Dec)

Kick-start this serious foodie season with the Kyrenia Olive Festival, then look for freshly harvested wild mushrooms, artichokes and winter greens. Closer to Christmas bakeries overflow with *kourabies* and *melomakarona* (almond and honey cakes), while on Christmas day, families traditionally make and smoke their own *loukanika* (sausages made from lamb and pork).

Where to Go

While there's not much difference between the regions *within* the Republic and Northern Cyprus, the overall Turkish and Greek influences of the North and South mean plenty of variety.

If you are seeking traditional cuisine anywhere in the country, ensure that a healthy percentage of the restaurant's customers are locals. For the best seafood and fish, head for the Akamas Peninsula.

Regional Specialities
Republic of Cyprus

Look for the following traditional dishes on the menu. Some of these may also be included in your meze line-up.

➡ **dolmades** stuffed vine leaves (other similarly stuffed veg, including tomatoes, aubergines and marrows, are also popular)

➡ **guvech** a combination of meat (traditionally beef or lamb), courgettes, aubergines, potatoes, garlic and onions

➡ **koupepia** meat and rice wrapped in young vine leaves and baked in a tomato sauce

➡ **louvia me lahana** greens cooked with black-eyed beans and served with olive oil and fresh lemon juice

⇒ **melintzanes yiahni** a tasty bake of aubergines, garlic and fresh tomatoes

⇒ **mucendra** a side dish that combines lentils with fried onions and rice

⇒ **ofto** a simple meat and vegetable roast

⇒ **pilaf** cracked wheat steamed with fried onions and chicken stock and served with plain yoghurt; generally accompanied by meat and vegetables

⇒ **souvla** large chunks of meat (usually lamb) cooked on skewers over a charcoal barbecue

⇒ **spanakopita** a combination of spinach, feta and eggs, wrapped in paper-thin filo pastry

⇒ **stifado** a rich stew made with beef or rabbit and onions, simmered in vinegar and wine

⇒ **tava** a lamb and beef casserole with tomatoes, onions, potatoes and cumin cooked in an earthenware pot

⇒ **trahana** a mixture of cracked wheat and yoghurt; traditionally eaten for breakfast.

⇒ **yemista** courgettes stuffed with rice and meat

Northern Cyprus

In the more touristy resorts like Kyrenia, be discerning with your restaurant choice; if you're opting for seafood, watch the cost: menus in the resorts frequently quote the price in grams.

⇒ **adana kebab** a kebab laced with spicy red pepper

⇒ **adana köfte** spicy, grilled veal or lamb patties with parsley, cumin, coriander and onions

VEGANS &VEGETARIANS

Vegetarianism is slowly gaining attention in Cyprus, particularly in Nicosia (Lefkosia) with its more cosmopolitan populace. Many tavernas will also have an option for a vegetarian meze and, even if they don't, a traditional meze typically includes both vegetarian and vegan options. Throughout the island, Middle Eastern mainstays like hummus, falafel and tabouleh are readily available. Most towns also have excellent produce markets where you can stock up on local fruit and vegies and health food stores are becoming increasingly common, particularly in the Republic.

⇒ **dolmades** the Turkish variety is meatless, stuffed with rice, currants and pine nuts

⇒ **kebab** meat (usually lamb, although there are also chicken and fish variations) wrapped in flat bread with salad; often accompanied by *ayran*, a cool, salty, refreshing yoghurt drink

⇒ **lahmacun** a kind of pizza equivalent, with a crispy, thin base topped with fragrant minced lamb and fresh parsley

⇒ **patlıcan** a meatball and aubergine kebab

⇒ **pide** a dough base topped with aromatic meat or fish and cheese and baked in a wood-fired oven

⇒ **şiş köfte** barbecued meat on a flat skewer

⇒ **urfa kebab** a kebab with plenty of onions and black pepper

Like a Local
When to Eat

Cypriots generally eat three meals daily; dinner is the main meal.

Breakfast Eaten around 8am; normally a combination of olives, grilled or fresh haloumi (in Greek; helimi in Turkish), bread and tomatoes and, of course, coffee. It's a wonderful combination to start your day.

Lunch Usually eaten at around 2pm or 3pm; meals don't usually last for more than an hour or so. Sunday lunch is the exception: on both sides of the island, this is when you will find entire families gathering, either at home or in restaurants, and staying for a good three to four hours, eating, drinking and chatting.

Dinner Generally eaten late, from around 9pm, which is when restaurants start to seriously fill up. This is the meal where the meze is typically served. Always shared between at least two – it's usually more like 10 – and dishes are passed around vociferously, so don't be shy to ask if you're dining with Cypriots and want to try something from the other end of the table.

Where to Eat

The taverna is where Greek Cypriots go to eat whenever they don't eat at home, and there is one in every Cypriot town and village. A taverna can be a no-frills village eatery, or a more upmarket restaurant with a leaning towards the traditional. The *psistaria* specialises in souvlaki, while the *psarotaverna* mainly serves fish.

SWEET DELIGHTS

Cypriot desserts reflect the rich flavours of Turkey and the Middle East. But despite these sweet delights, fruit is the most common Cypriot dessert on both parts of the island.

➡ **baklava** filo pastry layered with honey and nuts

➡ **galatopoureko** sweet, sticky pastry filled with custard

➡ **irmik kurabiyesi** nut-stuffed semolina pastries

➡ **kandaifi** (in Greek; *kadaif* in Turkish) strands of sugary pastry wound into a roll

➡ **katméri** a kind of crêpe filled with bananas, honey and cream

➡ **lokma** doughnuts in syrup

➡ **mahalepi** (in Greek; *muhallebi* in Turkish): an aromatic Middle Eastern rice pudding sprinkled with rosewater and pistachios

➡ **shammali** yoghurt and semolina cake

➡ **tahinli** tahina buns

The *kafeneio* is central to any self-respecting Greek Cypriot village's existence. Traditionally, *kafeneia* serve coffee and snacks of haloumi, tomatoes and olives, and are frequented only by (older) men.

Meyhanes are Turkish taverns where you can enjoy meze, meat, fish and anything else, swilled down with plenty of *raki*. In the North, a *lokanta* is an informal restaurant and a *restoran* is a more upmarket version. *Hazir yemek* ('ready food') restaurants specialise in dishes that are best eaten earlier in the day when they're fresh. You'll see signs for *kebapçi* (kebab shops) and *oakbaş* (fireside kebab shops) where you can watch your kebab being prepared.

Don't miss the *pastanes* (patisseries) selling sugary treats, such as *kiru* (biscuits), cakes and sweet, sweet baklava. Be aware of the difference between *pasta* (pastry) and *makarna* (noodles).

Cheap Treats

Traditional fast food on both sides of the island is the kebab or souvlaki, which is justifiably popular with locals. The meat is barbecued, stuffed into a pitta or rolled in a flat bread and accompanied by a large salad, dressed with lemon juice.

International Cuisine

Plenty of restaurants specialise in international dishes. Aside from the standard gut-busting Brit-style breakfast (supposedly good for hangovers), they can be good options for simple snacks like filled baked potatoes and toasted sandwiches.

Drinking

Don't miss out on the fabulous juice bars. Mango, papaya, strawberry, guava: endless combinations are whizzed up on the spot and packed full of all those five-a-day fresh-fruit essentials, at a very reasonable price.

If you are after something stronger, locals drink at bars and generally accompany their meal with locally produced wine. Cyprus produces a wide range of red, white and rosé wines, as well as a famous sweet dessert wine, *Commandaria*. Spirits are also popular, particularly the famous anise-laced ouzo and the stronger grape-based zivania.

The most popular cocktail here is Cypriot brandy sour, often cited as the national drink and with a somewhat bizarre history. Apparently the young (and Muslim) King Farouk of Egypt, who frequented the Forest Park Hotel in Platres, used to drink this as it resembled iced tea; the mix is slightly different from the brandy sour norm.

Beer drinkers normally go for the inexpensive local brew Keo, although imported beers are also available, as well as the Yorkshire-style bitters produced by the island's craft brewery, Aphrodite's Rock Brewery (p89).

Tap water is safe to drink and can be requested at any restaurant without raising an eyebrow. Locals, however, prefer the bottled variety as the water is very hard, which some people believe can lead to kidney stones if drunk to excess. It is advisable to drink bottled water in North Nicosia (Lefkoşa).

The Meze

Prepare yourself for a (pleasant) assault, a sampling of and gorging on around 30 dishes. The small plates may look unthreatening, but they keep on coming, promising a night of indigestion laced with wonderful taste-bud-tantalising memories.

The word meze is short for *mezedes* or 'little delicacies', and is used by both the Greeks and the Turks. Meze is almost never served for one: two is the minimum, and three's never a crowd but the beginning of a beautiful feast. Try to dine in a larger group, since sharing meze is as integral to the experience of eating as the variety of the dishes themselves. All the passing this and passing that and shouting across the table for more tahini or bread is a true bonding experience that Cypriots share many nights a week.

First on the table are shiny olives, a salad and fresh bread, along with tahina, taramasalata, *talatouri* (tzatziki) and hummus for dipping. Pace yourself, go easy on the bread, suck on an olive or two, and crunch on a salad leaf.

Next are the vegetables. Some are garnished with lemon, some are raw and a few are pickled or brought with haloumi. Sausages and Cyprus' own *lountza* (smoked loin of pork) follow. Again, eat the vegies, sample a coin of sausage and a strip of cheese, but remember, a bite of each will suffice because the biggies are still to come.

The next course is the meat (vegetarians may be able to order vegetarian meze). A meat meze is a parade of lamb, chicken, beef, pork, souvlaki, *kleftiko*, *sheftalia* (spiced, grilled sausage), meatballs and smoked meat. If you're having fish meze, then expect everything from sea bass to red mullet, prawns, octopus and, of course, calamari (squid).

Finally the waiter will bring fresh fruit and pastries. You will doubtless be on your last belt notch by now but, if possible, try some prickly pears – they're a real delicacy.

The best advice is to be sure not to have any lunch before you go for a meze dinner. Pace yourself and eat slowly and, as with every good meal, a nice wine is recommended, so choose yourself a bottle and *kali orexi – bon appétit!*

Dare to Try

If you want to play it safe with familiar ingredients, you can in Cyprus. But if you fancy being just a tad bolder, there's plenty to consider. You could also try Greek or Turkish coffee served *sketos* (in Greek) or *şekersiz* (in Turkish), which is without sugar, so very bitter and strong.

➡ **amelitita hirina vrasta** (boiled pork testicles) Cooked with onions and celery and served with a dressing of garlic, cloves, thyme, olive oil and lemon juice.

➡ **karalous keftedes** (fried snail balls) Minced and boiled with chopped onions, potatoes and eggs, then coated in flour and deep-fried.

➡ **karaolous me pnigouri** (snails with bulgur wheat) Boiled snails are fried with chopped onions and tomatoes and served on a bed of bulgur wheat.

➡ **kokorets** (offal wrapped in intestines grilled over charcoal) Lamb liver, lungs, heart, spleen, glands – you get the picture – chopped into medium-size pieces, wrapped in intestines and grilled over charcoal for approximately 1½ hours.

➡ **mialle arnisha vrasta** (boiled lambs' brains) Halved and served with olive oil, chopped parsley, lemon juice and salt.

➡ **zalatina** (jellied pork) Ingredients include one small pig's head, two pig's trotters, eight oranges and a few red-hot peppers.

MEALS OF A LIFETIME

Mattheos (p136; Nicosia) Where the locals come for delicious homestyle Cypriot food, with a gutsy *kleftiko* (oven-baked lamb), *stifado* (beef or rabbit stew) and similar.

Argo (p90; Pafos) This place has all the charm of a village taverna with mouth-watering specialities such as moussaka and *kleftiko*.

İkimiz (p165; Kyrenia) At this atmospheric spot, enjoy hearty and traditional Turkish Cypriot food, including *kleftiko* kebabs made in a traditional clay oven.

Stou Kir Yianni (p75; Omodos, Troödos Mountains) Tucked in the backstreets, this place serves superb Middle Eastern favourites like *fatoush*, plus moussaka, *kleftiko*... and snails.

Voreas (p110; Oroklini, Larnaka) Located in a hilltop village, this restaurant is famed for its fabulous meze.

Plan Your Trip
Life Outdoors

Small it may be but Cyprus punches above its weight in terms of outdoor pursuits. Whether it's sun, sand and sea on the coastline that tempts you or the rugged mountain terrain inland, this island has activities that suit every age and energy level.

Best Outdoors

Best Wreck Dive
Zenobia, 17m to 43m below sea level; *Vera K*, 10m below sea level; Helicopter Wreck, 16m below sea level; *M/Y Diana*, 21m below sea level

Best Wind- & Kitesurfing Spots
Pissouri Bay, Lemesos; Protaras, Agia Napa district; Makenzy Beach (including Cape Kiti), Larnaka

Best Hiking Zones
Aphrodite Trail and Adonis Trail, Akamas Peninsula; Kyrenia Mountain Trail, Kyrenia; Mt Olympus, Platres and the Troödos Mountains; Stavros tis Psokas forest reserve trails, Tylliria

Best Riding
Kiniras Horse Riding Centre, Pafos (www.horse ridingpaphos.com); Moonshine Ranch, Agia Napa

Best Cycling
Troödos cycling route; Cape Greco national park, Agia Napa; Lemesos to Pano Platres cycling route, Lemesos

Beaches

The azure blue waters of the Mediterranean are Cyprus' biggest drawcard and it's not difficult to see why. From May to late October sea temperatures rarely dip below 20°C, while during the peak summer months of July and August, water temperatures average between 24°C and 27°C, making Cyprus the perfect place to plunge right in.

In the South most beaches are well equipped with all the facilities you'd need for a day on the sand. Even quieter, less-developed beaches will have at least one or two tavernas on hand for supplies and sun-lounger and sunshade hire. From April to October the popular beaches all have lifeguards on patrol. South Cyprus has 57 beaches that have been awarded Blue Flag status and 11 beaches that are fully accessible for wheelchairs right down to the waterfront; visit www.blueflag.org for more information.

Some of the safest swimming on the island is in the calm sheltered waters of Coral Bay (Pafos) and Fig Tree Bay (Protaras). Konnos Bay on Cape Greco (Agia Napa) is also an excellent strip of sand for those more interested in swimming than sunning themselves.

Although the beaches of the North have lagged behind on the development front, they are fast catching up. North Cyprus' beaches are divided into public and private. The private beaches have an entrance fee (though between October and May they are usually free) and, unsurprisingly, have the most facilities on offer. Even the public beaches usually have toilets, though, and a restaurant or two that will rent sunshades and sun loungers.

Diving

Cyprus draws flocks of tourists to dive its pristine waters, which offer ancient remains, reefs, sea shelves and shipwrecks. Some of the best diving can be found along the Cape Greco Peninsula and Protaras bay.

Diving centres hiring full equipment and offering certified instruction are in Larnaka, Agia Napa, Protaras, Lemesos, Pafos, Coral Bay, Latsi, Kyrenia and Yenierenkoy. And check out www.oceanssearch.com to stay up to date with Cyprus' diving community.

Shipwrecks

Situated off the coast of Larnaka, where it sank in 1980, the *Zenobia* is rated as one of the world's top 10 diving wrecks. The 200m-long Swedish cargo ship is now home to giant tuna, barracuda, amberjack and eel.

The *Vera K* is a fascinating wreck located 5km from Pafos harbour. This Turkish cargo vessel sank in the 1970s and has since been used as a romantic background for underwater photography; its submerged arches are particularly special. It's also an ideal dive for beginners.

Officially called the Helicopter Wreck, this former British Army Air Corps helicopter is located 15 minutes by boat off Larnaka's shore. With excellent visibility to 25m, it attracts many divers and is a magnet for sea creatures such as octopus, jack and groper.

M/Y Diana, near Lemesos port, is a 15m Russian yacht that foundered in 1996. Now sitting upright on the seabed, it's frequently used for diver training and night dives. Its large squid and many fish make it popular with underwater photographers.

Sea Caves & Culture

Beautiful underwater caves such as the Big Country (23m below sea level), a multilevel cave site near Lemesos, and the Akrotiri Fish Reserve (9m below sea level) are ideal

SNORKELLING

Some of the best snorkelling areas are situated in the sheltered coves of eastern Cyprus, especially around Protaras. Waters here are warm and shallow with excellent reefs and plenty of active marine life. You can also see a variety of shells, sea urchins and hermit crabs. Snorkelling equipment like masks and flippers can all be purchased easily and cheaply or hired across the island.

dive sites for the inexperienced but enthusiastic. You can expect to see groper and sea bass among shoals of fish.

For marine life, North Cyprus' huge Zephyros reef, with its 18m to 28m drop off is an exciting dive while the Antique Shop site (25m below sea level) mixes archaeology with spotting shoals of soldier fish.

Serious divers should head to Mushroom Rocks (50m below sea level) near Larnaka; it offers mass fish sightings and canyons sprouting from the sea floor. Many of the rock formations are mushroom-shaped, hence the name.

Ancient history underwater is best found at the Amphorae Reef in Pafos (5m to 10m below sea level). An abundance of pottery and amphorae sit hauntingly on the sea bed, shadowed by a wreck beached on the reef.

Wind-, Kite- & Stand-Up Paddle Surfing

Thanks to the island's steady winds and mild weather, various forms of sea surfing (windsurfing, kitesurfing and stand-up paddle surfing) have become some of the most popular and widespread of all water sports.

The season runs from April to September with peak conditions for all these water sports from June to August.

For novices, the best location is Makenzy Beach, Larnaka, where you can hire everything you need, including an instructor. Expect to pay roughly €70 a day for equipment and tutelage.

Experienced windsurfers and kitesurfers rate Pissouri Bay (north of Lemesos) highly for its strong wind conditions in season.

Fishing

Surrounded by sea, and with a score of plentiful reservoirs, the age-old Tao of fishing is a popular pastime of local Cypriots as well as visitors.

Over 250 species of fish enjoy Cyprus' warm waters. Many fishing villages along the coastline hire out boats, and at the marinas of the resort towns, you'll find plenty of anglers willing to take you on board or out on organised fishing excursions (kids welcome). These trips usually include a village lunch.

BEST BEACHES FOR...

A Family Day Out

Shallow, gentle water and a gorgeous sweep of golden sand make Protaras' Fig Tree Bay (p125) one of the best spots on the island for family fun in the sun.

Romance

What could be more romantic than chilling out with a picnic at Petra tou Romiou (Aphrodite's Rock & Beach; p57)? If it's good enough for the goddess of love herself...

Leaving the Crowds Behind

Make a beeline for Lara Beach (p168) in the Akamas Heights or Golden Beach (p193) on the Karpas Peninsula where you'll find oodles of sand blissfully free of crowds.

Partying

Nissi Beach (p119) in Agia Napa is where everyone heads for fun and frolics galore.

Nature

Specifically left undeveloped to protect its seasonal nesting turtles, Alagadı Beach (p168) is perfect for nature lovers.

Deep-sea fishing is also possible, with bluefish, sea bass, barracuda, tuna, jack and amberjack all copious catches. In North Cyprus, Kyrenia is the main centre for organised deep-sea fishing trips, while in the South you'll find trips easy to organise in all the main resorts.

Mountain Biking & Cycling

Tracks through terrain that once took pack mules and camel trains are now some of the best-recommended mountain-bike areas on the island. The Troödos Mountains and its valleys take in both surfaced and unsurfaced roads. Long, sweeping and slowly increasing gradients lead up and down the mountains, providing riders with some of Cyprus' most scenic areas. Further west, the Akamas Peninsula offers kilometres of pine-forest trails, rocky tracks and twisting roads worthy of a yellow jersey. Bikes with a good range of gears, puncture kits and maps are essential.

Mountain bikes can be hired in Troödos and Platres or you can go to www.mountainbikecyprus.com for information on training, skills courses, tours, repairs and servicing in the Akamas.

Cycling (or road biking) has become very popular in Cyprus, largely with Northern Europeans, with many international cycling teams training on the island. The relatively short distances and quieter roads that run parallel to the motorways make ideal, clean and scenic runs. These old roads connect Nicosia (Lefkosia) with the major southern coastal towns of Larnaka, Lemesos and Pafos. Cyclists can enjoy the use of hard shoulders and well-paved roads throughout most of the island, and the weather, though hot on the tarmac, is conducive to training and fitness.

The Karpas Peninsula, in Northern Cyprus, offers some worthwhile traffic-free and flat rural roads along its cape. It has the added bonus of isolated beaches along its coastline, always available for a dip in summer. Got to www.cypruscycling.com for information on cycling clubs, races and events. Drink plenty of water and take it easy in the middle (hottest) part of the day. Aim for the spring and autumn months if cycling is your main activity while visiting the island.

Hiking

Cyprus has oodles of trails with plenty of wilderness and unspoilt nature to discover. Its many paths span the ages and history of the island, leading to Byzantine churches, picturesque monasteries, Venetian bridges, Gothic arches, crumbling ancient ruins and waterfalls.

In the South hikers can fully immerse themselves in the expanses of the Akamas Peninsula and Troödos Mountains. Cape Greco on the eastern coast also offers wonderful trails, filled with spring flora, leading to its majestic coast of sea caves and natural rock arches. Paths are well marked making independent hiking perfectly feasible for the less-experienced. For serious through-hikers and ramblers South Cyprus is part of the European Long Distance Path E4.

For those shorter on time, the Aphrodite Circular Route (four hours, Akamas Peninsula), Atalanti Circular Route (five hours) and Kannoures to Agios Nikolaos tis Stegis Church trail (three hours), in the Troödos Mountains, all offer good walking with a good slice of historic sites thrown in.

North Cyprus offers walkers vast tracts of empty trails in the Kyrenia Range and Karpas Peninsula. Many of the paths are part of the way-marked Kyrenia Mountain Trail (p169), which stretches for 230km across the full breadth of the coast. The hiking industry here lacks infrastructure and detailed maps are difficult to come by, so unless you're an experienced trekker it's generally best to hire a local guide.

Some of the best shorter hikes in North Cyprus are in the craggy hills between Buffavento Castle and Bellapais village.

Skiing

One of the most southerly ski resorts in Europe really comes alive over the winter months of early January to mid-March.

The spectacular 1952m peak of Mt Olympus, part of the Troödos Mountains, is the perfect venue, and its facilities have recently increased in quality and gained in popularity.

There are four ski runs close to Troödos, operated and maintained by the Cyprus Ski Club. On the north face of Mt Olympus you'll find two sweeping runs, one of 350m that's suitable for enthusiastic beginners, and a more advanced run of 500m. In the peaceful Sun Valley, on the southern side of the range, are two faster, shorter runs, each 150m long. One suits beginners and one is for intermediate-level skiers.

There's a ski shop on the southern side of the mountain with an ample supply of items for hire. The newest and best-quality equipment always goes first, though, so be sure to get in early or risk being left with slightly shabbier pieces. Check out www. cyprusski.com for ski-club information and snow updates.

Horse Riding

The island's diverse range of landscapes and scenery make it an exhilarating place for horseback riding. Cypriots' love of and respect for the big animal have led to well-organised riding facilities and networks across the south of the island. The various clubs and centres offer everything from sunset rides, scenic treks, skills improvement and kids' lessons to even letting you be a cowboy (or cowgirl) for a day.

Rates usually run from €25 to €40 per hour. Trails often take in ruins and the island's ancient history, which makes riding an unforgettable way to get to know Cyprus, so pony up.

Paintball

Perhaps it's the Cypriot penchant for a good hunt, or maybe it's the adrenaline rush of split-second strategy while you avoid the onslaught of paintballs whizzing by your mask. Whatever it is, paintball, both as a serious team sport and as recreational shooting at friends and family members, has taken off across the island.

The island now has a host of safe and well-equipped paintball-dedicated arenas, offering every kind of scenario for experienced gamers and novices alike. Some of the best paintball zones to check out are DNA Paintball in Geroskipou (Pafos), Lapatsa Paintball Ranch (Nicosia) and Souni Paintball Arena in Souni (Lemesos district).

Plan Your Trip
Travel with Children

Cyprus is superb for families, with cuisine that is guaranteed to offer something for the fussiest of eaters and superb beaches, fascinating sights and fun-filled attractions.

Best Regions for Kids

Pafos & the West

Pafos overflows with watery activities: boat rides, fishing trips, snorkelling and a water park. Or there's the spine-tingling trip to the Tomb of the Kings.

Lemesos & the South

The city beaches offer shallow waters and plenty of activities, while horse riding, a water park and an expansive sports centre all keep the adrenaline up.

Larnaka & the East

Older kids will really enjoy the underwater activities, plus sandy beaches, sea caves, camel rides and a fascinating museum on, you guessed it, the sea.

Kyrenia (Girne) & the North

Fairy-tale castles, deserted beaches, nature strolls and the hulking Kyrenia shipwreck in the town's main museum should blow their little socks off.

Famagusta (Mağusa) & the Karpas (Kırpaşa) Peninsula

Famagusta's medieval walled city captures the imagination. On the peninsula, stride out on endless beaches, enjoy a cycling trip, visit an eco village and see turtles in the wild.

Cyprus for Kids

Cyprus is definitely a family-friendly destination. The culture revolves around the (extended) family and children are adored. Stripped back to basics, beaches, castles, ancient sights and virtual year-round sunshine are pretty good raw ingredients. Add to this water sports, museums, parks, boat rides and loads of ice cream, and it becomes serious spoil-them-rotten time. Note that the majority of theme parks and man-made entertainment for children is in the Republic.

Always make a point of asking the staff at tourist offices for a list of family activities, including traditional fiestas, as well as suggestions about hotels that cater for children.

FAMILY-FRIENDLY ICON

A family-friendly icon (👪) has been added to sights, eating and sleeping entries in this guide that seem to be particularly appropriate for children or go out of their way to welcome kids. This does not imply that other places in the guide are not family friendly.

Children's Highlights
Activities

➡ **Zet Karting** (p155) An excellent go-kart circuit for kids of all ages.

➡ **Bubble Maker** (p89) Beginner scuba-diving courses for children aged eight years or older.

➡ **Santa Marina Retreat** (p51) Offers many activities, including horse riding.

➡ **Zephyros Adventure Sports** (p89) A wide range of organised activities for older kids, ranging from kayaking to trekking.

Theme Parks & Wildlife

➡ **Extreme Park** (p140) An enormous playground encompassing everything from trampolines to obstacle courses.

➡ **Parko Paliasto** (p120) A traditional funfair with plenty of head-spinning rides.

➡ **Lemesos Mini Zoo** (p50) A recently renovated small zoo with a large aviary.

➡ **Pafos Zoo** (p87) A superb zoo and bird park.

➡ **Mazotos Camel Park** (p113) Ride on camels, then freshen up in the swimming pool.

Water Parks

➡ **Water World** (p120) It's big, it's splashy and it's been the recipient of a tidal wave of international awards.

➡ **Octopus Aqua Park** (p169) A great place to cool down on those dusty hot summer days with plenty of rides.

➡ **Fasouri Watermania** (p51) Options range from paddling pools for tots to kamikaze slides for teens.

Museums & History

➡ **Shipwreck Museum** (p163) The real-life shipwreck here dates back some 2300 years and is sure to fire up young imaginations.

➡ **Natural History Museum** (p109) Great for kids, with a good playground and peacocks, pelicans and macaws, plus the all-time favourites: creepy-crawlies.

Fairy-Tale Castles

➡ **St Hilarion Castle** (p170) Walt Disney apparently drew inspiration from this castle for his *Snow White;* it's that sort of place.

➡ **Buffavento Castle** (p169) Older kids should enjoy the hilly hike to this lofty castle, with its corners to explore and sensational views.

➡ **Kantara Castle** (p194) This castle has a real magical appeal with turrets, towers and lookouts.

Planning

This is an easygoing, child-friendly destination with little advance planning necessary. Note that July and August can be very busy with tourists, and hotels in the main tourist resorts are often block-booked by tour companies. Late spring is a good time to travel with young children as the weather is still warm enough for beach days, without being too hot, and attractions are not too crowded – until the Easter holidays, that is.

Beaches

Overall, beaches in the main resorts have shallow waters, bucket-and-spade-worthy pebbles and sand, various activities (pedalos, boat rides, volleyball or similar), plus family-friendly restaurants and ice-cream vendors within tottering distance of the sand.

Restaurants & Mealtimes

Children are generally made very welcome at restaurants here. On the downside, few have nappy-changing facilities, although this is changing, albeit at a glacial pace. Most restaurants have a children's menu, and as Cypriot food is rarely spicy, kids tend to like it anyway. One challenge can be adapting to the later eating hours. However, it's generally easy to zip into the nearest kebab (or similar) fast-food place, and patisseries often sell savoury snacks as well as sweeter treats.

Regions at a Glance

This is an island where the word diversity takes on a whole new meaning. While the South has robustly developed its beachside towns and historic sites, the North's main attractions remain the quintessential Med-style resort of Kyrenia and the wild beaches north of Famagusta.

On both sides of the Green Line there are great opportunities for hiking, particularly in the Troödos Mountains and on the northwest coast. For more gourmet pursuits, consider Lemesos with its sophisticated restaurants or enjoy the delicious simplicity of a North Nicosia (Lefkoşa) kebab. History buffs have plenty to ponder as well, with some inspiring archaeological sites, particularly around Famagusta, Pafos and Lemesos. For a slice of rural life head to the interior where mountain villages around Lemesos and the Troödos Mountains provide tranquil respite from the clamour of the coast, as well as superb agrotourism accommodation.

Lemesos & the South

Restaurants
History
Villages

Superb Dining

Lemesos is famed for its innovative and sophisticated dining, particularly around the historic centre. Check out the Old Carob Mill, home to some seriously urban-chic culinary choices.

Into the Past

Ancient Amathous was one of Cyprus' former four kingdoms and is one of several magnificent archaeological sites in this region. Another is Ancient Kourion, located high on a bluff overlooking the sea. Plus there are museums, monasteries and a castle.

Lovely Villages

Some of the region's prettiest villages lie in the foothills of the Troödos Mountains. Enjoy cobbled streets, traditional architecture and atmospheric tavernas, as well as fascinating monasteries.

p46

Troödos Mountains

Hiking
Churches
Activities

Striding Out

There is a growing number of signposted nature trails here, ranging from a half-hour stroll to tumbling waterfalls, to climbing the dizzy heights to the peak of Mt Olympus.

Lavish Frescos

Many of the Byzantine churches located here have extraordinarily vivid frescos with a clarity of detail and colour that has remained largely unchanged for centuries.

Activities

Cycling, birdwatching, horse riding, picnicking or just touring the villages; this region's appeal lies in its lack of commercialism, compounded by an abundance of natural beauty.

p63

Pafos & the West

Beaches
Archaeology
Nature

Best Beaches

You can still find unspoiled beaches here, especially on the Akamas Peninsula. Closer to Pafos, there are pleasant stretches, many with adjacent tavernas or beach bars where you can grab a bite overlooking the surf with sand between your toes.

Mosaics

The Pafos Archaeological Site, with its superb mosaics, should be your first stop, but don't make it your only one; visit the other sites, including the Tombs of the Kings and the catacombs.

Wild Countryside

For a glimpse of untamed Cyprus, consider one of the Akamas Peninsula's treks, visit the villages in the western foothills or wonder at the towering trees in the bucolic Cedar Valley.

p82

Larnaka & the East

Activities
Nightlife
Beaches

Water Sports

One of the world's top 10 diving wrecks is just off the coast at Larnaka, plus there is plenty of scope for snorkelling, windsurfing, kite-boarding, boat rides and swimming (particularly around the sea caves).

Nightlife

Although it has tamed down a double measure or more since its wild heyday, Agia Napa still has the most concentrated (and spirited) nightlife on the island – and the promenade in Larnaka also has plenty of bar-hopping choice.

Beaches & Capes

The east of the island has some good beaches, particularly around Agia Napa, where you will find sweeps of golden sand instead of the more usual pebble and shingle.

p104

Nicosia (Lefkosia)

Museums
Shopping
Restaurants

Museums & Galleries

The Cyprus Museum, the island's best, should not be missed. Folk art, local history, Ottoman memorabilia and world-class art can also be enjoyed in the culturally rich capital.

Superb Shopping

Shift your credit card into overdrive with an extensive choice of classy stores. For more unusual finds, head for the idiosyncratic small family-owned shops in the backstreets of the Old City.

Capital Dining

This is a foodie city with restaurants ranging between spit-and-sawdust style tavernas serving just one main homestyle dish and ultra-sophisticated places with menus that read more like a book.

p126

North Nicosia (Lefkoşa)

Architecture
Fast Food
Souvenirs

Architectural Gems

The city is studded with sometimes crumbling, sometimes renovated but always fascinating historic buildings. Highlights include the mosque, the Bedesten and the Büyük Han.

Best Fast Food

Forget the corner kebab house back home, this is the place to enjoy the succulent, spicy, unforgettable real thing. Head to Girne Caddesi for several good meaty choices.

Souvenirs

A former Ottoman inn, the Büyük Han is now home to two floors of exceptional arts and crafts shops selling items like embroidered silk, hand-painted cards, fruit preserves, ceramics and jewellery.

p148

Kyrenia (Girne) & the North

Castles
Beaches
Hiking

Castles

Kyrenia's castle is home to the fascinating shipwreck museum, while nearby are the crowning glories of St Hilarion and Buffavento Castles with the added plus of sweeping panoramic views.

Beach Life

For wild deserted beaches head for the coastal tip of Koruçam, while east of Kyrenia there are more tempting stretches of sand, including Alagadı Beach, one of the Mediterranean's prime turtle nesting spots.

Walks

The Kyrenia Mountain Trail is a well-mapped path that follows the entire crest of the Kyrenia Range and is surrounded by deserted beaches and beautiful scenery.

p160

Famagusta & the Karpas Peninsula

Archaeology
Nature
Architecture

Archaeology

One of the island's prime and most extensive archaeological sites and the most significant of the 10 ancient city kingdoms in Cyprus, Ancient Salamis is located here and should not be missed.

Wild Nature

The Karpas Peninsula is wonderfully wild and isolated and where you can enjoy hiking, cycling and swimming surrounded by a uniquely beautiful landscape.

Architectural Legacy

Once seen, never forgotten, the historical centre of Famagusta is an extraordinary, albeit harrowing, landscape of Frankish and Venetian ruins, with gap-toothed frontages and looming facades.

p179

On the Road

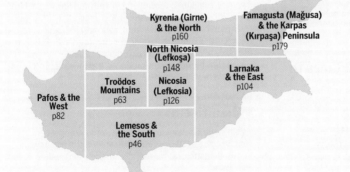

Lemesos & the South

Best Places to Eat

➡ Syrian Arab Friendship Club (p52)

➡ Dino Art Cafe (p52)

➡ Il Gusto (p62)

➡ Old Stables (p59)

➡ Karatello (p52)

Best Places to Stay

➡ Apokryfo (p201)

➡ Vouni Lodge (p201)

➡ Chrielka (p200)

➡ Bunch of Grapes Inn (p201)

Why Go?

The south coast is Cyprus at its most diverse. Beaches hem the shore offering relaxed holiday fun. Impressive sites like Ancient Kourion showcase the island's rich history. Travellers seeking vestiges of traditional rural life are charmed by the gentle pace of the hill villages scattered on the Troödos Mountains' slopes. And centred around it all is cosmopolitan Lemesos.

Hotel developments may have taken over much of the coast but drive a little further afield and the natural beauty of this region is revealed. The beaches around Episkopi Bay nestle against verdant farmland and dramatic bluffs while inland the countryside rolls upward in hilly waves with roads edged by olive and almond trees and vineyard rows. Once exploring is done for the day, lively Lemesos is the place to head. With its cafe culture and restaurants, this city is developing a reputation as a rising star in Cyprus' foodie scene.

When to Go

➡ Join in the fun-time revelry along the seafront at Lemesos' annual carnival (50 days before Easter), full of traditional music and dance, family-friendly parades and modern festivities.

➡ Springtime is an ideal time for touring with the Troödos foothills blanketed by a riot of wildflowers and the sun still warm enough for beach days.

➡ The height of the holiday season is July and August, so beaches are busy. Enjoy the full gamut of the coast facilities with water sports galore then escape to the hills to catch a breeze while strolling picturesque village lanes.

➡ Raise a glass (or three) at Lemesos' famed Wine Festival in September when Dionysus' favourite tipple takes centre stage.

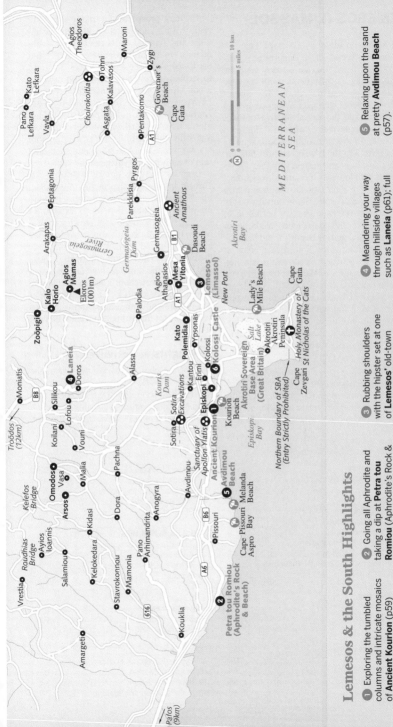

Lemesos & the South Highlights

1 Exploring the tumbled columns and intricate mosaics of **Ancient Kourion** (p59) and then sitting on your lofty Roman theatre perch to enjoy the sweeping coastal view.

2 Going all Aphrodite and taking a dip at **Petra tou Romiou** (Aphrodite's Rock & Beach; p57), the legendary spot where the goddess emerged from the sea.

3 Rubbing shoulders with the hipster set at one of **Lemesos'** old-town restaurants (p51), where Cypriot classics are given fresh new tweaks.

4 Meandering your way through hillside villages such as **Laneia** (p61); full of honey-toned stone and cobblestone loveliness.

5 Relaxing upon the sand at pretty **Avdimou Beach** (p57).

6 Playing king of the castle at **Kolossi Castle** (p61).

LEMESOS (LIMASSOL)

POP 101,000

Still known to many as Limassol, Lemesos is one of Cyprus' most underrated cities. Although fringed on its eastern edge by bland-looking developments with an eye firmly on the tourism industry, the core of this city is full of character. Wrapped around the dinky castle, the central old town radiates out in a squiggle of lanes where old shuttered houses and modern boutiques both squeeze themselves into the fray. It's an area buzzing with cafes, bars and restaurants that are as popular with locals as they are with visitors.

This is the international business centre of Cyprus, and despite the financial woes of recent years there's a sense of optimism in the air again. The construction of the long-planned flashy marina beside the old harbour is still grinding along and grittier areas of town are being tagged for a revamp. For travellers looking for a holiday that takes in more than sun and sea, Lemesos is at the very heart of one of the island's richest areas for exploration. Basing yourself here puts you in easy striking distance to some of Cyprus' best historical remnants and the verdant mountains of the Troödos region are within easy reach.

History

In 1191 the crusader king Richard the Lionheart put Lemesos on the map when he defeated then ruler of Cyprus, Isaak Komninos, and took Cyprus and Lemesos for himself.

The city prospered for more than 200 years with a succession of Knights Hospitaller and Templar as its rulers until earthquakes, marauding Genoese (1373) and Saracens (1426) reduced Lemesos' fortunes to virtually zero. The city was still creating a bad impression in the mid-20th century: Lawrence Durrell, writing in 1952 in *Bitter Lemons of Cyprus,* noted upon arrival in Lemesos that 'we berthed towards sunrise in a gloomy and featureless roadstead, before a town whose desolate silhouette suggested that of a tin-mining village in the Andes'.

Lemesos grew up quickly following the Turkish invasion of Cyprus in 1974, replacing Famagusta (Mağusa) as the nation's main port. It also needed to expand to keep up with the Republic's growing tourist boom. Originally comprising what is today known as the old town, around the historic fishing port, Lemesos has outgrown its original geographic limits to now encompass a sprawling tourist suburb. Signposted as the 'tourist centre', this is a riotous confusion of hotels, bars and restaurants, and you could be excused for forgetting that the sea is there at all.

◎ Sights & Activities

Most of the main sights are set within the compact historic quarter. Beach lovers should head west out of town, where several popular beach resorts are strung along the coast. Less commercialised, more attractive

Lemesos (Limassol)

beaches are located further west, including Kourion, Melanda and Avdimou.

★**Lemesos Castle** CASTLE
(admission €4.50; ⏲9am-5pm Mon-Sat, to 1pm Sun) This 14th-century structure, built over the remains of a Byzantine castle, has been utilised by conquerors throughout Cyprus' turbulent history. The Venetians vandalised it, the Ottomans gave it a facelift for military use, and the British used it as a colonial prison. Apparently, Richard the Lionheart married Berengaria in the chapel of the original castle in 1191, where he also grandly

Lemesos (Limassol)

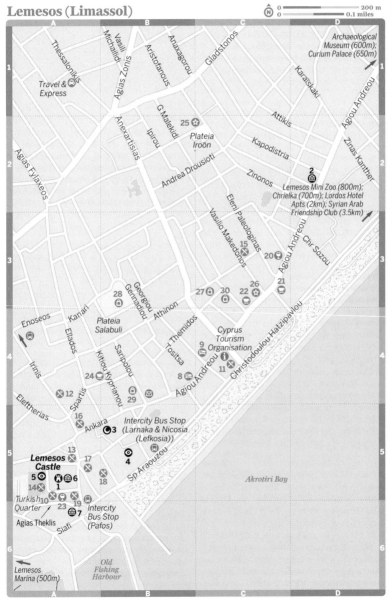

DON'T MISS

CYPRIOT FOLK ART

Folk Art Museum (Agiou Andreou 123; admission €2; ⊘ 9am-2.30pm Mon-Fri) Although small, this museum hosts beautifully put together ethnographical displays of traditional costumes and agricultural implements as well as some stunning examples of tornaretto embroidery (a traditional style of silk needlework) and other textiles. The museum is set in a finely restored stone house that showcases the typical architecture of old Lemesos.

crowned himself King of Cyprus and his wife Queen of England.

In the courtyard surrounding the castle walls there's an old olive press that dates from the 7th to 9th centuries.

The interior of Lemesos Castle contains a series of chambers on varying levels which are home to the **Medieval Museum**. The collection of Byzantine and medieval artefacts on display include tombstones, suits of armour, weaponry, religious objects and Ottoman pottery. Climb up to the rooftop terrace afterwards for views of the city.

Archaeological Museum   MUSEUM
(cnr Vyronos & Kaningos; admission €2.50; ⊘ 9am-4.30pm Mon-Sat) This museum includes an extensive collection of pottery, and a selection of items dating from neolithic and Chalcolithic times (primarily shards and implements for domestic use) through to Mycenaean pottery. A multitude of terracotta figures on show are thought to be the remains of votive offerings. There is a display of classical pottery, jewellery and oil lamps, as well as curiously modern-looking glass bottles and vials. Although it pales in comparison to the Cyprus Museum in Nicosia (Lefkosia), it's well worth a browse.

Cyprus Wine Museum   MUSEUM
(www.cypruswinemuseum.com; Pafos 42, Erimi; admission €4-7; ⊘ 9am-5pm) Just west of town, off the Lemesos–Pafos highway, the Cyprus Wine Museum offers an insight into the history of Cypriot winemaking. There are three tour options for visitors with the difference in price essentially relating to whether you want to do a wine tasting after viewing the winemaking exhibits. The museum displays include medieval drinking vessels and jars, as well as explanatory information on all aspects of winemaking. There's also a short audio-visual presentation.

Grand Mosque   MOSQUE
(Kebir Camii; Genethliou Mitella) At the heart of the old Turkish quarter, the Grand Mosque is surrounded by palms almost as tall as its minaret. It is used by the remaining Turkish Cypriot population and Muslims from the Middle East who live in Lemesos. As with any mosque, visitors are requested to dress conservatively; leave shoes by the door and avoid visiting at prayer times. There are no fixed opening hours; if the gate is open, step within and take a look.

Hammam   STEAM BATHS
(☏ 9947 4251; Loutron 3; steam bath & sauna €15; ⊘ 2-10pm Mon-Sat) This tiny hammam isn't really a tourist site, since many count on privacy when going in for a steam bath. If you do decide to indulge, don't come here expecting anything too luxurious; it's a very basic place where people go to relax. Keep in mind that all sessions are mixed. Also on offer are full-body massages, shiatsu, Swedish massage, Indian head massage and antistress massages from €20.

Lanitis Art Foundation   EXHIBITION CENTRE
(www.lanitisfoundation.org; Old Carob Mill; ⊘ 10am-6pm Mon-Sat) This arts centre runs a rolling schedule of events throughout the year, often highlighting interesting local artists and edgy exhibitions. Check the website for what's on show when you're in town.

Lemesos Mini Zoo   ZOO
(http://limassolzoo.com; Municipal Gardens; admission €1; ⊘ 9am-noon & 3-7pm May-Sep, 9am-6.30pm Oct-Apr) This renovated, albeit modest, zoo has an aviary, ostriches and some cheeky cheetahs. The zoo is within Lemesos' leafy Municipal Gardens, 1.5km from the central old district walking along seafront Christodoulou Hatzipavlou.

Natural Sea Sponge Exhibition Centre   MUSEUM
(Agias Theklis; ⊘ 9am-7pm Mon-Fri, to 3pm Sat) Sponges have a life of their own and the cartoon here, duly dedicated to a talking sponge, will amuse younger kids. The exhibition goes through the process of harvesting sea sponges, and how the living creatures become the soft things we use in our baths. Naturally enough, you can purchase sponges here too.

Fasouri Watermania   WATER PARK

(🖉2571 4235; www.fasouri-watermania.com; adult/child €29/16; ⊙10am-6pm Jun-Aug, to 5pm Sep-Oct & May; 🖬) Sitting in the Fasouri area, a 15-minute drive out of Lemesos, this place has all the usual watery options including a kamikaze slide, the 'big orange wet bubble', 'lazy river', a wave pool, and both children's and adult pools. There are also sunbeds and parasols for run-off-their-feet parents.

If you're driving, the water park is off the Lemesos–Pafos highway, 5km northwest of town. If you don't have your own wheels, there's a shuttle to the park; phone for pick-up times and location.

Santa Marina Retreat   OUTDOOR ACTIVITIES

(🖉9954 5454; www.santamarinaretreat.com; Pareklisia village; adult/child €3/free; ⊙9am-7pm Tue-Sun; 🖬) Offers horse riding, archery, quad biking, mountain biking, wall climbing, nature trails (via battery-run buggies) and a lot more besides – including golf for the grown-ups. Santa Marina Retreat is 17km east of Lemesos, just outside the village of Pareklisia.

Diving

Most of the dive sites just offshore are perfect for beginners, including Marina Wall (a favoured night diving spot) and Julie Reef (where you'll usually be surrounded by shoals of barracuda and sea bream). For more experienced divers the major site is exploring the *Diana* wreck with its plethora of sea life in residence. For more information on diving, see p37.

Crest Dive Centre   DIVING

(🖉2563 4076; www.crestdive.com; St Raphael Marina, Amathous; ⊙9am-6pm) This 5-star PADI centre offers the gamut of PADI courses (discover scuba is €70) as well as a good range of diving and snorkelling trips.

Dive-In Limassol   DIVING

(🖉2531 1923; www.dive-in.com.cy; Four Seasons Beach Hotel, Tourist Area; ⊙9am-5.30pm) This PADI centre offers the full range of PADI, BSAC and DAN courses and offers good-value dive and accommodation packages (seven-nights and five dives costs €230).

👉 Tours

There are three walking tours in Lemesos, all organised by the Cyprus Tourism Organisation (CTO). They're free, but it's wise to book in the high season.

The Historic Limassol Walk, at 10am on Monday, takes you around Lemesos' historic centre, monuments, markets and main sights.

At 10am every Wednesday, from October to April, there are alternating tours: the first, 'Germasogeia: A Village Blessed by Water', goes to Germasogeia village, where the water theme is covered by a visit to the village dam. You also get to see the architecture and street life of the village itself. The second is the 'Discover the Natural Environment of Germasogeia', which is a walk in the hills (some fitness required) following a nature trail laid out by the forestry department.

⭐ Festivals & Events

Lemesos Carnival   CARNIVAL

(www.limassolmunicipal.com.cy/carnival) Lemesos is the only town in Cyprus with a full-blown carnival atmosphere, enjoyed particularly by children. The 11-day carnival, held 50 days before Easter, starts with the 'King of the Carnival' entering town, escorted by a motley parade. There's also a children's carnival parade; the festivities close with a fancy-dress extravaganza.

Kataklysmos Festival   RELIGIOUS

(Flood Festival) Lemesos is one of the best places in Cyprus to experience the Kataklysmos festivities which commemorate both the Biblical flood of Genesis and the Greek myth of Deukalion. Celebrations take place in June on the seafront and include boat races and folk dancing.

Lemesos Wine Festival   WINE

(www.limassolmunicipal.com.cy/wine) Held in the Municipal Gardens annually from 30 August to 11 September, this festival provides a chance to sample a wide range of local wines. As you might predict, the festival is extremely popular with young, fun-seeking tourists, here for the Cypriot food, traditional music and dancing, and did we mention the wine?

Musical Sundays   MUSIC

(⊙Feb-May & Nov-Dec) Throughout spring, autumn and winter the CTO organises a series of free concerts every Sunday at the Seaside Theatre in the tourist area. It's a great way to experience traditional Cypriot music.

🍴 Eating

Eating in Lemesos equals a culinary combo of variety, quality and modern cuisine, particularly in the old town (most of the tourist area's eating options are fairly forgettable). The aesthetically restored Old Carob Mill, next to the castle, is home to several restaurants and bars sharing a cool, sophisticated vibe. For quick bites head for the pedestrian Plateia Salabuli next to the refurbished municipal market, which is surrounded by inexpensive kebab houses, traditional coffee shops and similar.

★ Syrian Arab Friendship Club   MIDDLE EASTERN €€

(SAFC; Iliados 3; full meze €15; ⏱ 7-11.30pm; 🅟) A delight for all lovers of Arab cuisine; the SAFC puts on some of the best meze in Cyprus. Have a nargileh (water pipe) afterwards for the full experience. To find the Syrian Club (as it's known), head east of the centre via the coast road for around 3.5km. The restaurant is located just behind the Apollonia Beach Hotel.

★ Dino Art Cafe   MEDITERRANEAN €€

(🖉 2576 2030; Irinis 62-66; mains from €8; ⏱ 10am-11pm; 🛜🅟) Dino's has a great reputation and a loyal local following thanks to its smart decor, friendly owner Dino Kosti and great food. It's known for its massive salads with quirky choices such as duck and orange or strawberry with blue cheese. Dino's also exhibits photography and other works by Cypriot artists.

Noodle House   ASIAN FUSION €€

(🖉 2582 0282; www.thenoodlehouse.com; Ankara 3; mains €10-15; ⏱ 11.30am-midnight; 🛜🅟🅟) A welcome addition to Lemesos' eating scene, Noodle House's menu fuses Singaporean, Thai and Chinese favourites for a trip through Asia in Cyprus. If you like spicy – ask; they tend to tame down the heat for the Cypriot palate. Sunday lunch is kids' time, with face-painting and balloons.

Bono   INTERNATIONAL €€

(Anexartisias 3; breakfast from €4.50, mains from €8; ⏱ 8am-6pm Mon-Sat; 🛜) We love the casual, friendly vibe of this place. Bono's owner spent several years in the US, where he learned how to whip up cheesecake that is the best in town. The breakfasts, burgers, quesadillas, salads and homemade soups are similarly a couple of notches above the norm.

Meze Taverna   CYPRIOT €€

(🖉 2536 7333; Athinon 209; mains €10-15; ⏱ 11am-2pm & 7.30-11pm; 🅟) This sweet family-run tavern serves up traditional Greek dishes with straight-up home cooking flair. If you're looking for somewhere cosy to munch on mousakka and meze this is just the ticket; red-and-white checker tablecloths and all.

Ousia   MEDITERRANEAN €€

(🖉 2510 9040; Irinis 30-32; mains from €8; ⏱ 11.30am-11pm; 🛜🅟) Fashionable arty decor and a menu that covers all the bases from classy burgers to Cypriot staples with a modern twist. The cocktails veer on the potent side.

Il Castello   INTERNATIONAL €€

(Irinis 22; sandwiches & salads €6-12, mains €15-25; ⏱ 10am-11pm; 🛜🅟) Don't be put off by the touristy look of this place. It's a local favourite for its huge salad dishes and interesting sandwich and wrap combinations. For lunch after viewing the castle it's a great choice.

Stretto Cafe   INTERNATIONAL €€

(🖉 2582 0465; Old Carob Mill, Vasilissis; light meals €6-12, mains €12-25; ⏱ 10am-11pm; 🛜🅟) This snazzy cafe attracts Lemesos' hipster set with a menu of pasta, sushi, steaks and light bites. There are comfy sofas, great streetside tables and superb people-watching potential.

Rizitiko Tavern   CYPRIOT €€

(Tzamiou 4-8; mains from €8; ⏱ 11am-11pm) Tucked away by the mosque on a newly pedestrianised street, this is a reliably good, low-key establishment with tables that spill out onto the cobbles at night. The *afelia* (pork cooked in red wine and coriander) and *kleftiko* (oven-baked lamb) are homemade quality – or better.

★ Karatello   CYPRIOT €€€

(🖉 2582 0464; Old Carob Mill, Vasilissis 1; mains from €10-15; ⏱ 11am-2pm & 7.30-11pm; 🛜) A modern take on Cypriot classics is the name of the game at this stylish restaurant, which is part of the Old Carob Mill complex. The hearty traditional tavern food here has been given a thorough touch of finesse for modern foodie palates.

Artima Bistro   MEDITERRANEAN €€€

(🖉 2582 0466; Old Carob Mill, Vasilissis; mains €12-25; ⏱ 11am-2pm & 7.30-11pm; 🛜🅟) This is where Queen Sofia of Spain chose to eat during an official trip to Cyprus in March 2011 (to open the Miró exhibition). Inspired by Italy's cuisine, the menu includes lots of pasta and seafood options with clever and innovative tweaks.

Trata Fish Tavern SEAFOOD €€€

(☑ 2558 6600; Ioanni Tompazi 4; seafood meze €20; ☺ 7-11pm) This is arguably one of Lemesos' best fish restaurants, particularly famed for the seafood meze. Despite the 'plain Jane' decor and unassuming atmosphere, the place attracts shoals of locals, particularly at weekends. It's just behind the prominently located Debenhams department store, around 400m east of the Municipal Gardens.

🍸 Drinking & Nightlife

Most places in Lemesos are quiet until at least 10pm. Bars on the seafront strip are predictably tourist-geared, with bitter on tap and football on the big screen. For a more authentic Cypriot experience, head for bars in and around the Old Carob Mill and the historic centre. The city also has a handful of contemporary, slightly bohemian cafes, the sorts of places where you can surf the net (along with the froth on a frappé) while checking out the effortlessly stylish locals.

★**Antithesis** CAFE

(Agiou Andreou 201; ☺ 9.30am-7pm Mon, Tue, Thu & Fri, to 3pm Wed & Sat) We love this snug cafe that whips up a mighty fine slice of cake as well as some great coffee, pots of tea and delicious smoothies. If you're peckish they have a small menu of pies, pitta-pockets and soups that make a tasty lunch.

Draught BAR

(Old Carob Mill, Vasilissis; ☺ 11am-late; ☎) This lively place has ace bartender Krisztian Gyokeres (who represented the island in the world bartending competition in 2010) mixing up cocktails as well as a full range of lagers, ales and wheat beers. On weekends a resident DJ hits the decks.

Adiexodo CAFE

(Agiou Andreou; ☺ 9.30am-4pm) Grab a table under the ancient ficus tree, order a syrupy coffee just like the locals do and challenge one of the elderly regulars to a game of backgammon.

Pi CAFE

(Kitiou Kyprianou 27; snacks €5; ☺ 10am-11pm) A relaxed, gay-friendly cafe with a lovely garden, light meals, excellent salads, 10-plus choice of beer, good (mainly Italian) wines and elaborate cocktails.

Tepee Rock Bar BAR

(www.tepeerock.com; Ampelakion; ☺ 11am-11pm) Chomp on Mexican burritos while enjoying live rock bands at this popular restaurant bar with a great foot-stomping atmosphere. It's located in the tourist centre, around 4km east of the historic quarter on the coastal road.

7-Seas CLUB

(www.7seaslive.com; Columbia Plaza, Agiou Andreou 223; ☺ 10.30pm-late) This hip club and live music venue attracts a roll call of Cyprus' best DJs as well as hosting live music events. The regular Tuesday Latin night and Friday DJ night are free entry. Put your glad-rags on if you want to get in. This place is strictly no beach-wear allowed.

Guaba Beach Bar CLUB

(Agia Varvara Beach; ☺ 10pm-late) This popular bar located 5km east of the historic centre next to the Aquarius Hotel has seats right on the beach. There are parties, as well as relaxed evenings, with DJs who play anything from reggae to electro, depending on the night and their fancy.

Sesto Senso CLUB

(www.sestosensoclub.com; Promaxon Elevftherias 45; ☺ 11pm-late) One of the most fashionable places in town, with stunning decor and extremely expensive drinks. It's about 3.5km east of the centre.

★ Entertainment

Rogmes Live Music LIVE MUSIC

(☑ 2534 1010; Agiou Andreou 197; ☺ 10pm-5am) A highly praised bouzouki bar touting a mad, wonderful tempo on weekend nights, when the musicians stay and play as loud and as late as the crowd wants.

Rialto Theatre

THEATRE

(☎ 2534 3900; www.rialto.com.cy; Andrea Drousioti 19) Exquisitely restored to its former art-deco glory, the Rialto is the main venue in town for theatre, concerts and film festivals.

K Cineplex

CINEMA

(www.kcineplex.com; Ariadnis 8) The multiscreen K Cineplex shows new-release movies. It's located in the tourist centre, 6km east of the historic quarter. See the website for current screenings.

🛍 Shopping

Most of Lemesos' clothes, shoe and appliance shops are clustered along the pedestrian street of Agiou Andreou in central Lemesos. Head for the backstreets here for more idiosyncratic gift shops, boutiques and similar.

Municipal Market

FOOD & DRINK

(Georgiou Gennadiou; ⊘ 6am-3pm Mon-Sat) The restored municipal market, full of fresh produce, is a must-visit for self-caterers and is also an excellent source of foodie-style souvenirs such as local honey, nuts and scrumptious Cypriot sweets. It's housed in a lovely old stone structure that was first built in 1917.

Cyprus Handicrafts Centre

SOUVENIRS

(Themidos 25; ⊘ 9am-7pm Mon-Fri, to 2pm Sat) As in other cities across the country, this government-sponsored store is the best place for seeking out authentic, traditional and fairly priced handmade crafts.

Violet's Second Hand Shop

CLOTHING

(Salaminos 10; ⊘ 9am-6pm Mon-Fri, to 2pm Sat) A great place for clothes and jewellery, including some interesting Cypriot vintage pieces.

Pana's Patchwork

ACCESSORIES

(www.panas-creations.com; Saripolou 21; ⊘ 9am-7pm Mon, Tue, Thu & Fri, to 2pm Wed & Sat) Crammed with a colourful jumble of ornaments, tapestries, dolls and embroidered pieces, all made by the owner, Pana.

🛈 Information

Bank of Cyprus (Agiou Andreou; ⊘ 8.30am-1.30pm Mon-Fri)

CyberNet (Eleftherias 79; per hr €2.50; ⊘ 1-11pm Mon-Fri, 10am-11pm Sat & Sun) Internet access in a convenient old-town location.

Cyprus Tourism Organisation (CTO; www.visitcyprus.com; Agiou Andreou 142; ⊘ 8.15am-2.30pm & 3-5.30pm Mon, Tue, Thu & Fri, to 2.30pm Wed, to 1pm Sat Apr-Oct, shorter hours rest of year) Also has a **branch** (Georgiou 1, 22a) in the tourist centre. Helpful staff and good maps.

Salamis Tours (☎ 2535 5555; www.salamis-international.com; Salamis House, Oktovriou 28; ⊘ 9am-6pm Mon-Fri) Organises cruises to Greece and issues tickets to transport your vehicle by boat to Greece or Israel.

🛈 Getting There & Away

AIR

Lemesos is more or less equidistant from Pafos and Larnaka airports.

Limassol Airport Express (☎ 7777 7075; www.airportshuttlebus.eu; adult/child €9/4) Has regular services between Larnaka airport and

---

LIMASSOL MARINA

Lemesos' decrepit former fishing harbour is undergoing a €300-million facelift. The competition for the new Limassol Marina was won in 2007 by Nicosia-based architects Dickon Irwin and Margarita Kritioti from Irwin & Kritioti Architects. The company's innovative and lush idea for Lemesos' marina sees the harbour's shape mimic the sea with a series of steel, wavelike shapes. But aside from its impressive aesthetics, the marina is meant to bring life back to the city centre year-round so that when the high-tourist season wanes in the early winter months, the harbour will turn into a vibrant conference and lecture centre as well as having a super-exclusive residential district and becoming a high-class shopping and dining destination.

The marina itself is now open for yachts to berth but, as the project continues to be fraught with delays, the proposed swish residential district has yet to be completed. When finished the marina is expected to be the most luxurious place on the island.

Check out the flashy website www.limassolmarina.com, and make sure you bring your yacht or, at the very least, your deck shoes.

Lemesos. Service or private taxis also operate to both airports. The latter will charge you around €20.

BOAT

Expensive two- and three-day cruises depart from Lemesos all year. They go to Haifa (Israel), Port Said (Egypt), a selection of Greek islands and sometimes (in summer) to Lebanon. You can book at most travel agencies.

BUS

InterCity Buses (www.intercity-buses.com; one way/return €4/7) has regular buses to Nicosia (Lefkosia; 1¼ hour), Larnaka (one hour) and Pafos (one hour) from its bus station at the new port, inconveniently 3.5km west of the castle. It also picks up and drops off passengers to Nicosia and Larnaka at the bus stop in front of Agia Napa Church and in front of Debenhams department store (in the tourist area) on the main coast road. To Pafos, its central pick up point is the roundabout in front of the old harbour.

SERVICE TAXI

Travel & Express (☑ 7777 7474; www.travelexpress.com.cy; Thessalonikis 21; ☺ 6am-7.30pm Mon-Sat, to 3pm Sun) operates service taxis to Nicosia (€11, 1¼ hours), Larnaka (€10, one hour) and Pafos (€9.50, one hour) every 30 minutes between 6.30am and 6pm Monday to Friday, and every hour between 7am and 5pm on weekends. They will also drop you off at Larnaka airport (€13) and Pafos airport (€13).

❶ Getting Around

BUS

Emel (www.limassolbuses.com; Irinis) provides an urban-wide as well as regional network of buses. Fares cost €1.50 per journey, €5 per day or €15 per week within the district of Lemesos, including rural villages.

The useful and frequent **Bus 30** operates along the seafront road between the new port and the Le Meridien Hotel via the old harbour, tourist area and Ancient Amathous.

Emel's main local bus station, known as the Old Hospital bus station, is located 1km north of the central port area along Irinis. Useful regional bus lines departing from this station include:

Bus 16 To Episkopi village and Ancient Kourion; 45 minutes

Bus 17 To Kolossi Castle; 40 minutes

Bus 22 To Akrotiri village; 30 minutes

CAR & MOTORCYCLE

There are convenient car parks all along the waterfront.

AROUND LEMESOS

Whether you're searching for some sun, sea and sand action or want to dig into Cyprus' ancient history, there's plenty to do and see in the area around Lemesos.

❶ Getting There & Around

You can easily get to Ancient Kourion, Episkopi and Kolossi Castle all in the same day using a combination of Emel Bus 16 and 17. Pissouri Bay, Ancient Amathous and even the Holy Monastery of St Nicholas of the Cats (if you don't mind a one-hour walk there and back from Akrotiri village) can also be visited using Emel buses. Travelling this way does take time though, and if you're in a hurry, or want to properly explore the beautiful villages to the north of Lemesos, you're going to require rented transport or expensive taxis.

Cycling in and around Lemesos is fairly easy once you have cleared the confines of the city and its surrounds. The terrain is reasonably flat until you encounter the first slopes of the Troödos Mountains.

🏊 Beaches

Lemesos' city beaches are popular enough and decent for a quick swim but they don't have any particular wow factor. For a quieter, and more picturesque, strip of sand look a little further afield.

🏖 Kourion Beach

This is a lovely beach of sand and small pebbles; the area is windy and attracts windsurfers and kite-boarders, as well as those who just want to chill out amid the unspoilt setting and backdrop of white cliffs.

The beach is around 17km west of Lemesos, within Great Britain's Akrotiri Sovereign Base Area (SBA), which is the reason for the lack of development. There's no natural shade, but the adjacent tavernas rent sunbeds and parasols for the day (€4).

The eastern end of the beach is unsafe for swimming (note the sign), so head west if you fancy a dip. This beach is best combined with your trip to Ancient Kourion. (You can get a taster here: the remains of a 6th-century port basilica, complete with 11 columns, back on to the centre of the beach.)

Locals rate the **Blue Beach Bar & Restaurant** (mains €9-15 ; ☺ 10.30am-10pm; ☑) as the best on this short culinary strip. You can select your fish or tentacled choice from the large tank, or go for a fish meze (€21 per person). Vegetarians are thoughtfully catered for with vegie burgers and various salad choices.

The beach is also home to the respected **Curium Beach Equestrian Centre** (☑9956 4232; curiumequestrian@hotmail.com; classes from €25; 🌐), which offers guided horse treks and classes, including dressage.

The beach can be reached by public transport (Bus 16) from Lemesos.

Lady's Mile Beach

This 7km stretch of hard-packed sand and pebbles is a popular weekend beach. Named after a horse owned by a colonial governor who exercised his mare here, it runs south beyond Lemesos' New Port along the eastern side of the British-controlled Akrotiri Peninsula. Keep driving away from the blight of cranes at the port, as the beach and the view improve the further south you go.

On summer weekends, the citizens of Lemesos flock here in large numbers to relax in the fairly shallow waters. A couple of beach taverns serve the crowds and provide some respite from an otherwise barren beachscape. Bring your own shade if you plan to sit on the beach all day, as well as mosquito repellent if you are staying here until dusk – the nearby salt lake provides a ripe breeding ground for these little nippers.

Governor's Beach

Lemesos' tourist appeal starts 30km east of the city, at Governor's Beach, with several coves of dark sand contrasting with the white, chalky rocks. On the downside, the Vasilikos power station looms 3km to the east, blighting the otherwise seamless sea views.

A good restaurant choice here (signposted from the approach road) is **Panayiotis** (☑2563 2315; www.panayiotisgovernorsbeach.

OFF THE BEATEN TRACK

ANOGYRA

Just inland, 39km west of Lemesos, sleepy Anogyra is all honey-coloured stone houses, painted window shutters and narrow lanes that twist and turn in lazy squiggles. This is the only village that still produces carob *pasteli* (a Cypriot sweet) the traditional way, and if you're passing through in September, don't miss the annual Pasteli Festival here when the village celebrates its sweet-treat industry heritage.

It's a charmingly peaceful place with an unhurried atmosphere far removed from the bustle of the coast. The higgledy-piggledy alleyways, offering a slice of Cypriot village life, were made for idle wandering. Park by the central plaza, dominated by the stately Church of the Archangel Michael (home to some lovely icons), and stroll out to explore from there.

Anogyra, and the surrounding area, is also home to a couple of interesting foodie-focussed sights that are well worth a look.

Oleastro Olive Park (☑9952 5093; www.oleastro.com.cy; 3km north of Anogyra; adult/child €3/2; ⊙10am-7pm) All you ever wanted to know about the humble olive and were afraid to ask. Oleastro is devoted to the story of this mainstay of Cypriot cuisine. The museum walks you through Olives 101, highlighting its long history of cultivation on the island. There are exhibits of traditional olive oil extraction machines and if you visit between October and February you can see olive oil being extracted. There's a good restaurant here as well, serving traditional Cypriot dishes.

The gift shop on-site sells (what else) all manner of olive-related gifts made from organic olive oil.

Pasteli Museum (☑2522 1500; ⊙10am-4pm Jun-Sep, shorter hours rest of year) This cute museum explains the traditional process behind manufacturing carob *pasteli* (a Cypriot sweet), which was every Cypriot child's favourite treat long before Cadbury's hit the market here. Outside of summer it's sometimes shut so phone beforehand to make sure it's open.

Nicolaidis Winery (☑2522 1709; www.facebook.com/nicolaides.winery) Part of the CTO's 'Wine Routes', this third generation boutique winery produces some interesting tipples. Stock up on their rosé (which they're known for) while there.

com; mains €9-20; ⊙11am-10pm), which has had the same ebullient owner, Andreas, since 1963. Order the specialty, fish meze, and sit surrounded by lush, mature gardens, with eucalyptus, pines, oleanders and olive trees, overlooking the sea below. Andreas also has a couple of reasonable apartments to rent.

Avdimou Beach
This lovely stretch of beach is home to **Zias Beach Club** (mains €10-14; ⊙10am-11pm Apr-Nov) with its dining area and classy wooden sun-loungers. You can rent a sunbed and parasol and staff will throw in a main course meal for €15 – or bring a picnic and pay just €3.20. For something a little more traditional head to the adjacent long-standing **Kyrenia Beach Restaurant** (mains €9-16; ⊙11am-10pm), which serves up some superb seafood dishes.

Melanda Beach
This is one of the best beaches in the region: an arc of fine pebbles and sand sheltered by low white cliffs and backed by olive trees. It's signposted off the B6; the approach road is fairly rough, but still accessible, and passes by vines and lush agricultural land.

Melanda Beach Restaurant (mains €10; ⊙11.30am-10pm) has a terrace on the beach, and rents sunbeds and parasols for €4.

July and August are months to avoid, but otherwise Melanda is a good choice for a beach day out.

Pissouri Bay & Village
Pissouri Bay resort, 10km west of Avdimou, has jet skis, surfing, banana rides and other entertaining sea activities. It's a popular spot for visitors with plenty of holiday villas in the surrounding area as well as a couple of luxury resorts. Despite the holiday overtones (and the fact that Pissouri is a free wi-fi zone) the original village still has some authentic corners but most people come here simply for the beach and all the facilities it offers.

Activities
Cyprus Diving Adventures   DIVING
(☑9766 1046; www.cyprusdivingadventures.com; Kolokotroni 26, Pissouri; ⊙9am-6pm) Offers the whole range of PADI and TDI courses as well as dive tour packages that take in dive sites

across the country. Discover scuba costs €60 and bubblemaker (for first-time children divers) costs €45.

Pissouri Bay Divers   DIVING
(☑9653 0761; www.pissouribaydivers.com; Pissouri Beach; ⊙9am-6pm) PADI discover scuba (€65) for first-timers and PADI bubblemaker (€45) for children are offered, as well as a range of other PADI courses. For qualified divers, two shore dives start from €90 and boat-dive tours start from €110.

Eating
Bunch of Grapes Inn   MEDITERRANEAN €€
(☑2522 1275; Ioannou Erotokritou 9; mains from €8; ⊙11am-late) This atmospheric place in the village centre offers excellent dining under the thick shade of grapevines and fig and plane trees. Feast on dishes such as crispy roast duck in apricot and brandy sauce, and red mullet in garlic. Cypriots flock here; reservations recommended.

Two Friends   CYPRIOT €€
(☑2522 2527; Pissouri; mains from €8; ⊙noon-11pm) Two Friends prides itself on its homemade cuisine. Everything is made from scratch, including the cheese ravioli, filled with fresh cheese and mint, and the tahini dip with freshly ground sesame seeds, garlic and olive oil. It's located on the main road to the beach, just outside the village.

Limanaki   INTERNATIONAL €€
(☑2522 1288; Pissouri Beach; mains €12-20; ⊙noon-11pm Tue-Sun) Down at Pissouri beach, the best place to eat is in this old carob mill. The restaurant is famous for its homemade curries and elaborate meze spreads. Reservations recommended.

Petra tou Romiou (Aphrodite's Rock & Beach)
Possibly the most famous beach in Cyprus, Aphrodite's Beach is distinctive for its two upright rocks, which are easy to spot, particularly as swimmers are generally perched somewhat precariously on top of them. To get here, take the old B6 road from Lemesos to Pafos (a recommended scenic journey).

The reason the spot is called the Rock of Aphrodite in English is because legend has it that Aphrodite, ancient patron goddess of

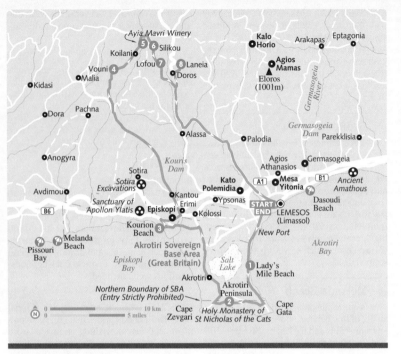

Driving Tour
Cats, Mountain Villages & Wine

START LEMESOS
FINISH LEMESOS
DISTANCE 74KM; FOUR TO SIX HOURS

From Lemesos, head west towards Pafos on the E602, passing the KEO winery and turning left to the signposted **1 Lady's Mile Beach** (p56). After a quick dip in the sea, take the long loop with the beach on your left to visit **2 St Nicholas of the Cats Monastery** (p62); see the exquisite small chapel and pick up some fruit or biscuits for your journey. Continue past the salt lake to dramatically located **3 Kourion Beach** (p55) for a coffee and mid-morning snack. Visiting Ancient Kourion takes a good two to three hours, so you may want to save this for another day. Get an inkling of what's to come by checking out the remains of the 6th-century port basilica backing Kourion Beach.

Next, double back towards Lemesos on the B6 and take the Erimi E601 exit heading north towards Omodos, passing a dam to the east. Follow the signs to **4 Vouni** and

have a stroll around this pretty town, pausing for lunch at Takis, part of the CTO's Vakhis scheme, which supports traditional Cypriot cuisine. Continue north for 5km and swing by the **5 Ayia Mavri Winery** (www.ayiamavri. com), with an excellent cabernet sauvignon and a sweet muscatel that has won the prestigious French Moscats du Monde award four times. The village is also home to Cyprus' leading producer of organic wines, Gaia Oinotechniki, which offers weekday tastings.

Around 2km after this hiccup of a detour, turn towards **6 Silikou** and **7 Lofou**; the road passes through dramatic mountain scenery and terraced agriculture with distant sea views. Wander the streets of Lofou, its cobbled lanes bordered by traditional warm limestone buildings. The village is also home to three more Vakhis restaurants.

Next stop is lovely **8 Laneia** (p61), arguably the prettiest village in these parts. Enjoy a Cypriot coffee at Kapudia restaurant (next to the car park) and a leisurely stroll through the cobbled backstreets before returning to Lemesos on the speedy, well-signposted B8.

Cyprus, emerged from the sea at this point in a surge of sea foam before, no doubt, going off to entertain some lovers. The same thing is claimed by the residents of Kythira island in Greece. But who's to say she didn't do it in two places? She was a goddess, after all.

Most visitors either stop when en route to somewhere else and have a swim, or come for the sunset, best seen from either the **Petra tou Romiou tourist pavilion**, or from a roadside car park about 1.5km further east. Skip any kind of eating at the tourist pavilion cafeteria, where you'll be overcharged for indifferent snacks; bring your own food and have a picnic instead.

A pedestrian underpass leads to the beach from the kiosk and car park on the other side of the road, around 500m further on towards Pafos from the tourist pavilion; it's well signposted.

Ancient Amathous

The remains at this **archaeological site** (admission €2.50; ☉ 9am-7.30pm Jul-Aug, to 5pm Sep-Jun), about 11km east of Lemesos, belie its original importance. Amathous was one of Cyprus' original four kingdoms (the others were Salamis, Pafos and Soloi). Founded about 1000 BC, the city had an unbroken history of settlement until about the 12th century. As much of the stone has long been looted for other building projects, imagining the ancient city layout can be baffling. At the entrance an excellent explanatory pedestal helps interpret the ruins.

Legend has it that the city was founded by Kinyras, the son of Pafos. It is also said that Kinyras introduced the cult of Aphrodite to Cyprus.

Amathous suffered badly at the hands of corsairs during the 7th and 8th centuries, and by 1191, when Richard the Lionheart appeared on the scene, the city was already on the decline. Since its harbour was silted up, King Richard was obliged to disembark on the beach to claim the once proud and wealthy city. He promptly applied the royal coup de grâce by destroying it, and Amathous was no more.

Occasional free summer concerts are held within the grounds at Amathous. Look for posters at the site or check with the CTO in Lemesos.

Episkopi

POP 3170

One of the main reasons for visiting the village of Episkopi, 14km west of Lemesos, is the **Kourion Museum** (admission €2.50; ☉ 8am-7.30pm Jul-Aug, shorter hours rest of year). The collection mainly comprises terracotta objects from Ancient Kourion and the Sanctuary of Apollon Ylatis, and is housed in what used to be the private residence of archaeologist George McFadden. The museum is signposted off the Lemesos–Kourion road, as well as in Episkopi itself.

For dining, grab a table at the **Old Stables** (☎ 2593 5568; mains €10; ☉ 6-11pm Mon-Sat). The *kleftiko* is tender and juicy, and the mezes are excellent. Takeaway is also available. It's out on the Lemesos–Pafos road opposite the Eko petrol station and looks like the kind of place that was established many generations before there were roads here, with a small and shady front terrace that deserves a better view than this.

Ancient Kourion

Defiantly perched on a hillside with a sweeping view of the surrounding patchwork of fields and the sea, **Ancient Kourion** (admission €4.50; ☉ 8.30am-7.30pm Apr-Oct, to 5pm Nov-Mar) is a spectacular site. Most likely founded in neolithic times because of its strategic position high on a bluff, it became a permanent settlement in about the 13th century BC, when Mycenaean colonisers established themselves here.

There's a small visitor's centre where you can see a scale model of the whole site, which will help orientate your visit.

The settlement prospered under the Ptolemies and Romans, and a pre-Christian cult of Apollo was active among the inhabitants of Kourion in Roman times, as evidenced by the nearby Sanctuary of Apollon Ylatis. Christianity eventually supplanted Apollo and, despite the disastrous earthquakes in the region, an early Christian basilica was built in the 5th century, testifying to the ongoing influence of Christianity on Kourion by this time.

Pirate raids 200 years later severely compromised the viability of the Christian bishopric; the Bishop of Kourion was obliged to move his base to a new settlement at nearby Episkopi (meaning 'bishopric' in Greek). Kourion declined as a settlement from that

---

ℹ TIPS FOR ANCIENT KOURION

➡ Ancient Kourion is firmly on the coach-tour and school-excursion trail. Come early in the morning or late in the afternoon, when the site is usually less crowded.

➡ If you do get there at the same time as a bus load don't fear. Most groups only tour the Roman theatre and the House of Eustolius. Start your visit at the Northern Plateau Ruins and by the time you get to the theatre the crowds should have dispersed.

➡ Ancient Kourion is close to two other attractions in the immediate vicinity: the Sanctuary of Apollon Ylatis and Kolossi Castle; all three can be visited in the same day. As a cooling break, incorporate a swim at Kourion Beach, spread out temptingly below the ancient site of Kourion itself.

---

point on and was not rediscovered until tentative excavations at the site began in 1876.

The ticket office is at the entry gate half way up the hill. From there the road continues to the hilltop to the visitor's centre and ruins.

Roman Theatre
ARCHAEOLOGICAL SITE

More interesting for its lovely coastal views than the actual structure, Kourion's Roman Theatre is a reconstruction of a smaller theatre that existed on the same spectacular site, high on the hill overlooking the sea, but which was destroyed by earthquakes in the 4th century. Nevertheless, it gives a good idea of how it would have been at its peak. Today it's often used for cultural events by Cypriot and visiting Greek singers and bands.

House of Eustolius
ARCHAEOLOGICAL SITE

Originally a palace dating from the early Roman period, this complex was subsequently altered in the 3rd century AD and made a more communal space for the local residents, with extensive baths, courtyards and halls. Its colourful, Christian-influenced mosaic floors are well preserved and make a mention of the builder, Eustolios, and the decidedly non-Christian patron, Apollo. Look for the Christian motifs of cross-shaped ornaments and fish.

Early Christian Basilica
ARCHAEOLOGICAL SITE

The early Christian basilica displays all the hallmarks of an early church, with foundations clearly showing the existence of a narthex, diakonikon (a storage area for agricultural products used by priests and monks), various rooms, a baptistery and an atrium. Some floor mosaics are also visible among the remains.

Northern Plateau Ruins
ARCHAEOLOGICAL SITE

The ruins of Hellenistic and Roman Kourion lay on the northern plateau. The Roman Agora and Stoa, with its colonnade of 16 marble columns, sit alongside the early Christian basilica.

Just to the north, a wooden walkway leads you over the substantial remnants of the Roman city baths, irrigation system, and the nymphaeum. The foundations of the public baths with the layout of the frigidarium (cold room), tepidarium (warm room) and caldarium (hot room) can still be clearly seen.

House of the Gladiators
ARCHAEOLOGICAL SITE

At the northwestern edge of the site you come to the House of the Gladiators, so called because of two fairly well-preserved floor mosaics depicting gladiators in combat dress. Two of these gladiators, Hellenikos and Margaritis, are shown practising with weapons. Just to the north is the **House of Achilles** where a fragment of a beautifully intricate floor mosaic depicting Achilles meeting with Odysseus has survived.

Sanctuary of Apollon Ylatis

About 2km west of Kourion's main entrance, and prominently signposted off the highway, is the **Sanctuary of Apollon Ylatis** (admission €2.50; ⊙ 8.30am-7.30pm Apr-Oct, to 5pm Nov-Mar), which is part of the larger site of Kourion.

Apollon Ylatis' main sanctuary has been partly restored; the beautiful, imposing columns mark the extent of the restoration. Also discernible are the priests' quarters, a palaestra (sports arena) and baths for the athletes, and a rather depleted stadium 500m to the east, which once seated up to 6000 spectators.

The precinct was established in the 8th century BC in honour of Apollo, who was considered god of the woods (*ylatis* means 'of the woods' in Greek). The once woody site now has far less vegetation but retains a good scattering of remains that give a reasonable idea of the layout of the original sanctuary. The remnants that you see are Roman structures that were levelled by a large earthquake in AD 365.

Kolossi Castle

A dollhouse of a castle (more like a fortified tower) that perches on the edge of Kolossi village, Kolossi Castle (admission €2.50; ⊙8.30am-7.30pm Apr-Sep, to 5.30pm Oct-Mar) is is an interesting reminder of the rule of the Knights of St John in the 13th century, who started producing wine and processing sugar cane at a commandery that stood on this land. The current structure dates from 1454 and was probably built over the older fortified building.

Kolossi Castle is accessible by a short drawbridge that was originally defended by a machicolation (a parapet for protecting the castle) high above, through which defenders would pour boiling oil on the heads of unwanted visitors. Upon entering, you come across two large chambers, one with an unusually large fireplace and a spiral staircase that leads to another two chambers on the second level. The only tangible remnant of occupation is a mural of the crucifixion in the first-level main chamber. The spiral staircase continues onto the roof, where the battlements, restored in 1933, lend a final touch.

To the east of the castle is a large outbuilding, now called the sugar factory, where cane was processed into sugar.

Akrotiri Peninsula

Akrotiri Sovereign Base Area

Cyprus' past is full of stories of colonisers, raiders and armies generally coveting the small island's strategic position. So when Cyprus finally and belatedly received its independence from colonial administration in 1960, Britain negotiated terms that saw the newly formed Republic of Cyprus ceding 158 sq km (99 sq miles) of its territory to its former colonial master. This territory, now known as the Sovereign Base Areas (SBAs), is used for military purposes by the British.

WORTH A TRIP

LANEIA VILLAGE

Some of the prettiest Cypriot villages are located north of Lemesos in the mountainous Mandaria region. Vouni, Silikou and Lofou are all worth visiting and within easy distance of each other, but the most photogenic village here is arguably Laneia, signposted off the B8 road, just beyond Doros (another gem).

Popular with artists and foreign residents, the flower-filled cobbled streets and warm limestone buildings have real picture-postcard appeal. This is just the sort of place where the real joy is simply wandering the streets with your camera at the ready and fantasising about buying that hideaway home for regular, annual escapes.

There's a modest agricultural museum displaying olive oil and grape presses just off the main square and a couple of good local tavernas if you fancy lunch but don't miss the other Laneia highlights on your stroll.

Church of the Virgin Mary (Main Square) This 16th-century church (restored in 1903) lies at the very heart of Laneia village. The icon panel here dates from 1676 and displays beautiful examples of religious icon paintings and decorative wooden panels from this period. The church is also home to the 12th-century Virgin Mary of Valana icon, to which many miracles are attributed.

Michael Owen Gallery (www.michaelowengallery.com; ⊙10am-5pm) British artist Michael Owen has been living in Cyprus since 1971 and his work is alive with the spirit of the Cypriot landscape. His gallery in Laneia is well signposted from the village centre.

Pleiades (⊙9.30am-5pm) Part art gallery, artists atelier, shop and cafe, Pleiades sells local pottery, jewellery and the exquisite glassware and mosaics of the owner, Phoebe. The cafe here sells tempting homemade cheesecake so it's the perfect place to put your feet up after your stroll around the village. Located near Laneia's main square.

The only indication that you are on 'foreign soil' is the odd sight of British SBA police, who patrol the territory in special police vehicles. To the immediate west of the peninsula, along the old Lemesos–Pafos road (beyond Episkopi), you'll come across green playing fields, cricket pitches and housing estates more reminiscent of Leicester than Lemesos.

The most southerly portion of the peninsula is out of bounds since it's a closed military base, complete with its own large airfield. The village of Akrotiri itself is the only true settlement within the SBA (borders were set in order to exclude most settlements). British military personnel often eat here at the several tavernas; they may be seen on their days off riding flashy mountain bikes and tackling the dirt tracks surrounding the large salt lake in the middle of the peninsula.

They also have easy access to one of the region's best restaurants: Il Gusto (☑2529 2638; Akrotiri Vasilissis Elisavel 11; mains €10-15; ☺11.30am-11pm), definitely something to write home about, with superb cuisine that's an innovative twist on classic Italian cooking. Reservations are essential. Easy to find, it is situated among the strip of restaurants on the main street here, wedged in between Chinese, Indian and fish-and-chips restaurants, but vastly superior to them all.

Akrotiri's salt lake is an important habitat for migratory birds including flamingos, cranes and ibis. Just south of Akrotiri village you can stop in at the Akrotiri Environment Centre (☑2582 6562; http://english.akrotirienvironment.com; Akrotiri Village; ☺8am-3pm Mon-Sat), which has exhibits on the area's flora and fauna, a wildlife observation kiosk and a short cultural trail.

The area is also known for its Fasouri plantations, a swathe of citrus groves across the north of the peninsula, interwoven with long, straight stretches of road overhung by tall cypress trees. They create wonderfully cool and refreshing corridors after the aridity of the southern peninsula.

Holy Monastery of St Nicholas of the Cats

This monastery (☺8am-2pm & 3-6.30pm) was founded in AD 327 by the first Byzantine governor of Cyprus, Kalokeros, and patronised by St Helena, mother of Constantine the Great. A delightful small chapel here dating from the 13th century has noteworthy icons painted by the original two nuns in residence. The actual monastery building has received a modern (and somewhat bland) refurbishment. You can buy the sisters' preserves, jams, honey and sweets, plus bags of oranges when in season.

There's a curious story behind the monastery's name. At the time of construction the Akrotiri Peninsula, and indeed the whole of Cyprus, was in the grip of a severe drought and was overrun with poisonous snakes, so building a monastery was fraught with practical difficulties. A large shipment of cats was therefore brought in from Egypt and Palestine to combat the reptilian threat. A bell would call the cats to meals and the furry warriors would then be dispatched to fight the snakes. These days, the many cats you'll find snoozing in the shade of the monastery colonnades far outnumber the six solitary sisters who now look after the place.

Positioned on the edge of the salt lake with its back to the Sovereign Base Area (SBA) fence, the monastery can be reached by a good dirt road from Akrotiri or via a not-so-obvious route west from Lady's Mile Beach.

Troödos Mountains

Best Places to Eat

➜ Mylos Restaurant (p77)

➜ Mimi's Restaurant (p69)

➜ Elyssia (p71)

➜ Stou Kir Yianni (p75)

➜ Psilo Dendro Restaurant (p71)

Best Places to Stay

➜ New Helvetia (p202)

➜ Linos Inn (p204)

➜ The Mill Hotel (p204)

➜ To Spitiko tou Arhonta (p202)

➜ Elyssia (p203)

Why Go?

Home to Mt Olympus (1952m), the island's highest peak, this stunning mountain range provides visitors with a forested flipside to the coastal resorts and big city clamour. Overlooking the valleys of Lemesos, Larnaka and the greater Mesaoria plain, this region covers over 90 sq km and is a protected natural park which safeguards its wildlife, ecology and geology. In winter, skiers and snowboarders populate the ski resorts of the northern slopes while, at other times of the year, the park is ideal for camping, picnicking, hiking, cycling and birdwatching.

As well as the natural beauty of the landscape, Troödos is home to a variety of postcard-pretty villages with their cobbled streets, terraced slopes and vernacular architecture. The region's peaks and valleys also hide some of the island's most important medieval frescoed churches, along with unexpected monasteries, museums and some of the Republic's finest wineries.

When to Go

➜ From January to April you can ski and board the slopes by day and and enjoy a hearty tavern meal by night.

➜ April to September is ideal for wine tasting; explore some of the fine wineries hidden among the sprawling vineyards and steep, breezy valleys.

➜ Ramble over 65km of diverse nature and hiking trails across the region in early summer (May and June).

➜ Beat the July and August heat by camping 1000m above sea level at verdant sites in the ranges.

Troödos Mountains Highlights

1 Visiting **Panagia Forviotissa** (p79) and the other world-famous painted churches on the Unesco World Heritage–listed Byzantine churches route.

2 Breathing in the fresh mountain air while hiking and cycling in the shadow of **Mt Olympus** (p66), and surrounded by stunning natural scenery.

3 Staying at some of the island's most authentic accommodation and getting a taste of traditional Cypriot rural life in villages such as **Kakopetria** (p76).

4 Sampling the best in Cypriot wines and visiting the vineyards along the wine routes around **Omodos** (p76).

5 Enjoying a laid-back picnic at scenic picnic sites such as **Kelefos Bridge** (p74) with its river setting and surrounding nature trails.

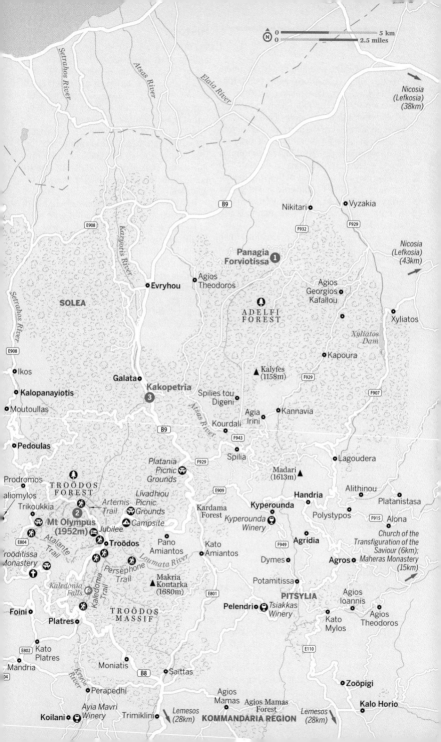

Troödos

POP 24

Located near the summit of Mt Olympus, Troödos village is the focal point for all hiking, cycling and snow-related activities in the region. At over 1900m above sea level, it's far cooler than the plains below and offers superb views of the surrounding valleys.

The village itself is minimal, centred on a simple square *(plateia)* known as Central Troödos (Kentriko Troödos in Greek). The square has a playground with some benches and a handful of souvenir shops selling everything from wind chimes to *soujoukko,* a traditional sweet made from almonds and sun-dried grape juice.

Opposite the park is the Troödos Hotel, with a couple of neighbouring restaurants and cafes. Nightlife here is practically non-existent, as most travellers are generally exhausted from the day's activities and head to bed early. A further 200m downhill to the west is Troödos Visitor Centre. The skiing facilities (open in winter) are just to the north near the Jubilee Hotel.

From the square the road north heads towards the Solea Valley and Nicosia (Lefkosia). To the west is the road to Prodromos and the Marathasa Valley. The third approach (and most common) is from the south, which takes in Platres (sometimes Pano Platres on maps), and the *krasohoria* (wine villages) of the Kommandaria region.

Central Troödos is best reached from Lemesos (via the B8) or Nicosia (via the B9). It can also be accessed from Pitsylia, in the east, and from Pafos in the west, via good but slow winding roads. On Sunday evening traffic can be very heavy on all the roads off the mountain, as weekend visitors head home to Nicosia and the coast.

History

The Troödos ocean crust, created over 90 million years ago, was the first part of the island to emerge from the sea around 15 million years ago. Rocks such as serpentinite, dunite, wehlite, pyroxenite, plagiogranite, gabbro, diabase and volcanic rock can be found at high altitudes in the region.

According to Strabo, the Greek geographer (born c 63 BC), Mt Olympus was the site of a temple to the goddess Aphrodite during the Hellenistic period. It was said to be not only unapproachable for women but completely invisible to them.

In AD 1571, Venetian generals built a fort on the mountain to keep invading Ottomans at bay, according to Cypriot nobles who visited the surrounding monasteries and summer recreation areas.

In the late 1800s, Troödos became the summer residence of the island's British governors, who came to avoid the scorching sunshine, and the area was considered the summer seat of government during British rule. At different points in its history it has provided a refuge for religious communities, freedom fighters and outlaws, as well as the wealthy of the Levant.

Nowadays, nature lovers, natural-history buffs and activity-seekers flock here for the camping, hiking trails and skiing during the winter months.

⊙ Sights & Activities

Hiking

Troödos has 13 nature trails, varying in length from 1.6km for novices to 14km for the more experienced. Together they provide an excellent insight into the diversity of the region. Most trees and plants on the trails are marked with their Latin and Greek names, and there are frequent wooden

---

DON'T MISS

KALEDONIA TRAIL: NIGHTINGALES & WATERFALLS

A perfect summer hike, the Kaledonia Trail is well shaded and well marked. Around 3km long, it starts approximately 1km downhill from Central Troödos and ends just outside the town of Platres. The trail winds down through a thickly wooded valley alongside the Kryos River, a gurgling stream with stepping-stone crossings and log bridges. The track is steep in parts and is best tackled from north to south, as it drops about 400m in altitude.

It offers a variety of vegetation like black pines and Cyprus mint and an abundance of small birds like Cyprus and Sardinian warblers and nightingales. The last kilometre brings you to picturesque Kaledonia Falls, a 15m drop of cascading water from an immense gabbro-rock precipice. Allow yourself two hours for an uplifting and relaxing hike.

benches positioned beneath trees to allow you to take breaks and admire the views.

Booklets outlining the flora, fauna and geology of each trail are available from the Troödos Visitor Centre.

Artemis Trail
HIKING

(Chionistra Circular Trail) Ideal for a first hike, this trail goes around the summit of Mt Olympus in a roughly circular loop, beginning and ending in the small car park off the Mt Olympus summit road. The track runs alternately through shaded and open areas with spectacular views to the south. It takes in vegetation such as St John's wort, Troödos sage, alyssum and barberry, and the geology includes a chromite pit and veins of pyroxenite and dunite.

The route also features the 'Walls of the Old Town', which legend says are remnants of the Venetian fort. The ski lift is conveniently located on this trail, should you come in winter. The 7km trail is fairly flat and takes three to four hours to complete. Come prepared with drinking water and a hat.

Persephone Trail
HIKING

Named after the mountain it ascends, this trail takes you on an attractive out-and-back hike through tall pines, rich vegetation and open areas with views to the horizon. The trail is 3km long and takes about an hour and a half to complete.

There's a lookout at the top of Makria Kontarka, where you can see the spread of vineyards and wine villages as far as Lemesos port to the south. On the northern side look for the enormous scar in the earth left by the now-closed asbestos mine at Pano Amiantos.

Atalante Trail
HIKING

Starting at the square in Troödos, this 12km trail is great for walkers as it's relatively easy-going and well marked. Named in honour of forest nymph Atalante, it runs at a lower altitude than the Artemis trail but follows nearly the same route. While the views are not as spectacular as those from the higher trail, it's still an enjoyable walk.

There's a fresh spring with drinking water about 3km from the trail's beginning. To get back to the village take the main Prodromos–Troödos road. Allow around five hours.

Birdwatching

Cyprus is blessed with nearly 400 bird species, and many visitors come to Troödos for its tranquillity, excellent visibility and variety of habitats. You can spot everything from

> ### CHILDREN'S CYPRUS: HORSE RIDING
>
> The small horse- and donkey-riding outfit that operates from the south side of the village (near the public toilets) is ideal if you want to give your kids an introduction to riding. The beasts are very friendly and gentle, so don't expect any galloping chases. A 10-minute escorted ride around Troödos costs €6, 20 minutes will set you back €10, half an hour €15.

Griffon vultures to warblers, wagtails and pipits. Check out www.cyprusbirding.com for comprehensive bird lists and locations.

Cycling

Troödos has a growing number of routes dedicated to cycling and mountain biking, including several forest tracks. The booklet *Troödos Cycling Routes* is available at the visitor centre and CTO offices, and has detailed information on bike tracks in the mountain range. Troödos' most common cycling route comprises three tracks making up one large circular run of the Mt Olympus summit:

Psilo Dendro (Platres)–Karvounas

A 16.2km flat ride through easy terrain including good-quality tarmac, forest and dirt track.

Karvounas–Prodromos A 22.7km ride

with a decent incline, a medium to hard degree of difficulty and good all-surface conditions.

Prodromos–Psilo Dendro An 18.2km

simple ride downhill with good roads mixed with stony tracks that can be tough on tyres.

Check out www.cypruscycling.com for information on bike runs and events held on the island.

Picnicking

With nine well-organised sites ranging in capacity from 250 to 2000 visitors, Troödos Forest Park attracts flocks of picnickers. You can set up practically anywhere and all sites have facilities such as wooden tables, fresh drinking water, toilets, playgrounds and parking. Barbecuing is allowed in the pits provided, if you wish to join the locals in grilling chops or spit-roasting *kontosouvli* (chunks of lamb).

Kampos tou Livadi, a great little picnic ground among the pine trees, is located 3km down the Troödos–Nicosia road (B9). A further 8km along this road is the popular **Platania** (Plane Trees) picnic ground and camp site. It can get busy with weekend visitors, but it offers plenty of shade and includes a children's adventure park, making it ideal for families.

Skiing

Troödos has four slopes, ranging in length from 150m to 350m. The two longer slopes are on the north face of the mountain; the Hera lift takes you to the 350m beginners' slope, and the Zeus lift takes you to the peak for the advanced 500m-long Jubilee run and the racing runs. The **North Face Ski Centre** (☑2542 0105; Tröodos; ⊙9am-7pm Jan-Mar), which offers ski equipment rental, is located here at the Dias Restaurant.

On the southern shoulder are the ski lifts to the shorter Aphrodite and Hermes runs, great for beginners and intermediates. The **Sun Valley Centre** (☑2542 0104; Tröodos; ⊙9am-6pm Jan-Mar) and a ski shop are located here.

Visit www.skicyprus.com for snow reports and the latest information on slope conditions.

✗ Eating

Choice here is not great unless you're after a simple snack. If so, **Fereos Park Restaurant** (☑2542 0114; mains from €12; ⊙9am-7pm) is your best bet for a good-sized kebab or souvlaki. Otherwise, head for Platres, where there are many more restaurants with a variety of food and far better quality.

ℹ Getting There & Away

Buses to the Troödos Mountains run regularly from Nicosia (Lefkosia) or Lemesos. Call ahead to confirm routes and times and even request a stop at an in-between village.

Service taxis don't operate out of Troödos. A standard taxi will take you there, but it can be expensive due to the time it takes to drive up the mountain.

Osel Buses (☑2246 5546; www.osel.com.cy; one way/all day/return €1.50/5/3) Buses run twice daily from Constanza Bastion, Nicosia, to Central Troödos at 5.45am and 11.55am weekdays and 8am and 2pm weekends. There is the same frequency of return trips. The journey takes approximately 1½ hours.

Emel (☑7777 8121; www.limassolbuses.com; one way/all day/return €1.50/5/3) Buses run from Lemesos to Central Troödos at 9am daily and return at 3.30pm.

ℹ Getting Around

The best way to explore the expanse of Troödos and the more remote villages is via your own wheels, rather than being at the mercy of the limited public transport. The roads, although windy, are good.

Platres

POP 200

The nightingales won't let you sleep in Platres. *Georgos Seferis, Eleni, 1953*

Platres (formerly Pano Platres) is the highest of the mountain communities, with an altitude of approximately 1200m. Located in a lush and fertile pocket of dense forest, it receives some of the highest rainfall in Cyprus.

A popular health retreat with British colonialists and personalities from the past, Platres has hosted Nobel Prize–winning Greek poet Georgos Seferis, whose most famous poems were inspired by the village, and King Farouk of Egypt, who crossed the Mediterranean to seek summer refuge here. Modelled somewhat on the hill stations of colonial Asia, it has all the trappings of a cool mountain retreat: forest walks, bubbling streams, relief from the heat of the plains, and gin and tonics on the balconies of old-world hotels.

ℹ TROÖDOS VISITOR CENTRE

Just south of Troödos' main street and worth checking out, the **visitor centre** (admission €1; ⊙10am-3pm Jun, to 4pm Jul-Aug, shorter hours rest of the year) includes a small museum with displays dedicated to examples of all the region's flora, fauna, geology and wildlife. A mini theatre plays an informative 10-minute audiovisual presentation detailing the park's history, and a geographic display in the foyer outlines the park's boundaries, mountains and environs. Importantly, all maps, brochures and published information about the region, including hiking trails and vegetation, are available here. The 250m botanical and geological trail surrounding the centre is an easy introduction to the area's attractions for children and adults alike.

Nowadays it's popular with hikers, retirees and travellers who prefer the hills to the beaches. Platres has now merged its former charm with modernised restaurants and hotels to become a delightful place to stay while visiting the mountains. It's a perfect retreat during the heat of summer with its dry climate, scenic surroundings and overall tranquility, and in winter, it converts into the perfect ski resort, with cosy restaurants and roaring log fires.

Platres is off the main Lemesos–Troödos highway (B9) and consists of a series of snaking roads, an upper road that's home to a number of hotels, and a lower road populated with restaurants, shops and bars.

It's a great base for day trips to surrounding sites such as the monasteries at Kykkos and Troöditissa, the Byzantine churches and the wine villages of the Kommandaria region. You'll definitely need a car or suitable alternative to explore the greater area.

Check out www.platres.org to keep up with local information.

◉ Sights

The village has some wonderful examples of traditional stone buildings, now mostly held (and still used) by the municipality. As you walk around the streets, look out for examples like the **police station** (built by the British) near the CTO office, the **old gymnasium** (now the Platres Hospital) 600m south of the village centre, the two-storey **community council offices**, and the well-kept building of the **Electricity Authority**, built in 1930 using local stone.

🏃 Activities

Only 10km from Central Troödos and its nearby hiking trails, Platres has some good hikes, such as the downhill route to Foini, 9km to the west, the slightly easier 7km route to Perapedhi, and an excellent 3km uphill ramble to Pouziaris. These hikes and others are mapped in the CTO brochure *Platres,* available at the Troödos Visitor Centre.

🍴 Eating

Enjoy local dishes accompanied by some superb wines from the nearby *krasohoria* valley and Kommandaria region.

★**Mimi's Restaurant**　CYPRIOT €€
(☑ 2542 1449; Olympou; mains from €8, meze €15; ⊙ 9am-10pm) Located just past the police station on the main road through town, this

HANDMADE CYPRUS CHOCOLATES

Cyprus Chocolates (☑ 9976 6446; www.cypruschocolate.com; Leoforos Archiepiskopou Makariou III; ⊙ 9.30am-5.30pm) This place would happily fit in on a big city high street, instead of on a quiet corner of Platres, although word is out and, apparently, even Queen Elizabeth II is a fan. Beautifully packaged handmade chocolates are available, including *flava* chocolate enhanced with Cyprus royal jelly, and promoted as being beneficial to your health (as if we needed any persuading...).

It also produces chocolates infused with herbal flavours such as fresh cardamom, wild rosemary and garden mint. Workshops are held both in making chocolates and creating art with chocolate (from €35 per person).

may not be the most atmospheric place to eat in town, but ask any local where they like to dine and this is the place they will probably cite. You won't hear that dreaded ping of the microwave, everything here is freshly made. The meze is the menu highlight.

Skylight Restaurant Bar & Pool　MEDITERRANEAN €€
(www.skylight.com.cy; Leoforos Archiepiskopou Makariou III 524; mains from €10; ⊙ noon-10pm) This popular restaurant offers an excellent choice of grills and seafood dishes, as well as an extensive choice of close to a dozen salads. Unusually, you can enjoy your meal in between taking a dip in the restaurant pool (admission per day €5).

Skylight also has a vast and sunny terrace, from where you can enjoy views over the rooftops to the mountains beyond.

To Anoi　CYPRIOT €€
(Olympou 37; mains from €10; ⊙ 10am-10pm) A large stone building, this family tavern serves traditional dishes like *kleftiko* (oven-baked lamb) and *souvla* (skewered meat, usually lamb) cooked over hot coals.

Village Tavern　CYPRIOT €€
(Leoforos Archiepiskopou Makariou III; mains €8; ⊙ 8am-9pm) Open views from the terrace, a cosy taverna-style interior and simple traditional food served in good-sized portions,

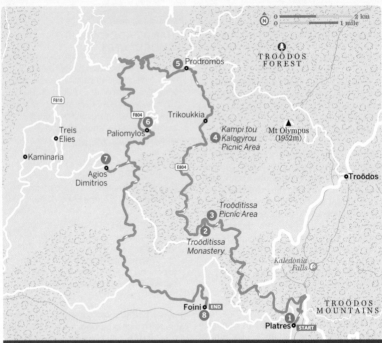

Driving Tour
Monasteries & Mountain Villages

START PLATRES
FINISH FOINI
DISTANCE 44KM; THREE TO FOUR HOURS

First stop is the Cyprus Chocolates shop in ❶ **Platres** to pick up a bag of scrumptious handmade chocolates for the trip. Next, take the E804 from Platres for a peek at some of the valley's hidden villages. This route includes the 13th-century ❷ **Troöditissa Monastery**, located amid thick pines at the top of a steep gorge.

The monastery was founded after the discovery of a priceless silver-plated icon of the Virgin that was brought from Asia Minor. Believed to assist fertility, the icon had been guarded in a nearby cave by two hermits until their deaths. The monastery's existing church, built in 1731, is currently closed to the public as it is part of a working religious order. However, if you are polite and patient the monks may well let you in.

Continuing along the mountain road, you pass the picnic areas of ❸ **Troöditissa** and

❹ **Kampi tou Kalogyrou** in the cool pine forests. From there you reach the village of ❺ **Prodromos** (www.prodromos.org.cy). This small village still has some hill-station clientele but is not as well known as Troödos and Platres. At 1380m, it's Cyprus' highest village and is surrounded by lush orchards with apple, peach, plum, almond and chestnut trees. Looping back towards the south brings you to ❻ **Paliomylos** and ❼ **Agios Dimitrios**, a pair of timeless villages barely touched by tourism, buried beneath the greenery and grapevines.

A little further on is ❽ **Foini**, a great place to stop for some *loukoumades* (similar to Turkish Delight, but flavoured with bergamot rather than traditional rosewater) and a strong coffee. It's also very popular for its handmade pottery and *pitharia* (earthenware storage jars). For lunch, a good choice is the fresh trout at Neraida. Located on the western side of the village, near the stream, it's open Thursday to Tuesday for lunch, and for dinner Friday and Saturday.

make this a pleasant spot to recharge after a hike. Try the fresh Cypriot salads with the lightly browned moussaka.

Psilo Dendro Restaurant CYPRIOT €€€
(Aïdonion 13; trout €14; ⏰11am-5pm) Close to the southern end of the Kaledonia Trail from Troödos, this restaurant receives many hungry hikers. It has an adjoining trout farm, from which it serves some of the freshest fish on the island.

ℹ Information

The **Cyprus Tourism Organisation** (CTO; ☑2542 1316; www.visitcyprus.com; F825 Platres; ⏰9am-3.30pm Mon-Fri, to 2.30pm Sat) has information on the Troödos hiking trails.

To report a **forest fire** call ☑1407.

ℹ Getting There & Away

All public transport arrives at and departs from the area adjoining the CTO office.

Emel (☑7777 8121; www.limassolbuses.com; one way/all day & return €3/5) Bus 64 runs to/from Platres to Lemesos six times daily from 6.05am to 3.15pm Monday to Friday, four times on Saturday and twice on Sunday. A single/return costs €1.50/3. Check the website for more detailed information.

Travel Express Taxis (☑2587 7666; www.travelexpress.com.cy) Runs from Lemesos to Platres for approximately €50 one way.

Marathasa Valley

This scenic valley to the northwest of Troödos cradles some of the mountain's most important and impressive sights, such as the splendid Kykkos Monastery, the beautifully frescoed church of Archangelos Michail in Pedoulas; and the humble Agios Ioannis Lambadistis Monastery in Kalopanayiotis.

Spring and autumn are particularly lovely times to visit, when wildflowers display their dazzling rainbow of colours. There's also some excellent agrotourism accommodation (p203) to be found in the valley, mostly in restored traditional houses.

Pedoulas

POP 195

Pedoulas (www.pedoulasvillage.com) is the main town and tourist centre in the Marathasa Valley with some reliably good eating and sleeping options. Famous for its spring water (sold all over Cyprus), it's particularly cool and breezy in summer.

ℹ BUG BEACON

Make sure you bring bug or insect repellent. The mountains are wonderfully picturesque, but they do have their share of creepy-crawlies. Many of the big flies and tree bugs appear to be especially attracted to white T-shirts and skirts, so consider wearing alternative colours, particularly during the hotter months and around the summit.

◉ Sights

★**Archangelos Michael** CHURCH
(⏰10am-6pm Tue-Sun) Most people visit Pedoulas to see this extraordinary Unesco-listed church. Dating from 1474, the gable-roofed building sits in the lower part of the village. Its evocative and brightly coloured frescos, restored in 1980, show a move towards the naturalism of the post-Byzantine revival, and are credited to an artist known only as Adamos. The key to the church is held at the Byzantine Museum across the street.

Also depicted are, of course, the Archangel Michael, looming above the faithful, as well as the denial of Christ, the sacrifice of Abraham, the Virgin and Christ, and a beautiful baptism scene where an unclothed Christ is exiting the River Jordan with fish swimming at his feet.

Be sure not to mistake the looming white Church of the Holy Cross just up the road for this far more famous and historic church.

Byzantine Museum MUSEUM
(⏰10am-4.30pm Tue-Sun) FREE The rich collection of 12th- to 15th-century icons come from six ancient Byzantine churches in the village and include the late-13th-century icon of the Virgin Vorinis. Many pieces have featured in exhibitions worldwide.

Folk Art Museum MUSEUM
(⏰10am-4pm Tue-Sun) FREE Near the village centre, this museum houses clothing, furniture and agricultural tools that provide a snapshot of the culture, customs and history of the Marathasa region.

✗ Eating

★**Elyssia** CYPRIOT €€
(☑9975 3573; Filoxenias 47; mains €10, meze €20; ⏰10am-11pm) The moussaka here apparently attracts regulars from Pafos – it is that good. The congenial owner (who also runs the hotel of the same name) loves to cook –

and it shows. Aside from meals, she sells a tantalising range of homemade preserves and chutneys. Rumbling tummies can opt for the meze comprising 20 plates and is another crowd pleaser. The fireplace gets going in winter.

Platanos CYPRIOT €€
(Vasou Hadjiioannou; mains €9; ⊘8am-6pm) In the cool shade of the *platano* (plane tree), this restaurant serves traditional dishes like *souvlakia* (souvlaki) and *afelia* (slow-cooked pork with wine and herbs). Cypriot coffee is a must, prepared using a tray of hot sand between the *brikki* (a small saucepan) and the open flame. This method allows the coffee to heat gradually, giving a richer taste.

ⓘ Getting There & Away

Osel Buses (p68) go from Constanza Bastion, Nicosia, to Pedoulas four times daily on weekdays, three times on Saturday and twice on Sunday (single/return €1.50/3, 1½ hours).

Kalopanayiotis

POP 290

Famous for its monastery and Byzantine museum, Kalopanayiotis is a relaxing place to stop for a few days, with natural **sulphur** springs (dedicated to the ancient god of healing, Asclepius) and good-quality agrotourism accommodation.

◉ Sights

Agios Ioannis Lambadistis Monastery CHURCH
(⊘9am-4pm Tue-Sun May-Sep, shorter hours rest of the year; ⓟ) This Unesco-listed site is a complex of three churches in one, dating from the 11th century and built over 400 years. The original Orthodox church has a double nave, to which a narthex and a Latin chapel were later added. Now under one huge pitched wooden roof, they represent one of the most wonderfully preserved churches in the region. The monastery is reached by following the narrow and winding main street to the opposite side of the valley.

The main domed Orthodox church exhibits colourful, intricate 13th-century frescos dedicated to Agios Irakleidios. These include Jesus' entry to Jerusalem on a donkey, with children climbing date trees to get a better look. Other featured frescos include the Raising of Lazarus, the Crucifixion and the Ascension, with vivid colour schemes suggesting artistic influence from Constantinople.

THE FRESCOED BYZANTINE CHURCHES OF CYPRUS

Many visitors come to the Troödos region to see the remarkable Byzantine churches, built and decorated with stunning frescos between the 11th and 15th centuries. Ten of these churches are Unesco World Heritage Sites.

When the French Catholic Lusignan dynasty took control of Cyprus in 1197, work on a series of small churches in the mountains had already begun. But it was the repression and discrimination exercised by the Lusignans against the Orthodox Greek Cypriots that prompted the Orthodox clergy, along with artisans and builders, to retreat to the northern slopes of the Troödos Mountains. Here they built and embellished private ecclesiastical retreats where Orthodoxy flourished undisturbed for 300 years.

The culmination of this activity was many churches built in a similar fashion. Most were little bigger than small barns; some had domes, some did not. Because of the harsh winter weather, steeply inclined overhanging roofs were added to protect the churches from accumulated snow. Inside, skilled fresco painters went to work producing vivid images.

Not all churches were lavishly painted, but the Unesco-designated churches represent the finest examples. The frescos are remarkable for their clarity of detail and the preservation of their colour. The later didactic-style frescos are unusual in that they are painted like a movie strip, ostensibly to teach illiterate villagers the rudiments of the gospels.

You will need at least two days to visit all the churches. A number of them are kept locked, so you'll have to track down their caretakers. Donations of €1 to €3 are appreciated. A car is the easiest way to visit most of the churches, as public transport is sporadic.

In viewing order, the Unesco churches are: Archangelos Michail, Agios Ioannis Lambadistis Monastery, Panagia tou Moutoulla, Agios Nikolaos tis Stegis, Panagia tis Podythou, Panagia Forviotissa (Asinou), Stavros tou Agiasmati, Panagia tou Araka, Church of Timios Stavros and Church of the Transfiguration of the Saviour.

The antechamber and Latin chapel have more frescos, dating from the 15th and 16th centuries. Those in the chapel are considered to be the most comprehensive series of Italo-Byzantine frescos in Cyprus. The scenes representing the Akathistos hymn (praising the Virgin Mary in 24 verses) are shown as 24 pictures, each carrying a letter of the Greek alphabet. The Arrival of the Magi depicts the Magi on horseback, wearing crusader armour and grandstanding red crescents (a Roman symbol for the Byzantines and later the Turks). Photographs of the iconography are not permitted.

Note that the opening hours can fluctuate; if closed you can generally find the priest (plus key) at the nearby coffee shop.

Byzantine Museum MUSEUM
(admission €1; ⊗9am-4pm Tue-Sat, 11am-4pm Sun May-Sep, shorter hours rest of the year) Part of the monastery, this museum displays a collection of 15 icons discovered in 1998. Dating from the 16th century, the icons were hidden underground for many years by Orthodox priests escaping the invading Ottomans. The iconostasis (screen that holds icons) is covered in carvings of local ferns found at the river in Kalopanayiotis, confirming its origins.

Moutoullas

This small village, on the road between Pedoulas and Kalopanayiotis, is the site of Panagia tou Moutoulla, another Unesco-listed church with frescos. The village is also well known for its traditional woodcarvings, as well as its bounty of apples and cherries, thanks to the vast surrounding orchards.

The oldest of the painted churches in the Tröodos mountains and believed to have once been a private chapel, **Panagia tou Moutoulla** (⊗dawn-dusk) `FREE` has the steep aisle and pitched roof common to the region. Its rare unrestored paintings include depictions of St Christopher, St George and the Virgin and date back to AD 1280. You will need to seek out the key, held at the village coffee shop.

Kykkos Monastery

The island's most prosperous and opulent Orthodox **monastery** (⊗dawn-dusk; `P`) `FREE` was founded in the 11th century by Byzantine emperor Alexios I Komninos after a bizarre series of events. Over the cen-

turies, a series of fires all but destroyed the original monastery. The surviving building is an imposing and well-maintained structure dating from 1831. To enter you will need to dress conservatively; shawls and cover-up clothing are provided for scantily clad visitors. It's located about 20km west of Pedoulas.

The story behind the monastery started with a hermit called Esaias (Isaiah), who lived in a cave close to the site. One day in the forest, Esaias crossed paths with a hunter from Nicosia, Manouil Voutomytis, who was also the Byzantine governor of Cyprus. Voutomytis was lost and asked directions from the recluse, only to be ignored because of Esaias' ascetic vows. The self-important hunter became outraged at what he perceived to be the hermit's insolence, cursing at him and shoving him as a lesson.

Upon returning to Nicosia, Voutomytis began to suffer incurable lethargy. He recalled how he had mistreated Esaias and set out to beg forgiveness, in the hope of restoring his failing health. Meanwhile, a vision from God appeared to Esaias, telling him to charge Voutomytis with the task of bringing the Icon of the Virgin Mary from Constantinople to Cyprus.

At the hermit's request, and after much soul-searching, Voutomytis was eventually able to bring the icon to Cyprus. He convinced the Byzantine emperor in Constantinople, whose daughter suffered the same lethargic affliction, that she would be saved if they did what the hermit (and therefore God) had asked.

The icon, said to be painted by St Luke, is one of only three that survive. For the last four centuries it has sat in a sealed, silver-encased box within the Kykkos Monastery.

Byzantine Museum MUSEUM
(⏱2294 2736; admission €5; ⊗10am-6pm Jun-Sep, to 4pm Oct-May; `P`) This museum houses much of the monastery's fabulous wealth, including Byzantine and ecclesiastical artefacts. On the left when you enter is an antiquities display. In the large ecclesiastical gallery are early Christian, Byzantine and post-Byzantine vestments, vessels and jewels. A small circular room houses old manuscripts, documents and books, and a rich display of icons, wall paintings and carvings can be found in the larger circular chamber.

Tomb of Archbishop Makarios III

The tomb of the first president of Cyprus is located on Throni Hill, 2km past Kykkos Monastery. Makarios was buried here at his request, close to the place where he served as an apprentice monk in 1926. The simple stone sepulchre is overlaid with black marble and covered by a round, stone-inlaid dome. A huge bronze statue of the archbishop, moved from Nicosia's Archepiscopal Palace in 2008, now stands on the hill, adding to its grandeur.

Higher up on the path from the tomb is the **Throni Shrine** to the Virgin Mary. It has spectacular, endless views of the valleys and roads leading to Kykkos from the east. A **wishing tree** is located just near here, where the pious tie paper and cloth messages in the hope that the Virgin Mary will grant their requests.

Treis Elies

Southwest of Prodromos via the F10 and F811 is Treis Elies, a quiet hamlet perfect for relaxation. There's a small river and nature trail around the village and just outside is the Iamatikes (signposted as 'Ιαματικές') **sulphur spring**, spurting through large rocks. Its location is convenient for hikes to the Kelefos, Elies and Roudhias medieval bridges, which were built during Venetian rule in an effort to streamline the camel-caravan route near the village. The camels transported copper from Troödos to Polis and Pafos, where it was traded. Unfortunately the original path is now all but lost.

The three bridges are connected by the European Long Distance Path E4, which is ideal for walking.

Closest to Treis Elies is **Elies Bridge**, just after the village of Kaminaria. Set in dense

ARCHBISHOP MAKARIOS III: PRIEST & POLITICIAN

The ethnarch and religious leader of Cyprus during its brief period of independence as a united island, Makarios was born Michael Christodoulou Mouskos on 13 August 1913, in the small mountain village of Pano Panagia in Pafos.

He studied in Cyprus and at the University of Athens, and graduated from the School of Theology at Boston University. Ordained Bishop of Kition in 1946, he became archbishop four years later.

Initially a supporter of the enosis (union with Greece) movement for Cyprus, he later opposed its notions of independence, commonwealth status and *taksim* (the Turkish objective for separation). However, during the three-year uprising of the 1950s, the British suspected him of collaboration with the rebel pro-enosis movement Ethniki Organosi tou Kypriakou Agona (EOKA; National Organisation for the Cypriot Struggle) and he was exiled to the Seychelles.

Still, Makarios was a politician, not an insurgent, and he was welcomed back to Cyprus in 1959. Negotiating an independence agreement with the British, he was elected president of the newly independent Republic of Cyprus in a landslide victory on 13 December of that year.

Distancing himself from the enosis movement in favour of independence, Makarios tried to appease the Turkish Cypriot minority on the island and forge a foreign policy of nonalignment. However, he was seen by some Turkish Cypriots as anti-Turkish, and serious sectarian violence broke out in 1963. The US saw his disinterest in the west as being too communist and pegged him as the 'Castro of the Mediterranean'.

The Greek junta, abetted by the American CIA and pro-enosis EOKA-B (the post-independence version of EOKA) radicals, launched a coup in 1974 behind Greek general Grivas with a view to assassinating Makarios and installing a new government. The coup backfired: Makarios escaped, and Turkey (already preparing for partition) used the coup as a reason for invasion, politically sabotaging any hope of peace between the two communities. Turkey started bombing villages and invaded the north of Cyprus.

The junta fell and Makarios returned from England to preside over a now truncated state. He died unexpectedly on 3 August 1977 aged 63. Today he is remembered by many as a leader, a statesman and the embodiment of the people's aspirations for independence and identity.

EUROPEAN LONG DISTANCE PATH E4

Treis Elies is a fantastic base from which to explore **European Long Distance Path E4**, a famous trail that starts at Gibraltar and passes through Spain, France, Switzerland, Germany, Austria, Hungary, Bulgaria, Greece and Cyprus. The E4 is linked to Cyprus by air and sea, starting at Larnaka and Pafos airports, and covering the Troödos Mountains. It continues on to the Akamas Peninsula and stretches across to the eastern regions of the Cypriot areas of Famagusta.

You can download the mapped route via the www.wandermap.net website and the Cyprus Tourism Organisation (CTO) booklet *European Long Distance Path E4 & Other Cyprus Nature Trails* also gives an overview of the Cypriot walks, stating lengths, degrees of difficulty, starting and ending locations, and points of interest. The path is a rambler's delight, with detailed maps an essential. Conquering the Cypriot portion is a soul-stirring start to being part of the greater project, so lace up those hiking boots and stride out.

forest, with an underground fresh stream, it was believed to be the easterly link of the caravan route.

Kelefos Bridge is the most elegant, with a strong single-pointed arch over a wide waterway. It takes about two hours to hike from Elies to Kelefos, where you'll find an excellent picnic spot. You can also reach Kelefos Bridge by car, following the signs towards Agios Nikolaos.

The third, **Roudhias Bridge**, is impressive but far more remote. It's a long-distance four-hour hike away, along the trail past the Pera Vassas forestry station and picnic ground. The bridge can be difficult to find, so take a good map. If you choose to drive, the direct road is a narrow track with limited access. There is also a river crossing that requires a 4WD.

Omodos

POP 600

Omodos is a popular destination for day trippers from the coastal resorts. And for good reason. Despite the proliferation of souvenir shops, there are several worthwhile sights and the backstreets have a timeless cobbled charm and are home to an excellent restaurant and guesthouse, plus a quirky museum, and some smaller more idiosyncratic shops.

◎ Sights

Timiou Stavrou (Holy Cross) Monastery   MONASTERY
(◎9.30am-1pm & 2-7pm Thu-Tue, 9.30am-12.30pm Wed) Fronted by the town's impressive (and massive) cobbled square, at the monastery's entrance stands a statue commemorating a former abbot, Dositheos, who was murdered by Turkish troops during the Greek War of

Independence in 1821. Acting as the parish church today, the monastery was originally built around 1150 and was extended and extensively remodelled in the 19th century. Several of the outbuildings now house small museums.

These include the harrowing **National Struggle Museum**. This museum is small and simple but the memories evoked by the black-and-white photos of the men and women killed (some reputedly tortured) by British forces between 1955 and 1959 might linger in your mind long after you leave.

Another outbuilding houses the **Museum for the Preservation of Lace** with delicate examples of the *pipilies* (needlepoint lacework) for which the village is famed.

Socrates Traditional House   MUSEUM
(Linou; ◎9.30am-7pm) **FREE** Located in the backstreets but well signposted, this quirky museum in a traditional house has an eclectic assortment of exhibits and furnishings including historic wine presses, wedding attire, old photos, looms, a corn mill, typical village furniture and objects from rural life.

✖ Eating

★**Stou Kir Yianni**   CYPRIOT €€
(☏2542 2100; Linou 15; mains €10-17; ◎10am-10pm; 🖐) Head for the courtyard with its cool colour palette of limestone and whitewash, plus local art on the walls and a menu that includes *fatoush* salad with pomegranate juice. There is also *kleftiko*, vegetarian moussaka, kebabs and *karaolous me pnigouri* (snails with bulgur wheat) – you may think Heston Blumenthal has stopped by, but actually this is a traditional Cypriot dish.

KOMMANDARIA REGION

Homer made mention of its amber colour and rich sweetness in his writings. The Knights Templar were so fond of it they named it after their Commanderie (headquarters) in Lemesos, exporting it to the royal courts of Europe. Upon Richard the Lionheart's marriage in Lemesos, he declared it 'the wine of kings' and 'the king of wines'. For over 4000 years it has been made at the vast vineyards in the Kommandaria valley, exposed to the southerly sun. Made from dark and white grapes, Kommandaria is as excellent as ever, with over a dozen villages still producing it. Try **Revecca Spirits** (www.reveccaspirits.com) in Agios Mamas for a large selection. You can also visit a number of the wineries and sample their produce.

There's live music Thursday to Saturday, ranging from blues to Greek, as well as an ouzo bar (tasting €5).

George's Bakery　　　　　　　BAKERY
(📞 2542 2142; 1 Oct; breads from €1.20; ⊘ 9am-6pm) This bakery and deli serves a vast range of breads, cakes, halvah, nut brittle and similar, most happily available for tasting. Try the local *apkatena* bread with ingredients including chickpeas, cinnamon, nutmeg and citrus peel. Located adjacent to the car park.

🔒 Shopping

Byzantine Icon Studio　　　　　SOUVENIRS
(maria.icon.painter@gmail.com; Linou; ⊘ 9.30am-6pm) Maria Aristou is an icon painter and sells her work at this small shop in the backstreets. Prices range from €80 to €120.

Around Omodos

The extensive vineyards of the *krasohoria* occupy the scenic slopes around Omodos. This is a traditional winemaking region where, up until around the 1960s, every house had its own winemaking tools. To this day you'll find that many villages sell a variety of traditional grape products such as *soujoukos* (grapes blended with almonds), *espima* (grape honey) and *palouze* (grape sweets).

Zenon (📞 2542 3555; Dimitri Liperti, Omodos; ⊘ noon-7pm) winery is just outside Omodos and offers free wine tasting along with a small wine museum. Try their award winning shiraz-maratheftiko. **Vlassides** (📞 9944 1574; www.vlassideswinery.com) offers aromatic, full-flavoured reds and is located in Kilani village. **Yiaskouris Winery** (📞 2594 2470), in Pachna village, has great shirazes and dry whites.

There are more than 50 boutique wineries in the region, many open by appointment only; visit www.wineriescyprus.com for profiles and seasonal opening times.

Solea Valley

The Solea Valley, bisected by the Karyotis River, has significant frescoed churches built during the late Byzantine era, when the area was revered for its importance as a stronghold.

The valley's reputation as a strategic refuge was furthered in the 1950s, when it served as the prime hideout area for Ethniki Organosi tou Kypriakou Agona (EOKA; National Organisation for the Cypriot Struggle) revolutionists during their anti-British campaigns. With its concealed terrain and proximity to Nicosia, it was an ideal location.

Today it's still perfect for accessing the mountains and beyond, with roads to both the east and west. The main village in the valley is Kakopetria, which is convenient for day trips and longer stays, with decent hotels and good facilities.

Kakopetria

POP 1200

Kakopetria, or *kaki petra* (meaning 'bad rock'), gets its name from the line of huge rocks along the ridge around the village that were clearly a hindrance to the first settlers. Situated across both banks of the Karyotis River, expect steep roads, hanging trees and the sound of natural storm drains.

The area is very popular with wealthy Cypriots, who retire to their homes in the mountains for the summer months. The old quarter of the village is heritage listed, and many of the houses have been restored accordingly, enabling it to retain its charm.

Kakopetria has good restaurants and accommodation. It's also another ideal place to base yourself while exploring the frescoed churches and the surrounding area.

✖ Eating

Village Pub   CYPRIOT €
(mains from €6; ⊙12.30-3.30pm & 6-10pm Tue-Sat) This place has a wooden terrace overlooking the village, and provides good and simple summer meals such as fresh salads, *fassolia* (white beans) and *faggi* (lentils).

★ Mylos Restaurant   MEDITERRANEAN €€
(Mill Hotel; ☑2292 2536; www.cymillhotel.com; Mylou 8; mains from €10; ⊙noon-4pm & 7-11pm; 🖘) This excellent restaurant at the Mill Hotel is ideally situated next to the river, with a slow-turning mill wheel and a shady terrace with superb views. The trout here is legendary and served either grilled or in a delicious garlic-spiked sauce. In winter they light up the historic fireplace inside. You'll need a reservation on weekends.

Linos Inn   CYPRIOT €€
(☑2292 3161; www.linosinn.com; Palea Kakopetria 34; meze per plate from €5; ⊙restaurant 10am-midnight year-round, cafe 10am-10pm May-Sep; 🖈) An atmospheric restaurant (part of the same name hotel) with an excellent meze and great local reds like *ktima malia* (€20), a rich cabernet. There's also a relaxing terrace cafe and bar (open in summer) where you can try smoking the nargileh (water pipe). This is a very popular venue, so reservations are essential.

ℹ Getting There & Away

There's no direct public transport to the Unesco-listed churches in the valley.

Osel Buses (p68) run from Constanza Bastion, Nicosia, to Kakopetria about every hour from 5.45am to 8pm on weekdays and less frequently, from 8am, on weekends. There are roughly the same number of buses doing the return trip. A single/return fare costs €1.50/3.

Around Kakopetria

These valleys are great for hiking and picnics, as well as being home to some of the area's most historic churches.

⊙ Sights

Agios Nikolaos tis Stegis   CHURCH
(⊙9am-6pm Tue-Sat, 11am-4pm Sun) This Unesco-listed church, known in English as St Nicholas of the Roof because of its large, heavy-pitched top, was founded in the 11th century and contains frescos which are a mix of images and styles, the best including the Crucifixion and the Nativity. The dome and narthex were added in the 15th century, along with the roof, to protect against the region's snowfall.

Situated 5km north of Kakopetria, it was originally part of a monastery complex.

Panagia tis Podythou   CHURCH
(☑2292 2393; Galata; ⊙sporadic) Located in the village of Galata, on the Nicosia road, is this 16th-century Unesco-listed church that was established in 1502 by Dimitrios de Coron, a Greek military officer, in the service of James II (King of Cyprus). It was occupied by monks until the 1950s.

Internally, its 17th-century frescos cover the pediment of both the east and west walls. The two striking frescos on the north and south walls appear to be uncompleted. They depict the apostles, Peter and Paul, in a Renaissance-influenced (Italo-Byzantine) style with vivid colours that provide a three-dimensional appearance.

The church is rectangular, with a semi-circular apse at the eastern end and a portico (built later) that surrounds it on three sides. It also has the characteristic pitched roof you would expect.

If the church is closed, ask for the caretaker at the Galata village coffee shop.

TROÖDOS MOUNTAINS SOLEA VALLEY

KAKOPETRIA'S HISTORIC QUARTER

To find the most picturesque and historic part of town, take the lane east of the Village Pub, past a large boulder known as the *Stone of the Couple* which has a plaque describing how it was thought to bring good luck to newlyweds until it toppled over and crushed one such – very unlucky – couple. The houses here have traditional trussed roofs, covered with reeds and tiles and supported by beams with overhanging wooden balconies. Seek out the simple Metamorposis Sotiros chapel, as well as a small wine museum, tucked up a side street but well signposted.

Driving Tour
Wine Route 6

START PLATRES
FINISH AGROS
DISTANCE 110KM; SEVEN TO EIGHT HOURS

Wine Route 6 takes in over 14 villages, two wineries and some of the best family-owned vineyards in the region. It is well signposted the whole way: look out for the green and burgundy signs that have a grape symbol and the number six on them. The route is one long, winding loop, so make lots of rest stops, allocate a designated driver or watch the amount of wine you consume. Visiting times at the wineries are fairly flexible, so it's a good idea to call beforehand. The wineries offer vineyard tours and are happy for you to taste freely. You ought to buy at least one bottle, though, which isn't much of a hardship.

Take the B8 south from Platres, then turn onto the E806 towards Pelendri. Look for the signs to the ❶ **Tsiakkas Winery** and make a stop to taste some excellent dry whites and a commendable cab sav. Just before you come to Pelendri, take the right-hand turn to the ❷ **Church of Timios Stavros** (p81), one of the region's most magnificent painted churches with rare 12th-century paintings. Continue on the F949 past Potamitissa and Dymes villages until you reach ❸ **Kyperounda** and the Kyperounda Winery. This contemporary winery has a large range of whites and reds and a particularly palatable red blend called Andessitis. Next stops are the high-altitude villages of ❹ **Handria** and ❺ **Lagoudera**, on the F915, with abundant vineyards. Here you can stop and see the Unesco-listed 12th-century Byzantine church of ❻ **Panagia tou Araka** (p80). Double back a short way then wind past ❼ **Polystypos** and ❽ **Alona** on the F915, then turn onto the E903 to reach the village of ❾ **Agros**, home of many mavros (dark red) grapevines. Here you can finish the day perusing a number of gourmet specialty shops and stay overnight at the lovely Rodon Hotel.

Panagia Theotokou (Arhangelou) CHURCH
(Galata; ☺ sporadic) Dating from around 1514, this smaller chapel is just near Panagia tis Podythou. It's quite dark inside, so you may want to bring a torch. It has vivid didactic style (teaching) panels with frescos depicting an interesting panoply of images from Jesus' life. To access the church you will need to ask for the caretaker at the Galata village coffee shop.

Panagia Forviotissa CHURCH
(Panagia Asinou; ☎ 9983 0329; ☺ 9.30am-1pm & 2-4pm Mon-Sat, 10am-1pm & 2-4pm Sun) This Unesco-listed church is in a stunning setting, on the perimeter of the Adelfi Forest 4km southwest of Nikitari village. Dedicated to the Virgin of 'Phorbiottissa', it has arguably the finest set of vibrant and colourful Byzantine frescos in the Troödos Mountains. They date from the 12th to the 17th centuries.

To view the church, you'll need to ask its priest and caretaker, Father Kyriakos, who can usually be found at Nikitari's coffee shop.

Panagia Forviotissa can be reached by following the signs off the B9 from Nicosia, via Vyzakia. There's also a 5.6km (roughly two hour) forest hike to the village of Agios Theodoros from just before you reach the church, plus the shady, well-equipped Asinou Picnic Site and a good local taverna across the road.

Pitsylia

This wide-reaching region stretches east from Mt Olympus and Troödos village, encompassing around 40 villages across to the Maheras Monastery. Its northern slopes are covered in tall, aromatic pines and its valleys are full of vines and nut and fruit trees. There are also a number of Byzantine churches, as well as challenging walks for long-distance hikers.

Agros is the hub of the region. Other villages with significant sites include Kyperounda, Platanistasa, Paliaiochori and Pelendri. Public transport to the Pitsylia region is limited.

Agros

POP 1000
Situated at 1100m in a cool valley, Agros (www.agros.org.cy) is well placed for hiking and driving forays into the surrounding

NECTAR OF THE GODS

Archaeologists have traced the island's winemaking history back to around 4000 BC, with amphorae, wine jugs and even grape pips excavated in the Lemesos region, suggesting Cyprus could be the oldest wine manufacturer on earth. Wine god Dionysos is making his presence felt once more, as Cypriot wines are growing in stature and popularity, perhaps regaining their former glory.

Troödos, with its fertile hills and valleys, is where some of the island's finest grapes are cultivated. Indigenous mavro (dark red grapes) and xynisteri (white grapes) vines are cultivated here, along with 11 other varieties. They contribute to red wines such as ofthalmo, maratheftiko, cabernet sauvignon, mataro, mavro, lefkada and shiraz, and to whites such as xynisteri, sauvignon blanc and chardonnay.

hills. Renowned in the region for its locally made rose products, including rosewater and Cypriot delight, it also specialises in preserved fruit and traditional Cypriot meats such as *loukanika* (spiced sausages) and *lountza* (smoked pork fillet). As such, most of the activity centres on its traditional warehouses and workshops.

🛍 Shopping

Venus Rose TRADITIONAL WORKSHOP
(www.venus-rose.com; Anapafseos 12; ☺ 8am-5pm Mon-Fri, 10am-5pm Sat & Sun) At this rose-product store you can check out the workshop for a glimpse of the many ways roses can be used. Great examples include flower water, skin cleanser, candles, rose liqueur and rose oil – one of the most sought after beauty ingredients in the world. This is an excellent place for gifts. If you happen to be visiting in May, you can volunteer to help collect the rose petals.

Niki's Sweets TRADITIONAL WORKSHOP
(www.nikisweets.com.cy; Anapafseos 5; preserves €3-5; ☺ 9am-6pm) Selling her products all over Cyprus, and exporting as far as Australia, Niki makes marmalades, fig preserves and walnut sweets. Many of her preserves offer natural soothing and healing properties.

You can also purchase carob syrup here, a natural treatment for osteoporosis.

Kafkalia Sausages TRADITIONAL WORKSHOP
(Kyriakou Apeitou St; prices by weight; ⊘ 8.30am-4pm Mon-Fri, 9am-3pm Sat) Some of the tastiest Cypriot meat products, including *lountza*, *hiromeri* (traditional smoked ham), *loukanika* and *pastourmas* (spicy smoked beef), are made fresh on the premises. Check out the smoke room next to the store.

❶ Getting There & Away

Emel (☑ 7777 8121; www.limassolbuses.com; one way/all day & return €1.50/3/5) buses run from Agros to Lemesos five times daily from 5.25am to 2.40pm weekdays, three times on Saturday and twice on Sunday.

Osel Buses (☑ 2246 5546; www.osel.com.cy; one way/all day/return €1.50/5/3) run to Nicosia from Agros twice daily.

Around Pitsylia & Agros

Stavros Tou Agiasmati CHURCH
(Orounda-Platanistasa; ⊘ sporadic) This Unesco-listed Byzantine church is famous for its 15th-century murals by Orthodox Syrian painter Philippos Goul. In two tiers, the images decorate the ceilings and interior beams of the gabled roof, depicting scenes such as the discovery of the Holy Cross.

If the priest cannot be found, ask for the key at the coffee shop in Platanistasa village. The church itself is 5km from the village, off the Orounda–Platanistasa route (E906). Follow the Unesco signposts.

Panagia tou Araka CHURCH
(Lagoudera; ⊘ 9am-6pm) This 12th-century Unesco-listed church is on the outskirts of Lagoudera village. From the outside it appears enormous, the pitched roof and wooden trellis concealing the church within. Inside, it has some of the finest examples of late Comnenian style (1192) frescos in the Orthodox world. Its wide selection of neoclassical works, by artists from Constantinople, display images like the incredible Pantokrator featured in the tholos (beehive-shaped stone tomb). Other excellent frescos include the Annunciation, the Four Evangelists, the Archangel Michael and the Panagia Arakiotissa.

The unusual name of the church derives from *arakiotissa* (meaning 'of the wild pea') and owes its origins to the vegetable that grows profusely in the district. The priest can

---

HIKING IN PITSYLIA

Pitsylia has some well-marked hiking trails, including two short circular trails. Most take an out-and-back approach, unless you're hiking to the next village. Routes traverse forests, orchards, villages, valleys and mountain peaks, offering some of the best recreational hiking on the island.

The CTO's pamphlet *Cyprus: Nature Trails* provides good maps of these trails, but it's still advisable to take detailed maps of the greater region. The www.maps-and-walks.com/cyprus is another reliable resource for self-guided walks and maps in the region.

Doxasi o Theos to Madari Fire Station (3.75km, two hours) A panoramic ridge-top hike with excellent views. The trail starts 2km outside Kyperounda.

Teisia tis Madari (3km, 1½ hours, circular) A continuation of the first route, this involves a circular cliff-top hike around Mt Madari (Adelfi; 1613m) with first-rate views.

Panagia tou Araka (Lagoudera) to Agros (6km, 2½ hours) A longer hike through vineyards and orchards, with a great viewpoint from the Madari-Papoutsas ridge.

Panagia tou Araka to Stavros tou Agiasmati (7km, 3½ hours) Takes in two of the most important Byzantine churches and weaves through forests, vineyards and stone terraces. This is the longest hike.

Agros to Kato Mylos (5km, two hours, circular) A gentle hike through cherry and pear orchards and past vineyards and rose gardens.

Petros Vanezis to Alona (1.5km, 30 minutes, circular) A shorter hike around the village of Alona, passing through hazelnut plantations.

Agia Irini to Spilies tou Digeni (3.2km, 1½ hours) A simple out-and-back hike to the concealed Digenis caves, where EOKA members hid during the insurgency of 1955–59.

usually be found next door; check with him before you take any photos of the frescos.

Timios Stavros CHURCH

(☉10am-5pm) Built in the 12th century, this Unesco-listed church was originally dome shaped with a single aisle. In the 13th and 14th centuries it was added to; only the frescoed apse is original.

The frescos (1178) include Jesus depicted (rather oversized) in prayer from the waist up, with the Virgin Mary and John the Baptist, painted as miniatures, flanking him.

Other depictions include the altar and the grail near the small window in the apse and St Stephen on the north side. These latter frescos (painted by the same hand) are considered a preface to the great works found in other Troödos churches, with simple straight lines and shiny earth colours. The rest of the images are from the 14th century, when the church was completely repainted.

The church is at the southern end of the village of Pelendri. If the church is closed (which is likely) ask at the village coffee shop for the whereabouts of the priest.

Agia Sotira tou Soteros CHURCH

(☑9997 4230; ☉10am-1pm Tue & Wed) Perched on the slope overlooking Palaichori village, is this Unesco-listed early-16th-century chapel containing one of the island's most complete groups of late Byzantine wall paintings. The work of an unknown master, the paintings depict complete figures like St Mamas Upon the Lion. The church also holds a series of iconostases painted by Mt Athos monk Mathaios. To see inside you may have to call the custodian or ask in the village centre at the Byzantine Heritage Museum.

Spilia-Kourdali

POP 460

These two traditional villages, situated in the Adelfi Forest, were established in the 16th century near the monastery and church of Virgin Mary Chrysokourdaliotissa (Kourdali). Like many villages in the region, they grew as refuges from constant invasions by conquerors like the Francs and later the Turks.

The narrow valley of Kourdali (www.kourdali.org) saw it expand towards the village of Spilia, which derived its name from the Roman graves (*spilioi* in Greek) found in the area. Local asbestos mining was the main proficiency of the villagers for many years; thereafter they became skilled tailors and cobblers. Now the villages' cafes and craft shops are the main attraction.

☉ Sights

Olive Mill of 'Paphitaina' HISTORIC SITE

FREE In operation until 1955, the well-preserved olive-stone mill and wooden press are now housed in a traditional building in Spilia's village centre.

The mill, originally privately owned, was usually turned by a donkey, with the broken olives later being crushed by the presser. Olive oil was then extracted into *tzares* (clay urns). Eventually the mill was superseded by modern presses in nearby villages. You can obtain the key from the Friends of Spilia-Kourdali, in the building next door.

Pafos & the West

Best Places to Eat

➡ Psaropoulos Beach Tavern (p99)

➡ Kiniras Garden (p90)

➡ Hondros (p91)

➡ Imogen's Inn (p96)

Best Places to Stay

➡ Axiothea Hotel (p204)

➡ Bougainvillea Hotel Apartments (p206)

➡ Pyramos Hotel (p204)

➡ Ayii Anargyri Natural Healing Spa Resort (p206)

Why Go?

Pafos was nominated joint European Capital of Culture for 2017 in recognition of its extraordinary archaeological sights. Unsurprisingly, tourists have flocked here for these for decades – plus more hedonistic pursuits. If you find the beach strip at Kato Pafos too developed, duck into the backstreets or head up to Ktima on the hillside, which has a more tangible traditional feel. More beach resorts are strung out north along the coast towards Agios Georgios.

To seriously sidestep the crowds, consider renting a car and searching out traditional rural villages where some of the best tavernas are located. If you have sturdier wheels, check out the unspoilt Akamas Peninsula, where there are remote beaches and some of the best walks on the island. To the east, the vast Pafos Forest is equally enticing, melting almost imperceptibly into the sombre tracts of the Tyllirian wilderness.

When to Go

➡ Pafos is the island's top tourist destination, which is worth bearing in mind when planning your visit.

➡ July and August are, obviously, when you find the most sunbeds on the sand, the most sunburned noses and the highest hotel prices.

➡ May, June, September and October are less crowded, with plenty of long sunny days.

➡ Spring and autumn can also be pleasantly warm, though evening temperatures cool down considerably.

➡ In winter, some restaurants and hotels close down altogether; if you head to the western Troödos, you may even see some snow.

Pafos & the West Highlights

1 Exploring Pafos' ancient past by visiting its Roman **mosaics** and the **Tombs of the Kings** (p84) necropolis.

2 Driving the wild and rugged **Akamas Peninsula** (p97).

3 Swimming on **Lara Beach** (p95), the Republic's wildest stretch of sand.

4 Having a wander around pretty, unspoiled **Polis** (p98), followed by a seafood lunch at Latsi harbour.

5 Enjoying delicious *kleftiko* at **Argo** (p90), a long-time Pafos restaurant that has built its reputation on this traditional oven-baked lamb dish.

6 Watching the weavers at work in **Fyti** (p103), a scenic village famous for its cotton and silk craftwork.

7 Relaxing in lovely **Akamas Heights** (p95) and spending time in its simple traditional villages.

PAFOS

POP 64,900

Linked by a traffic artery, Kato Pafos (Lower Pafos) and Ktima (Upper Pafos; 3km to the northeast) form a schizoid whole. Kato Pafos, the tourist centre, is blatantly geared towards English tourists, with the inevitable all-day English breakfasts and bars. It could be worse: construction along the palm-fringed seafront is low-rise and, as well as being home to a vast archaeological site, Kato Pafos has backstreets hiding other historic gems like medieval baths, catacombs and a simple fishermen's church. The official Pafos Archaeological Site is the grand-slam sight, however, being one of the South's richest archaeological locales. When you're standing (relatively) alone here, surrounded by acres of history, a vast blue sky and the wild fennel and caper plants that grow on the Mediterranean's edges, you feel a thousand years away from Guinness on tap.

Ktima, the old centre of Pafos, is overall a calmer place, where locals go about their daily business much as they have for decades. The neighbourhoods are rich with handsome colonial buildings that house government institutions and many of the town's museums. Ktima is also home to some good hotels.

☉ Sights

★ **Tombs of the Kings** ARCHAEOLOGICAL SITE
(☑2694 0295; Kato Pafos; admission €2.50; ☉8.30am-7.30pm; Ⓟ) Imagine yourself surrounded by ancient tombs in a desert-like landscape where the only sounds are waves crashing on rocks. The Tombs of the Kings, a Unesco World Heritage Site, contains a set of well-preserved underground tombs and chambers used by residents of Nea Pafos during the Hellenistic and Roman periods, from the 3rd century BC to the 3rd century

---

ⓘ TOMB TIPS

➡ Allow at least two hours for the Tombs of the Kings site.

➡ Try to visit during the early morning as it can get very hot walking around the sprawling necropolis later in the day.

➡ Bring a hat and bottled water.

➡ Be very careful when descending into some of the tombs, as the stone steps are large and can be slippery.

AD. Despite the name, the tombs were not actually used by royalty; they earned the title from their grand appearance.

Located 2km north of Kato Pafos, the tombs are unique in Cyprus, being heavily influenced by ancient Egyptian tradition, when it was believed that tombs for the dead should resemble houses for the living.

The seven excavated tombs are scattered over a wide area; most impressive is No 3, which has an open atrium below ground level, surrounded by columns. Other tombs have niches built into the walls where bodies were stored. Most of the tombs' treasures have long since been spirited away by robbers.

★ **Pafos Archaeological Site** ARCHAEOLOGICAL SITE
(Kato Pafos; admission €4.50; ☉8am-7.30pm; Ⓟ) Nea Pafos (New Pafos) is, ironically, the name given to the sprawling Pafos Archaeological Site, to the west of Kato Pafos. Nea Pafos was the ancient city of Pafos, founded in the late 4th century BC and originally encircled by massive walls. Despite being ceded to the Romans in 58 BC, it remained the centre of all political and administrative life in Cyprus. It is most famed today for its mesmerising collection of intricate and colourful mosaics based on ancient Greek myths.

Palea Pafos (Old Pafos) was in fact Kouklia, southeast of today's Pafos and the site of the Sanctuary of Aphrodite. At the time of Nea Pafos, Cyprus was part of the kingdom of the Ptolemies, the Greco-Macedonian rulers of Egypt whose capital was Alexandria. The city became an important strategic outpost for the Ptolemies, and the settlement grew considerably over the next seven centuries.

The city originally occupied an area of about 950,000 sq metres and reached its zenith during the 2nd or 3rd century AD. It was during this time that the city's most opulent public buildings were constructed, including those that house the famous Pafos mosaics.

Nea Pafos went into decline following an earthquake in the 4th century that badly damaged the city. Subsequently, Salamis in the east became the new capital of Cyprus, and Nea Pafos was relegated to the status of a mere bishopric. Arab raids in the 7th century set the seal on the city's demise and neither Lusignan settlement (1192–1489) nor Venetian and Ottoman colonisation revived Nea Pafos' fortunes.

The archaeological site is still being excavated since it is widely believed that there

Kato Pafos

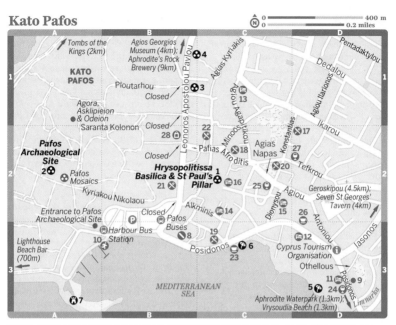

Kato Pafos

are many treasures still to be discovered. The following sections detail the major sights.

⇒ Pafos Mosaics

This superb collection of mosaics is located in the southern sector of the archaeological site, immediately to the south of the Agora. Discovered by accident in 1962 by a farmer ploughing his field, these exquisite mosaics decorated the extensive floor area of a large, wealthy residence from the Roman period. Subsequently named the **House of Dionysus** (because of the number of mosaics featuring Dionysus, the god of wine), this complex is the largest and best known of the mosaic houses.

The most wonderful thing about the mosaics is that, apart from their artistic and aesthetic merits, each tells a story, mostly based on ancient Greek myths.

The first thing you'll see on entering is not a Roman mosaic at all but a Hellenistic monochrome pebble mosaic showing the monster **Scylla**. Based on a Greek myth, this mosaic was discovered in 1977, underground in the southwestern corner of the atrium.

The famous tale of Narcissus is depicted in a mosaic in Room 2, while the Four Seasons mosaic (Room 3) depicts Spring crowned with flowers and holding a shepherd's stick, Summer holding a sickle and wearing ears of corn, Autumn crowned with leaves and wheat, and Winter as a bearded, grey-haired man.

Phaedra and Hippolytos (Room 6) is one of the most important mosaics in the house. It depicts the tragic tale of a stepmother's bizarre love for her stepson.

Another stunning mosaic in the house is the **Rape of Ganymede** (Room 8). Ganymede was a beautiful young shepherd who became the cupbearer of the gods. The mosaicist had apparently miscalculated the space allowed to him, which is why the eagle's wings are cropped.

In the **Western Portico** (Room 16) is a mosaic based on a tale familiar to any lover of Shakespeare: the story of Pyramus and Thisbe, first narrated by Ovid in his *Metamorphosis,* and adapted in *Romeo and Juliet* (and *A Midsummer Night's Dream*).

A short walk away are the smaller **Villa of Theseus** and the **House of Aion**. The latter, a purpose-built structure made from stones found on the site, houses a 4th-century mosaic display of five separate panels. The house was named after the pagan god Aion, depicted in the mosaics. Although the image has been damaged somewhat, the name Aion and the face of the god can still be clearly seen.

The Villa of Theseus is thought to have been a 2nd-century private residence and is named after a representation of the hero Theseus fighting the Minotaur. The building occupies an area of 9600 sq metres and, so far, 1400 sq metres of mosaics have been uncovered. The round mosaic of Theseus and the Minotaur is particularly well preserved and can be seen in Room 36. Other mosaics to look out for are those of Poseidon in Room 76 and Achilles in Rooms 39 and 40.

Allow at least two hours to see the three houses properly.

➡ **Agora, Asklipieion & Odeion**

The Agora (or forum) and Asklipieion date back to the 2nd century AD and constitute the heart of the original Nea Pafos complex. Today, the Agora consists mainly of the Odeion, a semicircular theatre that was restored in 1970 but does not look particularly ancient. The rest of the Agora is discernible by the remains of marble columns that form a rectangle in the largely empty open space. What is left of the Asklipieion, the healing centre and altar of Asklepios, god of medicine, runs east to west on the southern side of the Odeion.

➡ **Saranta Kolones Fortress**

Not far from the mosaics are the remains of the medieval Saranta Kolones Fortress, named for the '40 columns' that were once a feature of the now almost levelled structure. Little is known about the precise nature or history of the original fortress, other than it was built by the Lusignans in the 12th century and was subsequently destroyed by an earthquake in 1222. A few desultory arches are the only visual evidence of its original grandeur.

★ **Hrysopolitissa Basilica**
& St Paul's Pillar ARCHAEOLOGICAL SITE
(Stassándhrou, Kato Pafos) **FREE** This fascinating site was home to one of Pafos' largest religious structures. What remains are the foundations of a 4th century Christian **basilica**, which aptly demonstrates the size and magnificence of the original church; it was ultimately destroyed during Arab raids in 653. Several magnificent marble columns remain from the colonnades, while others lie scattered around the site, and **mosaics** are still visible. Further incarnations of the basilica were built over the years, leading to the present small **Agia Kyriaki** church, which is now used for Anglican, Lutheran and Greek Orthodox services.

A raised walkway provides excellent views of the extensive site and has explanatory plaques in English. Look also for the tomb of Eric Ejegod, the 12th-century King of Denmark who died suddenly in 1103 on his way to the Holy Land.

On the western side of the basilica is the so-called St Paul's Pillar, where St Paul was allegedly tied and scourged 39 times before he finally converted his tormentor, the Roman governor Sergius Paulus, to Christianity.

Pafos Castle   CASTLE

(Kato Pafos; adult/child €2.50/free; ☺8.30am-7pm) This small, empty fort guards the harbour entrance and is entered by a small stone bridge over a moat. Most visitors climb to the roof to enjoy the sweeping harbour views. The castle also serves as an event venue during the Pafos Aphrodite Festival.

The castle is all that remains of an earlier Lusignan fort built in 1391; the rest of it was destroyed by the Venetians less than a hundred years later. The Ottomans subsequently used the ground floor as dungeons.

Agia Solomoni & the
Christian Catacomb   ARCHAEOLOGICAL SITE

(Leonoros Apostolou Pavlou, Kato Pafos) FREE This modest tomb complex is the burial site of the seven Machabee Brothers, who were martyred around 174 BC. Their mother was Agia Solomoni, a Jewish woman who became a saint after the death of her sons. It is thought that the space was a synagogue in Roman times. The entrance to the catacomb is marked by a collection of votive rags tied to a large tree outside the tomb. This ostensibly pagan practice of tying rags is continued by Christian visitors today and visitors will see more rags surrounding the tombs, some attached to copies of icons.

Be wary of the lowest section at the base of a set of steep stairs; entering from the bright sunlight, it is hard to discern the water-filled cave and deep well which constitutes a potentially dangerous hazard.

Agios Lambrianos
Rock-Cut Tomb   ARCHAEOLOGICAL SITE

(Kato Pafos) FREE A little further north, on the side of Fabrica Hill, are a couple of enormous underground caverns dating from the early Hellenistic period. These are burial chambers associated with the saints Lambrianos and Misitikos. The tomb interiors bear frescos that indicate they were used as a Christian place of worship. There are ongoing excavations here which have, more recently, revealed remains of a classical theatre.

Byzantine Museum   MUSEUM

(☑2693 1393; Andrea Ioannou 5, Ktima; admission €2; ☺9am-3pm Mon-Fri, to 1pm Sat) This noteworthy museum is worth visiting for its ecclesiastical vestments, vessels, copies of scripture and collection of impressive icons, including a 9th-century representation of Agia Marina, thought to be the oldest icon on the island, and an unusual double-sided icon from Filousa dating from the 13th century.

Ethnographical Museum   MUSEUM

(www.ethnographicalmuseum.com; Exo Vrysis 1, Ktima; admission €3; ☺9am-6pm Mon-Sat, to 1pm Sun) This privately owned museum houses a varied collection of coins, traditional costumes, kitchen utensils, Chalcolithic axe heads, amphorae and other assorted items. There's more of the same in the garden, including a Hellenistic rock-cut tomb. The €5 guidebook available at the entrance helps you sort out the seemingly jumbled collection.

Archaeological Museum   MUSEUM

(Leoforos Georgiou Griva Digeni, Ktima; admission €1.70; ☺9am-5pm Mon-Fri, 10am-1pm Sat & Sun) Essentially for admirers of archaeological minutiae, this small museum houses a varied and extensive collection of artefacts from the neolithic period to the 18th century. Displayed in four rooms, exhibits include jars, pottery and glassware, tools and coins.

Agios Georgios Museum   MUSEUM

(Hlorakas; ☺9am-6pm) FREE This unusual museum is located 4km north of Kato Pafos on the spot where the caïque *Agios Georgios* (now the museum's prime exhibit), captained by EOKA rebel Georgios Grivas, landed in November 1954. It carried a large supply of arms and munitions, with the aim of overthrowing British colonial rule. Grivas' rebels were finally arrested two months later while attempting another landing. The museum walls document the capture, including the mug shots, as well as some of the seized rifles and ammunition.

The site, known as 'Grivas' Landing', is easily identified by the large Agios Georgios church, built to commemorate the event, as well as the adjacent St George Hotel.

Agia Paraskevi   CHURCH

(Geroskipou; ☺8am-1pm & 2-5pm) One of the loveliest churches in the Pafos area is this six-domed Byzantine church in Geroskipou, 4.5km east of Pafos. Most of the surviving frescos date back to the 15th century. The first frescos visible when entering are the Last Supper, the Washing of Feet and the Betrayal. A primitive but interesting depiction of the Virgin Orans (the Virgin Mary with her arms raised) can be seen in the central cupola.

Pafos Zoo   ZOO

(☑2681 3852; www.pafoszoo.com; Pegeia; adult/child €15.50/8.50; ☺9am-6pm; ℗) A superb zoo and children's attraction rolled into one.

Ktima

Ktima

◉ Sights
1 Archaeological Museum	D3
2 Byzantine Museum	A3
3 Ethnographical Museum	B3

🛏 Sleeping
4 Agapinor Hotel	A2
5 Axiothea Hotel	A3
6 Kiniras	B1

✪ Eating
7 Fetta's	B2
Kiniras Garden	(see 6)
8 Laona	A1
9 Plato	B2

◉ Drinking & Nightlife
10 Omnia	B3

◎ Shopping
11 Municipal Market	A1

Apart from birds (it started as a bird park), there are giraffes, antelopes, deer, gazelles, mouflon, reptiles, giant tortoises, emus, ostriches, small goats and so on. There is also a restaurant and snack bar, and a kiddies' playground. It's located in the Pegeia region near Coral Bay, approximately 3km from Pafos.

🏖 Beaches

Main Municipal Beach BEACH

In the centre of Kato Pafos, the Main Municipal Beach is not your standard holiday-brochure-style sweep of sun-kissed sand: the beach area is paved and partly pedestrianised. Comprising a collection of wooden decks, rocks, sand and diving points, it's still pleasant and the water is sparkling clean. Facilities include showers, toilets and a cafe-restaurant.

Alykes Beach BEACH

Heading east, you come to Alykes Beach, which is better known locally as Sopab Beach after a factory that once stood here. Wedged between the Deck Cafe & Bar and the Alexander the Great hotel, this is a perfect spot for families with paddling tots, with rock pools and shallow, clear water, as well as sufficient sand for sandcastles. The sprawling terrace of the overlooking cafe is also convenient for refreshments and drinks (including grown-up cocktails at sunset).

Vrysoudia Beach BEACH

East from Alykes Beach, you come to arguably the best municipal beach, Vrysoudia Beach, stretching some 400m and where you can rent sunbeds and parasols (€5 per day). There is also a popular beach bar here.

Faros Beach
BEACH

You will need wheels to reach Faros Beach, located north of Pafos Archaeological Site. It's an exposed, sandy beach with some sandstone rocks and a couple of on-site snack bars. Keep in mind, however, that the open sea often develops a swell, which can be dangerous for swimming.

Kissonerga Bay
BEACH

Around 8km north of Kato Pafos, Kissonerga Bay is a long, sandy undeveloped beach, where you can find banana plantations and solitude. There are almost no facilities, so bring a book, food and water, and relax.

🏃 Activities

Aside from the organised tours offered by myriad companies (look for the flyers all over town), most activities here are centred on the sea. Check out the wide range of options from the kiosks at the harbour, including boat trips, pedalos and (if you must) the ubiquitous banana ride.

Coastal Path
WALKING

(Kato Pafos) Over recent years, the Kato Pafos promenade has been extended and it now stretches some 5km from west of the Alexander the Great Hotel to the Louis Phaethon Beach Club en route to Coral Bay. The most scenic stretch sets off from just east of the castle in Kato Pafos and curves around the coastal point. There are shady benches located along the walkway and if you are here in springtime, the meadows to your east are a dazzle of wild flowers.

A good place to aim for (if you haven't packed the right footwear or have dodgy knees) is the Lighthouse Beach Bar (p91), situated some 1.6km from the castle.

Paphos Sea Cruises
BOAT TRIPS

(☑8000 0011; www.paphosseacruises.com; Pafos Harbour, Kato Pafos) A reputable choice; most cruises include extras such as an onboard barbecue, snorkelling gear, children's entertainment and canoes. Day trips cost from a reasonable €20 per person. Children under 12 are free or pay half, depending on the cruise.

Aphrodite's Rock Brewery
BREWERY

(☑2610 1446; www.aphroditesrock.com.cy; Polis Rd, Tsada; ☉10am-4pm; 🐾) Originally from Yorkshire, the family owners offer visitors a 100ml tasting of five beers for €3.50 and tours by master brewer (and daughter) Melanie. Production is a frothy 4000L a year and the favourite brew is Yorkshire Rose. There's a small outside bar with terrace; a pint costs around €1.80.

An on-site shop sells some gourmet goodies like mustard infused with beer. The brewery is located around 9km northeast of Pafos, just after the turn-off to Tsada, on the B7 towards Polis.

Cydive
DIVING

(☑2693 4271; www.cydive.com; 1 Posidonos, Myrra Complex 33, Kato Pafos; 🐾) The waters off Pafos are ideal for diving, with around 50 sites to explore. This is a professional, long-standing company which has its own swimming pool and a large store selling diving kits, swimwear and similar. Single dives, including all equipment, cost €53; a package of 10 dives costs €451.

Cydive also offers Bubble Maker (€40 to €45), a full scuba gear diving experience for children between eight and 10 years old. There are two programs: the first in a pool, the second taking that grand leap to the sea. It's a great watery way to get youngsters interested in diving, and this PADI-trained team ensures a safe and confined environment at all times.

Mickys Tours
BOAT TRIPS

(☑2694 2022; www.mickys-tours.com; Posidonos, Kato Pafos; €30 per person) Organises day-long trips to the Akamas Peninsula.

WORTH A TRIP

ZEPHYROS ADVENTURE SPORTS

Zephyros Adventure Sports (☑2693 0037; www.enjoycyprus.com; The Royal Complex, Shop 7, Tafon Ton Vasileon; 🐾) Parents, if you're on holiday with your teenage kids – or equally, teenagers, if you're on holiday with your parents – and you want a break from, well, each other, get over to Zephyros Adventure Sports and take your pick of activities. You can choose from mountain biking, kayaking, climbing, trekking, snorkelling, scuba diving and, in the winter months, skiing. It's a perfect way to play happy families.

Alternatively, go on one of the hikes around the Akamas Peninsula. Plenty of outfits offer 4WD safaris, but bear in mind their environmental impact, including soil erosion, excessive fossil-fuel use and noise pollution, and resist if you can.

Aphrodite Waterpark
WATER PARK

(☑2691 3638; www.aphroditewaterpark.com; Posidonos, Kato Pafos; adult/child €30/17; ⊙10am-5.30pm) A place for all-day entertainment (at a price to match) where the adults can have a massage while the kids battle the mini volcano. A wristband keeps track of your daily shell out, which you then pay at the end of the day. The waterpark is located off Poseidonos Avenue, around 1.5km south of the centre. Take Bus 11 or 611 from the Harbour Bus Station in Kato Pafos.

✨ Festivals & Events

Pafos Aphrodite Festival
MUSIC

(www.pafc.com.cy) Enjoy opera under the stars every September when a world-class operatic performance takes place in the suitably grandiose surroundings of Pafos Castle. Recent operas include the classic Bizet's *Carmen*.

Solar Car Challenge
CAR RACE

(www.cyi.ac.cy/solar-car-challenge.html; Geroskipou) This annual solar car race revs into action in June, attracting local teams and international participants who compete in creating and racing their solar-powered cars with some truly ingenious results.

🍴 Eating

Pafos' food scene varies considerably. In general, stay away from restaurants along the front-line strip in Kato Pafos, especially those with HP sauce bottles on the tables. Instead, wander back a street or two for more genuine local food. Ktima has more quality over quantity choice, including a couple of superb options.

🍴 Ktima

★ Kiniras Garden
CYPRIOT €€

(☑2694 1604; www.kiniras.cy.net; Leoforos Archiepiskopou Makariou III 91; mains €8-15; ⊙8am-midnight; 🛜🛗) 🍴 This restaurant is a green oasis with trees, statues and trickling waterfalls. Still family-run after four generations, owner Georgios is passionate about his traditional cuisine; most of the recipes have been passed down from his grandmother and the produce comes from his own 60-hectare garden. A member of the Vakhis scheme (p136), the restaurant also has a lighter snack menu.

There are homemade desserts and the wine list includes excellent vintages from family-owned local vineyards. Special diets are catered to and the dining space is expanding to encompass a spanking new spa.

Laona
CYPRIOT €€

(☑2693 7121; Votis 4-6; mains €9, meze €10; ⊙10am-3.30pm Mon, Wed, Thu & Sat, 10am-10pm Tue & Fri; 🛗) Tucked up a side street behind the Municipal Market, with all the atmosphere of a village taverna, Laona has been a family-owned restaurant since the '80s. There's no microwave or deep fat fryer in this kitchen – Cypriot owner Chris has a purposefully limited menu of freshly made and tasty traditional Cypriot dishes such as rabbit *stifado* (stew made with beef or rabbit and onions, simmered in vinegar and wine), stuffed vegetables and meze.

Plato
INTERNATIONAL €€

(☑7000 0785; Grigori Afxentiou, Kennedy Square; mains from €8.50; ⊙8.30am-1.30am) This slick contemporary wine bar and restaurant has a limited menu of well-prepared dishes such as spinach and wild mushroom pasta and salmon teriyaki. There are also salads, sandwiches and platters for sharing as well as a fine selection of wine – touted as being the most extensive in town.

Chill out music and a minimalist light wood-and-bamboo-style decor add to the fashionable flavour of the place.

Fetta's
CYPRIOT €€

(☑2693 7822; Ioanni Agroti 33; mains from €10, meze €18; ⊙7pm-10.30pm Tue-Sun) Fetta's specialises in classic regional fare made with salutary (and salivatory) attention to detail. The dining space is a typical taverna style, only larger, with a small outside terrace overlooking the fountain and park. Dishes include a superb meze of grilled meats. Reservations recommended.

🍴 Kato Pafos

Christos Steak House
CYPRIOT €

(☑9916 5934; 7 Kostantias; mains from €7; ⊙5pm-late) This no-frills, long-established place has bright lights, fake flowers and a menu illustrated with faded pics, but it is still well worth recommending for the homestyle traditional food. Steaks may be the specialty, but the typical dishes and sides like pasta with grated haloumi (helemi) are good choices as well. The owner is a delight.

★ Argo
CYPRIOT €€

(☑2693 3327; Pafias Afroditis 21; mains €10; ⊙6-11pm) Located in a (relatively) quiet part of Kato Pafos, this place oozes rustic charm with its natural stone, original wooden shutters and walls washed in warm ochre. The speciality, such as moussaka, are reliably authentic, as is the twice-weekly (Tuesday and Saturday) *kleftiko;* on these days it's advisable to book as word is out and the place gets busy.

★**Hondros** CYPRIOT €€
(www.facebook.com/HondrosTaverna; Leonoros Apostolou Pavlou 96; mains €10; ☺11am-11pm; 🖶) This is the oldest traditional restaurant in Pafos, dating back to 1953, and still in the same family. Highlights include a succulent *souvla* (spit-roasted pork, chicken or lamb) and *kleftiko* cooked in a traditional clay oven (along with the baked potatoes and bread). There is live music at weekends and a delightful rambling terrace.

Take a look at the old photos of Pafos and the fine paintings, done by the original owner, in the dining room.

Almond Tree FUSION €€
(Konstantias 5; mains from €8; ☺6.30-11pm; 🖉) Features unusual Thai-Cypriot tastes to titillate the palate – try the chicken satay or salmon cakes with mango – along with a smattering of stock Cypriot and international dishes. Vegetarians are also well catered to with stir-fries and similar.

Kyra Frosini CYPRIOT €€
(Pafias Afroditis & Filoktitou 4; mains €8; ☺10.30am-10.30pm) Kyra Frosini is a relaxed place, with a pretty courtyard shaded by palm trees and a cosy winter interior. Owner Andri is famed for her Greek classics like moussaka and *pastitsada* (lamb with pasta, onions and tomatoes), as well as her homestyle soups and cakes. There is live music in summer.

Chloe's No 1 CHINESE €€
(☎2693 4676; Posidonos 13; mains €10; ☺3-11pm; 🖉🖶) The best Chinese restaurant in town with a vast menu of standard dishes including plenty of veg choices. The decor is plushly oriental (but without the migraine-inducing moving pictures) and the service is top notch – if anything, a little *too* attentive.

🍷 **Drinking & Nightlife**

The traditional street for clubs: Agiou Antoniou in Kato Pafos is a sorry sight these days with the majority of places shuttered up a result of the economic woes of recent times. A few places have survived, including a handful of English pubs with big screen sports – as well as a lap dancing club, or two. Away from here, closer to the promenade the bar scene has fared slightly better, and

WORTH A TRIP

GOURMET GEROSKIPOU

Seven St Georges' Tavern (☎2696 3176; www.facebook.com/7StGeorges; Geroskipou; meze €25; ☺noon-3pm & 7-11pm Tue-Sat; 🖉🖶) Geroskipou's main appeal in the exceptional meze available here. Owner George and his family have grown, dried or pickled (organically) everything you eat and drink in this place. Your meze only includes what is in season so you might get hand-picked wild asparagus, wild mushrooms with fresh herbs, aubergines in tomato, or tender *kleftiko* (oven-baked lamb).

The restaurant is in an old house with a vine-and-palm-leaf-covered terrace, in the centre of this pretty, traditional village near a striking 9th-century Byzantine church.

there is also, encouragingly, a trend towards more sophisticated venues.

★**Lighthouse Beach Bar** BAR
(☎9968 3992; www.facebook.com/lighthouse.beachbar; Lighthouse Beach, Kato Pafos; ☺7am-10pm; 🖶) The recommended route here is via the 1.7km coastal path from Pafos Castle; by car it is trickier, but still possible via the Tombs of the Kings road. When you do arrive, you'll find this is what a beach bar should be: Bob Marley on the soundtrack, seamless sea views and sand between your toes while you sip something long and cool.

Light eats are available and kids will love the homegrown-style playground with rope swings and tyre tunnels. Live music in summer completes the laid-back boho feel. You can also rent sunbeds (€2.50 per day).

Alea CAFE, BAR
(☎9952 4000; 5 Posidonos, Kato Pafos; ☺8am-2am) A thong's throw from the waves, this former restaurant has happily morphed into a fashionable cafe-cum-lounge bar, famed for its seven choices of daiquiri (€5.50). The music is suitably chilled with regular live bands in the summer. Sit on the sprawling terrace or duck into one of the more intimate spaces within, decorated with eclectic antiques and heavy wooden furniture.

Old Fishing Shack Pub PUB
(Margarita Gardens, Tefkrou, Kato Pafos; ☺7pm-late Mon-Sat, 1-11pm Sun; 🕿) Owner Athos

REVITALISING PAFOS KTIMA

Plans are underway to treat Pafos Ktima to a subtle and aesthetic facelift. This neighbourhood has suffered from recent economic woes with a worrying number of local shops closing their shutters for good and an influx of generic bargain-basement-style stores. The centre is due to be gradually pedestrianised from 2015 and local artisans and craftspeople will be encouraged to set up shop with cheaper rental rates and other incentives.

loves good beer and good music (classic rock and blues), so come here for both. He also makes his own headily recommended cider spiked with ginger, and holds an annual beer festival in the last weekend in September with live music and a tasting of some 200-plus beers.

La Place Royale
CAFE, BAR

(Posidonos, Kato Pafos; ⊙8am-11pm) This is one of the classiest cafe-bars, right on the busy pedestrian strip at the eastern end of Posidonos. This little oasis of glass, cane, wrought iron and mini waterfalls in a shaded paved patio is perfect for a pre-clubbing cocktail. Food is served here but it's fairly forgettable.

Omnia
BAR

(Martiou 25, Ktima; ⊙8am-late) A delightful location across from a leafy small park with a sprawling white wicker-and-leaf, green-themed terrace contrasted with the late-night look of a hot pink-and-black interior. A couple of TVs screen music videos or sports, and there are some light eats to accompany the drinks (cocktails €5.50).

Different Bar
BAR

(Agias Napas, Kato Pafos) Popular gay bar with an attractive dark ochre colour scheme and tables on the terrace overlooking the street

Deck Cafe & Bar
BAR

(Posidonos, Kato Pafos; ⊙8am-midnight) Situated beside the Alexander the Great hotel, this is a choice place to kick back while listening to feel-good lounge music and sipping a (feel-good) cocktail. The terrace is vast and overlooks the sand and rocks. Avoid the indifferent food.

🛍 Shopping

Kings Avenue Mall
MALL

(www.kingsavenuemall.com; Leoforos Apostolou Pavlou, Kato Pafos; ⊙9.30am-8pm Mon-Sat, 11am-7.30pm Sun; 🛜) The largest shopping mall in the Republic opened here in 2013 with around 125 stores, plus restaurants, coffee shops and a cineplex.

Gabriela & Silvana
CERAMICS

(www.gabrielasilvanapotterycyprus.com; 92 Leonoros Apostolou Pavlou, Kato Pafos; ⊙9am-9pm Mon-Sat, 5-9pm Sun) Colourful and highly original ceramics are on display here; you can watch the potters at work in the adjacent workshop.

Municipal Market
MARKET

(Agora St, Ktima; ⊙8am-6pm Mon, Tue, Thu & Fri, to 2.30pm Wed & Sat) As well as colourful fruit and veg, the municipal market houses a large number of souvenir stalls with the occasional more tasteful place selling locally produced embroidery and jewellery.

ℹ Information

Wi-fi is widely available in Pafos hotels, as well as in a number of cafes and bars, where you can generally connect free with a drink.

Cyprus Tourism Organisation (CTO; www.visitcyprus.org.cy) Airport (☑2642 3161; Pafos International Airport; ⊙9.30am-11pm); Kato Pafos (☑2693 0521; Posidonos; ⊙8.15am-2.30pm & 3-6.30pm Mon-Tue, Thu & Fri, 8.15am-2.30pm Sat); Ktima (☑2693 2841; Agoras 8; ⊙8.15am-2.30pm & 3-6.30pm Mon-Sat, closed Wed & Sat afternoons) Has decent maps, useful brochures and booklets on hiking, biking and agrotourism, a hotel guide, transport information and other useful information about Cyprus. It also organises free guided tours around Ktima every Thursday at 10am from the Ktima office. You need to book in advance.

ℹ Getting There & Away

TO/FROM THE AIRPORT

Bus 613 runs to the airport from the Karavella Bus Station in Ktima at 7.25am and 6.30pm, while buses from the airport to Ktima run at 8am and 7pm. Bus 612 runs roughly hourly from the harbour between 7am and 12.30am to/from the airport, with stops or pick-up points including Coral Bay and Posidonos in Kato Pafos. A single journey is €1.50. A taxi between the airport and Pafos costs about €30.

AIR

Pafos International Airport is 8km southeast of the town. Both scheduled and budget airlines fly here, and it is a hub for Ryanair, which flies to 14 destinations (at the time of research) from Pafos.

BUS

InterCity (www.intercity-buses.com) Has six daily buses weekdays to Nicosia (Lefkosia; €7, two hours) and eight daily buses weekdays to Lemesos (€4, 45 minutes) departing from Karavella Bus Station in Ktima. There is a reduced service at weekends.

SERVICE TAXI

Travel & Express (☑0777 7474; www.travel-express.com.cy; Leoforos Evagora Pallikaridi 9, Ktima) Operates service taxis to Lemesos (€9.50, one hour), to Larnaka (change at Lemesos; €19.50, 1½ hours) and to Nicosia (change at Lemesos; €20.50, 1½ hours).

ⓘ Getting Around

Pafos Buses (www.pafosbuses.com; Pafos Harbour) provides an urban-wide and regional network of buses from their two stations: **Harbour Bus Station** (Harbour, Kato Pafos) in Kato Pafos and Karavella Bus Station in Ktima. A comprehensive bus schedule booklet is available at both bus stations. Fares cost €1.50 per journey, €5 per day or €15 per week within the district of Pafos, including rural villages.

Frequent services from Kato Pafos (harbour):

Coral Beach Bus 615, 616; 25 minutes.

Geroskipou Beach Bus 611; 25 minutes. (The beach is 4.5km east of Kato Pafos.)

Kato Ktima (market) Bus 610; 15 minutes.

Polis Bus 626; one hour.

In Kato Pafos, there's a large free car park near the entrance to the Pafos Archaeological Site. In Ktima, there are car parks on the main square (cnr Gladstonos and Leoforos Georgiou Griva Digeni) and by Karavella Bus Station.

If you need a **taxi** (☑2693 3301), you can call, flag one down or head for one of the plentiful taxi stands across the city. Be aware that taxi drivers will charge an extortionate €8 for the 3km Kato Pafos–Ktima ride.

AROUND PAFOS

The area around Pafos is superb for beaches, walks, traditional villages and overall exploring. To visit, however, you'll generally need to take a tour or organise your own transport. While a scooter is great for pottering around beach resorts, a car is preferable, especially for visiting the western Troödos, the wild and desolate Akamas Peninsula or the sparsely populated Tyllirian wilderness of northwest Cyprus.

Coral Bay

Coral Bay is located 12km northwest of Pafos, with several different stretches of beach, all accessible from different parts of the approach road. Although rows of umbrellas and crowds of bathers are no longer conducive to finding coral on this lovely beach, the atmosphere is lively and the facilities are good for families. The restaurants are largely indifferent unless you like burgers and chips.

The construction of a luxurious new 1000-berth marina in nearby Potima has been indefinitely postponed.

✖ Eating

Tweedie's INTERNATIONAL €€€
(☑9912 6590; Kissonerga; mains from €15; ☺7pm-late Thu-Sun) Located on the main street in Kissonerga, roughly halfway between

THE MUCH-MALIGNED CYPRIOT MOUFLON

Featured as a stylised graphic on the tail fin of Cyprus Airways planes, the Cypriot mouflon (*Ovis orientalis ophion*), known as *agrino* in Greek, is Cyprus' de facto national symbol. Similar to a wild sheep and native to the island of Cyprus, it has close cousins on the islands of Sardinia and Sicily, and in Iran. Today, Cyprus' mouflon population is limited to the dense vegetation of the Pafos Forest on the western side of the Troödos Mountains.

Once treated as vermin, the mouflon was fair game for trigger-happy hunters – by the 1930s there were only 15 alive in Cyprus. Since then an enlightened preservation program has seen numbers rise to around 3000. The mouflon is a shy, retiring animal and is rarely seen in the wild, as it will disappear into the forest long before your arrival. The male mouflon sports enormous curved horns and, while not aggressive to humans, uses its horns in mating battles with other males.

While numbers have reached stable levels, the mouflon is still considered an endangered species. The main threats nowadays come from forest fires and poachers. For more mouflon info, check the www.moa.gov.cy/forest website.

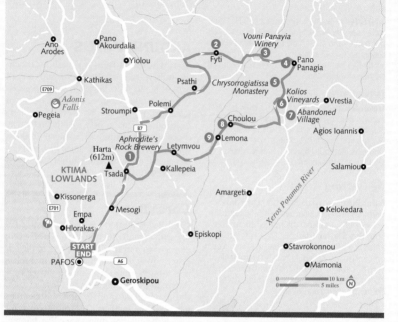

Driving Tour
Wineries, Weaving & Abandoned Villages

START PAFOS
FINISH PAFOS
DISTANCE 86KM; FOUR TO SIX HOURS

From Pafos, take the B7 north towards Polis. After around 14km, look for the sign for ① **Aphrodite's Rock Brewery** where you can taste (and buy) craft beers. After a further 3km head towards Fyti on the signposted E703; this pretty country road winds between vineyards and orchards. Pass through Polemi and Psathi, then take the signposted left turn towards ② **Fyti**. Park by the church, stop at the Fyti Village Tavern (also known as Maria's Place), duck into the Folk Art Museum and then leave on the F725 towards Pano Panagia via Kritou Marottous and Asprogia; the scenery is lovely, with vineyards, citrus groves and distant mountains.

Watch for the sign for the ③ **Vouni Panayia Winery** and stop for a wine tasting; the Barba Yiannis dry red comes particularly recommended. Continue on to ④ **Pano Panagia**, the birthplace of Archbishop Makarios (p74); have a quick nose around his childhood home, a typical peasants' house with just two rooms.

Head south out of town on the F622, stopping at the well-signposted ⑤ **Chrysorrogiatissa Monastery** for lunch on the terrace, accompanied by beautiful countryside views. A couple of kms on from here is another excellent winery, ⑥ **Kolios Vineyards**, which offers free tastings. Its Shiraz is highly regarded. Follow signs to the E702 and Choulou. After around 3km you will pass through a fascinating ⑦ **abandoned village** where just a couple of residents, one donkey and several goats remain after a 1969 earthquake forced the vast majority of villagers to relocate.

In ⑧ **Choulou** have a look at the simple whitewashed mosque (this was a Turkish village before 1974) and enjoy a coffee at the traditional Antoyaneta Taverna across the way. Make the last stop on your tour the village of ⑨ **Lemona**, home to an excellent micro-winery: Tsangarides Winery. Continue back to Pafos on the B7, via Letymvou and Tsada.

Pafos and Coral Bay, Tweedie's offers a different menu daily and innovative dishes with creative combos like beetroot and bacon or cauliflower and brie (as in soups), homemade ravioli with unusual fillings, and fabulous art-on-a-plate desserts. Tweedie's works strictly on advance reservations only.

Akamas Heights

If you're spending any time in the Pafos area, make sure you check out the Akamas Heights region. Most of the villages have great agrotourism-restored traditional houses for rent (check www.agrotourism.com.cy); the food in the tavernas, cooked for the locals, is generally delicious; the atmosphere is peaceful; and the hiking possibilities are fantastic. And did we mention the beaches? This area has some of the best in the South.

The villages of Akamas Heights can be visited en route to Polis, on the picturesque western road (E701/709). There's no public transport to get to these villages, the beaches or Avgas Gorge. The climb to the heights starts at Pegeia, populated mainly by well-heeled Brits. From here you can head northwest towards the southern approach to the Akamas Peninsula.

Lara & Agios Georgios Beaches

There is a real treat on the southwestern side of the Akamas Peninsula. Approached by a rough but driveable track from Agios Georgios, around 21km north of Coral Bay, the famous Lara coastal area is mercifully undeveloped. Backed by desertlike scrubland, tinged with dark ochre, and studded with gorse, bushy pines and seasonal wildflowers, it is set against a distant backdrop of low-lying hills. Look for the signs to Lara Restaurant, where you can stop for a drink or snack on the vast terrace overlooking pristine **Lara Bay**, with its shingle and dark sand.

The more famous **Lara Beach** lies in the next cove, separated by a headland and cupped by lime rocks. Aside from the modest cafeteria-bar near the entrance, there is no development here; the beach is sandy and the water is clean and calm. Also serving as a **turtle hatchery**, this is one of the few remaining havens for green and loggerhead turtles to nest, so sun loungers and umbrellas are not allowed. Monk seals also dwell in the sea caves around the peninsula.

The path towards the beach is a dirt track but can be driven on by 'normal' (2WD) cars, in dry weather – although you should take care when parking not to get stuck in the sand. Also, if you are renting a car you may be specifically told that you should not drive off road. If you feel uneasy, go for a 4WD rental vehicle or take a tour.

If you would rather not retrace your path to Agios Georgios, take the signposted paved road to **Ineia** (8km) near the entrance to Lara Restaurant; this is a pretty drive which winds between pine-clad hills and valleys.

Agios Georgios Beach can be reached by road from Polis (via Pegeia) or Pafos (via Coral Bay). It is a 100m stretch of shadeless sand and rock with a modest harbour, but beach umbrellas and loungers are available for hire. There is a small beach bar and, up on the bluff, one of the region's most popular seafood restaurants, **Saint George's Fish Tavern** (⚑ 2662 1888; Agios Georgios; mains €13; ⊙ 9am-11pm). Due to the restaurant's location right above the harbour, the fish here is the best in the region – and you know it's good when it's just grilled, with nothing but some olive oil and lemon. The squid and octopus are similarly superb. Weekends get busy and, despite the vast terrace, you may have to queue for a table, but you can enjoy the sea views while you wait. The owners also have a few rooms to rent.

The adjacent large open space is popular at sunset and a small daily market held here sells ceramics and deli-style products. There is also a modest archaeological site nearby, with ruins of a 6th-century basilica church, including a partly visible mosaic floor, and several rock-hewn tombs dating from the Roman period. Access times are a hit-and-miss affair.

Dhrousia, Kritou Terra & Around

POP 390 & 90

Once you are up in the heights, you will come across a series of villages that enjoy a cool climate, grow fine wine grapes and are truly picturesque. They also make a useful alternative base for travellers wishing to avoid the clamour of the coast further south.

Particularly appealing are the villages of **Dhrousia** and **Kritou Terra** with good places to stay, eat, drink and simply watch the world go by.

Dhrousia is a village of winding streets, moustached men sitting outside the *kafeneio* (coffee shop), lofty fig trees offering their fruit to passers-by, and an occasional donkey standing nonchalantly on the cobbles. Fortunately, the newish modern hotel sitting grandly on the outskirts of the village has not detracted too much from the sense of off-the-beaten-track tranquillity here.

Kritou Terra, a little east from Dhrousia, is an unspoilt village with some splendid traditional houses tastefully renovated by their inhabitants; several have been reborn as atmospheric places to stay. The late-Byzantine church of Agia Ekaterini, at the southern end of the village, is worth a photo.

Three other villages, not far from Dhrousia and Kritou Terra, are unspoilt **Inia** (population 350), **Miliou** (population 60) and **Goudi** (population 160), which also have places to stay.

◎ Sights

Kouyiouka Watermill HISTORIC BUILDING
(☑ 2663 2847; kouyiouka@cytanet.com.cy; Gioulou; ☺ 7.30am-5pm) **FREE** Located 7km south of Goudi on the B7, this 200-year-old listed watermill has been superbly renovated and now houses a museum, a coffee shop and a traditional bakery. The museum displays the traditional (and historical) equipment necessary for making bread while the bakery sells delicious rolls with haloumi which you can enjoy with a coffee or beer overlooking the stream with orchards across the way.

✖ Eating

Finikkas CYPRIOT €€
(☑ 2633 2336; Dhrousia; mains €9-11, meze €13; ☺ noon-9pm Tue-Sat Apr-Sep; 🚗) Located just off the crossroad in the centre of town, this is the village's most popular taverna sporting a traditional dining room and typical menu of meaty mains like grilled souvlaki and lamb kebabs, as well as a generous (some may say porky...) 15 dish meze.

Kathikas

POP 335
This is the most easily accessible village from Pafos, midway between Pafos and Polis on the E709. Famous for its vineyards and wine, it is home to several popular restaurants. You can also spy one of Cyprus' so-called tree monuments located just outside the village here: the Cypress tree of Agios Nikolaos is a lofty 14m high, with a pensionable age of more than 700 years.

✖ Eating & Drinking

★ Imogen's Inn CYPRIOT €€
(☑ 2663 3269; Georgiou Kleanthous St; meze €16.50, pizza €6.50; ☺ 10am-3.30pm Thu-Tue) For something different, head to Imogen's, located at the entrance to the village and which resembles a French bistro, with the sounds of jazz and blues tinkling into the garden that sprawls out under a large fig tree. Try the vegetarian meze, it's delicious.

Imogen has recently opened a small pizza restaurant and takeaway out front here, as well. All the pizzas are the same reasonable price and include four toppings.

Vasilikon WINE BAR
(☑ 2663 3999; www.vasilikon.com; Kathikas; ☺ 8am-7pm; 🕿) This winery has won several prestigious international awards for its wines. A wine bar opened here in 2014 serving platters of cheese and cold cuts to share while enjoying sweeping vineyard views. There is also complimentary wine tasting from 8am to 3pm daily. The winery and wine bar is signposted just after the turn-off to Kathikas on the Polis road.

Pano Akourdalia, Kato Akourdalia & Miliou

POP 35, 30 & 60
From Kathikas you can detour onto the B7 (the direct road between Pafos and Polis) via these three picturesque villages, where you have the option of staying overnight or just stopping for a relaxing lunch.

✖ Eating & Drinking

★ Pagratios CYPRIOT €€
(☑ 7000 3757; Milou Square, Milou; meze €17; ☺ noon-midnight Tue-Sun) This quintessential Cypriot tavern has its roots in the 1930s when it was the village coffee shop. There are just a handful of tables and reservations are essential on weekends. Popular with Cypriots, as well as visitors, most diners opt for the superb meze.

Amarakos Inn CYPRIOT €€
(☑ 2231 3374; Kato Akourdalia; mains €10; ☺ 11am-10pm; 🕿🚗) This restaurant is part of the Amarakos Inn (p206) guesthouse. Enjoy palate-pleasing fare such as village sausages with grilled mushrooms and *afelia* (pork cooked in red wine).

Avgas Gorge

Also known as the Avakas Gorge, this narrow split in the Akamas Heights escarpment is a popular hiking excursion. The gorge is reached by vehicle from its western end via Agios Georgios Beach. You can drive or ride more or less up to the gorge entrance, though low-slung conventional vehicles will have to take care. The hike up the gorge, which becomes a defile with cliffs towering overhead, is easy and enjoyable. There is usually water in the gorge until at least May, hence the lush streamside vegetation (keep an eye out for tree frogs). The walk will take no longer than 30 to 40 minutes one way, although some groups do press on upwards – with some difficulty – emerging on the escarpment ridge and then finding their way to the village of Ano Arodes (not much use if your vehicle is at the gorge entrance).

AKAMAS PENINSULA

This part of western Cyprus, jutting almost defiantly into the Mediterranean, is one of the island's last remaining wildernesses. Visitors can still traverse the Akamas as long as they're prepared to walk, ride a trail bike or bump along in a sturdy 4WD. Those with less stamina can take tour boats that sail the Akamas coastline from Latsi, west of Polis. The peninsula can be approached from two sides: from the east via Polis, or from the south via the little village of Agios Georgios. Tracks linking the two entry points are very rough, perhaps deliberately so as to discourage traffic.

The peninsula's big attraction is its abundant flora and fauna, resulting from Akamas' position as the easternmost point of the three major plant-life zones of Europe. There are around 600 plant species here, and 35 of them are unique to Cyprus. There are also 68 bird species, 12 types of mammals, 20 species of reptile and many butterflies, including the native *Glaucopsyche pafos*, the symbol of the region.

The only public transport to the area is the bus from Polis to the Baths of Aphrodite.

🏃 Activities

Hiking

Easily the most popular way to get a taste of the Akamas is to spend a few hours hiking one of the following trails, which run through the northeastern sector of the peninsula. All can start and end at one of two points: the Baths of Aphrodite, or Smigies picnic ground, which is reached via an unsealed road 2.5km west of Neo Chorio.

The two most popular trails are those that start and end at the Baths of Aphrodite. They are both longer than the Smigies trails and offer better views. The first is the **Aphrodite Trail**, a 7.5km, three- to four-hour loop. It heads inland and upwards to begin with; as this can be tiring on a hot day, make an early start if you can. Halfway along the trail you can see the ruins of **Pyrgos tis Rigainas** (Queen's Tower), part of a Byzantine monastery. Look for the huge 100-year-old oak tree nearby before you head up to the summit of **Mouti tis Sotiras** (370m). At this point you head east and down towards the coastal track, which will eventually lead you back to the car park.

The second hike, the 3½-hour, 7.5km **Adonis Trail**, shares the same path as the Aphrodite as far as Queen's Tower but then turns left (south) before looping back to the car park. In order to complete its circular path, the trail follows the main road connecting the Baths of Aphrodite and Polis for about 400m. Alternatively, you can turn right (south) just after the village of Kefalovrysi and continue on to Smigies picnic ground if you have arranged a pick-up beforehand.

Water is usually available at Queen's Tower and, on the Adonis Trail, at Kefalovrysi, but don't count on it in high summer. In

VIKLARI

Viklari (Last Castle; ☏ 2699 6088; mains €12; ⏱ 1.30-4pm; 🍴) If you haven't taken a picnic with you, excellent food is available near the entrance of Avgas Gorge at Viklari, better known as the Last Castle. For €12 you get a delicious *kleftiko* barbecue, accompanied by salad and a baked potato. You eat at heavy stone tables under grapevines, surrounded by petrified-rock 'sculptures', lovingly nurtured pot plants and a garden.

Owner Savvas Symeou has been greeting customers here since 1989, providing lunch for hungry hikers. Look for signs to the 'Last Castle' from the coastal road and enjoy stunning views of citrus and banana groves leading down to the sea.

PAFOS & THE WEST AKAMAS PENINSULA

any case, these trails are best attempted in spring or autumn; if you must do it in Cyprus' extremely hot summer, stride out at sunrise.

The CTO produces a step-by-step and plant-by-plant description of these two trails in a booklet entitled *European Long Distance Path E4 and other Cyprus Nature Trails,* available from the main CTO offices. Two other trails to consider (also outlined in the booklet) commence from Smigies picnic ground: the circular 2.5km or 5km **Smigies Trail** and the circular 3km, 1½-hour **Pissouromouttis Trail**. Both afford splendid views of Chrysohou Bay to the northeast and the Akamas coastline to the west.

PAFOS & THE WEST POLIS

Polis

POP 1890

Polis is mainly visited by Cypriots on their August holidays, although the number of coach tours from the coast has been increasing. It remains an appealing small town, however, with a beach, a good camp site, and some decent hotels and restaurants, as well as an overall welcome lack of overdevelopment – aside from a holiday village that was built several years ago near the centre of town. Notwithstanding, Polis makes an ideal base for hiking or mountain biking in the Akamas and touring the Akamas Heights winemaking villages.

Polis lies on wide Chrysohou Bay, on the northwestern sweep of Cyprus from Cape Arnaoutis at the tip of the Akamas Peninsula to Pomos Point at the start of the Tyllirian wilderness.

◎ Sights & Activities

There is plenty of scope for water sports at **Latsi harbour**, located 2km west of Polis.

Archaeological Museum   MUSEUM
(Leoforos Archiepiskopou Makariou III; admission €1; ☺8am-2pm Mon-Wed & Fri, to 6pm Thu, 9am-5pm Sat) Includes finds from the nearby graves at Marion and Arsinoe. There is an old olive tree close to the museum; its trunk is almost split in two, but it still produces olives after 600 years.

Agios Andronikos   CHURCH
(Iouliou; ☺10am-6pm; P) This 16th-century church was previously a mosque and the centre of local Turkish Cypriot religious life. Don't miss the fine Byzantine frescos that were hidden behind whitewash for decades.

Sitting on the western side of town, the church can only be visited in groups of 10 or more. The key is held at the Archaeological Museum.

Latsi Watersports Centre   WATER SPORTS
(☎2632 2095; www.latchiwatersportscentre.com; Latsi Harbour; ⊕) Offers diving courses (from €75), boat hire (from €45), parasailing (from €48) and windsurfing (from €28 per hour, including equipment rental).

Ride in Cyprus   HORSE RIDING
(☎9977 7624; www.rideincyprus.com; from €30; ⊕) For hour-long horse-riding treks, overnight safaris and picnic day rides, contact this company in Lysos, 12km southeast of town, on the road to Stavros tis Psokas.

🏖 Beaches

The best beaches easily accessible from Polis are those on the eastern side of Latsi, 2km west of Polis. These beaches tend to be mixed sand and pebble, and are somewhat exposed to the vagaries of the weather, but they are popular enough and well serviced with restaurants.

Camp Site Beach   BEACH
The nearest stretch of sand is a good beach and convenient if you don't want to move far from Polis and fancy a picnic, or are camping there. It's sandy, with natural shade from fragrant eucalyptus trees. There's a beach restaurant and lifeguards.

Aphrodite Beach Hotel Beach   BEACH
(⊕) This lovely, calm beach is clearly signposted on the way to the Baths of Aphrodite. It's good for children, with its clear, swimmable waters and comfortably small pebbles.

🧭 Tours

Wheelie Cyprus   BICYCLE TOURS
(☎9935 0898; www.wheeliecyprus.com; from €65; ⊕) Organises bike tours on little-known trails throughout the area. The price includes high-quality bike rental, all equipment and pick-up from your hotel. Book online.

🎉 Festivals & Events

Summer Nights in Polis   MUSIC
In summer the Plateia Iroön (Town Hall Sq) hosts various free concerts ranging from traditional dancing, music and folkloric events to classical music and jazz performances.

Polis

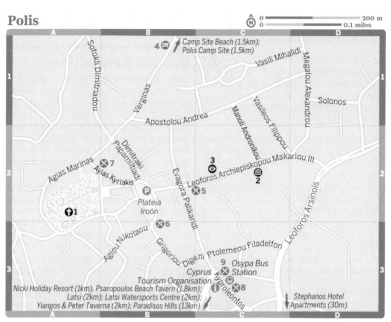

✖ Eating & Drinking

You'll find plenty of restaurants and bars in Polis.

★ Kivotis Art Cafe   CAFE €

(🖉 9955 5183; Ayias Kyriakis; waffles €4.50, cakes €2.80; ⏱ 10am-6pm; 🖟) The antithesis of the sanitised coach-tour-geared cafes up the road, this shady oasis has a welcoming informality with its rambling terrace of mismatched furniture, quirky sculptures and shelves of boardgames and books. Homemade cakes, waffles and ice cream are the scrumptious specialities plus light meals.

★ Psaropoulos Beach Tavern   SEAFOOD €€

(🖉 2632 1089; Polis-Latsi Rd; fish meze €17.50; ⏱ 10am-11pm; 🖟) This is an excellent choice for seafood and fish meze. Not only is the atmosphere superb, it's family run, packed with locals, right on the beach, and the seafood and fish are so fresh it is virtually flapping. Children are also made to feel very welcome. Located on the road to Latsi, look for the sign on the right-hand side, around 1km after the Polis crossroad.

Mosfilo's Tavern   CYPRIOT €€

(Kyproleontos; mains €8; ⏱ noon-10pm Tue-Sat; 🖟) This place exudes a traditional ambience with its high ceilings, original tiles and col-

Polis

◉ Sights

1 Agios Andronikos	A2
2 Archaeological Museum	C2
3 Olive Tree	C2

🛏 Sleeping

4 Bougainvillea Hotel Apartments	B1

✖ Eating

5 Archontariki Restaurant-Tavern	C2
6 Arsinoe Fish Tavern	B3
7 Kivotis Art Cafe	B2
8 Mosfilo's Tavern	C3
9 Old Town Restaurant	C3

umns, and gallery of historic pics of Polis. The menu includes classics like spinach and lamb, and grilled chicken. The location is less aesthetic – across from the petrol station on the B7 main road to Pafos.

Archontariki Restaurant-Tavern   CYPRIOT €€

(🖉 2632 1328; www.archontariki.com.cy; Leoforos Archiepiskopou Makariou III 14; mains €11; ⏱ 6-11pm Tue-Sun) This is a popular traditional tavern where the service is attentive and the food top class. Dine in an old renovated stone house and try chicken stuffed with haloumi and mushrooms, or *kathisto* (octopus cooked in wine and oregano). There's live music on Friday. Reservations recommended.

Arsinoe Fish Tavern SEAFOOD €€
(Grigoriou Digeni; fish meze €14; ⊙ 6-11pm) Locals continue to rate this as one of the top places in town for fresh fish. It is an atmospheric, traditional family-owned place. Try the succulent fish meze.

Old Town Restaurant MODERN CYPRIOT €€€
(☑ 9963 2781; www.facebook.com/oldtownpolis; Kyproleontos 9; mains €16; ⊙ 7-11pm Tue-Sun) This is a discreet and relaxing place with a leafy, secluded garden and a stripped-back, stone-clad dining room with crisp white tablecloths, shelves of wine, and plants. The menu is seasonal, but you can expect dishes like rabbit *stifado* with wild mushrooms and juniper berries, crispy duck spring rolls with honey and chilli, and lobster pasta. Reservations recommended.

Yiangos & Peter Taverna SEAFOOD €€€
(Leoforos, Latsi; mains from €12; ⊙ 8.30am-11pm) One of the first seafood restaurants to open here, dating from 1939, this longtime popular place is located at the entrance to the harbour, with a large terrace; most (though not all) of the fish on display here is caught on the day.

☆ Entertainment

Stop by the CTO office for details of events. Ticketed concerts, often given by top-name Greek artists, take place in the Eukalyptionas (Eucalyptus Grove) at Polis Camp Site. These outdoor events can be magical on a hot summer night. Tickets cost between €10 and €20.

ℹ Information

Cyprus Tourism Organisation (CTO; www.visitcyprus.org.cy; Vasileos Stasioikou 2; ⊙ 9am-1pm & 2.30-5.30pm Sun-Tue, Thu & Fri, 9am-1pm Sat) Very central.

ℹ Getting There & Around

Pafos Buses (www.pafosbuses.com) has daily service to/from Polis leaving from Karavella Bus Station in Ktima. All buses depart from Osypa Bus Station in Polis.
Baths of Aphrodite (bus 622; 30min; €1.50; hourly 6am-noon & 3-6pm Mon-Fri, 7 Sat & Sun)
Latsi (bus 623; 20min; €1.50; 2 daily)
Pafos (bus 645; 1hr; €1.50; up to 11 Mon-Fri, 5 Sat & Sun)

Pomos Bus 643A; one hour, €1.50. Three on weekdays, two on weekends.

Baths of Aphrodite

The myth surrounding the cool cave that is the Baths of Aphrodite (Loutra tis Afroditis) is great advertising. Aphrodite, goddess of love and patron of Cyprus, came to the island in a shower of foam and nakedness, launching a cult that has remained to this day. Legend has it that she came to this secluded spot to bathe after entertaining her lovers.

The baths attract a steady crowd, but it is easy to wonder if the visitors expect more than they find. Surrounded by fig trees and filled with the relaxing sound of running water, the grotto is a nice spot away from the heat, but it's far from the luxurious setting that may be associated with a goddess of such amorous prowess. The surrounding botanical garden is pretty, however, with labelled plants and trees, including carob trees, red gum and the slightly less exotic dandelion.

The baths are 11km west of Polis, along a sealed road. From the baths' car park with its adjacent gift shop, follow the well-marked paved trail for 200m. You are not allowed to swim in the baths.

There are various nature trails you can take from the grotto.

TYLLIRIA

If you love untouched, tranquil nature, head for Tylliria. It's a sparsely populated, forested territory with a few desultory beach resorts nestling between Chrysohou and Morfou Bays. Enjoying its wilderness, even if just for a few days, is highly recommended.

The only public transport in this area is the bus connecting Pomos with Polis.

Pomos

POP 570

The trip up the coastal road from Polis towards Tylliria becomes gradually more scenic but doesn't really unfold in all its glory until beyond Pomos, which is the first village you come to (at 19km). This is a lush agricultural area with olive trees, citrus groves and vines, and precious little development.

⊙ Sights

Museum of Natural History   MUSEUM
(admission €1; ⊙7.30am-2.30pm Mon-Fri, to 4pm Wed, 8am-1pm Sat; P🐾) Clearly signposted off the main street, this is an unexpected attraction to find here, with its two large galleries of animals and birds endemic to the island, as well as a modest display of rocks and minerals. While taxidermists may not be impressed with some of the mildly moth-eaten exhibits, the comprehensive display includes some surprises, such as pelicans, a mouflon, the large Caretta turtle and a prehistoric-looking *gyps fulvos* vulture – all native to Cyprus.

Don't miss the photo of the skeleton of a hippopotamus found in caves in the Akrotiri area, along with skeletons of the pygmy elephant, both dating back to neolithic times.

✖ Eating

★ **Kanali Fish Restaurant**   SEAFOOD €€
(Pomos Harbour; mains from €12; ⊙10am-10pm; 🛜🐾) The main draw is the stunning view from its terrace: the turquoise bay and the small, upgraded harbour with forested mountains in the distance; romantics should head here at sunset. The kitchen specialises in fresh fish, namely sea bass, bream, red snapper and red mullet, served with freshly made (rather than frozen) chips.

The homemade desserts are good too; opt for the deliciously moist carrot cake if it's on offer. Kanali is well signposted from the centre of town, located above the small harbour.

Sea Cave   SEAFOOD €€
(mains from €8; ⊙noon-11pm Apr-Sep; 🐾) A sound informal eating option located on the coastal road at the far side of town. Head for the outside terrace shaded by pomegranate trees and enjoy a classic seafood menu with an emphasis on the catch of the day.

Pahyammos

Located just 5km east of Pomos along a lovely stretch of highway flanked by colourful oleander bushes, Pahyammos means 'broad sand'. Its beach is indeed broad and sweeps around a large bay up to the UN watchtowers that mark the beginning of Kokkina, a Turkish Cypriot enclave.

The beach is made up of darkish sand and there's no natural shade, but the swimming is reasonable. There are no facilities on the beach, but there are one or two places to eat in the town, which is strung out along the main through-road.

Kokkina (Erenköy)

Tylliria really felt the pinch when it was partly isolated from the rest of Cyprus following the Turkish invasion in 1974. Since that time,

---

THE CULT OF APHRODITE

Cyprus is indelibly linked to the ancient worship of the goddess Aphrodite (known as Venus in Roman mythology). She is known primarily as the Greek goddess of sexual love and beauty, although she was also worshipped as a goddess of war – particularly in Sparta and Thebes. While prostitutes often considered her their patron, her public cult was usually solemn and even austere.

The name Aphrodite is thought to derive from the Greek word *afros,* meaning 'foam'. Cypriot legend has it that Aphrodite rose from the sea off the south coast of Cyprus. She was born out of the white foam produced by the severed genitals of Ouranos (Heaven), after they were thrown into the sea by his son Chronos (the father of Zeus, king of the Greek gods). The people of Kythira in Greece hold a similar view to that expressed in the legend; an enormous rock off the south-coast port of Kapsali is believed by Kytherians to be the place where Aphrodite really emerged.

Despite being a goddess, Aphrodite had a predilection for mortal lovers. The most famous of them were Anchises (by whom Aphrodite became mother to Aeneas) and Adonis (who was killed by a boar and whose death was lamented by women at the festival of Adonia).

The main centres of worship on Cyprus for the cult of Aphrodite were at Pafos and Amathous. Her symbols included the dove, the swan, pomegranates and myrtle.

Greek art represented her as a nude-goddess type. Ancient Greek sculptor Praxiteles carved a famous statue of Aphrodite which later became the model for the Hellenistic statue known as *Venus de Milo.*

this small Turkish enclave, known in Greek as Kokkina and in Turkish as Erenköy, has been surrounded by Greek Cypriot territory. Don't risk driving off the road trying to spot the place; it's hidden behind mountains and guarded by a couple of UN and Greek Cypriot army lookout points, with signposts forbidding photography.

Kato Pyrgos

POP 1135

This remote beach resort is as far out of the way as you can get in the Republic, yet it attracts a regular summer clientele of Cypriots who come for its laid-back ambience. Don't expect palm-fringed promenades and white sandy beaches; Kato Pyrgos has a mildly shabby, old-fashioned appeal, and many Cypriots come here just to get away from the rampant commercialism that they recognise has overwhelmed the more popular coastal resorts of their island. Since the opening of the border crossing here in 2010, the resort has attracted still more visitors, who stop here en route to the North.

The breezy village is dotted along a wide bay running from Kokkina Point to where the Green Line meets the sea. The border's proximity is emphasised by the frequent chatter of UN helicopters that fly in and out of the nearby base. You can bathe at a number of locations along the bay, though the most popular spot seems to be the far eastern end, close to the Green Line, which is also where the most attractive part of town is, its main street lined with leafy trees and a couple of traditional coffee houses.

Kato Pyrgos has a sprinkling of bars and tavernas. The best places to eat are down on the beach at the far eastern end of town, specialising, unsurprisingly, in seafood and open roughly from Easter to October.

Psokas

From Kato Pyrgos or Pahyammos you can strike out south into the Tylliria hinterland. Make sure you detour slightly to the lovely forest reserve of Stavros tis Psokas, also accessible from Pafos (51km) via a picturesque road that is unsealed for a considerable distance. This vast picnic site is a forest station responsible for fire control in the Pafos Forest. Nature-loving Cypriots come here to walk and enjoy the peace, and it can get quite crowded in summer. In a small en-

closure, signposted from the main parking area, you can get a glimpse of the rare and endangered native Cypriot mouflon. Move quietly and slowly if you want to see them, as they get rather skittish at the approach of humans.

You can do some hiking from the Stavros tis Psokas forest station. The **Horteri Trail**, a 5km, three-hour circular hike, loops around the eastern flank of the Stavros Valley. The trail starts at the Platanoudkia Fountain, about halfway along the forest station's approach road, which turns off the main through-road at Selladi tou Stavrou (Stavros Saddle). The hike involves a fair bit of upward climbing and can get tiring in the heat of summer; tackle the walk early in the day if you can.

The second trail is the **Selladi tou Stavrou**, a 2.5km, 1½-hour circular loop of the northern flank of the Stavros Valley. The start is prominently marked from Stavros Saddle (at the junction of the forest station approach road and the main through-road). A longer option (7km, 2½ hours) is to follow the trail anticlockwise and then branch south to the heliport. From there you can walk along a forest road to the forest station proper.

The CTO should be able to provide you with more information on these trails. Alternatively, consult www.visitpafos.org.cy.

You will need your own car to get here. There's a small camp site at Stavros tis Psokas with capacity for 60 people.

Kampos

POP 430

Few tourists make it to Kampos, the only substantial habitation in Tylliria. The scenery is beautiful and the locals don't see many foreigners.

Although technically part of the Kykkos Monastery sector of the Troödos, Kampos is stuck out on the southern edge of the Tyllirian wilderness with – these days – only one road out. The road that leads north from the village now comes to an ignominious end after 12km, at the Green Line.

However, this part of Tylliria is now less isolated than it was, thanks to the completion of the good sealed road that leads across the Tyllirian hinterland and northern extent of the vast Pafos Forest, linking the Kykkos Monastery with Kato Pyrgos and Pahyammos. Take it slowly, though; the road, while

WORTH A TRIP

FYTI

Easily accessible from Pano Panagia or Pafos, the picturesque village of Fyti is known for its distinctive weaving, with patterns passed down through generations. Park outside the church and have a mid-morning snack or lunch at the welcoming **Fyti Village Tavern** (Maria's Place; mains €8-10, meze €13; ☺7am-4pm), the most popular place in town with villagers, including the local priest. Courgettes with eggs, couscous with yoghurt and an excellent €13 meze are among the culinary treats. The interior is all beams and stone arches, with examples of local hand-woven cloth on the wall, although the shady terrace is where you really want to be.

Next, amble across the square to the **Folk Art Museum** (☺8am-1pm & 2-5pm) where former school teacher Charalambos will explain the exhibits, ranging from live silkworms munching on their bed of mulberry leaves to centuries-old donkey saddles and farm implements. Meanwhile, his cheerful wife, Theano, is busy at the loom, weaving exquisitely patterned silk-and-cotton fabrics. There are interesting historical photos here as well, including some of camels, which were used as pack animals until the late '50s. You can buy the hand-woven pieces, including cushion covers, runners and bags. At the very minimum, pick up a €2 embroidered bookmark memento. If you don't make a purchase, a small donation is appreciated.

good, is very winding and tiring to drive. Most maps still show it as unsealed. It's a much shorter, if more challenging, route into the Tyllirian region than the traditional road from the southeast, via Polis.

WESTERN TROÖDOS

The sparsely populated area flanking the western foothills of the Troödos Mountains is home to few attractions other than several delightful villages, where traditions hold fast and the local Cypriot dialect is just that bit more impenetrable. If you're looking for a route to central Troödos from the west coast, you can now easily follow a mixture of good sealed and unsealed roads into the mountains. The best route takes you to Kykkos Monastery via the village of Pano Panagia.

You'll need a vehicle to see these places, as public transport is patchy or nonexistent. Alternatively, you could join a tour from Polis or Pafos.

Pano Panagia

POP 560

This village is the birthplace of Makarios III, the island's famous archbishop president. A few tavernas and cafes on the main street provide very average (and overpriced) snacks and meals to the day trippers.

◉ Sights

Makarios Cultural Centre   MUSEUM
(admission €0.50; ☺9am-1pm & 2-5pm) This museum is a place for hard-core fans only, containing memorabilia from Makarios' life as a politician and priest, including plenty of photos. Housed in just one room, the exhibits include his overcoat, slippers and dressing gown (from the famous London department store Selfridges).

Childhood House of Makarios   NOTABLE BUILDING
(☺10am-1pm & 2-6pm) FREE A considerable-sized building, considering his family's peasant status, the childhood house of Makarios contains more photos and memorabilia from his younger years. If the house is locked, you can obtain the key from the nearby cultural centre.

Cedar Valley

This cool valley is the highlight of the western Troödos hinterland, home to a large number of the unusual indigenous Cypriot cedar (*Cedrus brevifolia*), a close cousin of the better-known Lebanese cedar. The valley is approached via a winding, unsealed forest road from Pano Panagia on the Pafos side of the Troödos Mountains, or along a signposted unsealed road from the Kykkos Monastery side of the Troödos. There is a picnic ground here and the opportunity to hike 2.5km to the summit of **Mt Tripylos**.

Larnaka & the East

Best Places to Eat

➡ Art Cafe 1900 (p110)

➡ Voreas (p110)

➡ Militzis (p110)

➡ Karousos Beach (p121)

➡ La Cultura Del Gusto (p125)

Best Places to Stay

➡ Hotel Opera (p207)

➡ Gabriel House (p208)

➡ Iosiphis House (p208)

➡ Alkisti City (p207)

➡ Golden Bay (p208)

Why Go?

Cyprus' east has more to offer than sunbathing and sandcastles. Hike Cape Greco's coastal path for glorious scenery and weird rock formations then follow the winding roads inland to wander snoozy villages which hug hillsides speckled with wild fennel. Delve into the very beginning of this island's human habitation at the neolithic site of Choirokoitia or whiz back not quite so far in history with a fresco-infused church-hop of this region's Byzantine relics.

Larnaka itself is an easygoing seaside town with a handful of excellent historic sites. It's an ideal base for further exploration.

Those golden strips of sand along the coast are what beckon most travellers here though. As resorts, hedonist-fuelled Agia Napa and family-friendly Protaras may be as different as chalk and cheese but both owe their success to this region's beach-sloth beauty. Pick a beach. Any beach. You're pretty much guaranteed to come up trumps.

When to Go

➡ Between February and March pink clouds of flamingos, waterfowl, wild ducks and many other migratory birds check in at Larnaka's salt lake for their annual spring break and turn the serene waters into birdwatcher central.

➡ June's Kataklysmos Festival in Larnaka is a great opportunity to witness how the traditional ties still play an important role in modern Cypriot life.

➡ From May to September someone turns the hot switch on and everyone makes for the beach. With excellent visibility and peak sea conditions, this is also the best time to head underwater and check out the famed *Zenobia* wreck dive (p109).

➡ In July and August Agia Napa's party scene reaches full throttle and all-night clubbing is the name of the game.

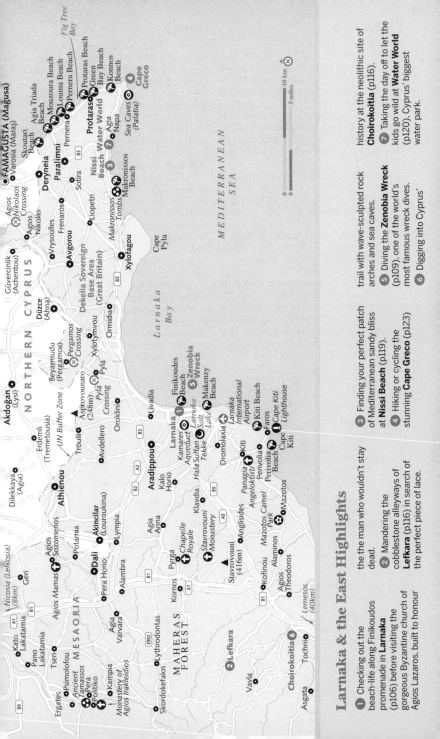

Larnaka & the East Highlights

1 Checking out the beach-life along Finikoudes promenade in **Larnaka** (p106) before visiting the gorgeous Byzantine church of Agios Lazaros, built to honour the the man who wouldn't stay dead.

2 Mandering the cobblestone alleyways of **Lefkara** (p116) in search of the perfect piece of lace.

3 Finding your perfect patch of Mediterranean sandy bliss at **Nissi Beach** (p119).

4 Hiking or cycling the stunning **Cape Greco** (p123) trail with wave-sculpted rock arches and sea caves.

5 Diving the **Zenobia Wreck** (p109), one of the world's most famous wreck dives.

6 Digging into Cyprus' history at the neolithic site of **Choirokoitia** (p116).

7 Taking the day off to let the kids go wild at **Water World** (p120), Cyprus' biggest water park.

LARNAKA

POP 51, 470

Larnaka revolves around its seaside position. The lively coastal promenade – known universally as the Finikoudes – is where locals and visitors alike come for a morning coffee or an evening beer, to flop out on the beach during the day and to stroll the wide pavement at sunset. It's the hub of the scene with restaurants, cafes and bars galore and during summer it fully revs up for the annual flood of holidaymakers.

Take a few steps inland though and a less tourism-centred side of Larnaka unfolds. The modern downtown district has stayed determinedly low-rise and has a proper community feel and working-town atmosphere. The old Turkish quarter of Skala is a slice of days-gone-by Cyprus full of whitewashed, quaintly dilapidated cottages where the arts and crafts traditions of the region are kept alive by the ceramic workshops which have moved in.

Between downtown and Skala you'll find the gorgeous Byzantine church of Agios Lazaros and Larnaka's little fort, which have both – in their own ways – been keeping a beady eye on the town for centuries.

History

Larnaka, originally known as Kition, was established during the Mycenaean expansion in the 14th century BC. An influential Greek city kingdom of the late Bronze Age, Kition prospered as a trading port through the export of copper. Withstanding rule by the Phoenicians and then the Persians, the city flourished into the Hellenistic period, even adopting the Phoenician fertility goddess Astarte, who was perhaps a precursor to Cypriot patron goddess Aphrodite.

During the Greek-Persian wars, Athenian general Kimon attempted to liberate the city from Persian rule in 450 BC. He died during the siege, urging his captains to conceal his fate from both enemies and allies. The episode is famously told as 'Kai Nekros enika' (Even in death he is victorious!). His bust now stands on the Finikoudes as a tribute.

Under Ottoman rule between the 16th and early 19th centuries, Larnaka attracted merchants, dignitaries and foreign consuls. Many of these participated in amateur archaeology, prevalent at the time and spirited away much of Larnaka's artefacts. The city's importance slowly decreased during

Larnaka

Britain's 88-year rule as trade moved through the port at Lemesos.

In 1974 the Turkish invasion of Northern Cyprus forced thousands of Greek Cypriots south, dramatically increasing Larnaka's population. Today Larnaka has Armenian, Lebanese, Pontian Greek and Palestinian settlers living alongside Cypriots and Europeans with mixed backgrounds of their own. Tourism is now the town's primary industry.

Larnaka

0 — 200 m
0 — 0.1 miles

Ancient Kition (500m)
Kimonos
Krikis
Kouriou
Kyriakou Matsi
Plateia Kalogreon
Sofroniou Christodoulou
Leoforos Archiepiskopou Makariou III
Filiou Tsigaridi
Louki Akrita
Kalogreon
Zinonas Bus Station
Leoforos Grigoriou Afxentiou
Gladstonos
Ermou
Iardou Vyronos
Stasinou
Ap Varnava
Larnaka Marina
Natural History Museum (320m)
6 Plateia Evropis
14
7
Italia Spagetteria (150m)
Galileou
Cyprus Tourism Organisation
Vasileos Pavlou
2
13
23
Vasil Evagorou
Pierides Archaeological Foundation
Stavrakis Taxi Office
9
12
Filiou Zannetou
Leoforos Athinon (Finikoudes Prm)
Stylianou Apostolidi
Agias Elenis
Stadiou
Kostaki Pantelidi
Konstantinou Kalogera
Armenikis Ekklisias
Zinonas Kitieos
Ev Pieridi
InterCity Bus Stop
20
25
19
22
Agiou Lazarou
Ermou
N Laniti
Love Buses Bus Stop
18
Diogenous
Adonidos
17
K Lysioti
Mihail Paridi
1
11
27
21
Agios Lazaros
Kalogera
Leoforos Faneromenis
10
8
Pavlou Valsamaki
3
El Alamein
Apollonioukitieos
Istanbul
5
Larnaka Bay
Paster
Okullar Haci Ömer Ali
Mehmet Ali
Menzil
Okullar
24
Zehra
16
Prevezis
Onisilou
Umm Haram
Mehmet Ali
Koca Tepe
Leoforos Artemidos
Piyale Pasha
26
Ak Deniz
28
Boz Dağu
15
Dive-In Larnaca (250m);
Zephyros (500m);
Psarolimano Tavern (650m);
Ammos & Makenzy Beach (800m)

LARNAKA & THE EAST LARNAKA

⊙ Sights & Activities

★ Agios Lazaros   CHURCH

(www.ayioslazaros.org; Agiou Lazarou; ⊙8am-12.30pm & 3.30-6.30pm Apr-Aug, 8am-12.30pm & 2.30-5.30pm Sep-Mar) This 9th-century church is dedicated to Lazarus of Bethany, whom Jesus is said to have resurrected four days after his death. The church itself is an astounding example of Byzantine architecture and further restoration in the 17th century added Latinate and Orthodox influences to the building, most prominently in the bell tower, which was replaced after being destroyed by the Ottomans. The beautiful interior is a showcase of unique Catholic woodcarvings and skilled gold-plated Orthodox icon artistry.

Lazarus has a close association with Larnaka. Shortly after he rose from the dead, thanks to Christ's miraculous intervention, Lazarus was forced to flee Bethany. His boat landed here in Kition, where he was ordained as a bishop and canonised by the Apostles Barnabas and Paul. He remained a bishop for a further 30 years and when he died for the second time was buried in a hidden tomb.

In 890 the tomb was discovered, bearing the inscription 'Lazarus friend of Christ'. Byzantine Emperor Leo VI had Lazarus' remains sent to Constantinople and built the current church over the vault to appease local Christians. The remains were moved again, to Marseille, in 1204.

The **Tomb of Lazarus** is under the apse of the Agios Lazaros. Several sarcophagi were supposedly found in this catacomb when it was first discovered but only the empty tomb now remains. In 1972 human remains were found under the church altar; some believe that the remains are those of St Lazarus, possibly hidden here by priests in anticipation of any theft.

Byzantine Museum   MUSEUM

(Agiou Lazarou; admission €1; ⊙8.30am-1pm & 3-5.30pm Mon, Tue, Thu, Fri & Sun, 8.30am-1pm Wed & Sat) Located in the courtyard of the Agios Lazaros complex, this museum originally contained many priceless relics and artefacts. Unfortunately, much of the collection was on loan to Lemesos' Archaeological Museum in the 1960s when sectarian violence broke out and the museum was looted. All that remains is the original catalogue of items, now on display.

The museum has worked hard to rebuild its collection and exhibits ecclesiastical artefacts, icons and utensils with many exhibits donated by Orthodox Russian clergy.

★ Pierides Archaeological Foundation   MUSEUM

(Zinonos Kitieos 4; adult/child €3/1; ⊙9am-4pm Mon-Thu, to 1pm Fri & Sat) This museum was established in 1839 by Demetrios Pierides as a protective answer to the region's notorious tomb raiders and illegal selling of precious artefacts from the area.

The collection, expanded by Pierides' descendents, is housed in the family mansion, built in 1825. It features artefacts from all over Cyprus, with detailed explanations in English. The museum's six rooms are arranged chronologically and present a comprehensive history of Cyprus.

The Pierides houses neolithic exhibits like the famous ceramic howling man, dating to c 5500 BC. If water is poured into the seated figure's mouth it will drain from his phallus. Archaeologists have debated whether the figure had a religious or a secular function, but no consensus has been reached.

The exhibits then wander through the Mycenaean and Achaean periods, the Iron Age, the Roman occupation, and Byzantine, Crusader, Lusignan, Venetian and Ottoman periods.

The collection also showcases intricate Greek and Roman glassware and offers fine examples of weaving, embroidery, woodcarvings and traditional costumes associated with Cypriot folk art.

Larnaka Fort   HISTORIC SITE

(Leoforos Athinon; admission €2.50; ⊙9am-7pm Mon-Fri) Built in the Lusignan era, the fort stands at the water's edge and separates the Finikoudes promenade from the old Turkish quarter. Its present form is a result of remodelling by the Ottomans around 1605.

The courtyard is home to some Medieval tomb stone exhibits and old cannons and you can climb up onto the ramparts for coastal views. The room on your right as you enter was where the British carried out executions during their rule over Cyprus.

There is a small and rather forlorn **Medieval Museum** with displays from the Hala Sultan Tekke and ancient Kition in the fort's upper-level room.

During summer the impressive courtyard is used for concerts and cultural events, which are heavily advertised on the Finikoudes.

Grand Mosque   MOSQUE

(Büyük Camii; Agias Faneromenis) Located at the beginning of Larnaka's Turkish quarter, with its maze of sleepy whitewashed streets, the Grand Mosque is the spiritual home of Larnaka's Muslim community. Left untouched when the Turkish community dispersed in 1974, it now predominantly serves Muslims from North Africa.

Originally built in the 16th century as the Latin Holy Cross Church, it was converted into a mosque. The current construction is the result of 19th-century restoration. There's a small graveyard in front, with gothic-looking tombstones.

Larnaka Archaeological Museum   MUSEUM

(Plateia Kalogreon; admission €2.50; ⊙9am-5pm Mon-Sat) A stop on the Aphrodite Cultural Route, Larnaka's archaeological museum houses a wide collection of pottery from ancient Kition and a reconstructed **neolithic tomb** from Choirokoitia. Spread out over five rooms, the collection's highlights are its terracotta votive figures.

Ancient Kition   ARCHAEOLOGICAL SITE

(Leoforos Arhiepiskopou Kyprianos; admission €2.50; ⊙8.30am-5pm Mon-Fri Apr-Oct, shorter hours rest of year) A lot of the original city-kingdom of Kition is still covered by present-day Larnaka. What is unearthed of the ancient city, referred to as Area II, is about 1km northwest of central Larnaka. The site appears sparse as you walk the raised runway that takes you over the remains of Cyclopean walls. Most remarkable is what remains of the five temples (from the 13th century BC) and ship depictions etched into the walls of the nearby ancient port. These confirmed that the city was founded by sea-trading Mycenaeans.

Municipal Cultural Centre   MUSEUM

(Leoforos Athinon, Plateia Evropis; ⊙9am-noon Tue-Sat) **FREE** Made up of five adjoining colonial-style stone warehouses built by the British in 1881, the cultural centre holds occasional exhibitions and is also home to the **Municipal Art Gallery**, which displays old and contemporary works of art from local artists.

Natural History Museum   MUSEUM

(Municipal Gardens, Leoforos Grigoriou Afxentiou; admission €1.70; ⊙10am-1pm & 4-6pm Tue-Sun Jun-Sep, 10am-1pm & 3-5pm Tue-Sun Oct-May) This museum presents an excellent introduction to the natural history of the island,

---

> **DON'T MISS**
>
> ## THE TURKISH QUARTER
>
> **Turkish Quarter** (Skala) Strolling the streets of the old Turkish neighbourhood of Skala is a glimpse of the Cyprus of old. This quaint district is a watercolour-worthy scene of squat cottages with peeling whitewash, coloured window shutters and flowerpot-studded doorways. Road signs here still carry their Turkish names; a reminder of Larnaka's mixed community before 1974. Today the quarter is being revived by a clutch of ceramic workshops that have made Skala their home giving the area a distinct bohemian edge.

with exhibits dedicated to fauna, flora, geology, insects and marine life. Situated in the Municipal Gardens, it is regularly visited by school groups and is a fun place for children, who can see pelicans, flamingos, peacocks and macaws in cages outside the museum. There is also a little playground in the gardens.

Dive-In Larnaca   DIVING

(☑2462 7469; www.dive-in.com.cy; Piyale Pasha 132; ⊙9am-6pm) With the famed *Zenobia* wreck dive site only a three-minute boat ride away, there's no better place to dive in Cyprus than Larnaka. This 5-star PADI dive centre has a whole range of technical, recreational dive safaris and learn-to-dive courses.

Alpha Divers   DIVING

(☑2464 7519; www.alpha-divers.com; Dhekalia, opposite Lordos Beach Hotel; ⊙9am-6pm) This 5-star PADI centre offers all the PADI dive courses from beginner to advanced and both technical and recreational dives to the *Zenobia*. The dive centre is 10km north of central Larnaka along Dhekalia Road and opposite the large Lordos Beach Hotel complex.

☞ Tours

The Cyprus Tourist Organisation (CTO) runs free guided walks that are a great introduction to the layout of Larnaka and its rich history. The 'Larnaka: Its Past & Present' walk starts at 10am every Wednesday at the CTO, and takes in the Finikoudes promenade, Agios Lazaros and the Pierides museum.

The second walk, 'Skala: Its Craftsmen', leaves at 10am every Friday from the fort. It

TOO HOT TO WALK?

Larnaka City Cruisers (☑ 9962 0749; Leoforos Athinon, Plateia Evropis; tour €12) These modern tricycles are powered by a friendly guide offering city-centre, arts-and-handicrafts and historical-themed bicycle tours (the latter is possibly the best). Each tour takes in 20 to 30 stops, giving you the opportunity to get out for a further look if you wish, and guides do their utmost to fill you with information.

Tours last about an hour and are a fun way to get to know the city. Cruisers depart from Plateia Evropis on the Finikoudes.

tours the old town with its traditional white-washed houses, balconies and arches. There are also stops at the pottery and handicraft workshops in its backstreets.

Walks take around two hours, with breaks to rest and refresh.

✦✦ Festivals & Events

Kataklysmos Festival RELIGIOUS
Held in June each year, 50 days after Orthodox Easter, this festival has special significance for Larnaka as a coastal town. Kataklysmos, meaning deluge or cataclysm in Greek, is a traditional celebration of Noah and his salvation from the Flood.

During the day there are all kinds of fun water-based activities like windsurfing, kayak races and swimming competitions.

At night the coastal promenade hosts open-air concerts and bazaar stalls selling everything from corn on a stick to tacky trinkets.

Musical Sundays MUSIC
(☻ from 11am Sun Jan-May & Nov-Dec) On the seafront stage at the Finikoudes, Musical Sundays feature a variety of rock, jazz, traditional music and dancing events. Line-ups are listed in the free brochure *Larnaka This Month,* available at all bookshops.

✖ Eating

Larnaka has a variety of eateries, ranging from souvlaki bars to gourmet restaurants. Most places can be found on or just off the Finikoudes promenade, with one or two hidden gems in the back streets. Dinners are usually available after 7pm, in keeping with Cypriots' big-lunch, late-siesta lifestyle. Often good restaurants won't be full until 10pm.

To Kafe INTERNATIONAL €
(Nikolaou Rossou 1; mains €6-12; ☻ 10.30am-11pm) This cute little cafe, squirreled away just off the main coastal drag, does excellent home-made soups, crispy salads and a mighty fine piece of cake. The outside seating – in a narrow alleyway off the street – is a good place to put your feet up for a light bite.

Chris' Kebab FAST FOOD €
(Piyale Pasha; mains €4-6; ☻ noon-10pm) This tiny souvlaki bar has just a handful of outdoor tables. Try the soft chicken pitta with homemade tahina sauce for extra tang. Watch out for the sea spray on windy days.

★ Art Cafe 1900 CYPRIOT €€
(☑ 2465 3027; Stasinou 6; mains €9-14; ☻ 6.30-11pm; ☑) With art prints and photos covering the wall, and shelves laden with bric-a-brac, Art Cafe 1900 is by far Larnaka's most atmospheric dining choice. The small menu dishes up cooking the way a Cypriot mamma would and there's a decent choice for vegetarians.

Italia Spagetteria ITALIAN €€
(Stylianou 1; mains €7-16; ☻ noon-3pm & 6-11pm Mon-Sat, 6-11pm Sun; ☑) This intimate venue has an extensive menu of well-priced, authentic Italian (loads of pasta, pizzas and steaks) with friendly service and imported Italian beers to wash it down. If you're after a carbohydrate-fix, it fits the bill nicely.

Militzis CYPRIOT €€
(Piyale Pasha 42; mains €9-12; ☻ 11am-11pm) This tavern has a traditional indoor-outdoor courtyard backing onto the domed *fourno* (traditional ovens) that 'all-day' bake incredibly soft lamb and chicken. Simple Cypriot meze is served with haloumi, giant beans and *bourgouri* (cracked wheat).

★ Voreas CYPRIOT €€€
(☑ 2464 7177; Agiou Demetriou 3, Oroklini; mains €9-17; ☻ 4pm-midnight Mon-Sat, noon-midnight Sun) Ten minutes outside Larnaka, in the village of Oroklini to the north, this traditional house and courtyard offers a taste of traditional foods, surrounds and hospitality. The aroma of herbs, the succulent variety of meat and the wild vegetable meze dishes leave you scrambling for space on the table and wondering if your stomach can take any more.

Zephyros

SEAFOOD €€€

(Piyale Pasha 37; mains €9-18; ⊘ 11am-11pm) Near the harbour, this contemporary tavern's service is only bettered by its high-quality fish meze. Calamari and silver sardines are an excellent choice. Dine here once and it's a safe bet you'll return.

Psarolimano Tavern

SEAFOOD €€€

(www.psarolimano.com; Piyale Pasha 118; mains €12-25; ⊘ 11am-11pm) This seafood tavern is known for its fish meze and it's well worth splashing out for it. The view, over the traditional fishing boat harbour, complements the food perfectly and service is friendly and efficient.

▼ Drinking & Nightlife

Larnaka's drinking scene centres on the Finikoudes, offering bars and cafes of every style. More intimate pubs and *kafeneia* (cafes) can be found in the side streets leading away from the coast and tend to have more reasonable prices.

While most serious party-goers head to Agia Napa for its club and bar scene, there are some easy-going spots to enjoy in Larnaka. Once more, the seafront and surrounding streets provide some good clubs, but in Larnaka the hottest spot is the up-and-coming area of Makenzy Beach.

In summer regular beach parties are held with guest DJs from around the globe and you can drink and dance all day at the beach bars on the sand. Watch for the leaflets posted around town advertising musical acts.

★ Ammos

BAR

(www.ammos.eu; Makenzy Beach; ⊘ 9am-late) Ammos (Greek for 'sand') is a splendidly bright white venue, perfectly located on the beach and open all day till late. You can eat in the classy kitchen bar or drink, chill and dance on the open rooftop to a mix of urban house and lazy funk. Don't be scared to kick off your shoes and enjoy the soft white sand featured in-house.

Times

BAR

(Leoforos Athinon 73; ⊘ 10am-1am) This popular cafe-bar on the seafront has a modern feel set off by cool white sofas stretched along the wall, perfect for lounging and sipping cocktails all night. There's live jazz on Sunday, Funky House Friday, and a rock night on Wednesday. Patrons dress smart and move on to Club Deep next door.

Savino's Rock Bar

BAR

(9 Ouotkins, Laiki Geitonia; ⊘ 7pm-late) With a hardwood bar and pictures of rock gods on the wall, this diminutive place is hidden just off the main promenade. It plays classic rock, jazz and blues and is a welcoming place to pull up a stool and enjoy a drink. It gets packed quickly, but fortunately Savino Live, its sister venue, is opposite for when the crowds expand and need to dance.

Brewery

BREWERY

(Leoforos Athinon 77; ⊘ 10am-1am) Pull your own pint from the micro-brew pumps brought to your table. There's a great selection of exclusive lagers, ales and well-hopped brews and a mix of fruity beers like cherry, lime and passion fruit. The burger menu is great for snacks but can be a bit pricy.

Geometry

CLUB

(Karaoli & Demetriou 8; ⊘ 10pm-late Fri-Sun) The entrance is a floor-lit mirrored ramp which looks like a cross between a retro spaceship and the 'Billy Jean' film clip. Inside is a decadent club kitted out with geometric light patterns and prisms. Aimed at a posh crowd, it plays a good selection of dance, club and Greek tracks. Dress well, so you feel at home with the locals.

Club Deep

CLUB

(Leoforos Athinon 76; ⊘ 11pm-late) Two floors of all-night clubbing right on the seafront. The lower club plays mostly chilled trance and progressive house. The main club (Deep) houses a huge dance floor melting with old school, R&B and mainstream dance. It gets busy after midnight with a young, easy-going crowd.

☆ Entertainment

Savino Live

LIVE MUSIC

(9 Ouotkins, Laiki Geitonia; ⊘ 8pm-late Wed-Fri & Sat) This live-rock venue fits up to 300 people and it needs to. With its well-amplified stage and open dance floor, it's a great night of vivacious dancing. Bands from all over Cyprus come to play classic blues, jazz and rock till late.

K Cineplex

CINEMA

(☑ Kmax bowling alley 7777 8373, box office 2436 2167; www.kcineplex.com; Peloponisou 1) A cineplex with six screens, wide reclining seats and all the usual Hollywood blockbusters on show. All films are subtitled in Greek except animated features, which have Greek or English alternatives. The site also houses the

20-lane **Kmax bowling alley** and Finnegan's Irish pub-restaurant. The complex is 10 minutes' drive west of the city centre, near the Kamares Aqueduct.

Shopping

Larnaka's signature collectable is pottery and there are some excellent ceramic workshops where you can pick up a piece of original Cypriot art.

★**Academic & General**   BOOKS
(⌨2462 8401; Ermou 41; ⊙9am-7pm) You could spend all day in here. The shop has thousands of English books, including the classics, history, philosophy and books on Cyprus. There's also a huge secondhand fiction section, ideal for beach reads. Cultural events are held here in summer. Feel free to make a coffee and lounge upstairs on the couches.

Studio Ceramics   CERAMICS
(⌨2465 0338; www.studioceramicscyprus.com; Ak Deniz 18; ⊙9am-1pm & 3-6pm Mon-Sat) The pottery here is inspired by ancient and medieval Cypriot art. The Pierides museum replicas are a standout.

Emira Pottery   CERAMICS
(⌨9940 4414; www.emirapottery.com.cy; Mehmet Ali 13; ⊙9am-1.30pm & 3-6pm Mon-Sat) Unique, delicately patterned plates and traditional Cypriot cooking pots are some of the many pieces on offer. You can even try your hand at your own creation.

Fotinis Pottery   CERAMICS
(Bozkourt 28; ⊙9.30am-1.30pm & 3-6pm Mon-Sat) Beautiful everyday bowls and plates embellished with pomegranates (the symbol of fertility during the island's pagan times).

Flamma Art Gallery   CERAMICS
(⌨2462 5530; Zinonos Kitieos 113; ⊙9.30am-1.30pm & 4-7pm Mon, Tue, Thu & Fri, 9.30am-1.30pm Wed & Sat) The dynamic pieces here are the work of local ceramic artist Stravros Stavrou whose creative work has a slightly whimsical edge.

Handworks Handmade   JEWELLERY
(www.handworkshandmade.com; Pavlou Valsamaki 22; ⊙9am-1pm & 3-6pm Mon-Sat) Just 50m from Agios Lazaros towards the sea is this eclectic store featuring myriad pendants, stones, anklets, rings and necklaces, in everything from wood to silver. This is a really well-priced shop for gifts and keepsakes.

🛈 Information

INTERNET ACCESS
Wi-fi is available all along the Finikoudes.
Amalfi Café (Lordou Vyronos 35; per hr €2; ⊙10am-1am) Centre of town, with billiards and gaming.
Replay (Leoforos Athinon; per hr €2.50; ⊙10am-1am) On the main promenade.

MEDICAL SERVICES
Larnaka Hospital (⌨2480 0500; Leoforos Grigoriou Afxentiou)
Night Pharmacy Assistance (⌨1414)

MONEY
Hellenic Bank (⌨2414 4141; Stasinou) Opposite the CTO.

POLICE
Police Station (⌨2480 4040; Leoforos Archiepiskopou Makariou III) Near to the Finikoudes promenade.

POST
Post Office (Plateia; ⊙7.30am-1pm & 3-6pm Mon-Fri, 9am-11am Sat) Near the CTO office.

TOURIST INFORMATION
Cyprus Tourism Organisation (CTO; ⌨2465 4322; www.visitcyprus.com; Plateia; ⊙8.15am-2.30pm & 3-6.15pm Mon, Tue, Thu & Fri, 8.15am-1.30pm Sat) Good maps of the city. Plenty of brochures. Up-to-date information on local events.

🛈 Getting There & Away

AIR
Larnaka International Airport (⌨flight info 2464 3000; www.hermesairports.com) is 7km southwest of the city centre. Direct flights come from all major European cities and northern Africa.

BOAT
Larnaka Marina (⌨2465 3110; ctolar@cytanet.com.cy) is an official port of entry into Cyprus offering a complete range of berthing facilities. It requires advance reservations.

BUS
InterCity Buses (⌨2464 3492; www.inter-city-buses.com) has regular buses to Nicosia (Lefkosia; one hour), Lemesos (45 minutes) and Agia Napa and Paralimni (45 minutes) from its Finikoudes bus stop, on the beach side in the middle of the coastal main promenade. All destinations cost one way/return €4/7.

SERVICE TAXI
Travel & Express (⌨2466 1010; www.travelexpress.com.cy; Kimonos 2) operates service

(shared) taxis to Agia Napa–Paralimni–Protaras (€11.50, 45 minutes), Nicosia (€8.50, 40 minutes), Lemesos (€10, one hour) and Pafos (€22, 1¾ hours) every half hour between 6am and 5pm Monday to Saturday, and to about 4pm on Sunday. The office is north of central Larnaka, about 200m east of the Ancient Kition site.

TAXI

There are several taxi stands along the Finikoudes. **Stavrakis Taxi Office** (☎ 2465 5988; Ermou 64) is in the centre of town. Sample journey fares and times:

Agia Napa €35, 30 minutes

Lemesos €50 to €60, one hour

Nicosia €45, 35 minutes

Pafos €105, one hour 40 minutes

Troödos €80 to €90, one hour

ℹ Getting Around

TO/FROM THE AIRPORT

A taxi stand operates 24/7 at the arrivals gate of Larnaka airport. The 10-minute ride costs approximately €15.

Alternatively local Zinonas buses 417, 419, 425 and 429 all make a stop at the airport bus stop (a short walk from the arrivals hall) and return (some by a rather roundabout route) to their central bus station near the marina. Tickets cost €1.50.

BUS

Larnaka's urban and regional bus network is run by **Zinonas Buses** (☎ 2466 5531; www.zinonas-buses.com; Filiou Tsigaridi) whose central bus station is opposite Larnaka marina. One-way tickets are €1.50 and all-day tickets are €5. Due to roundabout routes and irregular schedules, the bus network isn't used much by visitors. The website has route information in English but no timetables. The helpful staff at the bus station can provide timetables for you.

CAR & MOTORCYCLE

All the big international car rental firms are represented at Larnaka airport.

Andreas Petsas Rent-a-car (☎ 2464 3350; www.petsas.com.cy; Larnaka Airport) One of Cyprus' largest car hire companies.

Anemayia Car & Motorbike Rentals (☎ 9962 4726; www.anemayiacarsbikes.com; 19 Leoforos Archiepiskopou Makariou III) Also hires out cruisers, mopeds and buggies.

Thames Car Rentals (☎ 8004 1044; www.thames.com.cy; Vasileos Pavlou 13) Has another **branch** (☎ 2400 8700; Larnaka Airport) at the airport.

AROUND LARNAKA

ℹ Getting Around

It's no secret that the best way to see greater Larnaka (and the rest of Cyprus, for that matter) is with your own transport. A great alternative, though, is a **Love Buses** (☎ 9776 1761; Leoforos Athinon, Larnaka; per person €10; ☉ 11am-5.30pm, night tours 8.30pm & 10pm summer) sightseeing tour aboard a bright red double-decker open-air bus that would look more at home in central London.

Tours usually run twice a day and include stops at Larnaka Salt Lake, Hala Sultan Tekke and the Kamares Aqueduct. On Saturday there's a route to Panagia Angeloktisti in Kiti, and kid-friendly Mazotos Camel Park. It does get hot on the top level of the bus, so bring water and a hat.

🏖 Beaches

Larnaka's beaches can be bland compared to those in Agia Napa and the east coast. Most have hard-packed, greyish sand and occasional pebbles. The waters, though, are generally very shallow and great for kids.

Makenzy   BEACH
Probably the best beach in town with all the facilities needed for a day in the sun. It's about 2km south of Larnaka past Piyale Pasha.

Finikoudes   BEACH
Clean, shallow beach that is highly popular despite not being particularly pretty. Sunbeds and umbrellas can be hired for between €2 and €3 and there are kiosks and cafes galore all along the strip.

CHILDREN'S CYPRUS: CAMEL RIDES

Mazotos Camel Park (☎ 2499 1243; www.camel-park.com; Mazotos; adult/child €3/2, camel rides adult/child €9/6; ☉ 9am-7pm May-Sep, to 5pm Oct-Apr) Kids had enough of archaeological sites and church icons? The Mazotos Camel Park is a great family day out. Camels were once a mainstay of transport in Cyprus but this is the last place on the island where they can still be seen. As well as camel rides, there's a swimming pool, play area and a petting zoo.

Mazotos Camel Park is 20 minutes from Larnaka by car. The entrance fee is deducted from activity fees.

CTO Municipal Beach BEACH

On Dekelia road, east of Larnaka; popular with locals and backed by dozens of taverns, restaurants and hotels.

Cape Kiti & Perivolia BEACH

Southwest of Larnaka, these secluded, narrow beaches have large, white stones and shallow waters. The Perivolia side of the cape is often exposed to tremendous winds, ideal for kite and windsurfing. You'll need to have your own equipment, though.

Kamares Aqueduct

Sanctioned in 1746 by Ottoman governor Bekir Pasha, and built in classical Roman style – some historians believe it is actually a Roman creation that was simply refurbished by the Ottomans – the aqueduct was constructed to solve Larnaka's freshwater problems. It originally ferried water from a source 10km south using underground tunnels, hundreds of air wells and a series of overland arches, remnants of which can be glimpsed from the freeway to Lemesos. The aqueduct remained in use until the 1950s. Today it is known as 'the Kamares' or 'the Arches'. The Larnaka municipality holds open-air concerts on the lawns in front of the aqueduct, which is wonderfully illuminated by night. It can be found close to the K Cineplex on the old road to Lemesos.

Hala Sultan Tekkesi

Surrounded by date palms, cypresses and olive trees, this **mosque** (⊘ 9am-7.30pm May-Sep, to 5pm Oct-Apr) and *tekke* (shrine), built in the late 18th century, sit wistfully on the edge of Larnaka's salt lake. According to Muslim lore, during the Arab raids on Cyprus in 674 Umm Haram, the revered aunt of the Prophet Mohammed, fell from her mule and died at this exact spot. Her mausoleum and shrine are in the small room attached to the main mosque prayer hall.

The mosque itself is still used and is a place of great reverence for Muslims who consider it a place of major religious significance. If you wish to enter, dress modestly and remove your shoes before entering the prayer hall. The interior is very simple and modest with little decoration except for the floor layered with prayer mats.

The excavated tomb and sarcophagus of Hala Sultan (Umm Haram), meaning 'Great Mother' in Turkish, is found left of the entrance, in what feels like a cave.

The tekke is 1km from the main road between Larnaka and the airport.

Larnaka Salt Lake

During winter this protected reserve fills with rainwater, creating an important migratory habitat for flamingos, wild ducks and water fowl. As summer approaches the waters slowly dry up and the birds leave. They are replaced by a crusty layer of salt amid heat waves that bounce and shimmer off its white surface.

Archaeologists have determined that in prehistoric times the central lake (known to locals as Aliki) was a natural port that facilitated important trade to the island. It serviced a sizeable late–Bronze Age town that stood near where the Hala Sultan Tekke is now. In 1050 BC the town's population abandoned the site and shortly after the waterway dried up, thus creating the salt lake. For centuries afterwards salt was harvested from the lake and became a valuable export for Cyprus. Temporary harvest houses were set up and donkeys were used to cart salt in large woven baskets. By the 1980s rising costs and slowed production halted salt harvesting altogether.

There are walking trails around the banks which are great for birdwatching in spring. During summer, when the water has disappeared, you should still stick to the paths rather than walk on the salt crust.

Kiti & Around

POP 3140

This village 9km southwest of Larnaka is home to the 11th-century domed cruciform church of **Panagia Angeloktisti** (⊘ 9.30am-noon & 2-4pm Mon-Sat Jun-Sep). The church, literally meaning 'built by angels', houses an extraordinary 6th-century **Mosaic of the Virgin Mary**. It was only discovered in 1952 amid the remains of the original 5th-century apse, which has been incorporated into the current building. Wonderfully preserved, the mosaic portrays Mary standing on a jeweled pedestal with baby Jesus in her arms, bordered by the archangels Gabriel and

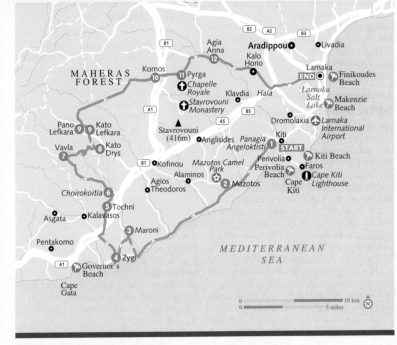

🏃 Driving Tour
Craftwork of Traditional Villages

START KITI
FINISH LARNAKA
DISTANCE 96KM; 5 TO 7 HOURS

From the church of **1 Panagia Angeloktisti** (p114) in Kiti take the 403 road west towards the agricultural village of **2 Mazotos**. Kids will love its camel park. From here take the old coastal road west through fields and sparse terrain. You'll travel about 17km, with a view of the sea on your left, before reaching attractive **3 Maroni** village, where you can buy some local cucumbers and have a Greek coffee. Then take the short road southwest to **4 Zygi**, a diminutive fishing village known for some of the island's best fish taverns. After you've had a bite to eat, it's back on track westward for 1km. Head inland and turn right onto the B1 underpass (crossing the A1 motorway) for about 6km, then head left towards the valley and the scenic village of **5 Tochni**. The north road out of the village takes you 4km to the impressive prehistoric settlement of **6 Choirokoitia** (p116). From

this neolithic site take a long stretch of climbing road inland northwest to **7 Vavla**, with its wonderfully restored homes. Next is the pretty, well-signposted stone village of **8 Kato Drys**, with its quaint balconies. A mere 4km more of winding road brings you to the lace- and silverwork village of **9 Pano and Kato Lefkara**, where you can wander the precipitous old town or barter for wares. From Pano Lefkara travel north for 7km on a good stretch of road until you see Lefkara dam on your left. Follow the road right over an incline for 16km to the pottery village of **10 Kornos**. After some clay hunting, follow the signs and road east, through the underpass (recrossing the motorway), to the town of **11 Pyrga**, home of the 14th-century Lusignan Chapelle Royale (signposted as 'Medieval Chapel'). This church is dedicated to St Catherine and houses some fine frescos. About 4km north of the village you can turn right (east) onto the 104 road, stop in **12 Agia Anna** for meze, then ease back into Larnaka.

Michael. The church is still a place of worship with regular services.

Further along the coastline you will find the village of **Perivolia** and **Cape Kiti**. The cape, complete with cliffs and lighthouse, has some wonderful getaway hotels and simple ice-cream parlours.

Stavrovouni Monastery

Perched 668m high at the peak of Stavrovouni (literally 'Mountain of the Cross'), this **monastery** (☉8am-noon & 3-6pm Apr-Aug, 8am-noon & 2-5pm Sep-Mar) is revered as the oldest on the island and is said to hold a piece of the Holy Cross, brought here by St Helena, mother of Emperor Constantine the Great, upon her return from Jerusalem in AD 327. Today this fragment from the Holy Land is preserved in an ornate 1.2m solid silver cross inside the church.

Ironically, nowadays St Helena herself could not view the cross, as the monastery grounds are closed to women. The site is still well worth the trip, though, for its uninterrupted views of the Mesaoria (Mesarya) plain. On a clear day you can see to Famagusta to the east, Troödos Mountains to the northwest, all the way around to Larnaka and the salt lake, and as far as the clear blue Mediterranean.

Once inside the monastery you can take a seat in the sun-filled courtyard entrance to the church, admire the bell tower and ponder monastic life. While male visitors are freely exploring the many icons and arched hallways, female travellers can spend their time at the smaller **Church of All Saints** just outside the monastery. All can meet in the souvenir and bookshop, with a grand array of Bibles, hymn books and icons for sale. There are also handmade prayer bracelets (€4), which are wonderful souvenirs.

Stavrovouni is still a working religious community with a score of monks dedicated to lifelong ascetic principles. Pilgrims and visitors are welcome and can take confession by request but should arrive during visiting hours only. Photos are prohibited inside the monastery, so leave your camera behind. If you are a dedicated pilgrim (and male) you may be invited, by the monks, to sleep the night, meditate and dine with them on their organically grown produce.

Stavrovouni monastery is located 17km from Larnaka off the Nicosia–Lemesos motorway (A1).

Choirokoitia

Occupying a well-defended hillside with a large perimeter wall, the small but well-preserved neolithic site of **Choirokoitia** (admission €2.50; ☉8.30am-5.30pm) is the earliest permanent human settlement found in Cyprus, dating back to 7000 BC. A walkway guides you around the settlement starting at the foot of the hill where reconstructions of huts, built by archaeologists, help visualise how Choirokoitia's people would have lived. The best remains are on the hilltop where you can also see sparse remnants of the settlement's walls.

Choirokoitia is believed to have been established by peoples from Anatolia and Asia Minor. The remains of over 50 cylindrical stone and mud dwellings have been discovered, along with prehistoric utensils, indicating that the Choirokoitians practised a sophisticated lifestyle that included well-developed hunting and farming. They also appear to have buried their dead under the floors of their dwellings, as indicated by the remains of over 20 skeletons including those of infants.

The site's significance in our understanding of neolithic culture was recognised in 1998 when it was added to the Unesco World Heritage List.

Choirokoitia is located 32km from Larnaka, just off the main Larnaka–Lemesos highway. If you continue a further 10km towards Lemesos, you can see the neolithic site at **Tenta** (Kalavasos), easily recognisable by the huge cone-shaped tent shielding it from the elements. It is a simpler version of Choirokoitia but just as important archaeologically.

Lefkara

POP 1100

During the Renaissance, with an affluent population of nearly 5000, this mountain village combining Pano and Kato Lefkara was one of the island's largest and most influential towns. It was already famous for its exquisite lace, handcrafted by the village women since medieval times, and for the men's fine silverwork, incorporating lacing techniques with silver smithing.

The area was a favoured destination for wealthy settlers and travellers, and it was poised to become a fully fledged city. Although it didn't quite make it, the village is still in a beautiful setting, surrounded by a steep valley of pines and wild carob trees. Its narrow cobbled streets and traditional houses charmingly show an obvious Venetian influence.

In 1481 Leonardo da Vinci is said to have visited Lefkara and obtained a fine piece of lace for the altar of Milan's cathedral. Lace and silver lovers the world over still come just for these crafts and are not disappointed. Shop owners sit outside in the streets, weaving lace and calling you to come and watch their work or look inside their stores with 'no obligation'. They can be overzealous but are genuinely pleasant about it. The lace is of exceptional quality, but it can be very pricy, so it's best to pick your favourite from the hundreds on offer and bargain about the cost. You will find the best quality and variety in the village itself. Keep in mind that the finest pieces are always found inside the stores and not displayed outside.

After souvenir shopping, it's fun to buy a bag of local, in-season fruit, walk around and check out the wonderful array of traditional doors, doorways and hidden courtyards.

Follow the signs through the backstreets to find the **Lefkara Folk Art Museum** (admission €2; ⊙9.30am-4pm Mon-Thu, 10am-4pm Fri & Sat). Formerly the home of one of Lefkara's wealthiest families, this restored building is set around a large courtyard complete with outdoor oven and pomegranate and citrus trees. The ground floor has information boards on Lefkara's history and a typical 19th-century dining area. Upstairs there are examples of original lace and silverwork as well as traditionally styled bedrooms, complete with antique dressers, mirrors and beds.

In nearby Skarinou is the weird and wonderful **Fatsa Wax Museum** (Georgiou Papandreou; adult/child €5/3.50; ⊙9am-5.30pm Oct-Mar, to 6.30pm Apr-Sep), inspired by Madame Tussauds. It houses over 120 waxworks that show Cypriot historical ages, events and culture, and prominent citizens such as presidents, war heroes and religious leaders. There's a cafe-restaurant for snacks.

The best lunch in town is at the **Lefkara Hotel & Restaurant** (www.lefkarahotels. com; 42 Timiou Stavrou Pano, Lefkara; mains €12; ⊙11.30am-3pm & 6.30pm-11pm), whose ancient walls encircle the diminutive church of **St Mamas** (c 974). Sit at a low-lit table and enjoy fresh organic vegetables grown on-site, blended with delights like soft smoked pork fillet stuffed with haloumi and served with sun-dried tomatoes and warm *bourgouri*.

You can get to Lefkara from the Nicosia–Lemesos motorway (A1) or by the scenic road from Choirokoitia via Vavla. A daily bus (one way €1, Monday to Saturday) runs between Lefkara and Larnaka, leaving Lefkara at 7am and returning at 1pm from Larnaka (Zinonas bus station opposite Larnaka marina).

AGIA NAPA

POP 2680

Phenomenal weather and perfect beaches have transformed this unassuming fishing village into every young hedonist's favourite European party-holiday destination. Gorgeous white sandy beaches and literally hundreds of clubs and bars have made it a Disneyland for clubbers the world over.

The central square is surrounded with every incarnation of themed club you can imagine, with places dedicated to the Flintstones, Arthurian legend and '70s cop shows, to name a few, and world-famous DJs play headline acts here every summer. High season is June to August, when it can be difficult to find a spot on the beach, let alone accommodation.

Agia Napa is not everyone's cup of tea and has its fair share of detractors, who decry its brash tackyness, as well as devotees. In recent years the municipality has made a push towards more family tourism, which has increased dramatically, but Napa (as many visitors refer to it) is still where the party is at its hardest. If you're looking for nightlife this is the place to come. If you just want to experience the gorgeous coastline that first brought this region into the spotlight you might be more comfortable in one of the resorts just outside town or in nearby Protaras.

◎ Sights

Agia Napa Monastery   MONASTERY
(Plateia Seferi; ⊙9am-6pm) Surreally surrounded by modern temples to partying, this beautiful monastery is a serene reminder of the great history Agia Napa has to offer over and above its nightlife. Built in 1500 by the Venetians, it protects a cave in which an icon of the Virgin Mary was hidden during the iconoclasm of the 7th and 8th centuries. Surviving Ottoman rule undamaged, it

Agia Napa

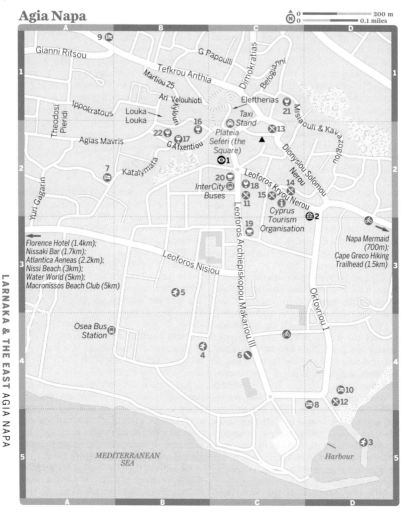

Florence Hotel (1.4km);
Nissaki Bar (1.7km);
Atlantica Aeneas (2.2km);
Nissi Beach (3km);
Water World (5km);
Macronissos Beach Club (5km)

Napa Mermaid
(700m);
Cape Greco Hiking
Trailhead (1.5km)

MEDITERRANEAN
SEA

Harbour

served as both a convent and a monastery during different periods until it was abandoned in 1758.

The structure is remarkably well preserved with the stout protective walls opening up onto a peaceful arcaded courtyard with a marble fountain, dating from 1530, covered by a domed stone spectator area. Also of interest is the enormous 600-year-old sycamore tree just outside the southern gate, complete with modern steel props designed to help hold its giant branches.

The modest church has steps down into the cave alcove where the Virgin Mary icon was hidden.

**Thalassa Municipal
Museum of the Sea**   MUSEUM
(Leoforos Kryou Nerou 14; adult/child €4/1.50; ☉9am-5pm Tue-Sat, 9am-1pm Mon, 3-7pm Sun Jun-Sep, shorter hours rest of year) This fantastic contemporary museum opened in 2005 and is dedicated to all things relating to the sea. It shows the enormous impact the ocean has had on Cypriot life and culture.

Agia Napa

The museum covers over 700 years of sealife history and also houses an exact replica of an ancient vessel that was shipwrecked off the coast of Kyrenia in the 3rd century BC. Dubbed Kyrenia II, it was reconstructed by scientists using traditional methods and materials.

On the upper floor, exhibits include fossilised fish, corals, shells and all manner of sea urchins and sea plants, but the star attraction is the complete skeleton of the pygmy hippopotamus (estimated to be more than 75,000 years old).

Most of the ground floor is taken up by the Kyrenia II replica but there are also exhibits of archaeological artefacts that take you step-by-step through the vast history of Cyprus.

The basement is home to the Tornaritis-Pierides **Marine Life Musuem** with displays of shells, sponges and preserved and stuffed Mediterranean fish, sharks, turtles and sea birds.

Makronissos Tombs   ARCHAEOLOGICAL SITE
(⊙dawn-dusk) Overlooking the sea, this ancient necropolis of 19 tombs cut into the rock is attributed to the Hellenistic and Roman periods. The chambers are practically identical, with wide steps leading down into the simple tombs, which have stone benches that were originally designed to hold sarcophagi. The site was heavily looted during the 1870s.

Further excavations have found remnants of a quarry and evidence of ancient Greek interments. The site is well-signposted on the main road west of Agia Napa.

🏖 Beaches

Nissi Beach   BEACH
The main attraction, Nissi Beach boasts crystal-clear, shallow water, soft white sand and a picturesque rock island about 60m from its shore. In summer it gets extremely crowded with sunbathers, umbrellas, music and beach loungers, but it all seems to work. Well stocked with bars, water sports and shower amenities, it's 3km from the centre square, so most arrive by scooter or bicycle.

Kermia Beach   BEACH
Ideal for those who prefer a quiet spot where it's easier to find a sunbed, Kermia Beach is about 2km east of Napa towards Cape Greco. This is a wonderfully secluded beach with golden sands and a rock break. A great choice for families.

Konnos Beach   BEACH
Bordering Paralimni, 2km past Kermia Beach, this lovely long stretch of white sand is sheltered by the bay and hills behind it. All kinds of water sports are on offer here, perfect with the placid waves.

Pantahou   BEACH
Starting from Agia Napa's fishing harbour this strip of sand swings east for 1km. There are loads of eating and snacking options and bundles of activities on offer. Be aware that it gets extremely crowded in July and August.

☞ Tours & Activities

A variety of big boats, glass-bottom boats and speedboats operate out of Agia Napa's remodelled harbour. Most offer round trips

LARNAKA & THE EAST AGIA NAPA

to Cape Greco, Konnos Bay, Protaras or Pernera.

The waters from Nissi Bay to Cape Greco and Konnos Bay up to Protaras are exceptional for diving, with calm seas that are both warm and clear. There are a multitude of inlets and natural caves to explore but the real highlight here for divers is the famed *Zenobia* wreck, one of the world's top 10 wreck dives; see p37.

Cyprus Tourism Organisation WALKING TOUR
(CTO; www.visitcyprus.com; Leoforos Kryou Nerou 12) The CTO runs free 'Agia Napa and the Sea' walking tours every Wednesday and Friday between November and March. Tours start at 10am at the CTO office.

Sunfish DIVING
(2372 1300; www.sunfishdivers.com; Leoforos Archiepiskopou Makariou III 26) This trusted operator caters for both novices and professionals and covers more than 10 diving spots, including reefs, caves, canyons and the famous *Zenobia* wreck. Certification programs are offered, ranging from discover scuba diving all the way through to master certification. Snorkelling to a depth of 2m is available and suitable for kids as young as eight. A two-dive package costs €90 with full equipment; PADI discover scuba try-dives for beginners are €60.

Water World WATER PARK
(www.waterworldwaterpark.com; Agias Theklis 18; adult/child €35/20; 10am-6pm Apr-Oct) With a Greek-mythology theme, this water park 5km west of central Agia Napa is easily the best in Cyprus. There are more than 18 rides, including all the usual suspects with the Atlantis activity pool and the Trojan Adventure perfect for young children and families. This is a safe and fun place for kids of all ages.

Parko Paliasto AMUSEMENT PARK
(www.parkopaliatsocy.com; Leoforos Nisiou; 6pm-1am Apr-Oct) The highlight here is the Slingshot – the highest ejection-seat ride in Europe – it shoots you 90m skyward in a caged ball in one and a half seconds. It's all caught on camera, too, so you'll have a keepsake of your contorted, petrified face. The park also offers less intense rides like bumper cars, carousels and a ghost train.

Napa Bungee BUNGEE JUMPING
(www.facebook.com/NapaBungee; off Leoforos Nisiou; jump incl photo, DVD & free drink €70-80;

10am-6pm May-Sep) Perfect for adrenaline junkies, Napa Bungee has an excellent safety record and a great set-up with a jump over 60m high. There are solo jumps, plus tandems for those in need of moral support. Wedding jumps and naked jumps have also been performed. These guys have seen it all before.

Black Pearl Pirate Boat BOAT TRIPS
(9940 8132; www.blackpearlayianapa.com; Agia Napa Harbour; adult/child €35/15; departs 11.30am May-Sep) This pirate-themed cruise on a large buccaneer ship is great fun for kids, with live pirates and treasure hunts. It stops at two picturesque swimming spots in the bays around Cape Greco. A full roast lunch, including Greek salad, is served afterwards on deck. There is also a bar on board (with rum, of course!), but drinks are additional.

Fantasy Boat Party BOAT TRIPS
(9940 8132; www.fantasyboatparty.com; Agia Napa Harbour; adult €55, drinks extra; departs 5.30-9pm daily Jul-Aug, Tue & Sat Apr-Jun & Sep-Oct) DJs pump music while the crowd dances and drinks away their time on the sea. It's a floating nightclub, though there are some swimming stops where diving games and screaming are encouraged. These cruises are not for the faint hearted and hardcore revellers are always expected.

✖ Eating

While most eating in Agia Napa is generic and uncultured, there are some decent places among the plethora of fast-food chains and burger joints. Prices, though not exorbitant, tend to reflect the high tourism in the area.

★**Limelight** CYPRIOT €€
(www.limelighttaverna.com; D Liperti; mains €11-25; 11am-11pm) This traditional, well-established and family-run restaurant excels at what it does best: chargrilled dishes. It also serves pasta and steak, lobster and seafood, but it's the yielding beef, lamb and *stifado* (beef or rabbit stew) that really bring folk flocking to the table. There's a proper children's menu here too.

Quadro ITALIAN €€
(Leoforos Kryou Nerou 7; mains €16-24; 10am-midnight) This modern Italian restaurant has an open dining terrace, comfortable seating, and affordable, great-flavoured

food. The menu includes a grand array of pizzas and pastas, and takeaway is also available.

★ Sage   INTERNATIONAL €€€

(www.sagerest.com; Leoforos Kryou Nerou 10; mains €25; ⊙11am-11pm) With modern decor like slated walls and concatenate doors, this place has an elegant feel about it. The menu features fillet steaks with a range of accompanying sauces. The food is expensive, but deservedly so. The umbrella courtyard is a very relaxing spot in summer.

Karousos Beach   SEAFOOD €€€

(Oktovriou 1; mains €22; ⊙10.30am-11pm) Beautiful fresh-fish meze (try the ouzo mussels) and local wines are served on intimate tables right on the sea's edge. The service is impeccable and personal.

Fiji   INTERNATIONAL €€€

(www.polynesian-ayianapa.com; Leoforos Archiepiskopou Makariou III 23; mains €17-25; ⊙6pm-midnight; 📝) There's a bizarre Pacific islands theme here with banana trees, oversized flowers and comfortable wicker furnishings. The food though – a kind of Asian-Polynesian-fusion – is excellent. Try the mango beef or salmon teriyaki.

🍸 Drinking & Nightlife

It all begins in 'the Square' with bars and clubs abounding in every direction. The sight of thousands upon thousands of tourists heaving together in this locale in the heat of a July night is mind-boggling. Revellers drink and dance in the bars between 10pm and 2am. Then it's time to hit the clubs, with a whole host to choose from. Most venues open after 1am and don't get full until 3am. A cover charge of €10 to €15 is normal – the best deals are found from ticket sellers in the Square.

Macronissos Beach Club   BAR

(Macronissos Beach; ⊙noon-late) Out of town (on the beach opposite Waterworld) Macronissos Beach Club is one of Agia Napa's premier drinking spots which morphs from cruisy lounge-type bar-restaurant to club as the night wears on. It's known for its weekly Ministry of Sound events, regular international acts, and beach parties.

Golden Arrow   BAR

(Leoforos Archiepiskopou Makariou III 21; ⊙9am-2.30am; 🛜) A stone's throw from the Square, this laid-back bar is super friendly and full

of entertainment. You can sit outdoors and watch the human traffic, pull up a spot at the bar, or watch football on the big screens.

Castle   CLUB

(www.thecastleclub.com; Grigoriou Afxentiou; ⊙1am-5am) The Castle is hard to miss. It holds over 2000 people, in three separate music rooms, and plays host to some of the world's best DJs during summer. Lovers of dance, house and garage will not be disappointed. If you're here to party, it continues to be Agia Napa's top venue.

Black & White   CLUB

(Louka Louka 6; ⊙1am-5am) A staple of the hip hop, R&B and soul scene since the 1990s, this dark little venue has multiple bars and an intimate dance floor. It gets full quickly and draws a big crowd.

Starsky's   CLUB

(www.starskysayianapa.com; Louka Louka; ⊙8pm-2am) This mainstay on the Agia Napa scene specialises in commercial dance and house and features an octagonal bar with dancing poles and retro disco balls. As the sign says 'All roads lead to Starsky's'.

River Reggae Club   CLUB

(Misiaouli & Kavazoglou; ⊙2am-late) An outdoor club with palm trees, a wooded dance floor, winding pool and reggae music. This is one of town's most popular late-night venues and it's usually best after 4am, when things can get crazy as revellers skinny dip and dance. So, if you're up for it...

Jello Bar   CAFE

(Leoforos Archiepiskopou Makariou III 43; ⊙9am-2am) This trendy bar serves everything from beers and cocktails to coffee and milkshakes. There's a decent menu of burgers and dessert treats. Happy hour starts at 8pm.

Nissaki Bar   BAR

(Sandy Bay; ⊙11am-late) If you're looking for a quieter venue this chilled-out restaurant-cafe-bar combo has a beautiful setting on the beach for drinks as well as a great menu of Cypriot dishes.

Kafenio   CAFE

(Leoforos Archiepiskopou Makariou III; ⊙10am-late) This relaxed cafe-bar-restaurant is a good central spot with a friendly vibe to chill out during the day or head to for pre-drinks before the real action starts. The roof terrace is a particularly nice lounging spot.

LARNAKA & THE EAST AGIA NAPA

ℹ️ Information

INTERNET ACCESS

3W Internet Café (☎ 2372 3032; Leoforos Nisiou 27; per hr €3; ☺10am-midnight) Internet, printing, photo downloads.

Backstage Internet Centre (☎ 2381 6097; Ari Velouchioti 7; per hr €3; ☺10am-midnight) Internet access with games and pool table.

MEDICAL SERVICES

After-Hours Pharmacy Assistance (☎192)

Napa Olympic Polyclinic (☎ 2372 3222; Chavares 24) Private hospital.

Paralimni Hospital (☎ 2382 1211; Paralimni) Located 15 minutes' drive away in Paralimni.

MONEY

ATMs are available on most streets.

Hellenic Bank (☎ 2372 1588; Leoforos Archiepiskopou Makariou III 18) Just south of Agia Napa main square.

POLICE

Police Station (☎2472 1553; Kavo Greko) North of central Agia Napa, at the big roundabout.

POST

Post Office (☎ 2472 2141; D Liperti 3; ☺9am-1.30pm Mon-Fri) Just east of the Square.

TOURIST INFORMATION

Cyprus Tourism Organisation (CTO; ☎ 2372 1796; Leoforos Kryou Nerou 12; ☺8.15am-2.30pm & 3-6.30pm Mon, Tue, Thu & Fri, to 2.30pm Wed & Sat) Helpful, friendly staff and good maps of town.

ℹ️ Getting There & Away

AIR

Larnaka International Airport, 48km away, is the closest airport.

BUS

InterCity Buses (☎ 2381 9090; www.intercity-buses.com; single €4, return trip €7) Inter City Buses drop-off and pick-up from official stops at the Marina Hotel on Leoforos Kryou Nerou and outside the Water World water park on Leoforos Nisiou. Although it is not stated on their official schedules, all InterCity buses also stop at the bus stand directly opposite Agia Napa Monastery on Leoforos Archiepiskopou Makariou III, right in the centre of town.

There are regular departures to Paralimni (15 minutes), Larnaca (45 minutes), and Nicosia (two hours).

SERVICE TAXI

Travel & Express (☎ 2382 6061; www.travel express.com.cy; George Griva Digeni 105, Paralimni; ☺6.30am-7pm Mon-Sat, to 4pm Sun) Operates shared taxis to Larnaka (€8.50), Larnaka airport (€11.50), Nicosia (€17), Lemesos (€18.50) and Pafos (€28). Services run every half hour from 6am with the last service (depending on destination) usually at 5pm. There are fewer services, and fares are higher, on Sunday. Ring beforehand to book a seat.

TAXI

Standard taxis can be found on the edge of the main square. Journey fares and times:

Larnaka €35 to €43, 30 minutes

Lemesos €60 to €70, one hour

Nicosia €45 to €52, 35 minutes

Pafos €120, one hour 40 minutes

Troödos €90 to €100, one hour

ℹ️ Getting Around

Central Agia Napa is compact enough to walk around. The urban bus network is pretty good or join the masses and hire a scooter, motorbike or buggy.

BUS

Agia Napa's local and regional bus network is run by **Osea** (☎ 2381 9090; www.osea.com. cy; Evagora Pallikaridi), which has a number of routes useful for visitors. Single ride tickets cost €1.50, one-day tickets cost €5.

Bus 101 From Water World water park, through Agia Napa, to Protaras and Paralimni (approximately every 40 minutes, between 7am and 11pm)

Bus 102 From Paralimni and Protaras, through Agia Napa, to Water World water park (approximately every 40 minutes. between 7am and 11pm)

Bus 201 (Agia Napa Circle Line) This circular route goes to Nissi Beach from Osea's bus station (every hour between 8.15am and 4.15pm)

CAR & MOTORCYCLE

Easyriders (☎2372 2438; www.easyriders.com. cy; Gianni Ritsou 1; ☺9am-9pm) Rents 50cc scooters (from €20 per day), quads, and Kawasaki or Suzuki 800cc heavies (from €55 per day). There's a second outlet at Dimokratias 17.

V&L Tsokkos (☎ 9968 4785; Leoforos Nisiou 58; ☺9am-7pm) Has cars, quads, buggies and scooters for hire at competitive prices.

AROUND AGIA NAPA

ℹ️ Getting Around

Other than the Osea and InterCity buses, the best option is to hire a scooter or buggy in Agia Napa or Protaras, where you can find reasonable rates.

Riding around the Paralimni region is wonderful, but you'll need a vehicle high in ccs. For beach-hopping along the Pernera–Protaras coastal strip, scooters, buggies or quad bikes will do nicely. The area is ideal for cycling enthusiasts, with designated paths between Agia Napa and Cape Greco.

If you want to explore the greater region, a car or small 4WD is more suitable.

Palaces & Sea Caves

Located at the inlet between Limnara Beach and Cape Greco are the unique rock formations known as the **palaces**. Carved into the cliff face by centuries of waves buffering the coast, they look like spy holes, framing the clear blue sea. The natural architecture plays host to divers, who can approach the rocks here only by boat.

Further east are the spectacular **sea caves** cut into the face of the rocky coastline. From lookout seats above you can hear the dynamic echoes created by the sea funnelling back and forth. When the sea is calm you can access some caves on foot, but on rough and windy days the spray reaches your face some 10m above, leaving you with tight cheeks and the taste of salt in your mouth. Again, the best views are from the sea, so consider one of the many charters that run from Napa's harbour.

Cape Greco

This national park has sweeping views of the sea and coast and is excellent for hiking and riding. A coastal track starting from Kryou Nerou in Agia Napa winds all the way to the lighthouse at the edge of the cape, approximately 3½ hours' walk. The region is unsheltered, so bring hats, water and sunscreen. There are some great picnic spots along the way. The track can get bumpy, so if you're cycling, mountain-bike tyres are more appropriate.

The region has 15km of walking tracks with interesting local flora, such as sea squill, wild orchids and sand lilies, which have managed to prosper in high-salinity soil. Once you reach Cape Greco itself, you can walk north towards the little bay and scamper down to the rock platforms, where swimmers jump and dive into the idyllic waters.

Paralimni

POP 11,100 (INCLUDING PROTARAS & PERNERA)

Paralimni is located inland near the seasonal lake from which it derives its name. The unofficial capital of the Famagusta district, it has grown due to migration from the occupied North and the success of nearby resort towns Agia Napa and Protaras. Many of its inhabitants work and own businesses in these areas.

The town itself has few sights. It has a simple paved square, a church (Agios Georgios) and a growing strip of restaurants and shops.

Deryneia

POP 7500

Deryneia is a traditional village with Byzantine churches dating from the 12th century and a Folk Art Museum worth visiting but it's primarily known for its location at the eastern rise of the closed 'border' that separates the occupied North from the Republic of Cyprus. Most people come to visit the Cultural Centre with its views across the UN buffer zone and the eerie abandoned ghost town of Varosia. For anyone interested in the Cyprus' modern history, it's well worth stopping in.

If you don't have a car, Osea bus 501 has regular services from Agia Napa to Deryneia and bus 502 makes the return trip.

◉ Sights

Cultural Centre of Occupied Famagusta MUSEUM

(Evagorou 35; ◷ 7.30am-4.30pm Mon-Fri, 9.30am-4.30pm Sat) FREE This centre is a sober reminder of the island's ongoing separation. There is an audio-visual presentation and information about Famagusta but the real reason to visit is for the panoramic views (binoculars provided) across the bizarre barbed-wire no-man's land to Varosia from the rooftop. The withered and empty remains of this one-time Mediterannean hot-ticket resort are a bitter and stark reminder of the ongoing separation.

Varosia's residents fled the invading Turkish troops in August 1974 and now, entirely fenced off by the Turkish military, this once thriving resort with its glossy hotels, sits slowly crumbling into ruin.

Folk Art Museum   MUSEUM
(Demetris Lipertis 2; admission €2.50; ☺ 9am-1pm & 4-6pm Mon-Sat) This little museum displays agricultural implements and other ethnographical exhibits of typical rural life.

Dekelia Sovereign Base Area

In 1960, during independence negotiations between the nascent Republic of Cyprus and the British administration, the rights to two major Sovereign Base Areas (SBAs) were brokered. Dekelia SBA is the second of these. The area comprises a large part of eastern Cyprus running from Larnaka Bay to the border with the North. You can pass through the base and even stop and enjoy fish and chips in the civilian area. It has a small beach populated with a few British-styled shops and a playground for kids.

The military site itself is off-limits. The base is still a critical centre for intelligence gathering and monitoring of the Middle East. The British government has stated that it is prepared to cede back some of the area if Cyprus becomes reunified.

The Kokkinohoria

POP 16,300
The Kokkinohoria ('The Red Villages') are so named because of the deep-red, mineral-rich earth found in the area. It comprises the inland rural villages of **Xylofagou**, **Avgorou**, **Frenaros**, **Liopetri** and **Sotira**. Most of these villages rely heavily on agriculture and are famous for their potato and *kolokasi* (a root vegetable similar to taro) produce. Wind-powered water pumps dot the landscape and prosperous crops are cultivated three to four times annually.

The region is indicative of rural Cyprus, where you can find some excellent country taverns with simple dishes and fresh produce. Take a good map, as signposting is limited.

Pyla

POP 1370
Pyla (Pıle) is the only village in the South where Greek Cypriots and Turkish Cypriots still live together. There's a token UN peacekeeping contingent in the village, but it's the inhabitants who have made it work. The village itself is located in the UN buffer zone. In the village square, a red-and-white Turkish Cypriot coffee shop stands opposite a blue-and-white Greek Cypriot *kafeneio* in peaceful harmony. The neighbourhood is a mix of Cypriots simply going about their daily lives.

The only differences that arise relate to local taxes and utility costs. These are paid by the Greeks only; as the Turks are citizens of the North, they pay nothing. The politics, though, come second, as it is understood here that they are all Cypriots.

There are nearby vehicle crossings to Northern Cyprus at the town of Pergamos.

Protaras

POP 11,100 (INCLUDING PARALIMNI & PERNERA)
With bags of child-friendly activities in the area, gorgeous sweeps of beach and a general air of easygoing holiday fun, the resort town of Protaras is a favourite holiday spot for families. Totally geared towards tourism its modernised beachfront comes complete with walking path and bike track and hosts sprawling hotels with manicured lawns and huge swimming pools while the main avenue has a concentration of shops, restaurants, hotels and bars.

◉ Sights & Activities

Ayios Elias   CHURCH
Rebuilt in 1980, this church is situated on a rocky peak just off the Protaras–Pernera road. A long set of stairs leads to the top, where you can enjoy magnificent views of Protaras and the bay. Follow the signs to get here.

Magic Dancing Water   WATER SHOW
(adult/child €15/8; ☺ 9pm) Young kids will love this show where water seems to dance and spin, accompanied by cheesy '80s music, laser lights and holograms.

Moonshine Ranch   HORSE RIDING
(✍ 9960 5042; Cape Greco; rides €40; ☺ 8am-7pm) This ranch has a glorious position with sweeping views of Cape Greco. It offers accompanied rides taking in Konnos Bay, the cape and the surrounding mountainous valley. All skill levels are happily catered for. The ranch is just off the coastal road between Agia Napa and Protaras.

🏖 Beaches

Protaras
BEACH

The main beach in Protaras has soft golden sand, a series of shallow rocky coves and a walkway backed by the green lawns of the resort hotels. Fully equipped, it's perfect for sunbathing and swimming, and a multitude of water sports are available.

Fig Tree Bay
BEACH

At the southern end of the Protaras main beach, Fig Tree Bay is very popular. It has a small sand island just off the coast, which is great for snorkelling with lots of fish to be seen. There are hotels and restaurants aplenty, so it's a great spot to eat, swim, drink and relax.

🍴 Eating

Most restaurants are on the main strip.

Kyklos Restaurant
CYPRIOT €€

(Protaras Ave; mains from €12; ⏰ 11am-11pm) Offers well-cooked, authentic food, like slow-baked meze (a standout item is lamb *souvla* tenderised with garlic and lemon). It's located at the southern end of Protaras' main street.

Nikolas Tavern
CYPRIOT €€

(Fig Tree Bay, Protaras; mains from €11; ⏰ 11.30am-11pm) Well-priced, consistently good Cypriot favourites with friendly service to boot. Try the *stifado* or *kleftiko* (oven-baked lamb) with one of the local wines.

Pernera

Just a couple of strides north of Protaras, Pernera is another coastal resort perfect for a peaceful getaway. It's so close to Protaras that the two towns have basically merged into one. This beach-bum haven is all about its beautiful sandy shores and pocket-sized bays. The town itself has a couple of really good restaurants, and shops dedicated to water sports.

🏖 Beaches

Louma
BEACH

A small, curving strip of beach which drops away gently, protected by an artificial bay. The sand is fine and the water is clear. Trees at the northern end provide shade.

Pernera
BEACH

Tiny Pernera beach is a curvy sliver of good, soft sand with shallow waters and a beach restaurant. It's highly popular with families.

Agia Triada
BEACH

This cute little beach with low water levels and coarse sand is an excellent boat-launching site.

Skoutari
BEACH

An isolated cove encircled by a cliff with hard-packed sand and rocks. It's ideal for snorkelling.

🏃 Activities

Under Sea Adventures
WATER SPORTS

(📞9956 3506; www.underseawalkers.com; Agia Triada Beach) At Under Sea Adventures kids eight years and up with a sense of adventure can choose between 'shallow-water helmet diving' (adults €45, children eight to 16 €35) or 'riding on a BOB' (Breathing Observation Bubble; 13 years and up €55). Both are a fun and safe way to experience underwater life.

The undersea walks go down to 3m, where you can see rock formations and sea life while your face remains completely dry inside your helmet.

🍴 Eating

⭐ La Cultura Del Gusto
MEDITERRANEAN €€€

(Ifaistou Skarou Markou 9; mains from €18; ⏰ 11am-11pm) This fashionable restaurant offers an innovative menu of mainly Italian-style cuisine. With courteous staff and specialities like lamb shank and succulent chicken, it makes for excellent dining.

Nicosia (Lefkosia)

Best Places to Eat

➡ Shiantris (p137)

➡ Mattheos (p136)

➡ Syrian Arab Friendship Club (p138)

➡ Zanettos Taverna (p137)

➡ Silver Pot (p138)

Best Museums

➡ Cyprus Museum (p128)

➡ Leventis Municipal Museum (p128)

➡ Nicosia Municipal Arts Centre (p128)

➡ AG Leventis Gallery (p133)

Why Go?

If you grow weary of the coast's sea and sunbed scene, and even if you don't, make sure you spend some time in the country's capital, Nicosia (or Lefkosia as it is known officially and to Greek speakers). It is an enticing city and is ideal for experiencing what modern Cyprus is all about. The ancient walls, traditional restaurants and an increasingly vibrant and young cafe and cultural scene effectively showcase the city's basic make-up.

Almost everything of interest lies within the historic walls, where a labyrinth of narrow streets reveals churches, mosques and evocative colonial-style buildings. The country's best museum is also here, housing an extensive archaeological collection.

The city has been labelled 'the last divided capital', a reality that, although still present, is slowly changing thanks to 24-hour checkpoint crossings into its Turkish northern half – North Nicosia (Lefkoşa).

When to Go

➡ The best time of year to visit is during spring and autumn, when the weather is pleasantly warm, interrupted by only an occasional outbreak of rain.

➡ Easter can be an extra-special time here, with traditional parades and a generally festive atmosphere.

➡ Avoid mid-summer when the capital is one of the hottest places on the island, albeit a dry heat, with temperatures generally hovering around 36°C.

➡ Many restaurants and hotels close their shutters in August to allow employees to substitute the relative cool of the coastal resorts for the hot, dusty capital.

NICOSIA (LEFKOSIA)

POP 213.500

History

Nicosia has always been the country's capital, mainly because the defences of the coastal cities were so weak and prone to attack. The city's position in the centre of a plain provided at least some protection against marauding invaders. Nicosia flourished during the Byzantine period. The Byzantines were followed by the Venetians who took command of the city in 1489 but failed dismally in repelling the Ottomans who took control in 1570. The city stagnated until the British arrived in 1878, which also marked

NICOSIA (LEFKOSIA) HISTORY

Nicosia (Lefkosia) Highlights

1 Exploring the emblematic and superbly preserved **Venetian walls** (p129) snaking around the Old City.

2 Seeing both sides of Europe's last divided capital by striding out north at the **Ledra St pedestrian crossing** (p129).

3 Perusing the world class art at the superb **AG Leventis Gallery** (p133).

4 Shopping for arts, crafts and souvenirs at small family owned shops in the Old City like **Atelier D'Art** (p141).

5 People-watching, accompanied by an ice-cold frappé, at one of the terrace cafes on **Ledra St** (p138).

6 Joining one of the tourist office's excellent free **guided walks** (p135) of the Old City.

7 Exploring the cobbled backstreets of Mesaoria villages such as **Pera** (p146).

the time that development started to spread beyond the city walls.

In the 1950s violence against the British instigated by the Ethniki Organosi tou Kypriakou Agona (EOKA; National Organisation for the Cypriot Struggle) saw considerable carnage on the streets of the capital.

Further violence in the form of intercommunal disturbances between Greek Cypriots and Turkish Cypriots in 1963 brought a de facto partition of the city. The so-called 'Green Line' came into being at this time when the British army defined the Greek and Turkish areas by using a simple green pen on a military map. The name has stuck to this day.

The Turkish invasion of 1974 cemented the division of the city, which has remained bisected ever since, chaperoned by the watchful, but increasingly weary, eyes of UN peacekeeping forces. In 2003 crossing the Green Line was made possible for ordinary citizens, resulting in a number of Turkish Cypriots going to work on the southern side of the capital. The Greek Cypriots, in turn, frequent the North's numerous casinos and head to the northeast's wild coastline.

The opening of the Ledra St pedestrian-only crossing in April 2008 has facilitated easier access in both directions while the Nicosia Master Plan continues to work with both sides of the Green Line in the generally agreed assumption that one day the city will be unified once again.

◎ Sights

The most interesting part of the city for visitors is the Old City, lying within the 16th-century Venetian walls. Note that a massive (albeit delayed) redesign project has currently cordoned off much of Nicosia's Plateia Eleftherias by the southern wall (p142). When completed, the area will encompass a park and a pedestrian walkway flanked by palm trees and the existing ancient Venetian walls, at the base of which are car parks and municipal gardens.

The New City sprawls southwards, and its main artery is the modern Leoforos Archiepiskopou Makariou III (Makarios Ave). In the past this street was full of cafes, bars, restaurants and shops. However, the recent economic recession has resulted in the closure of numerous businesses, while others have shifted to the more animated Ledra St in the Old City.

In addition to the crossover point at Ledra St, there is another at Ledra Palace Hotel, at the far west of the Old City; both are pedestrian only. Agios Dometios, northwest of the New City, is the car-only crossing point.

★**Cyprus Museum**   MUSEUM
(☑2286 5888; Leoforos Mouseiou 1; admission €4.50; ⊗8am-4pm Tue-Fri, 9am-4pm Sat, 10am-1pm Sun) Located opposite the municipal gardens, a 10-minute walk west of Plateia Elefherias, this excellent museum houses the best collection of archaeological finds in Cyprus. Highlights include a remarkable display of **terracotta votive statues** and **figurines** discovered in Northern Cyprus in 1929. The 2000 figures, dating back to the 7th to 6th centuries BC, are displayed as they were found, in a semicircular order. Another highlight is the collection of three **limestone lions** and two **sphinxes** found in the Tamassos necropolis south of Nicosia.

Also look out for the famous **Aphrodite of Soli** statue in Room 5, widely marketed as the 'goddess of Cyprus' on tourist posters. An enormous bronze statue of **Emperor Septimus Severus**, found at Değirmenlik (Kythrea) in 1928, is the magnificent main exhibit in Room 6.

A couple of lovely mosaics, such as **Leda & the Swan** from Palea Pafos, are exhibited in Room 7B, alongside various displays of gold objects excavated from tombs.

★**Leventis Municipal Museum**   MUSEUM
(www.leventismuseum.org.cy;   Ippokratous 17; ⊗10am-4.30pm Tue-Sat) **FREE** This museum concentrates on the history of Cyprus – in particular, Nicosia. The permanent collection includes traditional costumes, paintings, archaeological exhibits, and a historic and fascinating postcard collection; all are fittingly housed in a handsome neoclassical mansion. The gift shop is excellent.

★**Nicosia Municipal
Arts Centre**   MUSEUM
(Pierides Foundation; www.nimac.org.cy; Apostolou Varnava 19; ⊗10am-3pm & 5-11pm Tue-Sat, 10am-4pm Sun) **FREE** This contemporary art museum is housed in a former power station, and is the city's equivalent to London's Tate Modern. The former industrial setting is suitably dramatic, with looming pitched ceilings and some original equipment (pulleys etc) that blend well with the cutting-edge installations. The permanent collection includes

paintings, photography, videos, sculpture, and other works from the Dimitris Pierides Museum of Contemporary Art in Greece. Exhibitions vary monthly and often focus on edgy political and cultural themes.

To get here duck into the small arcade to the right of the National Struggle Museum and head along Apostolou Varnava for one block. The centre also has a sophisticated restaurant, gift shop and comprehensive art library for visitors.

Venetian Walls HISTORIC SITE
The Venetian walls form a border around the Old City so unusual that, once seen on a map, you'll never forget it. And that's partly to do with its odd snowflake-like shape.

Dating from 1567, the circular defence wall, was erected by the Venetian rulers to ward off the Ottoman invaders. Unfortunately it failed and, in July 1570, the Ottomans landed in Larnaka and three months later stormed the fortifications killing some 50,000 inhabitants. The walls have remained in place ever since.

Five of the bastions, **Tripoli**, **D'Avila**, **Constanza**, **Podocataro** and **Caraffa**, are in the southern sector of Nicosia. The **Flatro** (Sibeli) Bastion on the eastern side of the Old City is occupied by Turkish, Greek Cypriot and UN military forces. The remaining bastions, **Loredano** (Cevizli), **Barbaro** (Musalla), **Quirini** (Cephane), **Mula** (Zahra) and **Roccas** (Kaytazağa), are in North Nicosia (Lefkoşa).

The Venetian walls and moat around Nicosia (Lefkosia) are in excellent condition. They are used to provide car-parking spaces and venues for outdoor concerts, as

---

🛈 WHICH WAY NOW...?

The Cyprus Tourism Organisation (CTO) has a good map of the Nicosia city centre and, on the reverse side, greater Nicosia. This map is available free from all CTO offices. The *Street & Tourist Map of Nicosia*, however, has better coverage of the outer suburbs, plus a street index; it is available from most bookshops and stationery stores in Nicosia.

---

well as for strolling and relaxing. In North Nicosia, the walls are in poorer shape and have become overgrown and dilapidated in parts.

There are vehicle access points around the walls, which allow regular traffic access to the Old City.

House of Hatzigeorgakis Kornesios MUSEUM
(Patriarchou Grigoriou 20; admission €1.70; ⊙ 8am-2pm Mon-Fri, 9am-1pm Sat) From 1779 to 1809, the House of Hatzigeorgakis Kornesios belonged to Kornesios, the Great Dragoman of Cyprus, who accumulated his vast wealth through various estates and tax exemptions, and became the most powerful man in Cyprus. The house itself is more beautiful and interesting than the exhibits within. Only one room is set up as mock living quarters, with plush floor cushions and nargileh (water pipes) for smoking. The rest of the mansion is given over to displays of antiques and Ottoman memorabilia.

NICOSIA (LEFKOSIA) SIGHTS

LEDRA ST & LEDRA PALACE HOTEL CROSSINGS

These two checkpoints are the only places on the island reserved exclusively for pedestrian and bicycle crossings between the North and the South. Masses of tourists and locals now cross from one side to the other, and many cross in the middle of the night, too, after a late night out. Don't forget to take your passport or you will not be allowed through the border.

At the Ledra St crossing, you will pass a small office with army and police officials from the Republic of Cyprus, who will only check you on your return from the North and may well search your bags. They are generally friendly, though you should be careful not to exceed the amount of cigarettes and alcohol that you are permitted to bring from the North.

You'll then come to the Turkish Republic of Northern Cyprus' kiosks, where you will be asked to fill out a white 'visa form' with your name and passport number. You can keep one visa form for numerous entries into the North. After that, you're free to roam.

The process is the same at the Ledra Palace Hotel crossing.

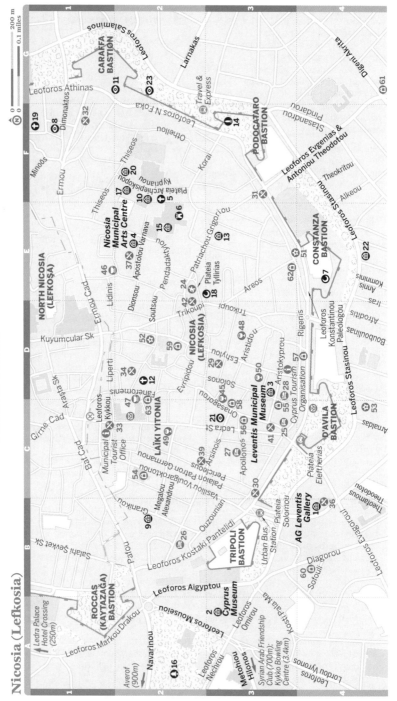

Kornesios was eventually driven from Cyprus to Istanbul by a peasant revolt in 1804, which was aimed at the ruling classes in general. When he returned from exile five years later, he was accused of treason, his property was confiscated and he was unceremoniously beheaded.

Makarios Cultural Foundation   MUSEUM
(Plateia Archiepiskopou Kyprianou; admission €1.70; ☺9am-4.30pm Mon-Fri, to 1pm Sat) The highlight of the foundation is the magnificent **Byzantine Art Museum**, which has the island's largest collection of icons relating to Cyprus. There are some 220 pieces in the museum, dating from the 5th to 19th centuries. Don't miss the six examples of the superb **Kanakaria mosaics** (p225), which were stolen from the Panagia Kanakaria (Kanakaria Church) in Northern Cyprus after the 1974 Turkish invasion and finally returned in 1991 after a lengthy court battle.

Among the more interesting pieces are the icons of Christ and the Virgin Mary (12th century) from the Church of the Virgin Mary of Arakas at Lagoudera, and the Resurrection (13th century) from the Church of St John Lambadistis Monastery at Kalopanayiotis.

Ethnographic Museum   MUSEUM
(Plateia Archiepiskopou Kyprianou; admission €2; ☺9am-5pm Mon-Fri, 10am-1pm Sat) The Ethnographic Museum houses the largest collection of folk art and ethnography on the island. The building dates back to the 15th century, though some later additions have been made. Here you will see exquisite examples of embroidery, lace, costumes, pottery, metalwork, basketry, folk painting, engraved gourds, leatherwork and woodcarving, the latter including beautiful, intricately carved chests.

National Struggle Museum   MUSEUM
(Plateia Archiepiskopou Kyprianou; admission €0.80; ☺8am-2pm Mon-Wed & Fri, 8am-2pm & 3-7pm Thu) This display is really for die-hard history buffs and bloodthirsty children. The National Struggle Museum exhibits documents, photos and other memorabilia from the often bloody 1955–59 National Liberation Struggle against the British. Exhibits include a harrowing copy of the gallows.

NICOSIA (LEFKOSIA) SIGHTS

Nicosia (Lefkosia)

Shacolas Tower Observatory OBSERVATORY
(11th fl, Shacolas Tower, cnr Ledra St & Arsinois; admission €2; ⊙10am-6.30pm) Shacolas Tower Observatory sits, rather bizarrely, above Debenhams department store and provides a superb vantage point across the city. You can use telescopes to gaze at the whole of Nicosia, and trace the Green Line and the distant mountain beyond; the mountainside bears a vast (and controversial) painted Turkish flag. Explanations of various buildings and neighbourhoods are written in English, French and German.

Pancyprian Gymnasium Museums MUSEUM
(Agiou Ioannou & Thiseos; ⊙9am-3.30pm Mon, Tue, Thu & Fri, 9am-5pm Wed, 9am-1pm Sat) FREE
Dating back to 1812, and the oldest school still operating in Cyprus, there are several museums here spread throughout a 12-room space. Highlights include an extensive natural history collection, an exhibit of Gothic sculptures and an art gallery with works by local painters. Lawrence Durrell, author of *Bitter Lemons of Cyprus,* taught English at the school for several years in the 1950s.

Omeriye Mosque
MOSQUE

(cnr Trikoupi & Plateia Tyllirias; ⊙ outside prayer times) Originally the Augustinian Church of St Mary, the Omeriye Mosque dates from the 14th century. The tall minaret can easily be spotted some distance away; the entrance to the mosque is about halfway along Trikoupi. Today the mosque is used primarily as a place of worship by visiting Muslims from neighbouring Arab countries. Non-Muslims may visit as long as they observe the general etiquette required – dress conservatively, leave shoes at the door and avoid official prayer times.

Faneromeni Church
CHURCH

(Plateia Faneromenis) Built in 1872 on the site of an ancient Orthodox nunnery, this is the largest church within the city walls and is a mixture of neoclassical, Byzantine and Latin styles. The **Marble Mausoleum** on the eastern side of the church was built in memory of four clerics executed by the Ottoman governor in 1821, during the newly declared Greek War of Independence.

Panagia Chrysaliniotissa
CHURCH

(Archiepiskopou Filotheou; ⊙ outside mass times) The church of Panagia Chrysaliniotissa is dedicated to the Virgin Mary and its name means 'Our Lady of the Golden Flax' in Greek. It's considered to be the oldest Byzantine church in Nicosia and was built in 1450 by Queen Helena Paleologos. It is renowned for its rich collection of old and rare icons.

Laïki Yitonia
NEIGHBOURHOOD

Laïki Yitonia, meaning 'popular neighbourhood', was restored after it served for many years as an area for painted ladies and dodgy merchants. This tiny southern part of the Old City is Nicosia's only tourist area. This means it's full of bad restaurants with tacky water features, where waiters try to lure you in with cheesy greetings and the food is often overpriced. However, it's still pretty and pleasant enough for a short stroll.

The Cyprus Tourism Organisation (CTO) has an office here, and you can stock up on most maps and other tourist brochures free of charge.

Famagusta Gate
HISTORIC SITE

(Caraffa Bastion; ⊙ 10am-1pm & 5-8pm Mon-Fri) Famagusta, the easternmost gate, is the most photographed and best-preserved of the three original gates that led into the Old

City of Nicosia. The gate's impressive wooden door and sloping facade open out onto a tunnel that leads through the rampart wall. Beyond the tunnel to the right is a small open-air arena, where concerts are held during the summer months.

Bayraktar Mosque
MOSQUE

This small mosque marks the spot where the Venetian walls were successfully breached by the Ottomans in 1570. The Ottoman *bayraktar* (standard bearer; after whom the mosque is named in Turkish) was promptly killed by the defending forces but his body was later recovered and buried here. The mosque has historically been the target of terrorist activity; in the early 1960s, EOKA-inspired attacks damaged the building. After being repaired, the mosque was closed to the general public.

Liberty Monument
MONUMENT

Near the mosque on the Podocataro Bastion is this thought-provoking monument. It represents the Greek Cypriots' liberation from the British colonial powers, with the figures of 14 Ethniki Organosi tou Kypriakou Agona (EOKA; National Organisation for the Cypriot Struggle) fighters being released from prison in 1959, alongside peasants and priests, representing the various strata of Greek Cypriot society.

Chrysaliniotissa Crafts Centre
CRAFTS

(Dimonaktos 2; ⊙ 10am-1pm & 3-6pm Mon-Fri, 10am-1pm Sat; ♿) This small arts centre is worth dropping into for its display of Cypriot arts and crafts. Several workshops and a vegetarian restaurant surround a central courtyard in a building designed along the lines of a traditional inn.

★ AG Leventis Gallery
MUSEUM

(www.leventisgallery.org; Leonidou St, New City; admission €5; ⊙ 10am-5pm Mon & Thu-Sun, to 10pm Wed; P 🛜) Located in the New City, this purpose-built art museum opened in 2014 and displays European paintings and sculpture from the 16th to 20th centuries. Divided into three sections, the gallery's **Paris Collection** features masters such as Chagall, Monet and Renoir, while the **Greek Collection** includes significant works by 19th- and 20th-century Greek artists. The highlight of the **Cyprus Collection**, located on the ground floor, is a magnificent and thought-provoking 17m painting entitled

NICOSIA (LEFKOSIA) SIGHTS

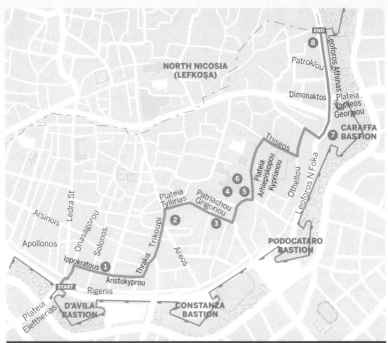

🏃 City Walk
Stepping Back in Time

START PLATEIA ELEFTHERIAS
FINISH FLATRO (SIBELI) BASTION
DISTANCE 2KM; TWO HOURS

This tour goes along the Old City's main streets and past many of its museums. Starting from Plateia Eleftherias, follow Ledra St and turn right onto Ippokratous where you'll find the ❶ **Leventis Municipal Museum** (p128), which traces the city's development from prehistoric times to the present.

Continue along Ippokratous (which becomes Aristokyprou), turn left onto Thrakis and take the dog-leg onto Trikoupi. Soon you'll see the ❷ **Omeriye Mosque** (p133) on your right with its imposing minaret and original 14th-century entrance. Turn right onto Plateia Tyllirias and shortly after you will reach Patriarchou Grigoriou. About 125m along this street on the right is the ❸ **House of Hatzigeorgakis Kornesios** (p129), an 18th-century house that is now a museum.

The next left leads you to Plateia Archiepiskopou Kyprianou, dominated by the

❹ **Archbishop's Palace**. Here you'll find the ❺ **Makarios Cultural Foundation** (p131), with its not-to-be-missed Byzantine Art Museum. In the grounds of the Foundation is the ❻ **Agios Ioannis Church**, which was built in 1662 and has frescos dating from 1736.

Continue north before turning right onto Thiseos. A left and then another right leads onto Leoforos N Foka. Turn left and you'll see the imposing ❼ **Famagusta Gate** (p133), which was once the main entrance to the city and now hosts exhibitions and cultural events. From here it's a 400m walk past Nicosia's trendy night-time dining area along Leoforos Athinas to where the street abruptly ends at the barbed wire and UN watchtowers of the ❽ **Flatro (Sibeli) Bastion**. The most direct way back to Laïki Yitonia is to take Leoforos N Foka, following the signposts to the Cyprus Tourism Organisation (CTO). Check out the Venetian walls along the way.

The World of Cyprus by renowned Cypriot artist, Adamantios Diamantis.

The art work on display is from the private collection of the late Anastosios G Leventis, a wealthy Cypriot businessman and philanthropist, as well as from the AG Levantis Foundation. The foundation was created after Leventis' death in 1978, and was also fundamental in the establishment of the Levantis Municipal Museum, also located in Nicosia. The Paris Collection is named after the Parisienne home of Levantis, where the paintings used to be displayed, away from public view. The Greek Collection is the result of a private purchase he made in 1973, while the Cyprus Collection was amassed more recently by the foundation.

State Gallery of Cypriot Contemporary Art
MUSEUM

(cnr Stasinou & Kritis, New City; ⊙10am-4.45pm Mon-Fri, to 12.45pm Sat) FREE This museum comprises a vast collection of quality Cypriot art, ranging from the mid-19th century to the late 1900s, and including some fine sculptures. Housed in a historic colonial-style building, the galleries cover three well-laid-out floors.

Cyprus Classic Motorcycle Museum
MUSEUM

(☑2268 0222; www.agrino.org/motormuseum; Granikou 44, Old City; ⊙9am-1pm & 3-6pm Mon-Fri, 9am-1pm Sat) FREE The owner of this private museum is more than happy to chat extensively about his 150-plus bike collection. It may just bring out your inner Hell's Angel (bring a bandanna, just in case).

Municipal Gardens
PARK

(Leoforos Mouseiou; ⊙8am-10pm) A pleasant park located right in the centre of the Old City with a large children's playground, ponds and water features, plus plenty of mature shady trees and at least a couple of ice cream vendors...

Omeriye Hammam
BATH HOUSE

(Ömeriye Hamam; ☑2246 0006; www.hamammomerye.com; Plateia Tyllirias; ⊙10.30-12.30pm & 1-9.30pm Tue-Sun) After two years of closure, the stunning 16th-century Omeriye Hamam Turkish steam baths reopened in May 2014. The tastefully restored building sports a luxurious Ottoman-inspired design with facilities that include a hot and cold room, as well as a range of massages, body scrubs and treatments.

⌖ Tours

The Cyprus Tourism Organisation (CTO; p143) runs free guided walks on Monday and Thursday, leaving at 10am from the CTO office in the Old City.

'Chrysaliniotissa & Kaimakli: the Past Restored' is a bus and walking guided tour that runs on Monday; Thursday is a walk through Old Nicosia. The walks last two hours and 45

WALKING THE GREEN LINE

Despite the fact that crossing into North Nicosia (Lefkoşa) is now straightforward, the Green Line and the evocative buffer zone, with its abandoned houses, are still fascinating. While there's not a lot to see once you are there (save for some creative graffiti work), its mere presence gives Nicosia a bizarre edge. You'll see the double minarets of the Selimiye Mosque, North Nicosia's most remarkable landmark, with the Turkish and Turkish Cypriot flags that hang between them like washing. The Green Line embodies the eeriness of the capital's and the country's division, especially when coupled with all those harrowing 1974 Cypriot stories.

UN and Greek Cypriot **bunkers** punctuate the line across the city, and you are not allowed to approach them too closely. The Cyprus Tourism Organisation (CTO) signposted walking tour takes you hard up to the line at the far eastern side of the city, close to the military-controlled **Flatro (Sibeli) Bastion**. Take the last turn left off Leoforos Athinas along Agiou Georgiou and look for the little street on the right named Axiothea. Walk to the end of this street and squeeze through the gap into the next street, following the walking-tour sign.

One area which was formerly one of considerable desolation and destruction is towards the end of **Pendadaktylou** where it meets **Ermou**, the street that originally bisected the Old City. Buildings here are gradually being resurrected and turned into artists' studios and similar.

minutes, and include a 30-minute half-time break.

Alternatively, pick up a CTO walking-tour brochure., or follow our walking tour around the Old City.

✕ Eating

Nicosia offers three basic locations for eating: the Old City, the New City and the burgeoning western and southern suburbs. Suburbs such as Engomi to the west and Strovolos to the south have their own culinary enclaves, and a drive to either may turn up some surprising finds.

Dining in Nicosia can be a real treat. Because the city is not a prime tourist target, it is thankfully bereft of low-quality, high-cost tourist traps. There are some excellent, simple local diners serving traditional Cypriot food, such as pulses, seasonal vegetables and stewed meat dishes. The growing internationalism of Cyprus has also equated to a rise in more sophisticated and ethnic cuisine.

Note that many restaurants in Nicosia close for a couple of weeks in August for the annual holidays.

Old City

Dining in the Old City is centred on two main areas, with a sprinkling of cheap, low-frills restaurants scattered in between. Laïki Yitonia is mainly popular with the lunch-time crowd of day-trippers, while the Famagusta Gate strip has several reliably good bars and restaurants that are frequented mainly at night by locals in the know.

★**Mattheos**　　　　　　　　　　CYPRIOT €
(Plateia 28 Oktovriou 6; mains from €6; ☺10am-4pm Mon-Sat; 🐾) A simple, atmospheric place next to the Faneromeni Church, with a clutch of outside tables set with colourful chequered tablecloths. Attracting lunching nine-to-fivers, the food is homestyle Cypriot, with gutsy *kleftiko* (oven-baked lamb), *stifado* (beef or rabbit stew) and stuffed vegetables on the menu. It's one of the most popular places in town, and an empty seat is as rare as a mediocre meal.

Christakis　　　　　　　　　　CYPRIOT €
(Leoforos Kostaki Pantelidi 28; mains €6; ☺8am-10pm Mon-Sat) Locals rate this rough-and-ready restaurant across from the bus station as the best place in town for souvlaki. Market-fresh salads, superb vegetable side dishes, traditional bean courses and a jovial family atmosphere complete the picture. Get here early to grab a table; there is only a handful.

Tospitikon　　　　　　　　　　CYPRIOT €
(Onasagorou 6; snacks €1; ☺9am-10pm) There are just a couple of tables inside and out at this stripped back place so grab one quick and order a specialty *pourekia* (small fried pasties) with a choice of fillings like spinach,

---

AUTHENTIC CYPRIOT CUISINE

If you want to dine on authentic Cypriot cuisine, seek a taverna that displays a Vakhis sign (though, at the time of writing, there are only around eight in the whole Republic). The Vakhis scheme was established in 2006 by the Cyprus Tourism Organisation in association with the Eurotoques International, a European chefs' association, among others, as part of an EU-funded island-wide drive to promote rural tourism. Vakhis is named after Cyprus' original Jamie Oliver–style celebrity chef, who lived and, more famously, cooked in the ancient city of Kition around AD 300.

Typical dishes you can expect today include ingredients like wild asparagus, artichokes, various leafy greens, extra-virgin olive oil and fresh herbs. At Kiniras Garden (p90) restaurant, part of the Vakhis scheme, owner Georgios uses at least 10 different herbs in the marinade for his slow-cooked lamb.

Aside from Kiniras, several other member restaurants of the Vakhis scheme are clustered together in the picturesque villages of the wine-growing area in the Troödos foothills southwest of Nicosia, including **Loufou-Agrovino** (☎2547 0202; mains from €8; ☺noon-4pm Mon-Sat) and **Kamares** (☎2547 0719; mains from €10; ☺11.30am-4pm & 7-10pm Tue-Sun) both located in the pretty village of Lofou, and **Takis** (☎2594 3631; mains from €1; ☺noon-4pm Tue-Sun) in nearby Vouni. In general, Vakhis restaurants sport pretty traditional decor, with chequered tablecloths, wooden tables, wicker chairs and similar.

mushrooms and haloumi (helemi). Or go for a *groat* (a fried pie traditionally filled with mincemeat). And don't forget that slice of sticky baklava for dessert.

★ **Shiantris** CYPRIOT €€
(Pericleous 38; mains from €8; ☯8.30am-9pm Mon-Sat; 🖫) Our top choice restaurant has moved from cramped premises to a super-spacious three-floor venue with a rooftop terrace. Shiantris is named after its ebullient owner, who cooks up a fantastic array of seasonal beans with lemon, parsley and olive oil. Other dishes include traditional Cypriot pasta and meat combos like beef cooked in tomato and pasta.

The new venue is light, airy and contemporary for enjoying cuisine which has remained firmly (and deliciously) in classical mode.

Zanettos Taverna CYPRIOT €€
(Trikoupi 65; mains from €9, meze dishes €2; ☯6.30pm-midnight; 🖫) This place has a great reputation in the city, as it's allegedly one of the city's oldest traditional taverns, dating back to 1932. Locals flock here in their dozens for the succulent Greek-Cypriot meze, and it's definitely worth joining them – once you find the place, that is. It's hidden away in the back streets.

There's no menu, but ask to read about the history of the place – it's fascinating. Note also that the meze dishes are very generously sized. Come here hungry.

Kathodon GREEK €€
(☎2266 1656; www.kathodon.eu; Ledra St 62; mains from €8; ☯9am-11.45pm; 🕾🖫) Large, noisy and touristy... All is forgiven when you taste the authentic Greek cuisine here, like *Cretan apaki* (smoked pork) and crispy pumpkin. Take a look at the wall full of photos of contented customers, including Bill Clinton, but sit on the sprawling outside terrace for the best views and ambience. Live Greek music nightly.

Da Paolo ITALIAN €€
(Leoforos Konstantinou Paleologou 52; pizza from €11, pasta from €9; ☯6pm-late) This small Italian restaurant has a terrace setting beside the Venetian walls. It has a proper wood-fired pizza oven, traditional strings-of-garlic-style decor and a wide choice of pizza and pasta dishes. Go for the *cipriota pizza* with feta, haloumi, olives, salami and tomatoes for a real taste-bud treat.

NICOSIA MASTER PLAN
....
In an effort to bring North Cyprus and the Republic closer together, close to 100 Ottoman, Frankish and Byzantine buildings on both sides of the border have been faithfully restored with funding from the UN and EU. Founded in 1979, the Nicosia Master Plan covers churches and mosques, *hammams* (Turkish baths) and tombs, mansions and monuments, museums and cultural centres – the aim being to promote understanding of the history shared by the two sides. Efforts have even been made to renovate some of the crumbling buildings in the Buffer Zone, neglected for over 40 years. For more information, check the UNDP in Cyprus website (www.cy.undp.org) .

Inga's Veggie Heaven VEGETARIAN €€
(Chrysaliniotissa Crafts Centre, Dimonaktos 2; mains €10; ☯9am-5pm Tue-Sat; 🍴) Inga is a friendly Icelandic chef who prepares several homely vegetarian dishes of the day, such as stuffed peppers or lentil burgers, always served with a salad and homemade bread. The lovingly created cakes are a calorific high point. Afterwards, check out the surrounding arts and crafts studios.

Casa Vieja SPANISH €€
(☎2267 3371; Archangel Michael; paella for two people €22, tapas €5-8; ☯7.30pm-11.30pm) Flaunting an appropriate *olé España* atmosphere with dark ochre walls, bullfighting posters and Andalusian tilework, the menu here ranges from tapas, such as *tortilla* (potato omelette) and *croquetas de queso* (cheese croquettes), to three different types of paella, including the classic *Valenciano* with chicken and seafood. Live Spanish music on Friday.

Egeon CYPRIOT €€
(☎2243 3297; Ektoros 40; meze from €18; ☯7-11pm Tue-Sat) The ever-so-discreet yet very popular Egeon draws a faithful following of mainly local devotees. The food, basically meze, is reliably good. You dine in the courtyard of an atmospheric old house in the summer and inside the house in winter. Reservations essential.

NICOSIA (LEFKOSIA) EATING

Power House INTERNATIONAL €€
(Apostolou Varnava 19; mains from €12; ⊙10am-11pm Tue-Sat; 🛜) Part of the Nicosia Municipal Arts Centre, this sophisticated restaurant is suitably decorated with striking paintings and sculptures. The menu includes steaks, kebabs, pasta and salads, and desserts are in the innovative mode of chocolate mousse infused with Earl Grey tea. There is live jazz most Saturdays in the summer.

New City

The economic crisis of 2013 saw many restaurants on Leoforos Archiepiskopou Makariou III shift to Ledra St in the Old City. Some of the surrounding residential streets, like leafy and affluent Klimentos, are still home to some top dining, however, while Themistokli Dervi is fast becoming *the* place to come for cool new coffee shops and cafes.

⭐**Syrian Arab Friendship Club** MIDDLE EASTERN €€
(SAFC; Vassilisa Amalia 17; meze from €15; ⊙noon-midnight; 🚗🪑) Apart from being one of the best places to eat in Nicosia, this is the ideal place for vegetarians and families (it has a large garden in which children can play). The meze is vast and varied, with lots of tasty dips like beetroot and aubergine, plus delicious falafel, juicy parsley-and-tomato-laden tabouli, and plenty of meat dishes.

PLATEIA FANEROMENIS

In recent years the square and pedestrian zone surrounding the Faneromeni Church in the Old City has evolved into a buzzing cafe scene. There are more than half a dozen independently owned coffee shops and cafes with tables and chairs sprawled across the Plateia Faneromenis within confessional distance of this picturesque church. Just as fast, it seems, idiosyncratic small craft shops and galleries are opening, contributing to the dynamic youthful feel of the place. Apparently rents have plummeted in this historic part of town as part of a conscious move by local authorities to revitalise the neighbourhood.

Silver Pot CAFE €€
(🖉2210 1722; www.silverpot.com.cy; Themistokli Dervi 3; mains from €7; ⊙8am-5pm Mon-Fri, 10.30am-3.30pm Sat; 🛜🚗) Tight on space but big on boho-urban atmosphere, the menu here features locally sourced produce which is, as far as possible, organic. Dishes change daily but typical mains are Thai curry, oven-baked pork chops marinated in lemon juice and thyme, and inventive salads with ingredients like blue cheese, figs, pecans and cranberries. The Saturday brunch is justifiably popular.

Pinakothiki CYPRIOT €€
(AG Leventis Gallery, Leonidou St; mains from €10; ⊙8.30am-midnight Wed-Mon; 🛜🪑) Set in a fittingly contemporary space with glossy black and soothing cream decor and a long bar with stools for sipping pre-dinner cocktails. Dishes are light and appetising, including oven-baked salmon, duck pancakes in ginger-spiked soy sauce, and six different salads. There's an ample children's menu.

Sawa MIDDLE EASTERN €€
(🖉2276 6777; www.abbarahbrothers.com; Klimentos 31; meze from €15; ⊙noon-11.30pm) Known throughout the town for its superb Syrian dishes and fabulous sultan's-palace-style setting, with an elaborate carved-stone exterior, bubbling fountains and an elegant dining room. The mezes are recommended, ideally accompanied by a bottle of Lebanese Ksara riesling. Reservations essential.

Mediterranean SEAFOOD €€
(Klimentos Towers, Klimentos 43; mains from €10; ⊙noon-3pm & 6-11pm) Seafood lovers should head here to enjoy superbly fresh fish dishes. A seafood platter for two costs a reasonable €25; or push the boat out with the lobster spaghetti with a whole lobster for just €18.

🍷 Drinking & Nightlife

From the Famagusta Gate area in the Old City to bars along Leoforos Archiepiskopou Makariou III, there are plenty of atmospheric and welcoming night-owl places to enjoy a drink or three.

Old City

You'll find more atmospheric choices within the Old City walls, and a more boho-chic crowd, than in the more conservative New City.

★**Patio Cocktail Bar**　　　BAR

(☑2266 4488; www.patiococktailbar.com; Megalou Alexandrou 55-56; ⊙6pm-2am; 🔊) Step inside the show-stopping leafy courtyard with its dazzling wall of shutters painted in primary colours. Inside the main bar, exposed brickwork, chic furnishings and plenty of glass and light have an equally punchy effect for enjoying that pre (or post) dinner cocktail. Great mood music as well.

Oktana　　　BAR

(Aristidou 6; ⊙10am-2am; 🔊) Rub shoulders with artists, actors and academics at this soulful place decorated with edgy art-deco posters. There's a delightful sunken patio out back under the shade of a massive fig tree, while the rambling interior encompasses a book shop and various rooms, including a basement space favoured by nargileh smokers. There are regular art exhibitions and poetry readings.

Haratsi　　　CAFE

(Lidinis; ⊙4pm-midnight) Dating from the 1930s, the joy of this traditional coffee shop is that it is little changed from those days. There is no chill-out background music, no cutting-edge decor and, somehow, it's not the sort of place where you feel tempted to whip out your iPad.

Owner Stavros stresses that this is a place where people come to, well, talk as well as drink coffee, down a beer or shuffle cards. The regulars are far from old fashioned though; this is one of the coolest cafes in town.

Kalakathou　　　CAFE

(Nikokleous 21; ⊙10am-1am; 🔊) One of a clutch of cafes here which share a laid-back alternative vibe. Come here for board games, buskers and to sip a frappé under the vines. This evocative building formerly belonged to the Faneromeni Church across the way. Light snacks and homemade cakes also available.

Plato's　　　BAR

(Platonas 8; ⊙8pm-2am) Atmospheric bars are spread over several rooms at this early 20th-century building complete with original tiles, arches and a courtyard. Expect rock and blues on the soundtrack and a convivial local crowd.

Erodós　　　BAR

(☑2275 2250; Plateia Tyllirias; ⊙11am-late) This handsome colonial-style building is home

---

ℹ **THE GREEN LINE AT NIGHT**

Nicosia is a remarkably safe city to walk around. However, the Old City streets, particularly near the Green Line, can appear dingy and threatening at night, and solo women should avoid them. Crossing into the North is allowed only at official checkpoints; you'd be ill-advised to try to cross at any other place. This illegal move would lead to serious trouble. Also, be sure that you don't inadvertently take any photographs of the Green Line or the so-called no-man's zone, as this will surely lead to your camera being confiscated and possibly some tough questioning.

---

to an atmospheric bar with dark burgundy walls, warm woodwork and several moodily lit rooms. There's live music on Thursday at 10.30pm, which ranges from jazz to blues.

Gym　　　BAR

(☑2200 2001; Onasagorou 85-89; ⊙10am-late; 🔊) This corner venue is always heaving. They do food but stick to drinks – you should find something to suit with 20-plus cocktails. There's a DJ at weekends and the space is cavernous and contemporary with a small art gallery out back.

Weaving Mill　　　CULTURAL CENTRE

(☑2276 2275; Lefkonos 69; ⊙4pm-late Tue-Sun; 🔊👪) Owner Leontios started this non-profit educational and cultural association as a teaching base for the children of immigrants. These days the Mill has a multicultural purpose, showing films, staging the occasional concert and providing a large comfortable space for wi-fi use, board games, reading (there is an extensive library) or just socialising. There is a modest bar for light snacks and drinks.

🍷 **New City**

If you're about to hit the streets of the New City for a night out, be aware that jeans and trainers just won't cut it; Nicosians like to seriously dress up. There are some pleasant day-time cafes here as well.

Brew Lab　　　CAFE

(www.brewlab.com.cy; Stasikratous 3; ⊙7am-8pm Mon-Sat; 🔊) Follow the rich aroma of freshly

NICOSIA (LEFKOSIA) DRINKING & NIGHTLIFE

roasted fair-trade Costa Rican coffee which is proudly served here, along with freshly made bagels, brownies and similar baked goodies. There's a small courtyard out back, as well as pavement seating.

Finbarr's   BAR

(Leoforos Archiepiskopou Makariou III 52b; ⊙ noon-3pm & 7pm-midnight) Popular with Nicosians and expats for its Guinness on tap, screened football matches and suitably blarney atmosphere. Happy hour is from 4.30pm to 8pm. Chicken 'n' chips pub-style grub also available.

Zoo   CLUB

(Leoforos Stasinou 15; ⊙ 7pm-late Thu-Sun) Zoo is the embodiment of style and sophistication on Nicosia's club scene, with music that ranges from international to Greek pop. The summer-only Zoo Lounge on the top floor is a great place for a little locked-eyes-over-cocktails time with chill-out soundtracks and laid-back live music.

Sfinakia   CLUB

(cnr Sypros Kyprianou & Themistokli Dervi; ⊙ 9pm-late Thu-Sat) On trendy Themistokli Dervi, this place attracts girls in ankle-cracking high heels and boys shimmering with both brilliantine and expectation.

☆ Entertainment

For entertainment listings, particularly classical music concerts and the theatre, pick up the *Nicosia This Month* and *Diary of Events* pamphlets, available from the CTO. A number of cinemas scattered around Nicosia show varying permutations of the latest films and occasional re-runs of English-language movies.

Academy 32   LIVE MUSIC

(Leoforos Konstantino Paleologou 32, Old City; ⊙ 7pm-2am Tue-Sun; ☎) Housed in the basement of the Cyprus Academy of Music (the owner is the Academy's artistic director) this is, unsurprisingly, one of the best places in town to hear live music with an emphasis on jazz, classical and world music. There is also an art gallery, along with fine wines and light eats.

K-Cineplex   CINEMA

(www.kcineplex.com; Makedonitissis 8; ▣) Located 2.5km out of the city in Strovolos, K-Cineplex shows all the latest movie releases on six screens and offers ample parking,

CHILDREN'S CYPRUS: NICOSIA

Unlike the seaside towns and resorts, Nicosia is not immediately appealing to children, although Nicosians are child-friendly, as are most Cypriots. There are no professional baby-sitting services in the city, as so many families seem to have their own live-in nannies.

The Cyprus Tourism Organisation (CTO) has a list of child-friendly events taking place throughout the year. If you're lucky your visit may coincide with a traditional Cypriot shadow-puppet theatre show; don't forget to ask at the tourist office.

Eleon Swimming Pool (☎ 2266 7833; www.eleonpark.com; Ploutarhou 3; adult/child €6.50/4; ⊙ 9am-6pm mid-May–mid-Sep) When it gets too hot to traipse around the streets of Nicosia, head to Engomi for this large swimming pool fringed by olive trees and with an elaborate children's play area.

Kykko Bowling Centre (☎ 2235 0085; Archimidous 15-19, Engomi; ⊙ 2pm-1am Mon-Fri, 1pm-1am Sat & Sun) One really great place for the kids, where they get to wear uncomfortable shoes and share in Homer Simpson's great passion, is this bowling centre, located right behind the Hilton Park Hotel to the west of the New City. The cafe, which has snacks and drinks, will allow kids to share in his other passion (the fast food one).

Extreme Park (☎ 2242 4681; www.extremepark.com.cy; 149 Strovolos Ave; adult/child free/€3 Mon-Thu, child €5/5.50 Fri, Sat & Sun; ⊙ 4-9pm Mon-Fri, 11am-9pm Sat & Sun) For more dedicated big-time playground entertainment, consider heading to the appropriately named Extreme Park southwest of the centre. The park has vast indoor/outdoor playgrounds complete with climbing wall, inflatable slides, bungee trampolines, rope obstacle course, minigolf, soccer, bowling, kiddie cinema and three cafeterias for essential downtime.

ℹ CULTURAL CENTRES

Want to wise up on Cyprus' extraordinary history and culture? You're in luck... There are several cultural centres with libraries that offer a wide range of periodicals and books for reference. They are generally open 9am to 7pm Monday, Tuesday, Thursday and Friday and 9am to 1pm Wednesday.

British Council (☑ 2266 5152; www.britishcouncil.com.cy; Leoforos Mouseiou 3)

Makarios Cultural Foundation (p131)

Ahilleios Library (☑ 2276 3033; Leoforos Konstantinou Paleologou 30)

Nicosia Municipal Arts Centre (p128)

Ministry of Education Library (☑ 2230 3180; www.moec.gov.cy; Leoforos Konstantinou Paleologou)

a cafeteria and high-tech sight-and-sound systems.

Theatre & Live Music

There is a thriving local theatre scene in Nicosia; however, plays performed are almost always in Greek. If this doesn't deter you, check at the tourist office for any performances that may be taking place. Unfortunately, the former main venue, the Lefkosia Municipal Theatre, has closed down indefinitely after a serious fire in 2008.

The best way to get to see and hear some traditional music is to head for any of the restaurants offering live music in Laïki Yitonia and Ledra St in the Old City. Otherwise keep your eyes peeled for posters over the summer advertising visiting musicians from Greece.

Sport

Football (soccer) is the main spectator sport in Nicosia. The football season is from September to May. The 16-times champion, APOEL Nicosia, held the top spot for many years. The city is also home to clubs Omonia and Olympiakos. Tickets can also be bought at the gate on the day of the match. For more information email tickets@apoelfc.com.cy.

The **GSP Stadium** (☑ 22874050; www.gsp.org.cy; Pangyprion Avenue) is the main and largest stadium in Cyprus with a capacity for 22859 people. It is mostly used for football matches (as well as major concerts). The stadium is located in Strovolos, southeast Nicosia, approximately 6.5km from the city centre.

🔒 Shopping

With its army of designer babes, it's no wonder Nicosia rules when it comes to clothes shopping. The so-called 'discount stores' offer clothes and shoes at 30% to 80% off their original price, and many Nicosians can be found elbowing their way to the best bargain.

There are two main shopping areas. Ledra St in the Old City has lots of old-style, as well as high-fashion, boutiques and shops, and is home to Debenhams department store, while Leoforos Archiepiskopou Makariou III in the New City has a smattering of international chain stores, like Mango and Zara (although several have moved to Ledra St in recent years).

Tourist shops are centred on Laïki Yitonia in the Old City and sell items like backgammon boards and lacework; don't forget to barter. There's a large and lively fruit, veg and produce market held at the Constanza Bastion on Wednesday from 6am to 5pm.

★ Diachroniki Gallery ART

(www.diachroniki.com; Arsinois 84, Old City; ☉ 10am-7pm Mon-Sat) This priceless collection of paintings, sculpture, etchings and prints has been lovingly collected by owner Chris Kikas who used to run a gallery in London's King's Road. Art collectors come from far and wide to peruse the art work here. Don't miss it.

Atelier D'Art CERAMICS

(Apollonos 16, Old City; ☉ 9.30am-6.30pm Mon-Sat) Prepare to be impressed with this highly original pottery, including homewares, colourful mobiles and jewellery, created by master ceramicist Stavros. He studied his craft in Italy, France and London.

NICOSIA (LEFKOSIA) SHOPPING

Phanero Menis 70   CRAFTS

(www.kyriakicosta.net; Phaneromenis 70, Old City; ⊙9.30am-6.30pm Mon-Fri, to 1pm Sat) The owner of this fascinating shop, Kyriaki, is an artist – and it shows in the quirky and quality crafts, textiles and artwork on sale here, including handmade children's clothes and toys, jewellery, artwork, bags, fashion and fanciful ornaments and decor items.

Cyprus Handicrafts Centre   CRAFTS

(Leoforos Athalassis 186, Old City; ⊙7.30am-2.30pm Mon-Wed & Fri, 7.30am-2.30pm & 3-6pm Thu) Get your Cypriot lace and embroidery here at decent prices, as well as leatherwear, mosaics, ceramics and pottery. Even better, watch these products being made in various workshops at this government-sponsored foundation committed to preserving Cypriot handicrafts.

Astor   SHOES

(Ippocratous 16b, Old City; ⊙10am-4.30 Tue-Sun) Locally produced handmade sandals and boots with simple designs and quality leather are the standout here with prices starting from just €25. The bags are imported from Greece.

Antiques   ANTIQUES

(☑9966 4722; Vasiliou Voulgaroktonou 5 & 6, Old City; ⊙10am-6pm Mon, Tue & Fri, 10am-2pm Wed & Sat) These two very dusty and intriguing antique shops are located on opposite sides of the street. You may have to ring the owner to come down for you to browse, but you'll find lots of great stuff, from retro bits and pieces to attractive ceramics, paintings and ornaments.

Utopia   FOOD & DRINK

(www.utopia-cy.com; Areos 48; ⊙9am-7pm Mon, Tue, Thu & Fri, 9am-2pm Wed & Sat) ✐ The owner is an organic farmer, so this is the place to come for the ecological self-caterer. It also serves lunches on Friday, as well as tea and drinks the rest of the week.

Yatanou   CRAFTS

(Papadopoulou 25, Old City; ⊙9am-7pm Mon, Tue, Thu & Fri, 9am-2pm Wed & Sat) One of the more colourful shop windows you'll find anywhere, selling handmade kids' toys and decorations, including mobiles, knitted dolls, jazzy cushions and similar.

Messa   BAKLAVA

(Aischylou 73; ⊙9am-7pm Mon, Tue, Thu & Fri, 9am-2pm Wed & Sat) Sticky and delicious Syrian baklava exquisitely boxed-up for gifts or serious self-indulgence.

Moufflon Bookshop   BOOKS

(www.moufflon.com.cy; Sofouli 1, New City; ⊙9.30am-6pm Mon, Tue, Thu & Fri, 9am-2pm Wed & Sat) Arguably the largest selection of English-language books in Cyprus, dating back to 1967 (when a lot more people read books...).

Municipal Market   MARKET

(Digeni Akrita, New City; ⊙7am-4pm Thu-Sat & Mon-Tue, 7am-2pm Wed) This Municipal Market in the New City re-opened in early 2014 after an extensive refurbishment. It sports a small, but select, array of stalls, selling fruit, veg, spices, bakery goods, cheeses and similar. There is also a good cafe here and an excellent restaurant-cum-deli called Limoncelli.

PLATEIA ELEFTHERIAS

A massive reconstruction project has been obstructing much of Nicosia's Plateia Eleftherias. The architect is Zaha Hadid, one of the world's best. Renowned for her socially aware projects, Hadid's impressive CV includes the Strasbourg tram station, a housing project for IBA-Block 2 in Berlin, and the Mind Zone in London's Millennium Dome. Together with her Cypriot associate, Christos Passos, Hadid plans to construct a green belt along the moat that currently surrounds the Venetian walls, turning the area within into Nicosia's central park, encircled by a palm-tree-lined pedestrian walkway. There will be a (concrete) square in the midst of the green belt, where pedestrians can stroll and congregate, giving the area a new town centre. Hadid calls the design an 'urban intervention'.

There has been some controversy – but what's a grand architectural work without controversy? – with local opponents complaining of too little public consultation on the project, concerns about the impact a large concrete structure will have on the ancient walls, and the reduction of access to the Old City. Work started in 2008 but there have been numerous delays (and economic woes) and word is that the project won't now be completed until 2015 (or thereabouts).

ℹ Information

EMERGENCY

The general emergency numbers for police and ambulance are ☑ 199 or ☑ 112.

Police Station (☑ 2247 7434) Located in the Old City, at the northern end of Ledra St, by the barrier.

INTERNET ACCESS

Most midrange and top-end hotels provide wi-fi access, as do many cafes if you purchase a drink. There are a few internet cafes in town; the tourist office can provide you with a list.

MEDICAL SERVICES

If you need a private doctor or pharmacy, ring ☑ 9090 1432. Visiting hours for doctors are normally from 9am to 1pm and 4pm to 7pm. Local newspapers list pharmacies that are open during the night, and on weekends and holidays, as well as the names of doctors who are on call out of normal hours. You can also check www.cytayellowpages.com.cy for details of doctors and dentists.

Lefkosia General Hospital (☑ 2280 1400; Leoforos Nechrou) West of the Old City.

TOURIST INFORMATION

Cyprus Tourism Organisation (CTO; www.visitcyprus.org.cy; ⊙ 8.30am-4pm Mon-Fri, to 2pm Sat) New City (☑ 2233 7715; Leoforos Lemesou 19); Old City (☑ 2244 4264; Aristokyprou 11) The CTO's head office is in the New City, though it's not really geared to handling over-the-counter queries from the public.

Municipal Tourist Office (Ledra St; ⊙ 7.30am-2.30pm daily & 3-6pm Wed) At the Ledra St crossing, this municipal office has multilingual leaflets about the city. Look for the large Peace sign on your left just before the border. There are also regular photographic exhibitions and similar, generally with an evocative, thought-provoking theme.

ℹ Getting There & Away

AIR

Nicosia's international airport is in the UN buffer zone and is no longer a functioning airport. All air passengers for Nicosia arrive at the smart new Larnaka airport in the South. Most airlines that serve the Republic of Cyprus have offices or representatives in Nicosia.

BUS

Local buses primarily leave from the Urban Bus Station on Plateia Solomou, abutting the Tripoli Bastion in the Old City.

ℹ AUDIO GUIDES

The Cyprus Tourism Organisation (CTO; www.visitcyprus.com) has introduced a series of audio guides, which you can download in mp3 or mobile-phone format with a choice of six languages. Sights covered are the Cyprus Museum (Nicosia); 10 Byzantine churches in the Troödos area; the archaeological site of Kourion (Lemesos); the Pafos Archaeological Site and the Tombs of the Kings (Pafos). For more information, visit the website.

InterCity Buses (www.intercity-buses.com; Plateia Solomou) runs regular buses to the main cities and resorts, including to the following destinations:

Agia Napa & Paralimni Six buses daily Monday to Friday and three on Saturday (€5, one hour).

Larnaka Twelve buses daily Monday to Friday and six on Saturday (€4, 45 minutes).

Lemesos Four buses daily Monday to Friday and two on Saturday (€5, one hour).

Pafos Five buses run daily Monday to Friday and four at weekends (€7, 1¾ hours).

CAR & MOTORCYCLE

Traffic approaching Nicosia tends to come from either the Troödos Mountains to the west or Larnaka and Lemesos in the South. The Larnaka–Lemesos motorway ends fairly abruptly on the outskirts of Nicosia, about 6km south of the Old City. By following the extension of the motorway into the city centre, you will eventually reach Leoforos Archiepiskopou Makariou III, the main thoroughfare in the New City. Traffic from Troödos will enter the city along Leoforos Georgiou Griva Digeni.

Parking is most easily found at the large car parks abutting the city bastions, to the right of Leoforos Archiepiskopou Makariou III, or to your left if you approach from Troödos. The most convenient for new arrivals is the large lot between the D'Avila and Constanza Bastions on Leoforos Stasinou. Parking for a day should cost no more than €10.

Getting out of Nicosia is made easy by the prominent signs all along Leoforos Stasinou. Be wary, however, of the many one-way streets and the numerous on-street parking restrictions. Avoid the peak period of 11am to 1pm on weekdays when traffic can be very slow.

SERVICE TAXI

Travel & Express (☎ 7777 7474; www.travelexpress.com.cy; Municipal Parking Place, Leoforos Salaminos) has several popular routes, including Lemesos (€11, 1½ hours), Pafos (change at Lemesos, €20.50, 1½ hours), Larnaka (€8.50, one hour) and Agia Napa (€17, one hour).

Although Travel & Express will pick you up at an appointed time from anywhere in urban Nicosia, delays of up to 30 minutes are the norm; similarly, passengers boarding at the Podocataro Bastion will usually spend up to 30 minutes picking up other passengers before actually departing Nicosia. Be prepared and allow for at least an extra hour.

TAXI TO NORTHERN CYPRUS

Things have changed significantly when it comes to crossing into the North, though you're not advised to take a rented car across the line. The easiest thing to do if you have luggage and don't want to walk is to get a taxi to take you anywhere in the North. Most drivers should be happy to do this – if one refuses, try another. Most taxi drivers who go to the North will generally have the visa leaflet you'll need to fill out. A journey from Nicosia to Northern Cyprus should cost anywhere between €28 and €45, though you'd be best advised to cross to North Nicosia on foot and rent a car there – it'll be cheaper and more flexible.

ⓘ Getting Around

TO/FROM THE AIRPORT

There is no public or airline transport between Nicosia and Larnaka or Pafos airports. You can, however, take a service taxi to either airport, but make sure you leave at least an extra hour for your journey, as picking up and dropping off other passengers can take a long time. This particularly applies to those flying from Pafos airport, because passengers travelling from Nicosia to Pafos with a service taxi have to change in Lemesos, which can sometimes include a wait of around 30 minutes.

A service taxi to Larnaka airport will cost around €15, and it's around €30 to Pafos airport. Service taxis will drop you off at the airports, but won't pick you up. The only way to get into Nicosia from either of these airports is by renting a car or hiring a taxi (which may turn out to be quite expensive). Check whether your hotel organises airport pick-ups.

BUS

Osel Buses (www.osel.com.cy) Nicosia's urban bus company has a network of routes covering the city and suburbs. Check the website for more information.

CAR & MOTORCYCLE

The car-rental agency **A Petsas & Sons** (☎ 2246 2650; www.petsas.com.cy) is located at Plateia Solomou. You can also opt for **Hertz** (☎ 2220 8888; www.hertz.com.cy; 16 Aikaterinis Kornaro, off Leoforos Athalassis) in Strovolos; it has some good online rates. Beware that the drop-off charge is €35 if you rent a car in Nicosia and leave it in another city. At the base of the walls there are car parks.

There are no motorbikes for rent in or around the Old City.

TAXI

There is a large taxi stand on Plateia Eleftherias.

Apostrati (☎ 2266 3358; Plateia Eleftherias)

Elpis (☎ 2276 4966; Leoforos Archiepiskopou Makariou III 63c)

Ethniko (☎ 2266 0880; Plateia Solomou)

AROUND NICOSIA

The plain of the Mesaoria (meaning 'between two mountains') is a sprawling, parched landscape during the summer months, when the land is totally exposed to the relentless sun. But come spring and winter, the Mesaoria, like most of Cyprus, transforms into a green, fertile plain. The two mountain ranges bordering the plain are the Kyrenia (Girne) Range to the north and the Troödos Mountains to the west and southwest.

For the visitor wanting to explore the Mesaoria, there are a couple of ancient archaeological sites and a sprinkling of churches and monasteries. Note that for some of the churches and monasteries, you need to be in a group for those with the keys to be willing to unlock the buildings.

ⓘ Getting There & Around

A car is necessary to reach some of the sites in this region. While public buses (often colourful and old-fashioned) connect most of the Mesaoria (Mesarya) villages with Nicosia, they're basically scheduled to service workers and schoolchildren, not curious travellers, and so will be of limited use.

Cycling in the area is easy because of the mostly gentle gradients, but bear in mind the weather gets very hot in summer and the traffic on the main highways can be heavy and dangerous.

Ancient Tamassos

The main claim to fame of Tamassos (admission €2.50; ⊙ 9.30am-5pm Mon-Fri, 10am-3pm Sat & Sun Jun-Sep, shorter hours rest of the year) was its seemingly endless supply of copper – the mineral from which the name of Cyprus (Kypros in Greek; Kıbrıs in Turkish) is derived. A copper-producing settlement here dates from at least the 7th century BC, and production ran well into the Hellenistic period. Excavations of the remains of the citadel began in 1889 and, around this time, two tombs dating back to the 6th century BC were discovered, which today comprise the site's major attraction.

Homer apparently mentioned Ancient Tamassos in *The Odyssey*, where it is referred to as Temese. The goddess Athena says to Odysseus' son, Telemachus: 'We are bound for the foreign port of Temese with a cargo of gleaming iron, which we intend to trade for copper.' The site of this otherwise obscure and little-known city kingdom is located on a small hillside about 17km southwest of Nicosia next to the village of Politiko.

It is thought that the tombs probably contained the remains of the citadel's kings. Looters have long since spirited away the rich burial treasures that may once have been buried here. You can even see a hole in the roof of the larger tomb showing where grave robbers broke in. The walls are unusually carved in such a way as to imitate wood – a feature that some archaeologists have linked to a possible Anatolian influence at the time of the citadel's zenith. Some theorists suggest that Tamassos was even part of the Hittite Empire.

Among the discoveries unearthen by archeologists on the larger site are three limesone lions and two sphinxes which are on display at Nicosia's Cyprus Museum and a

Around Nicosia (Lefkosia)

> ### ⓘ DRESS CODE FOR MOSQUES & MONASTERIES
>
> If you are planning to visit a mosque or monastery anywhere on the island, be aware that modest dress is obligatory. Neither men nor women should wear shorts or short-sleeved shirts and women, in particular, should cover up as much as possible. The good news is that, increasingly, mosques and monasteries are supplying expansive capes, or similar, for visitors to borrow free of charge – a veritable godsend if it's a hot sightseeing day.

magnificent bronze head of Apollo, now in London's British Museum.

Agios Irakleidios

Easily combined with an excursion to the nearby archeological site of Tamassos is a visit to the historic **Monastery of Agios Irakleidios** (⊘8.30am-6pm), which has been occupied by nuns since the 1960s. The original church was built in the 5th century AD, but the current monastic buildings date from the late 18th century. The church today boasts the usual panoply of frescos and icons. On a table to the eastern side of the church you can spot a jewelled reliquary containing the skull of Saint Irakleidios.

Saint Irakleidios was born in Tamassos and guided St Paul and St Barnabas around Cyprus. He was later made one of the first bishops in Cyprus by Barnabas. The bishop has been subsequently credited with the performance of a number of miracles, including exorcisms.

Agios Mamas

This is the somewhat forgotten site of the 16th-century Gothic church of **Agios Mamas**, whose arches were never finished in the first place; it's like an exercise in non-starters. Perhaps that's why the beautiful arches have a sense of nostalgia about them. The church was built in retrograde Lusignan style, and although the site is locked and cannot be entered, the arches, nave and two aisles can be easily seen and admired. The isolated ruins are in the deserted village of **Agios Sozomenos**, an area that has been abandoned since some inter-communal incidents in 1964.

The church and village can be reached from Nicosia on the A1, taking exit 6 (for Potamia) and going on to a minor, paved road about 2km before Potamia, following the sign for Agios Sozomenos.

Maheras Monastery

It's a fair hike out to this sprawling **monastery** (⊘9am-noon Mon, Tue & Thu) perched in the foothills of the eastern spur of the Troödos Mountains and under the all-seeing radar installation on Mt Kionia (1423m) to the south. The Maheras Monastery was founded in a similar way to the Kykkos Monastery (p73). In 1148 a hermit named Neophytos found an icon guarded by a sword (*maheras* means knife or sword in Greek) in a cave near the site of the present monastery.

The monastery developed around the icon and flourished over time. Nothing remains of the original structures; the current building dates from around 1900. The monastery has become a popular outing for Cypriots, who possibly come as much for the cooler climate as for spiritual enlightenment. There is a small cafeteria in the grounds and pilgrims may stay overnight.

The monastery is open for visits by groups of parishioners only at certain times. Ask locally or at the CTO in Nicosia about how you might join one of these groups, which will mostly consist of Cypriot pilgrims. Visits should be conducted with reverence and solemnity. Maheras Monastery is best approached via Klirou and Fikardou, since the alternate route via Pera and the E902, while very pretty, is winding and very slow.

Mesaoria Villages

Renting a car and driving around the Mesaoria is a good way to see the area's villages, but keep in mind that roads tend to fan out haphazardly along roughly defined valleys and ravines, and cross from one valley to another. The journey can therefore be slow as the roads are narrow and winding. 4WD tours often take travellers to see some of the villages of the Mesaoria as part of a wider tour around Cyprus.

One of the more popular villages in the area is **Pera** (population 1020), situated a couple of kilometres from Tamassos. While there are no specific sights here, Pera is nonetheless pretty. Head for the signposted Arghaggelou Michail church, where you can park and wander around the surrounding cobbled backstreets. Photographers will find some particularly evocative scenes: old houses covered in bougainvillea, ancient stone jars, pretty doors and cats on walls. Visitors stop for refreshments at the *kafeneio* (coffee shop), where the locals, and often the village priest, enjoy coffee and gossip in a world where time means little.

The villages of **Orounda** (population 660) and **Peristerona** (population 2100), west of Nicosia, have interesting and photogenic churches. The village of **Lythrodontas** (population 2620), 25km south of Nicosia, has a lovely large central square with a couple of atmospheric traditional cafes.

The postcard-pretty village of **Fikardou** (population 16) is close to the Maheras Monastery; visits to both are easily combined. Fikardou is the 'official' village in a clutch of well-preserved villages in the eastern Troödos Mountains. Its Ottoman-period houses with wooden balconies are gradually being restored and are a visual relief after the cement structures of many modern Troödos Mountain villages. That said, there's not a lot to Fikardou, and only a handful of people live here permanently.

The main street is no more than a few hundred metres long, dominated by the Church of Apostles St Peter & Paul. Opposite, there are some harrowing photos of four young local soldiers (aged 22 to 24 years) who were killed during the Turkish invasion in 1974. With little else to do, most visitors content themselves with a visit to the village's cafe-cum-restaurant before moving on. Still, if you are in the region, a visit is recommended since there are few places left in Cyprus that are as representative of the culture and archaeology of the recent past.

Just to the south, in pretty **Lazanias**, stop in at the **Magic Lazania** (☑9653 0129; ☺9am-4pm Tue-Sun) with its terrace overlooking the mountains and monastery. Owner Luis is a trained chef, and it shows in the excellently prepared local dishes, such as *kleftiko*, courgettes with eggs, and juicy chicken kebabs. Call ahead if you are a large group.

From these villages, roads lead by various routes to the higher reaches of the Troödos, via the Pitsylia region, offering a slow but scenic journey into the mountains. This option is particularly useful on weekends when Nicosians in their hundreds storm the Troödos via the main B9 road (through Astromeritis and Kakopetria) for picnics and a day out in order to escape the city heat.

You will find a tavern or restaurant in most villages and even in out-of-the-way places along the road. Many Nicosians come to the country to eat on weekends and usually have their favourite haunts.

Advertised widely around **Agia Marina** (population 630) is **Katoï** (☑2285 2576; Agia Marina Xyliatou; mains from €8; ☺noon-10pm), overlooking the village itself. Its lights are visible from some distance away at night, and it commands a great view over the Troödos foothills and the Mesaoria. The restaurant serves solid Cypriot staples and an imaginative selection of mezes.

There are, in the area, a number of pleasant picnic grounds, usually situated in cool and leafy spots. Try the **Xyliatos Dam** near the village of the same name, or **Kapoura**, on a picturesque back road (F929) linking Vyzakia with the B9; or, alternatively, higher up in the Maheras Forest south of Pera at **Skordokefalos**, along the E902 leading to the Maheras Monastery. All picnic grounds in this region have barbecue areas, tables, chairs and, most importantly, shade.

NICOSIA (LEFKOSIA) MESAORIA VILLAGES

North Nicosia (Lefkoşa)

Best Places to Eat

➡ Sabor (p156)

➡ Boghjalian (p156)

➡ Passport Cadde (p156)

➡ Old Mosaic (p155)

Best Cultural Sights

➡ Büyük Han (p150)

➡ Bedesten (p151)

➡ Selimiye Mosque (p150)

➡ Mevlevi Shrine Museum (p153)

Why Go?

Home to roughly a third of the population of North Cyprus, the northern half of Nicosia is another world. Approached from the smart boutiques in Ledra St, North Nicosia (Lefkoşa) sees the avenue fracture into a medina-style market of stalls and kebab houses. Thanks to the Nicosia Master Plan, however, many of the historic buildings are being restored and the area around the Selimiye Mosque, in particular, has a real sense of heritage.

This is essentially a daytime city where the appeal lies in observing daily life and exploring the dusty historic streets lined with ancient mosques and Frankish ruins. Many visitors take a day trip via the Ledra Palace or Ledra St checkpoints. Consider staying until dusk, when the minarets light up and release their evening call to prayer and the air is scented with an intoxicating combination of wild jasmine and freshly grilled kebabs.

When to Go

➡ North Nicosia can be an uncomfortably hot and dusty city in July and August, which is also when many inhabitants leave for cooler coastal climes.

➡ Take note of when Ramadan falls, although it's not as strictly observed here as on the Turkish mainland.

➡ In September the temperature cools but the action heats up, with the town taking centre stage for the International Cyprus Theatre Festival.

➡ The spring and autumn months are pleasantly warm, while December and January see the most rainfall and the temperature is at its coolest, hovering around 15°C.

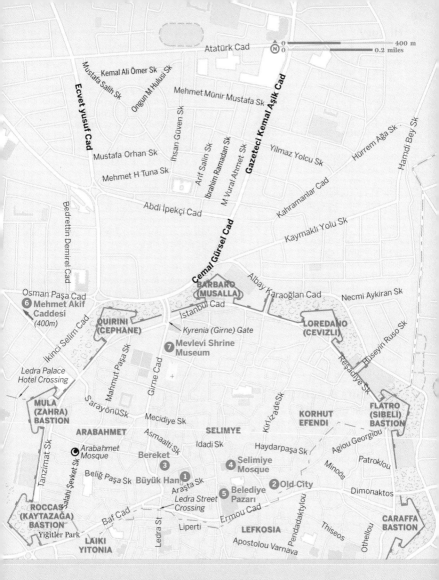

North Nicosia (Lefkoşa) Highlights

1 Visiting **Büyük Han** (p150), a grand Ottoman structure full of intriguing craft shops.

2 Strolling through the streets of the **Old City** (p150), an ancient and colourful maze.

3 Tasting a fantastic kebab, *pide* or *lahmacun* (Turkish pizza) at **Bereket** (p155), a traditional kiosk in North Nicosia.

4 Entering the sparseness and silence of the magnificent **Selimiye Mosque** (p150).

5 Walking between watermelon mountains at the **Belediye Pazarı** (p151).

6 Checking out the fashionable new restaurants and bars on cosmopolitan **Mehmet Akif Caddesi** (p157)in the New City.

7 Taking a twirl at the **Mevlevi Shrine Museum** (p153), a former shrine of the fascinating and mystic whirling dervishes.

History

Until 1963 North Nicosia, not surprisingly, shared much of the same history as its dismembered southern sector.

The capital was effectively divided into Greek and Turkish sectors in 1963, when violence against Turkish Cypriots by insurgents from the Ethniki Organosi tou Kypriakou Agona (EOKA; National Organisation for the Cypriot Struggle) forced them to retreat into safe enclaves or ghettos. The Green Line, as it has become known, was established when a British military commander divided up the city on a map with a green pen. The name has remained ever since.

The Turkish military invasion of 1974, which most Turkish Cypriots saw as a rescue operation, formalised the division between the two halves of the city. A wary truce was brokered by the blue-bereted members of the UN peacekeeping forces, who had been guarding the Green Line since sectarian troubles broke out in 1963.

It is now easy for visitors (and Cypriots) to cross over the border but, despite this, the city remains both physically and symbolically divided and many of the older generation (both Greek and Turkish) still bear grudges and refuse to cross the divide.

◉ Sights & Activities

To visit and appreciate the sights here, pick up a copy of the North Nicosia map from the friendly tourist office. If you get lost, head for the Venetian walls, which you can easily follow in order to reach a main point of reference. Running south from the Kyrenia Gate is Girne Caddesi, which leads onto

---

ⓘ CROSSING THE LINE

There are no time restrictions imposed when crossing the Green Line, so overnight stays (or longer) pose no problem. Pedestrian crossings are at Ledra St and Ledra Palace Hotel in Nicosia (Lefkosia); from the latter it's a 10-minute walk to the Kyrenia Gate. There are seven access points linking the Greek Cypriot and Turkish Cypriot sides of Cyprus; the latest is the Limnitis-Yeşilirmak crossing in the northwest of the island, which opened in October 2010.

Hire cars can only be taken from South to North, not the other way.

Atatürk Meydanı, the main square, surrounded by banks and shops.

★ Büyük Han   HISTORIC BUILDING
(Great Inn; Araşta Sk; ⊙10am-10pm Mon-Sat) **FREE** The Büyük Han is a wonderful example of Ottoman architecture and a rare surviving example of a medieval caravanserai. Built in 1572 by the first Ottoman governor of Cyprus, Musafer Pasha, it was renovated in the early '90s, and has once again become the centre of the Old City's bustle, with cafes, shops and traditional craft workshops housed in the small cells that originally served as the inn's sleeping areas.

During the medieval Ottoman period, travellers and traders could find accommodation at these *hans* (inns), as well as a place to stable their horses, trade their goods and socialise with fellow travellers.

The central courtyard has a *mescit* (Islamic 'chapel') in the centre, which is balanced on six pillars over a *şadrvan* (ablutions fountain). This design is found only in this inn and two others in Turkey.

★ Selimiye Mosque   MOSQUE
(Selimiye Camii; Selimiye Sk) North Nicosia's most prominent landmark, which is also clearly visible from the southern half of the city, is the Selimiye Mosque. This strange-looking building, a cross between a French Gothic church and a mosque, has a fascinating history. Today the mosque is a working place of worship and you are able to go inside. Try to time your visit either just before or just after one of the five Muslim prayer sessions.

Work started on the church in 1209 and progressed slowly. Louis IX of France, on his way to the Crusades, stopped by in 1248 and gave the building process a much-needed shot in the arm by offering the services of his retinue of artisans and builders. However, the church took another 78 years to complete and was finally consecrated in 1326 as the Church of Agia Sofia.

Until 1570 the church suffered depredation at the hands of the Genoese and the Mamelukes, and severe shakings from two earthquakes in 1491 and 1547. When the Ottomans arrived in 1571, they stripped the building of its Christian contents and added two minarets, between which the Turkish Cypriot and Turkish flags now flutter. The Gothic structure of the interior is still apparent despite Islamic overlays, such as the whitewashed walls and columns, and the

THE WHIRLING DERVISHES OF THE MEVLEVI ORDER

The founder of the Mevlevi Order was the poet Jelaluddin Mevlana, known in the West as Rumi, and born in the 13th century. His most famous work is *Mathnawi*, a long poem that details Mevlana's teachings and understanding of the world, and emphasises the belief that an individual's soul is separated from the divine during one's earthly life; only God's love has the power to draw it back to its source. Rumi's teachings were also based on the belief that everything was created by God, so every creature was to be loved and respected. The order paid special attention to patience, modesty, unlimited tolerance, charity and positive reasoning.

But most importantly, and shockingly to orthodox Muslims at that time, Rumi claimed that music was the way to transcend the mundane worries of life, and that one could connect with the divine through dancing, or indeed whirling.

The slow, whirling, trance-like dance of the dervishes is called *sema*, and it is accompanied by the sound of the *ney* (reed flute), an instrument central to Rumi's idea of yearning for the divine. The sound of the *ney*, whose tonal range is equal to that of a human voice, is supposed to symbolise the soul's cry for God. The *oud* (Levantine lute) and *kudum* (paired drums) are the other instruments that accompany *sema*. During their dance, the dervishes hold one palm upwards and the other downwards to symbolise humanity's position as a bridge between heaven and earth. The *sema* was performed exclusively as a spiritual exercise, and it was considered blasphemy to perform for money or show.

The Mevlevi order flourished for 700 years in Turkish life and spread from Konya in Turkey to the Balkans and southeastern Europe, until they were banned in Turkey by Atatürk in 1925. Today the dervishes perform in theatres all over the world, and it's possible to see their beautiful dance in most Western countries.

Whirling Dervish Performances

Performances of the mesmerising whirling dervishes take place daily at noon, 2pm, 3pm and 5pm, 50 metres north of the Selimiye Mosque from April to September. Performances last approximately 30 minutes and cost €7. Check the www.danceofcyprus.com website to confirm times.

reorientation of the layout to align it with Mecca. Note the ornate west front with the three decorated doorways, each in a different style. Also look out for four marble columns relocated from Ancient Salamis and now placed in the apse off the main aisles.

★**Bedesten** CHURCH
(St Nicholas of the English; Arasta Sk; ⊘ 10am-1pm Mon, Tue, Thu, Fri & Sat, 2-5pm Wed) Renovated as part of the Nicosia Master Plan, the imposing Bedesten dates from the 6th century, when it was built as a small Byzantine church. It was grandly embellished in the 14th century and reborn as a Catholic church.

More recently, at a cost of two million EU-funded euros, this magnificent building has been restored to its former glory and was recognised, in 2009, with the prestigious Europa Nostra Award for cultural heritage.

After the Ottomans' arrival in 1571, the church was used as a grain store and general market but was basically left to disintegrate. The north doorway has some splendid looking coats of arms originally belonging to noble Venetian families. These families may have been supporters of the Orthodox Church, which was nonetheless allowed to continue with its business, despite the Catholic dominance of religious life in Cyprus.

Explanatory panels outline the restoration works and the history of the building. Currently, the Bedesten is used primarily as a cultural centre.

Belediye Pazarı MARKET
(Municipal Market; Kuyumcular Sk; ⊘ 6am-3pm Mon-Sat) This is a fantastic place to check out local produce and local characters; the market bustles with action. Bargaining is rife and sellers either shout out their offers to shoppers or sleep on the counters amid piles of vegetables and fruit. There's also an area with souvenirs; don't forget to bargain.

North Nicosia (Lefkoşa)

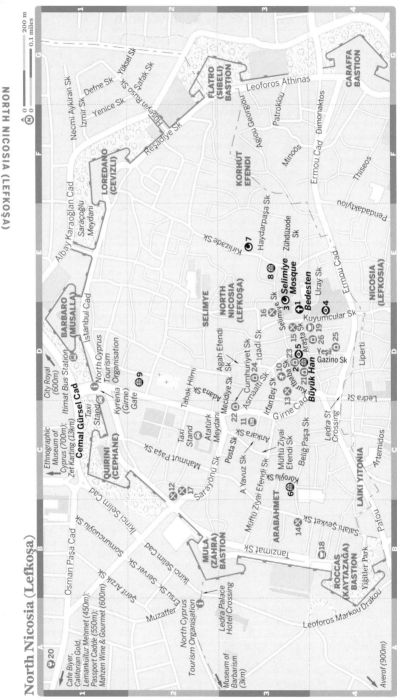

Mevlevi Shrine Museum MUSEUM

(Mevlevi Tekke Müzesi; Girne Cad; adult/child 5/3TL; ☉9am-12.30pm & 1.30-4.45pm Jun–mid-Sep, shorter hours rest of the year) The Mevlevi Shrine Museum is a former 17th-century *tekke* (Muslim shrine) of the mystic Islamic sect known as the Mevlevi order or, more famously, the whirling dervishes. Their spiritual philosophy, which started in the Turkish town of Konya, is based on the mystical branch of Islam called Sufism. This fascinating museum also houses a room with the coffins of the 16 Mevlevi sheiks.

The most captivating part of the museum is the former kitchen of the *tekke*, the centre of the hierarchical order in which the dervishes lived and moved from 'interns' to achieving dervish status. Each new intern would have to prove himself worthy by taking on the role of a kitchen servant for several years; at meal times, he would silently stand in the corner, watching out for subtle signals indicating the dervishes' needs. Lifting a piece of bread indicated that the dervish was thirsty and more water was needed.

Outside in the courtyard is a collection of Muslim tombstones.

Dervish Pasha Museum MUSEUM

(Derviş Paşa Konaği; Beliğ Paşa Sk; adult/child 5/3TL; ☉9am-12.30pm & 1.30-4.45pm Jun–mid-Sep, shorter hours rest of the year) This small ethnographic museum is housed in a 19th-century mansion. Built in 1807, it belonged to a wealthy Turkish Cypriot, Derviş Paşa, who published Cyprus' first Turkish-language newspaper.

The house became an ethnographic museum in 1988. Household goods, including an old loom, glassware and ceramics, are displayed in former servants' quarters on the ground floor. Upstairs is a rich display of embroidered Turkish costumes.

In the far corner, there's a a sumptuous *selamlık* (a retiring room for the owner of the mansion and his guests), replete with sofas and nargileh (Middle Eastern water pipes), and even some guests, in the form of eerie mannequins dressed up in suits.

Haydarpasha Mosque MOSQUE

(Camii Haydarpaşa; Kirlizade Sk; ☉9am-1pm & 2.30-5pm Mon-Fri, 9am-1pm Sat) FREE Originally built as the 14th-century Church of St Catherine, this mosque now functions as an art gallery. It's the second most important Gothic structure in North Nicosia after the Selimiye Mosque. The ornate sculptures, both inside and out, sprout gargoyles, dragons, shields and human heads.

Lapidary Museum MUSEUM

(Taş Eserler Müzesi; Kirlizade Sk; ☉9am-3.30pm Mon-Wed & Fri, to 5pm Thu) FREE Housed in a lovely 15th-century building, exhibits here include a varied collection of sarcophagi, shields, steles and columns, and a Gothic window rescued from a Lusignan palace that once stood near Atatürk Meydanı.

Ethnographic Museum of Cyprus MUSEUM

(☎227 1785; Ecvet Yusuf Cad 56; admission 10TL; ☉9am-4pm Mon-Sat) Arts and crafts dating back over 150 years comprise the eclectic

---

North Nicosia (Lefkoşa)

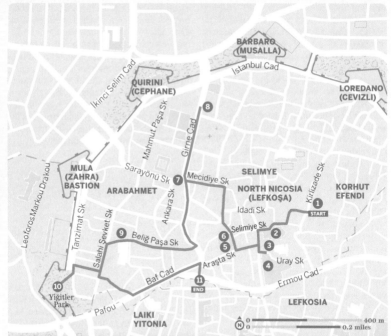

City Walk
Stepping Back in Time

START HAYDARPASHA MOSQUE
FINISH LEDRA ST CROSSING
DISTANCE 4KM; APPROXIMATELY TWO HOURS

Our self-paced walking tour starts at **1 Haydarpasha Mosque** (p153), originally the 14th-century Church of St Catherine. Close by you'll find the former Lusignan Church of Agia Sofia, now the **2 Selimiye Mosque** (p150), incongruous with its soaring minarets added after the Ottoman conquest.

Continue along Araşta Sokak towards the magnificent **3 Bedesten** (p151), across the street from the lively municipal market, the **4 Belediye Pazarı** (p151). Carry on down Araşta Sokak to the **5 Büyük Hammam** (p155) then head north to see magnificent Turkish caravanserai at the **6 Büyük Han** (p150) where you can peruse the craft shops and enjoy some refreshment.

Head west along Mecidiye Sokak, and make for the main square of **7 Atatürk Meydanı**, from where it's a short stroll north along Girne Caddesi to the Mevlevi Tekke, originally home of the whirling dervishes but now the **8 Mevlevi Shrine Museum** (p153).

Walk back down Girne Caddesi and turn right into Beliğ Paşa Sokak, in the lovely Arabahmet neighbourhood, where you can visit the **9 Dervish Pasha Museum** (p153), a small ethnographical collection housed in an old Turkish mansion. Follow Beliğ Paşa Sokak and turn left into Salahi Şevket Sokak, checking out the street life and the renovated or dilapidated old houses.

At the end of Salahi Şevket Sokak, you'll spot the small Yiğitler Park that sits atop the **10 Roccas (Kaytazağa) Bastion**. While crossing is easy now this was the only point along the whole of the Green Line where Turkish and Greek Cypriots could see each other at close quarters.

From here, trace your way along the Green Line on Baf Caddesi, noting the empty barrels and eerie atmosphere of the frontier, to surface at the **11 Ledra St crossing**.

private collection of the museum's amiable, English-speaking owner, Kibris Özei. Spread over three vast galleried floors, the exhibits include delicate Ottoman glass rosewater sprinklers, 19th-century carved Cypriot sideboards, traditional wedding dresses and a vast display of exquisite embroidery. A coffee shop serving light snacks is set to open.

Located a block north of Deniz Plaza, a taxi from Kyrenia gate should cost you around a 10TL.

Museum of Barbarism   MUSEUM
(Barbarlık Müzesi; Irhan Sk 2; ⊙9am-12.30pm & 1.30-4.45pm Jun-Sep, shorter hours rest of the year) FREE The gruesome posters and photographs that once greeted arrivals at the Ledra Palace Hotel crossing have been removed, but this museum has some similarly harrowing exhibits, including photo documentary displays, particularly of Turkish Cypriots murdered in the villages of Agios Sozomenos and Agios Vasilios.

The Museum of Barbarism is in a quiet suburb around 3km to the west of the Old City and takes a bit of seeking out. Best option is to hop in a taxi (around 12TL from the centre).

Cyprus Turkish Shadow Theatre   THEATRE
(⊉0542 850 3514; Büyük Han; 4TL; ⊙11am Sat; 📢) Considering the illustrious place of shadow theatre in Cyprus' history (it was introduced in the 16th century by the Turks), it's a surprise that this is the only place of its kind on the island. Shadow puppet plays take place on the 1st floor of the Büyük Han on Saturday at 11am in a tiny theatre with around 50 seats.

Puppeteer Mehmet Ertuğ laments the fact that he has so far found no successor, so don't miss an opportunity to see a show – kids *and* adults.

Büyük Hammam   STEAM BATHS
(Tarihi Büyük Hamam, Great Baths; Irfan Bey Sk 9; treatments 60-100TL; ⊙9am-3pm & 3.30-9pm) The Büyük Hammam baths are entered via a low ornate door, sunk 2m below street level. The door was originally part of the 14th-century Church of St George of the Latins. These days you can, more happily, choose from a choice of treatments, including mud baths, coffee-peeling and aromatherapy massage. Sessions are either for men, women or mixed. Wednesday and Saturday morning are for women only.

Inside is a nail that marks the height reached by the waters of the Pedieos River (Kanlı Dere), drowning about 3000 Lefkosians in 1330.

Zet Karting   KARTING
(⊉0533 866 6173; www.zetkarting.com; Lefkoşa-Güzelyurt Anayolu; per 10min 25-45TL; ⊙4pm-midnight Tue-Sun Jun–mid-Sep, shorter hours rest of the year) If you fancy yourself as a bit of a Formula 1 whiz, seek out this place which has a large and very professional-looking series of circuits. You can rent carts from 25TL for 10 minutes on the junior 300m course, 35TL for the medium 900m course, or 45TL on the 1200m professional circuit. Unwind in the Z1 Bar or Z1 Cafeteria.

Zet Karting is located on the road going north out of North Nicosia. At the roundabout, take the turn-off to Morfou (Güzelyurt); it's on the left, after the Alaykoy turnoff, around 13km from the Kyrenia Gate.

Eating

North Nicosia's eating scene is varied, with small kebab houses, *meyhane* (taverns), traditional restaurants, and chic, modern eateries. Lunchtime eating offers more choice in the Old City which, post sunset, grows very quiet and a little dark, so there aren't so many options. In the New City, Mehmet Akif Caddesi has several good restaurant choices for both lunch and dinner.

Old City

★Old Mosaic   TURKISH €
(⊉227 9551; Selimiye Meydani 4-5; meze dishes 5TL; ⊙10am-late) Head for the delightful interior patio with its tumbling bourgainvillea, terracotta pots, leafy plants and overall kitchen garden feel. Best choices are the meze dishes, like hummus, *patican salata* (eggplant in garlic), *pastirma* (spicy sausage) and *barbunya* (borlotti beans in olive oil). The same owners own the welcoming Old Mosaic Bar across the way.

Bereket   FAST FOOD €
(Irfan Bey Sk; pide & lahmacun 7-10TL; ⊙7am-1.30pm) A rough-and-ready kiosk a few metres away from the grand Büyük Han, Bereket is run by Ilker, who makes the best *pide* and *lahmacun* (Turkish-style pizza, topped with minced lamb and parsley) in town in his stone oven. There are a couple of chairs outside or you can munch on the go.

ℹ️ STREET WISE

North Nicosia is a safe city at any time of the day, and you should feel no concern about walking the streets.

At night, the Old City can seem uncomfortably quiet, especially for urban folk, and visitors may feel intimidated walking alone along dimly lit and often narrow streets. It's best to avoid them if you feel uncomfortable. The areas abutting the Green Line look threatening, with large black-and-red signs that clearly forbid photography or trespassing in the buffer zone.

Do not take photographs on the Roccas (Kaytazağa) Bastion, at the western end of the Old City limits, where you can still look over into Greek Nicosia (Lefkosia). Despite the loosening of the border-crossing laws, the buffer zone is still a military area. Watchful soldiers stationed not so obviously on the bastion may confront you and confiscate your camera.

★ **Boghjalian** TURKISH €€
(☎ 228 0700; Salahi Ševket Sk; meze dishes 10TL; ⊘noon-3.30pm & 7-11pm Mon-Sat) Housed in the former mansion of a wealthy Armenian, Boghjalian is a quality, popular restaurant. The set menu consists of either meze or mixed kebab, and food is served in a leafy courtyard or a choice of two elegant dining rooms. Try the sublime *ceviz macanu* (green walnuts and almonds with lemon, sugar and cloves). Reservations recommended.

Sabor MEDITERRANEAN €€
(Selimiye Sk 29; mains from 13TL; ⊘11am-midnight Mon-Sat) Right across from the Selimiye Mosque, this is North Nicosia's best choice for those who just can't quite handle another kebab. The menu specialises in Italian and Spanish food, with some Asian noodle dishes. The portions are generous, the prices are fair and the staff (and resident cat population) are friendly.

Bay Kahkaha TURKISH €€
(Queen's Pub; Tanzimat Sk 166; mains 18TL; ⊘noon-late Mon-Sat) Turkish Cypriot owner Mehmet returned from several years in Australia to open up this restaurant and bar. The evocative setting is a 1928 building with original tiles, several intimate rooms and a garden dining space with palms and olive trees. The cuisine is traditional, with *kah-kah tavuk dolma* (traditional stuffed chicken with mushrooms) a specialty.

The Queen's Pub, which shares the venue, is a vibrant night-time venue with live music in summer.

Sedirhan TURKISH €€
(Büyük Han; mains 18TL; ⊘8am-7.30pm Mon-Sat) This cafe is the best place to eat dishes such as pasta with artichokes and Turkish ravioli, while you admire the beauty of the Büyük Han; the Sedirhan enjoys prime position in the courtyard. You can also enjoy a coffee or a beer, and simple traditional local dishes like *börek* (meat or cheese rolled in thin pastry).

✗ New City

The main restaurant (and shopping) street in the new part of town is Mehmet Akif Caddesi, home to the city's most sophisticated restaurants, with at least a dozen options and an emphasis on modern Cypriot and international cuisine. There are laid-back bars here too, including at least one with Irish beer on tap. For parking, head for the residential side streets.

Lemankültur Mehmet INTERNATIONAL €
(www.lmk.com.tr; Mehmet Akif Caddesi 80; breakfast TL8-10; ⊘8am-midnight; 🖥) Not the place to come if you feel a migraine coming on. The decor is a full on, playful combination of pop art and cartoons in bright primary colours and patterns. Best meal to enjoy to the max is breakfast with a massive choice ranging from tasty filled bagels to American-style pancakes and omelettes .

★ **Passport Cadde** INTERNATIONAL €€
(www.caddepassport.com; Mehmet Akif Caddesi 88; mains 16TL; ⊘9am-1am Mon-Sat; 🖥) One of the most packed out and justifiably fashionable restaurants on this foodie street. It has a round-the-clock DJ, a vast interior and terrace seating space, and a menu that includes Asian-inspired cuisine, Italian choices, curries, fajitas and some good salads.

Seli
TURKISH €€

(Pencizade Sk 5; mains 15TYL; ⊘9am-midnight Mon-Sat) A little out of the way but this welcoming place attracts a local following with its menu of traditional dishes and ambience of white tableclothed elegance. The sunken kitchen allows you to watch (and savour the aromas) of the kebabs and meats being spit-roasted. Also on the menu are lighter bites, including pitta bread sandwiches.

Califorian Gold
INTERNATIONAL €€

(Mehmet Akif Caddesi 74; mains 14TL; ⊘8am-midnight; 🖉) This is one of the most popular restaurants among this energetic stretch of eateries. The sprawling terrace and two floors of tables are generally packed with a youthful, well-heeled crowd, here for the tasty international cuisine, including fajitas, pasta, steaks, kebabs and interesting salads, like a tasty vegetarian choice with lentils, red peppers and goats cheese.

Note that the name is intentionally spelled this way to avoid any potential copyright infringements from the US sunshine state.

Mahzen Wine & Gourmet
INTERNATIONAL €€

(www.mahzenwineandgourmet.com; Mehmet Akif Caddesi 75; mains 14TL; ⊘11am-11pm) In a historic building backing onto the old railway station, which dates to 1905 (it ceased operation in 1951). The menu includes pasta and chicken dishes with various sauces, and the excellent wine list offers vintages from South Africa, France and Italy.

🍷 Drinking & Nightlife

Turkish Cypriots will themselves admit that nightlife in their capital is not all that hot, at least in the Old City. In the New City, Mehmet Akif Caddesi is reasonably animated, but if you're looking for more vigour and choice, head over the Green Line or to Kyrenia, 25km away.

A popular drinking area in the Old City is behind the Belediye Pazarı within the restored old market building. Although it resembles a kind of warehouse, with tall ceilings and low-hanging lamps, the space has an upbeat, modern look. There are several bars inside and plenty of places to puff on a nargileh.

The Büyük Han has live music on Tuesday and Thursday evenings in its central courtyard.

Cafe Biyer
BAR

(Mehmet Akif Caddesi 61; ⊘11am-midnight; 🖹) A cosy cosmopolitan-style bar with live music Friday and Saturday and an impressive range of 14 specialty cocktails and eight brands of tequila. Bar snacks, including cheese platters and wraps, are also available or you can head to the swankier Biyer restaurant next door.

Özerlat
CAFE

(Araşta Sk 73; coffee 2.50TL; ⊘9am-7pm Mon, Tue, Thu & Fri, to 1pm Wed & Sat) This cafe and shop has been around since 1935 and is famous for its own brand of coffee which is even imported to the US. The friendly owner makes her own delicious cakes each day.

Street Corner Pub
BAR

(Osman Paşa Caddesi; ⊘noon-2am) Look for the pink Cadillac poised precariously on the roof at this popular Irish pub with its frothy ale on tap and live music on Wednesdays.

Atolye Cadi Kazani Cafe
CAFE

(Tanzimat Sk 77; ⊘5pm-1am; 🖹) Artist-run small cafe and bar tucked down a side street. The owner's artwork is on the walls and there is regular live jazz which accentuates the laid-back, cosmo mood of the place.

Solomajia
CLUB

(☑227 7901; Kurtuluş Meydanı; ⊘10pm-late) On the northern side of town, this is a popular venue for those who like some skirt-swirling salsa, starting with a 90-minute warm-up class, followed by a live band playing Latin, reggae and pop.

🛍 Shopping

The Büyük Han is the best place for tourists to pick up some memorable souvenirs, with genuine arts and crafts for sale.

ℹ SHOPPERS BEWARE

A word of warning: if you're visiting from the South and decide to go on a shopping spree in the North, or vice versa, beware the Greek Cypriot customs regulations: you can't take more than 200 cigarettes and 1L of alcohol or wine, plus €100 worth of other goods across the North–South border. So don't go indulging in expensive carpets!

Koza   SILK
(Büyük Han; ⊙10am-7pm) Cyprus' heritage of producing silk from silkworms and the once ubiquitous mulberry tree comes alive in this shop where owner Munise and her elderly mother hand weave the silk patterns. The patterns were traditionally used for picture frames, or simply as framed wall decorations themselves.

Senay Erkut   CRAFTS
(Büyük Han; ⊙10am-7pm) Beautiful handmade ceramic jewellery with a floral theme. Make fabulous, inexpensive and unusual gifts.

Shiffa Home   ORGANIC PRODUCTS
(Büyük Han; ⊙10am-7pm) Shiffa's owner makes handmade soaps, jams and preserves. She also sells and advises on local herbal and aromatherapy remedies.

Yumurtacioglu   SWEETS
(Bekediye Pazari; ⊙8am-7pm Mon-Sat) You can't miss the mouthwatering display of Turkish delight outside this shop, located near the main entrance of the market. This is where the locals shop for their sweet treats and it's a whole different taste experience to those suspiciously cheap boxes of the sugary delicacy sold at the souvenir shops.

Rüstem Kitabevi   BOOKS
(☑228 3506; Girne Caddesi 22; ⊙9am-7pm Mon, Tue & Thu, to 1pm Wed & Sat) This well-supplied store, with old and new books, and many English-language reads, plus a rack of all kinds of magazines. Also has a branch of Gloria Jeans Coffee, with 14 caffeine fixes to choose from, and a shady outside patio.

THC   CRAFTS
(Asmaalti Sk; ⊙9am-7pm Mon, Tue, Thu & Fri, to 1pm Wed & Sat) Specialises in stunning Iranian glassware and ceramics in that distinctive iridescent blue. Can arrange shipping.

Yağcioğlu   CRAFTS
(Yeşil Gazino Sk 46; ⊙9am-7pm Mon, Tue, Thu & Fri, to 1pm Wed & Sat) Hidden away among the endless stalls selling lycra leggings and similar is this shop that has been selling buttons since the 1950s. The choice is wonderfully diverse including translucent and delicate, big and brassy and enticingly retro. Local crafts also sold.

ⓘ Information

EMERGENCY
Call ☑155.
Police Station (☑228 3311; Atatürk Meydanı)

INTERNET ACCESS
Wi-fi is almost nonexistent in cafes in the North, so you'll be bound to use the internet cafes.
Orbit Internet Cafe (Girne Caddesi 180; per hr 2TL; ⊙24hr) Busy and central.

MEDICAL SERVICES
Poliklinik (☑227 3996; Gazeteci Kemal Aşik Caddesi) Where foreigners can seek medical treatment.

MONEY
You can change your money into Turkish lira (TL) at any of the money-changing facilities just past the passport-control booth at both the Ledra Palace Hotel and Ledra St crossings. ATMs can be found at **TC Ziraat Bankası** (Girne Caddesi) at the northern end of the road, or at **Kıbrıs Vakıflar Bankası** (Atatürk Meydanı). Both change foreign currency, as do private exchange offices nearby.

TOURIST INFORMATION
North Cyprus Tourism Organisation (NCTO; ☑227 2994; www.northcyprus.org) Kyrenia Gate (☑227 299; www.northcyprus.org; Kyrenia Gate; ⊙8am-5pm); Ledra Palace Hotel crossing (☑227 2994; www.northcyprus. org; Ledra Palace Hotel crossing; ⊙9am-5pm Mon-Sat, to 2pm Sun) The most useful office is at the Kyrenia Gate where the staff are English speaking and helpful.

ⓘ Getting There & Away

AIR
Ercan airport (Tymvou; ☑231 4703) is about 14km northeast of North Nicosia and is linked to the city by an expressway. Many visitors to the North now fly to Larnaka airport, as the flights are direct and less subject to delays. There are scheduled flights to London and several destinations in Turkey from Ercan airport. All charter flights operate from Ercan, although occasional flights are diverted to the military airport at **Geçitkale** (Lefkoniko; ☑227 9420; Lefkoniko), closer to Famagusta, when Ercan is being serviced.

Turkish Airlines (Türk Hava Yolları, THY; ☑227 1061; www.turkishairlines.com; Mehmet Akif Caddesi 32), **Pegasus Airlines** (www.flypgs. com) and **Onur Air** (www.www.onurair.com) are the main airlines that operate regular flights to Ercan, via Turkey.

BUS

The long-distance bus station is on the corner of Atatürk Caddesi and Gazeteci Kemal Aşik Caddesi in the New City. Buses to major towns leave from here. You may prefer the bus to the sometimes hair-raising rides in service taxis or *dolmuş* (minibuses).

CAR & MOTORCYCLE

Drivers and riders will enter North Nicosia via one of two main roads that lead directly to the Old City. If you come from Famagusta or Ercan airport, you will enter North Nicosia via Mustafa Ahmet Ruso Caddesi and then Gazeteci Kemal Aşik Caddesi. This road leads directly to Kyrenia Gate. Arriving from Kyrenia, you will enter North Nicosia via Tekin Yurdabay Caddesi and eventually Bedrettin Demirel Caddesi, which also leads towards Kyrenia Gate.

If you are entering North Nicosia from the Republic of Cyprus, the car crossing point is at Agios Dometios, west of the city. The easiest way into the Old City is to turn immediately right after passing the Ledra Palace Hotel crossing and enter via Memduh Asar Sokak. Turn left onto Tanzimat Sokak as soon as you cross the moat and you will reach Kyrenia Gate after about 200m.

Parking is usually not a problem, though finding a place in the Old City may get tricky if you arrive late in the morning on a working day. If you arrive early, you can easily park on Girne Caddesi.

SERVICE TAXI & MINIBUS

Minibuses to local destinations and further afield start from various stations outside the Venetian walls and from the Itimat bus station, just outside the Kyrenia Gate. The most con-venient stop for service taxis to Kyrenia is just southeast of the Mevlevi Shrine Museum. City destinations include Famagusta (15TL, one hour) and Kyrenia (12TL, 30 minutes). Service taxis also leave from the Itimat bus station.

ⓘ Getting Around

TO/FROM THE AIRPORT

Kibhas airport shuttle (www.kibhas.org) has regular buses (35 minutes, 8TL) that run to Gazeteci Kemal Aşik Caddesi in the New City. A taxi from Kyrenia Gate to the airport will cost around 40TL.

BUS

While there are public buses in North Nicosia, they tend to mainly service the suburbs outside the Old City. Buses leave from near Kyrenia Gate.

CAR

For local inexpensive car hire **Sun Rent a Car** (☑ 227 2303; www.sunrentacar.com; Abdi Ip-ekçi Caddesi 10) is a good choice. If you're coming from the South, you can call ahead and see if they'll pick you up from Kyrenia Gate. Rates start at around 85TL a day. In high season there is a minimum hire period of three days.

TAXI

There are plenty of taxi ranks in North Nicosia; the most convenient and easiest to find are at Atatürk Meydanı and Kyrenia Gate. A ride to anywhere in town should cost from between 5TL and 10TL, and the drivers are usually good about turning on the meter.

Among the more reliable taxi companies in North Nicosia are **Ankara Taxi** (☑ 227 1788), **Özner Taxi** (☑ 227 4012), **Terminal Taxi** (☑ 228 4909) and **Yılmaz Taxi** (☑ 227 3036).

Kyrenia (Girne) & the North

Best Places to Eat

➡ İkimiz (p165)

➡ Tervetuloa Restaurant (p166)

➡ Kybele (p172)

➡ St Kathleen's Restaurant (p169)

➡ Kıbrıs Evi (p165)

Best Places to Stay

➡ Bellapais Gardens (p212)

➡ Nostalgia (p211)

➡ White Pearl Hotel (p211)

➡ Lapida Garden (p212)

Why Go?

Castles cling to craggy hilltops. Lonely churches peek out amid wild-flowered slopes. Fields of gnarled olive trees march across the coastline where the harbour town of Kyrenia, backed by the imposing silhouette of jagged mountain ranges, looks out towards the sea. This bite-sized region combines the best of Cyprus' natural charm with oodles of history.

Most visit for sun and sea holidays which has led to a flurry of less-than-pretty developments being flung up along the shore. Ignore the concrete-block oddities though and you'll find there's plenty left to explore. From Bellapais Abbey to the fairytale-fluff of St Hilarion Castle, there are ruins with million-dollar views galore.

This region is famed for its outdoor potential with hiking, turtle-spotting, orchid-hunting and bird watching on the agenda. The trails are under-promoted and gloriously quiet; a perfect incentive to get your walking shoes on and discover them before everyone else.

When to Go

➡ From February to April a vibrant palette of wildflowers and rare orchids bloom across Kyrenia's coastline, splashing the rolling fields with a paintbox of colours.

➡ April is also the prime hiking period with gloriously clear and warm weather nearly guaranteed.

➡ In May musicians and singers serenade crowds amid the Gothic arcades where Augustinian monks once trod at the Bellapais Music Festival.

➡ Turtle nesting season begins in June and continues through August.

➡ July and August's fierce humidity is the perfect time to take to the water. Hop on a gulet (Turkish wooden ship) and sail out of Kyrenia's harbour to catch a sea breeze.

Kyrenia (Girne) & the North Highlights

1 Climbing up onto the **Kyrenia Castle** (p163) ramparts before sitting back on the Old Harbour to watch sunset cast its golden glow across the Mediterranean.

2 Getting your literary-pilgrimage fix wandering the lanes of **Bellapais** (p171), then exploring the village's beautiful medieval abbey.

3 Reliving the golden days of hermit monks and shining armoured knights at **St Hilarion Castle** (p170).

4 Delving even further into history with a visit to **Ancient Vouni** (p178) and then taking the precarious curving road up the cliff to **Ancient Soloi** (p177).

5 Savouring bird's-eye views of the coast from the heights of **Buffavento Castle** (p172).

KYRENIA (GIRNE)

POP 33,200

Kyrenia has always been governed by the sea. Its natural harbour, once so attractive to those with empirical ambitions, is today just as popular with visitors whose only desire is to stroll the seaside strand and hop on a boat cruise around the bay. Climb up the honey-coloured fortifications of the Byzantine castle, lording-it-up over the horseshoe-shaped inlet, and stare down at the fishing boats bobbing in the water. Then join the flocks of day-trippers and travellers taking up residence outside the former carob warehouses that house harbour-side cafes and restaurants to ponder this ancient port's mammoth history while staring out to sea.

The traders and exporters that once bustled through here may be long gone – replaced by boat-excursion and restaurant touts – but you can still catch a whiff of the days long-gone by wandering the narrow twisty lanes of the Old Town which hug the harbour. Stroll the area in the early morning before business starts for the day and you'll experience Kyrenia at its most picturesque. Or join everyone else promenading shoreside in the evening to witness the town's buzzing holidaymaker modern soul.

History

Once one of the ancient city kingdoms of Cyprus, Kyrenia was founded by Mycenaean Greeks around 1200 BC. From this point Kyrenia's history is, in essence, the history of its castle. Little more is known about the town until the castle's construction by the Byzantines in the 7th century to ward off continuing Arab raids.

In 1191 the castle was captured by Richard the Lionheart of England, on his way to Jerusalem and a third crusade. The castle was then used as both a residence and prison. It was sold to the Knights Templar and then gifted to Guy de Lusignan when he became king of Cyprus.

In the 14th century the Venetians extended the castle and built the bulbous sea-facing fortifications still seen today. During Ottoman rule, changes to the castle were again made, while Kyrenia itself functioned primarily as the island's only northern port.

Kyrenia has long since given up this port role, as the Old Harbour's size and depth only allow it to service tourist crafts, fishing boats and the small yachts commonly found in its cluttered quays. Two kilometres to the east of Kyrenia, there is now a large purpose-built harbour created to receive commercial and passenger ships from Turkey.

Kyrenia (Girne)

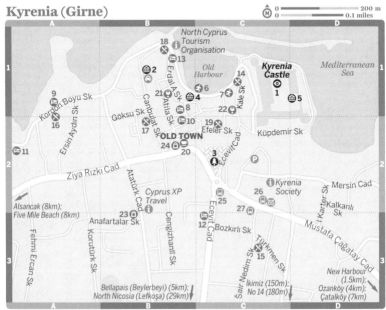

During British rule, the town became a favourite with retiring (ex-colonial) British civil servants. When Turkey invaded Cyprus in 1974, it used the beaches to the west of Kyrenia as the prime location for landing its army. Almost all Greek Cypriots and many British retirees fled.

Now, 40 years later, Kyrenia supports a large and growing tourist industry, mainly from Britain, Germany and Turkey.

◉ Sights

The compact Old Harbour and Old Town district just behind the bay are home to Kyrenia's major sights.

★**Kyrenia Castle** HISTORIC SITE
(Girne Kalesi; Old Harbour; adult/student 12/2TL; ⏱9am-7pm Jun-Sep, to 4pm Oct-May) If the grand fortifications of Kyrenia Castle could talk, they could sure tell some tales. First built by the Byzantines – possibly over the remains of an earlier Roman fort – every era of conquerors from Richard the Lionheart to the Ottomans has added their own touch to its bulk.

A large rectangular structure, the castle contains a cistern, dungeon, chapel and museum, though the real highlight is walking along the ramparts high above the harbour.

You enter the castle via the stone bridge over the former moat, which leads to the small 12th-century Byzantine **Chapel of St George**. Its broken mosaics and Corinthian columns, originally outside the walls, were incorporated into the larger structure by the Venetians.

The western side of the inner castle is home to the infamous dungeon where King Peter I's pregnant mistress, Joanna L'Aleman, was tortured by order of the king's jealous wife, Queen Eleanor.

Across the courtyard, the northeast Lusignon bastion tower features mannequins dressed in armour. The Venetian bastion tower is in the southeast corner. Between the towers are two small museums.

You can walk between the castle's four towers via the handrailed ramparts, but follow the marked routes as some sections can be quite dangerous. Keep younger children close by at all times. Views of the Old Harbour are fantastic from here, especially in the morning light.

➡ Shipwreck Museum
The Kyrenia Shipwreck chamber contains the remains of the oldest shipwreck recovered from Cypriot waters. This wood-hulled (Aleppo pine) Greek merchant ship sank off the Kyrenia coast around 300 BC, and was discovered by a local diver in 1967. Its cargo consisted of amphorae, almonds, grain, wine and millstones from the Greek islands of Samos, Rhodes and Kos. Its crew most

Kyrenia (Girne)

likely traded along the coast of Anatolia and as far as the islands of the Dodecanese in Greece.

Evidence suggests that the boat, 80 years old at the time, sank because of piracy. Much of its cargo seems to have been plundered, and it has what appear to be spear marks in its hull. A curse tablet was also found with the wreck. At the time, pirates believed that placing these tablets on a sinking ship would conceal its fate, by keeping the wreck forever at the bottom of the sea.

An excellent modern reconstruction of the ship (using the same materials) can be viewed in Agia Napa's Thalassa Municipal Museum of the Sea.

➡ **Gallery of Tomb-Finds**

This small but interesting exhibit from the neolithic and Bronze ages as well as the Hellenistic and Byzantine periods includes amphorae, gold jewellery and ancient coins. Another display shows a reconstruction of the Neolithic II Period houses (4500–3900 BC) made from mud and stone, found at the archaeological site of Ayios Epiktitos Vrysi, just outside Çatalköy.

Old Town   NEIGHBOURHOOD

Wrapping around the Old Harbour, between Canbulat Caddesi and Kale Sokak,

---

KYRENIA'S CAROB HISTORY

The Old Harbour may be chock-a-block full of restaurants and cafes today but the beautiful stone buildings that line the waterfront once played an important role as carob warehouses for the port's carob industry.

Carob has been cultivated in Cyprus since the 1st century AD and was one of the island's major exports from the medieval era right up to the end of the British Mandate period. As the Kyrenia region harvested nearly 30% of Cyprus' carob tree pods, Kyrenia port became the centre for the trade.

The harbour-front buildings were used as warehouses to store the carob (as well as other exports such as olive oil and cotton) before being shipped out to Europe. Although the international carob trade collapsed in the 1960s, carob continues to be harvested in North Cyprus to be made into the beloved *pekmez* (molasses) condiment.

---

the diminutive Old Town is Kyrenia's most atmospheric area for a wander. Its winding alleyways hold a jumble of abandoned old stone buildings slowly slipping into disrepair, mixed with newer concrete houses.

Walk down Ağa Cafer Paşa Sokak to see **Agha Cafer Paşa Mosque** (built in 1589) and the dilapidated remains of the 16th-century **Chysopolitissa Church**. There is also an ancient Greco-Roman tomb on Canbulat Caddesi.

Cyprus House   MUSEUM

(Old Harbour; adult/student 5/2TL; ⊙9am-6pm Mon-Sat) This lovingly restored old carob warehouse on the harbour contains interesting ethnographic exhibits of traditional clothing, furniture and Cypriot textile craft work. There are also displays on the harbour's history as a major trading port exporting carob to Europe.

Archangelos Michael
Icon Museum   MUSEUM

(Canbulat Caddesi; admission 5TL; ⊙8am-3.30pm Mon-Wed, Fri & Sat, to 5pm Thu) The 19th-century St Archangelos Michael Church, easily distinguished by its prominent bell tower, displays icons dating from the 18th and 19th centuries. The collection is made up of icons salvaged from Orthodox churches throughout North Cyprus. Notable depictions include Saint George and the Dragon, the beheading of John the Baptist, and Virgin and child.

🏃 Activities

Scuba diving and boat trips are the most popular activities in town.

The Old Harbour boat-cruise scene is like a market where everyone is selling the same thing. For 50TL to 60TL you can expect to get a day cruise on a gulet (Turkish wooden ship) with two swimming/snorkelling stops, usually finishing with an on-board barbecue lunch (drinks are extra). The boats typically leave at 10.30am and return at 5pm, taking up to 20 passengers.

Cyprus Wildlife Ecology   OUTDOOR ACTIVITIES

(📱224 0850; www.cypruswildlifeecology.com) 🐾 These excellent birdwatching trips are led by conservation-biologist duo Robin Snape and Damla Beton. Hugely involved with the North Cyprus Society for Protection of Birds, these two design tailored trips to spot the incredible wealth of bird life in both the Kyrenia and Famagusta areas.

Highly recommended for anyone interested in discovering North Cyprus' wealth of wildlife and nature.

Aphrodite Boat Charters & Fishing
BOAT TRIPS

(☏0533 868 0943; musa-aksoy@hotmail.co.uk; Old Harbour; cruises per person €35, fishing trips per person €70; ☺Mar-Oct) This gulet offers cruises around the bay and fishing excursions. Captain Musa Aksoy was the first to start sport-fishing tours in North Cyprus, so if you're after hooking the big catch, you're in safe hands.

Musa's leisure cruises (for up to 12 passengers) include snorkelling and swimming at isolated bays that the bigger boats don't go to.

It's a more intimate and peaceful way to explore the Kyrenia coastline than on the party boats.

Highline Tandem
PARAGLIDING

(☏0542 855 5672; www.highlineparagliding.com; Old Harbour; adult incl transport, flight & insurance €89) Run by a New Zealander-Cypriot couple, Highline helped a 100-year-old Scottish woman paraglide her way into the *Guinness Book of Records* as the oldest woman ever to take up the adventure sport. Weather permitting, tandem fights run throughout the year from an altitude of 750m, allowing incredible panoramas across the countryside.

Ladyboss Fishing
FISHING

(☏0542 855 5672; www.fishingnorthcyprus.com; Old Harbour; per person €60) The same team behind Highline paragliding also operate these great fishing trips which set out to sea for some angling action on the 34ft *Ladyboss*. Trips are usually five hours long and your catch of the day can be cooked for you afterwards.

Scuba Cyprus
DIVING

(☏0533 865 2317; www.scubacyprus.com; Camelot Beach, Alsancak; 1 dive €22, 5-dive package €105; ☺9am-5pm) Has regular PADI and SSI diving courses as well as good value dive packages and dive cruises. The boat is often moored in Kyrenia's Old Harbour while the main office is based 12km west of Kyrenia.

Amphora Diving
DIVING

(☏0542 851 4924; www.amphoradiving.com; Kervansaray Beach, Karaoğlanoğlu; 1 dive €30, Zenobia Wreck excursion €115) As well as operating all the usual PADI and BSAC courses, Amphora Diving operates regular *Zenobia*

wreck excursions and dive safaris. They're based approximately 6km west of Kyrenia.

Örnek Holidays
HIKING

(☏815 8969; www.ornekholidays.com; Dedekorkut Plaza 13, Karakum; ☺9am-5pm Mon-Sat) Specialists in North Cyprus walking and hiking tours, with excellent guides who have expertise in flora and bird life as well as history.

✗ Eating

The most atmospheric place to dine in Kyrenia is the Old Harbour. Although many of the restaurants depend on their setting rather than their menus to get you in the door, there are a couple of gems among the more mundane places. There are also some excellent restaurants in Kyrenia's old Turkish Quarter.

Self-caterers should head to central and well-stocked supermarket **Ordu Pazarı** (Atatürk Caddesi ; ☺8am-9pm).

Old Harbour & Turkish Quarter

Özgulen Restaurant
TURKISH €

(☏868 6872; Canbulat Sokak; lahmacun 3.50TL; mains 9-16TL; ☺11am-10.30pm) This cheerful canteen is the place to come for tasty, filling Turkish staples of lentil soup, *lahmacun* (Turkish pizza) kebab plates and *dürüm* (kebab wraps).

★İkimiz
CYPRIOT €€

(Meşeli Sokak 22, Turkish Quarter; mains 15-25TL; ☺11.30am-2.30pm & 6.30-11pm Mon-Sat; ☏) The mother and daughter duo behind this cute as a button restaurant dish up Cypriot soul food at its best. The small menu (which changes regularly) features hearty and wholesome specialities such as *molehiya* (mallow-leaf stew) and *pirohu* (haloumi ravioli). To find it, take the second left-hand turn on Şair Nedim Sokak.

Kıbrıs Evi
CYPRIOT €€

(Kale Sokak, Old Harbour; mains 16-18TL; ☺10.30am-11pm; ☏) Traditional Cypriot cooking is dished up with unbeatable harbourside views at this restaurant just beside the castle. Grab a table on the rooftop, or on one of the teensy balconies for panoramic dining at its best. Try the *bumbar* (sausages) and the stuffed artichokes for a true feast of Cyprus' flavours.

Corner Restaurant INTERNATIONAL €€
(Old Harbour; mains 16-30TL; ☺10.30am-11pm; 🛜🍽) This welcoming harbourside restaurant serves the best coffee you're going to get in Kyrenia so those after a caffiene-fix should make this their harbour hang-out. The menu of seafood and European-modern dishes with some contemporary tweaks on Turkish flavours is also a winner.

Kyrenia Tavern CYPRIOT €€
(Türkmen Sokak, Turkish Quarter; meals 30TL; ☺6.30-11pm) If you like it authentic and rustic this is the spot for you. Serving simple and tasty Cypriot favourites: meze, moussaka and *kleftiko* (clay-pot cooked lamb), usually prepared daily. It's on the first left-hand corner of Şair Nedim Sokak, after the small fire station.

No 14 INTERNATIONAL €€
(Yazıcızade Sokak 14, Turkish Quarter; mains 18-28TL; ☺6.30-11pm Mon-Sat) This poolside garden restaurant offers home-cooked delights such as pork with peppercorn and stuffed calamari. Its simple menu is accompanied with excellent service. Follow the signs from Namik Kemal Sokak and turn left at the mosque.

Niazi's Restaurant & Bar TURKISH €€
(Kordon Boyu Caddesi; kebab 20-30TL; ☺11am-11pm) Meat-lover's heaven, Niazi's is a favourite spot for a kebab-fix. Turkish staples of *Adana kebap, köfte* (meatballs) and *pathcan kebap* (aubergine kebab) rule the menu as well as the Cypriot *sheftalia* (spiced-mince sausages, called *şeftalı* in Turkish).

Six Brothers Restaurant TURKISH €€
(Kordon Boyu Caddesi; mains 18-35TL; ☺10.30am-midnight) With a menu like a novella, Six Brothers offers up a mind-boggling array of meze, kebabs, fish and international dishes – plus friendly service. The best tables are located outside, across from the restaurant, overlooking the bay.

Stone Arch INTERNATIONAL €€€
(Efeler Sokak 13, Old Harbour; mains 30-40TL; ☺6.30-11pm; 🛜🍽) A top spot for a special meal, Stone Arch is all starched white table cloths and romantic lighting. The small menu offers seafood and steaks, there's a decent wine list, and the service is unobtrusive.

🍴 Out of Town

Tervetuloa Restaurant TURKISH €€
(Ufuk Sokak, Alsancak; meals 25-35TL; ☺11am-3pm & 6-11pm) If you like your meze don't miss Tervetuloa. It's a charmingly casual place with little pretension that serves up some of the freshest, tastiest meze spreads in North Cyprus. Just off the main coast road, it's about 10km west of Kyrenia.

Jashan's INDIAN €€
(Karaoğlanoğlu Caddesi; mains 18-25TL; ☺noon-3pm & 6-11pm Sat-Thu, 6-11pm Fri) If you're hankering for a taste of the subcontinent, Jashan's has everything from kormas and chicken tikka to more authentic Punjabi meals. It's set back off the main road, approximately 4km west of Kyrenia.

Çatalköy Kebapcısı TURKISH €€€
(Uğur Mumcu Bulvarı, Çatalköy; set menu 40TL; ☺6-11pm) Possibly one of the best kebab houses in North Cyprus. Bring your appetite because the full set-menu kebab blow-out of 10 meze and seven different chargrilled meats will satisfy even the most hungry. Its on the main road, about 7km east of Kyrenia.

🍸 Drinking & Nightlife

The harbour area is where most travellers in Kyrenia congregate for a drink. The outdoor tables spread across the waterfront are just the ticket for a coffee break or beer. If you're looking for something less low key, some of the bigger beach resorts along the coast have attached clubs. Most are quite cheesy. Single male travellers should be aware that they are unlikely to gain entry to a nightclub unless they bring a female companion.

Ali's Special Cafe CAFE
(Ziya Rızkı Caddesi; ☺10am-7pm) Take a break with a syrupy Cypriot coffee, or freshly squeezed orange juice, at this cute little place under a shady tree and watch the world go by.

Ego Bar BAR
(Doğan Türk Sokak, Old Town; ☺6pm-2am) With its chilled-out atmosphere, this is a great spot for an evening drink within the stone walls of an open-air courtyard. In summer it showcases live bands, playing a mix of jazz, rock, blues and soul.

Casablanca
BAR

(Atila Sokak; ☺8pm-late Thu-Sat) This little bar in the Old Town has decently priced drinks and attracts a good mix of locals, expats and travellers.

Escape Beach
CLUB

(www.escapebeachclub.com; Yavuz Çıkarma Beach, Alsancak; 10pm-late Thu-Sat) Located right on the waterfront, Escape Beach gets packed with clubbers enjoying a mix of R&B, hip-hop and Turkish pop. It's 10km west of Kyrenia, just off the main road.

Ice Lounge
CLUB

(Yavuz Çıkarma Beach, Alsancak; ☺10.30pm-5am) Found above Yavuz Çıkarma beach, in the Alsancak quarter, this club is one of the most popular spots for nightlife. Iridescent lights glow on its outdoor bars and stage. Also plays host to international DJs during the summer.

🛍 Shopping

Ziya Rızkı Caddesi is the main shopping street.

Round Tower
CRAFTS

(Ziya Rızkı Caddesi; ☺10am-5.30pm Mon-Sat) Inside the restored Lusignan-era Round Tower, is this small art-and-crafts shop with a selection of interesting souvenirs including books, local art, old photographs and ceramics. There's also a section of secondhand English language books for 5TL each.

Green Jacket
BOOKS

(Temmuz Caddesi 20; ☺9am-5pm Mon-Sat) West of the town centre near the Astro supermarket, this shop is the place to go for foreign-language books.

ℹ Information

INTERNET ACCESS

Cafe Net (Mustafa Çağatay Caddesi; per hr 3TL; ☺10am-midnight) The best place for checking your email. English-speaking owner Mehmet Çavuş serves hot and cold drinks and jacket potatoes. It also runs a small book exchange. Located southeast of the town centre.

City.Net Internet Cafe (off Ziya Rızkı Caddesi; per hour 2TL; ☺10am-midnight) In the shopping arcade between Ziya Rızkı Caddesi and Ecevit Caddesi. Fast internet and friendly service.

MEDICAL SERVICES

Akçiçek Hastahanesi (☑ 815 2254; Mustafa Çağatay Caddesi) Kyrenia's hospital is 300m southeast of the post office.

MONEY

Banks and ATMs are clustered along Ziya Rızkı Caddesi.

Türk Bankası (Ziya Rızkı Caddesi; ☺8am-noon & 2-5pm Mon-Sat) Near Belediye Meydanı.

Gesfi Money Exchange (Kordon Boyu Sokak 40; ☺8.30am-8pm) Opposite the Dome Hotel.

TOURIST INFORMATION

North Cyprus Tourism Organisation (NCTO; Old Harbour; ☺8am-6pm May-Sep, to 4pm Oct-Apr) Extremely helpful staff and free maps of the city.

Kyrenia Society (Mersin Caddesi; ☺10am-noon) Located behind the post office. It advertises upcoming events and excursions, particularly in summer. Check the noticeboard for more information.

ℹ Getting There & Away

AIR

Ercan airport (Ercan Havalimanı; ☑ 600 5000; www.ercanhavalimani.com) is 40km southeast of Kyrenia.

Cyprus XP Travel (☑ 815 1453; Atatürk Caddesi ; ☺9am-5pm Mon-Sat) is the North Cyprus representatives for Pegasus Airlines.

BOATS

A car ferry leaves for Taşucu in Turkey every Tuesday and Thursday at 2pm, and Friday at midnight (passenger only/with car 75/175TL, departure tax 25TL, seven hours) from the New Harbour, east of town.

The express passenger ferry to Turkey hasn't run since 2013 but there is talk of reinstating the service. Enquire for updates and buy tickets for ferries at **Mavi Tur** (☑ 815 2344; Ziya Rızkı Caddesi 6; ☺9am-6pm Mon-Sat), located on the roundabout in front of Belediye Meydanı.

BUSES & MINIBUSES

Kyrenia's transport hub is Belediye Meydanı. From here a jumble of private buses and minibuses (dolmuşes) depart to destinations across the country.

Buses to Famagusta (Mağusa; 8TL, 1¼ hours, hourly from 7am to 6pm) leave from the **Libra Tur office** (☑ 815 7248; Ecevit Caddesi; ☺7am-9pm).

Minibuses to North Nicosia (Lefkoşa; 4.50TL, 35 minutes, half-hourly from 7am to 6.30pm), Lapta (4TL, 20 minutes, roughly every 20 minutes from 7am to 6pm) and Güzelyurt (Morfou; 5TL, 1¼ hours) among others depart from Mustafa Çağatay Caddesi.

CAR HIRE

There are plenty of car-hire outlets. Prices are similar all over the island; €40 to €50 per day is average.

Oscar Car Rentals (☑ 815 2272; Kordon Boyu Sokak) Opposite the Dome Hotel.

SERVICE TAXIS

Service taxis (called kombos) go to North Nicosia (5TL) and Famagusta (10TL). They leave from near the Libra Tur office on Belediye Meydanı when full.

❶ Getting Around

TO/FROM THE AIRPORT

Kibhas (☑ Ercan airport 0533 870 7848, Kyrenia 0533 870 7846; www.kibhas.org; ticket 11.50TL) runs airport shuttle buses between Kyrenia and the airport with several departures a day. The pick-up and drop-off point is the Libra Tur office in the centre of town.

A taxi to/from the airport costs around 80TL.

TAXI

Private taxis are useful for going to Bellapais (15TL) and St Hilarion Castle (80TL return), both of which aren't serviced by public transport.

AROUND KYRENIA & THE RANGES

Kyrenia is perfectly placed for excursions to other parts of the North, which offer beaches, trekking, mountains and natural wilderness. There are also some incredible medieval castles and ancient sites. The whole area is quite condensed, with short driving distances. Nearly all roads are easily accessible by regular-drive cars.

🏖 Beaches

Northern Cyprus has separated many of its beaches into paid and public beaches, called *halk plajları*. The paid beaches are designed to be tourist friendly and entry usually costs around 6TL to 10TL.

Five Mile Beach   BEACH

(Yavuz Çıkarma Plajı; Alsancak; admission 10TL) Five Mile (also known as Yavuz Çıkarma) is one of Kyrenia's best swimming beaches. Run by Escape Beach Club, it's hugely popular and during summer you should get here early to find space. Hire a sun lounger and umbrella to counter the lack of shade. Swimmers should be mindful of the strong wind that can come in off the open water, which also makes it great for water sports. Five Mile is about 10km west of Kyrenia.

The sandy cove actually has three names: Altınkaya, after the rock next to it; Beşinci Mil, meaning five mile; and Yavuz Çıkarma, meaning the resolute outbreak. This was one of the beaches used by the Turkish Army to launch the 1974 invasion. On the road overlooking the beach you'll notice a phallic-looking monument (known locally as 'the Turkish erection') which commemorates the event.

Çatalköy Beach   BEACH

(Çatalköy) FREE Çatalköy, 7km east of Kyrenia, is a quiet beach with a less-developed feel than others in the region. The beach here is narrow with soft sand, in a protected and attractive little bay. You can rent sunbeds here and dive from the pontoon. The beach is 1.5km to the right, off the main road.

Vrysi (Acapulco) Beach   BEACH

(Çatalköy; admission 25TL) Now commonly called Acapulco Beach, thanks to the mega resort of Acapulco Holiday Village which manages it, Vrysi caters mainly to package tourists. Day visitors are welcome as well though and the (rather expensive) admission fee includes access to all the hotel facilities such as pools, changing rooms, sunbeds and umbrellas. The beach itself is lovely and clean, though it can get extremely crowded.

Lara Beach   BEACH

(Vakıflar Plajı; 3km east of Çatalköy) FREE If you're not one of those beach-goers obsessed with golden sand, the greyish sand of Lara Beach will be perfectly fine. This is a good swimming spot which also has clean toilets and changing-room facilities as well as a small snack bar.

Alagadı Beach   BEACH

(Turtle Beach; Alagadı) FREE Alagadı (Turtle) Beach, approximately 19km east of Kyrenia, is where the Society for the Protection of Turtles (SPOT) has its small monitoring station called the **Goat Shed** (☑ 0533 872 5350; www.cyprusturtles.org; Alagadı Beach; ⊙ 9am-8.30pm 1 Jun-15 Sep) where you can find out about turtle conservation. This is not really used as a swimming beach, but you are able to enjoy the habitat. Its twin sandy beaches are intentionally undeveloped, as they are considered turtle territory, and the beach is closed from 8pm to 8am from May to October.

If you get hungry, family-run **St Kathleen's Restaurant** (☑ 0533 861 7640; Main Rd, Alagadı; mains 15-25TL; ☺ 11am-10pm) is on the nearby main road. The meze, grills and fish dishes are excellent and good value.

🏃 Activities

Turtle Watching Tours OUTDOOR ACTIVITIES
(☑ 0533 872 5350; www.cyprusturtles.org; Alagadı Beach; ☺ 1 Jun-15 Sep) Between June and August the Society for the Protection of Turtles (SPOT) runs night tours where visitors can watch female turtles covering up their nests. Numbers are limited to 10 people per night. From late July to late September there are also opportunities to witness hatchling releases and nest excavations.

Bookings can be made through the Goat Shed (SPOT's research centre) on Alagadı Beach.

Octopus Aqua Park WATER PARK
(☑ 853 9674; Beşparmak Caddesi, Çatalköy; ☺ 8am-5pm Jul-Aug) Octopus Aqua Park, 8km east of Kyrenia, is a haven of water, where the little ones can climb, swing, slide and bounce on watery and dry spaces, while their parents relax at the pool bar and restaurant.

Hiking

The **Kyrenia Mountain Trail** is an excellent hiking option. It is 240km in total, traversing Northern Cyprus west to east, from **Koruçam Burnu** (Cape Kormakitis) to **Zafer Burnu** (Cape Apostolos Andreas). You can choose a section that appeals to you, or for serious ramblers, it can constitute one long amazing trek.

Spring is the best season, as you'll get to see a large number of the impressive 1600 plant, 350 bird and 26 reptile species that live in North Cyprus. This is also prime orchid spotting time. Autumn is also ideal for walking.

Unfortunately the NCTO have stopped producing their Mountain Trails brochure and decent maps of hiking trails can be difficult to come by. Check out www.kyreniamountaintrail.org for route planning information and to buy maps. All sections of the Kyrenia Mountain Trail are marked with green and white trail blazes.

Bellapais Walk HIKING
Starting at the end of the road just past the Ambelia Holiday Village in Bellapais, this circular hike takes you uphill to walk on the lofty ridge above the dinky village for astonishingly beautiful panoramas over the entire countryside.

Karaman to İlgaz Walk HIKING
One for wildflower and orchid spotters, this flora-filled easy walk begins in the village of Karaman. Head west on the road for 400m and then take the main dirt track from here, still heading west. There are great views across the hills to St Hilarion Castle along the way, though most people walk here for the flora.

Buffavento Castle Walk HIKING
Starting from the Buffavento Cafe on the Beşparmak Pass road, you can hike up the mountain road to where the remnants of Buffavento Castle cling to the cliff top. Two and a half kilometres uphill, a walking track

---

LOCAL KNOWLEDGE

TURTLE WATCHING AT ALAGADI BEACH

Kutlay Keço is a founding member of North Cyprus' Society for the Protection of Turtles (SPOT).

Why is Alagadı Beach so important in turtle conservation? Alagadı Beach is a major turtle nest site for both green and loggerhead (*caretta caretta*) turtles. It's recognised as the second most important nesting area for green turtles in the Mediterranean.

How does SPOT help to protect North Cyprus' turtles? At Alagadı we have 100% control over the area and can protect the nests from stray dogs and foxes, which are the biggest threat. We also research and monitor turtle nesting throughout North Cyprus. Our greatest achievement is that now everyone is aware of the turtles here, Alagadı has been designated as a special protected area and the population is increasing.

How can travellers see the turtles? We run free night tours at Alagadı throughout the nesting season. We only take a small number of people out each night so it's important to book as soon as you arrive to make sure you get a place.

(marked by red trail blazes) verges off to the right winding its way to the castle car park at the top.

This is a great day walk for those who don't have their own transport, as the Kyrenia–Famagusta bus passes right beside the Buffavento Cafe.

Beşparmak Range Trek   HIKING

The ultimate trek for mountain view fans is the hike along the spine of the Beşparmak (Pentadaktylos) Range which takes in forest trails and several villages along the way. Again, this is best walked in sections, staying in one of these villages. The section starting from Buffavento Castle and ending at Bellapais is one of the most beautiful.

Alevkaya to Kantara Trek   HIKING

Alevkaya to Kantara is a long easterly trail, with over 40km of hiking, connecting the Alevkaya Herbarium Forest Station to Kantara Castle.

Ağirdağ to Geçitköy Trek   HIKING

The hike from Ağirdağ to Geçitköy is a good trek for experienced walkers. Best tackled in sections over a few days, it runs west along the southern flank of the Kyrenia Range. It starts at Ağirdağ village on the Kyrenia–North Nicosia road and finishes at Geçitköy on the Kyrenia–Güzelyurt (Morfou) road.

❶ Getting Around

Public transport in the Kyrenia region consists of buses, dolmuşes (minibuses) and service taxis (known as kombos) that run during the day between the major towns and larger villages. Fares are cheap (around 4TL to 6TL), but services can be late and infrequent.

Cycling is a good-weather alternative, as the region's east–west routes are mostly flat and well serviced with places to stay, eateries and beaches.

St Hilarion Castle

The full fairytale outline of **St Hilarion Castle** (Hilarion Kalesi; ☑0533 161 276; adult/ student 7/3TL; ⊘9am-6.30pm Apr-Oct, to 3.30pm Nov-Mar) only becomes apparent once you're directly beneath it. The stone walls and half-ruined buildings blend, near seamlessly, into the rocky landscape creating a dreamscape castle plucked from a child's imagination with hidden rooms, tunnels and crumbling towers.

The site consists of three main parts, the lower enceinte, the upper enceinte and Prince John's Tower, all linked by steep staircases. The stunning views are well worth the arduous climb to the top.

Rumour has it that Walt Disney drew inspiration from the jagged contours of St Hilarion when he created the animated film *Snow White*. And a local folk legend tells that the castle once boasted 101 rooms, the last of which leading to a secret internal garden that belonged to a fairy queen. This enchantress was known for seducing hunters, shepherds and travellers who stumbled into her lair and robbing them by placing them into a deep slumber.

The castle's real history is a bit less fantastic. The lofty fort is named after the monk Hilarion, who fled persecution in the Holy Land. He lived (and died) in a mountain cave that overlooked the Kyrenia plain, protecting the pass between the coast and Nicosia (Lefkosia).

In the 10th century, the Byzantines built a church and monastery over Hilarion's tomb. Due to the site's strategic position, it was used as a watchtower and beacon during the Arab raids of the 7th and 8th centuries and was an important link in the communication chain between Buffavento and Kantara Castles further east.

In 1191 Guy de Lusignan seized control of St Hilarion, defeating the self-proclaimed Byzantine emperor of Cyprus, Isaak Komninos. The castle was then extensively expanded and used as both a military outpost and a summer residence of the Lusignan court. Later, during Venetian rule, the castle was neglected and fell into disrepair.

In 1964 the (TMT) Turk Müdafaa Teskilati, an underground Turkish Nationalist group, took control of the castle, again for its strategic position. It has been in Turkish Cypriot hands ever since, with a sheltered Turkish military base located on the ridge below.

You enter by the barbican main gate into the lower enceinte, once used as the main garrison and stabling area. Then follow the meandering path up to the middle enceinte, originally protected and sealed by a drawbridge. Here, remains of the church, barrack rooms, four-level royal apartments and a large cistern, vital to the storage of water, are found.

Access to the upper enceinte is via a paved winding track, which leads to the Lusignan

Gate. Guarded by the Byzantine tower it opens on to the central courtyard, adorned with more royal apartments, kitchens and ancillary chambers.

Finally one last climb takes you to Prince John's Tower. Legend has it that Prince John of Antioch became convinced his two Bulgarian bodyguards were plotting to assassinate him and had them thrown from the cliff, to their deaths.

From the tower on clear days you can see the Taurus Mountains, 100km away in Turkey.

In summer it's best to arrive early and avoid climbing in the heat of the day.

Bellapais (Beylerbeyi)

Charmingly sleepy, the little village of Bellapais sits snugly into the mountainside offering spectacular views of the Mediterranean coastline below. The impressive remnants of Bellapais Abbey are positioned on the village's lower flank from where narrow lanes rimmed by pot-plant festooned houses creep up the hill. Just past the monastery there is a large car park on the left, so you can avoid stopping in the main street.

Bellapais found literary fame after being immortalised by British writer Lawrence Durrell, who lived here during the Ethniki Organosi tou Kypriakou Agona (EOKA; National Organisation for the Cypriot Struggle) uprising against British rule. His entertaining memoir of his time here, *Bitter Lemons of Cyprus,* is a love letter to the village and a way of life now long gone.

◉ Sights

Bellapais Abbey   HISTORIC SITE
(Zafer Caddesi; adult/student 9/3TL; ⊙9am-8pm Jun-Sep, to 4.45pm Oct-May) The exquisite ruins of this Augustinian monastery are reason enough to drive up the mountain. It was built in the 12th century by Augustinian monks fleeing Palestine after the fall of Jerusalem to Saladin (Selahaddin Eyyubi) in 1187. The monks who established the monastery called it *Abbaye de la Paix* (Abbey of Peace), from which the corrupted version of the name, Bellapais, evolved.

The original structure, built between 1198 and 1205, was augmented between 1267 and 1284, during the reign of Hugh III. The cloisters and large refectory were added after that by Hugh IV (1324–59), and these embellishments are most of what remains today.

The 13th-century **church** is in fine condition, and remains much as it was in 1976, when the last of the stoic Orthodox faithful had to leave.

Behind, is the 14th-century **cloister** lined with towering cypress trees and rimmed with Gothic arched arcades that have survived the centuries almost intact. From here there are stairs up to the rooftop where you can savour tumbling views across the plains down to the sea. On the western side of the cloister is the kitchen court which has all but a few walls remaining.

The **refectory** on the north side of the cloister is frequently used for gatherings, events and wedding photos. Note the lintel above the main entrance with its Lasignan coat of arms.

THE TREE OF IDLENESS

When writer Lawrence Durrell took up residence in Bellapais (Beylerbeyi) between 1953 and 1956, he little realised the minor controversy he would leave behind almost 50 years later. His famous book *Bitter Lemons of Cyprus* described life in the then blissfully bucolic mixed community and his trials and tribulations while purchasing and renovating a house in the village, along with the intrigues and gossip of local life.

Among the villagers' favourite activities was spending many hours in idle conversation under the so-called 'Tree of Idleness', which dominated the main square. However, throughout the book, Durrell never once mentioned what kind of tree it was. Maybe it was a plane, or a mulberry, or perhaps an oak?

Today there are two trees that vie for the title. One is a leafy mulberry tree, overshadowing the coffee shop next to the monastery ticket office. The other contender, hardly 20m away, is a Robinia casting shade over the Huzur Ağaç (Tree of Idleness) Restaurant. In fairness, both trees qualify for the role pretty well: both have their supporters and draw idle crowds of onlookers who like to sit and drink coffee or a cold beer, just as the villagers did in Durrell's day. So pick your tree, sit idly by, and ponder.

Home of Lawrence Durrell NOTABLE BUILDING
(admission 13TL; ⊙11.30am-1pm Sep) A yellow plaque above the door marks the house where Lawrence Durell lived in the early 1950s, forever marking Bellapais on the literary map with his descriptions of the village's idyllic, mixed-community life in his memoir *Bitter Lemons of Cyprus*.

To reach the house, follow the signs uphill for 200m on the main street, to the right of Huzur Ağaç (Tree of Idleness) Restaurant. The house is now a private residence and is only open to visitors during September.

✦✦ Festivals & Events

Bellapais Music Festival MUSIC
(www.bellapaisfestival.com) Held annually during May and June, the festival takes place in and around Bellapais Abbey. It consists of concerts, recitals and brass-band performances in the refectory. Look out for event details in Kyrenia and around town.

✗ Eating

Paşa TURKISH €
(Zafer Caddesi; meals 12TL; ⊙11am-10pm) This teensy joint serves up cheap and cheerful portions of homemade flavour on Bellapais' main road. Filling plates of *lahmacun* and *manti* (Turkish ravioli) are dished up with large salads and lots of smiles.

Huzur Ağaç (Tree of Idleness)
Restaurant INTERNATIONAL €€
(☑815 3380; Zafer Caddesi; sandwiches & snacks 10-15TL, mains 20-35TL; ⊙10am-11.30pm) Across the road from Bellapais Abbey, the shady varanda at Huzur Ağaç is a great spot for lunch with a menu of filling sandwiches, kebabs and classic Cypriot favourites. Outside is the 200-year-old Robinia which may (or

not) be Lawrence Durrell's famed 'Tree of Idleness'.

Tarihi Değirmen Historic Mill Cafe CAFE €€
(Değirmen Sokak; mains 15-20TL; ⊙11am-6pm) Follow the signs from the road up Bellapais hill from the abbey and you'll find this cafe, set in an old mill (with grinding machines on show) where locals once produced their olive oil. It's a good option for coffee or cold drinks as well as snacks and traditional Cypriot grills.

★Kybele CYPRIOT €€€
(Bellapais Abbey grounds; mains 30TL; ⊙11am-11pm) Even if the food was so-so, the atmospheric garden setting and fantastic views of Bellapais Abbey next door would still make Kybele the prime spot for dining in the village. Luckily the traditional dishes (and international favourites such as steaks) are top notch. Come for dinner to experience the romantic floodlit abbey ambience.

Buffavento Castle

Buffavento (Buffavento Kalesi; ⊙dawn-dusk)
FREE perches precariously at 940m, overlooking the Mesaoria (Mesarya) plain. The constant pummelling it endures from high winds is how it derived its Italian name, 'challenger of the winds'.

The castle is divided into two sections, the lower enceinte and the upper enceinte, which occupies a smaller area on the rocky peak. Built in such a way that no fortifications other than its outer walls were needed, its naturally guarded location has only one entrance approach.

Little is known about the castle's early history. In medieval times, it was known as the Castle of the Lion, when Richard the Lionheart took it from the daughter of Byzantine emperor Isaak Komninos in 1191. The Lusignans later used it as a prison and a beacon tower, connecting both Kantara Castle to the east and St Hilarion Castle to the west.

Although it has deteriorated more than the other castles – and some of its buildings have been sadly defaced by graffiti – its surviving towers and walls have an ambience of lingering grandeur topped off by the dizzying views sweeping downwards over the forested slopes.

Prominently signposted (as Buffavento Kalesi) off the Beşparmak (Pentadaktylos) Pass, it's a 15-minute drive along the uphill

---

WHAT'S IN A NAME?

Since 1974, all the original Greek place names have been replaced by Turkish names. Road signs to Kyrenia (Girne) and Famagusta (Mağusa) usually state both names but road signs for smaller towns and villages just display the Turkish name. Those only familiar with the pre-partition names may find it difficult to navigate without a new road map (available from the Tourist Information Office in Kyrenia).

Driving Tour
Combing the North Eastern Ridge & Coast

START OZANKÖY (KAZAFANI)
FINISH BELLAPAIS (BEYLERBEYI)
DISTANCE 95KM; SIX TO EIGHT HOURS

Barely 4km east of Kyrenia, pretty **1 Ozanköy** is noted for its olive oil and carob *pekmez* (molasses). Cypriots swear a tablespoon of *pekmez* every day wards off illness so don't forget to pick up a bottle. After taking a look at the medieval church, head east on the coast road (signed 'Uğur Mumcu Bulvan') to **2 Çatalköy**. Its caves provided sanctuary to the hermit Epiktitos in the 13th century. Another 10km east and you arrive at **3 Alagadı Beach** (p168), great for a sandy stroll. Continue along the coast for another 10km to the turn off for Esentepe and head inland to the Byzantine **4 Antifonitis Monastery**.

After visiting the monastery take the scenic ridge road for 17km west, parallel to the mountains until you come to **5 Alevkaya (Halevga)** where nature lovers can check out the Alevkaya Herbarium. Continuing 2.5km to the west (on the main road), you'll see the

battered ruins of the 11th-century Coptic Armenian **6 Sourp Magar Monastery** nestled in pine trees below. To get there, turn right at the picnic site and follow the forestry track that winds down to the church.

Backtrack onto the main road and head west for 9km onto the Beşparmak (Five Fingers) pass until you get to the Buffavento Cafe. Turn left here and take the winding road for 6km up to **7 Buffavento Castle** for some of the best views in North Cyprus. When you've finished scrambling around the ruins, exit the castle car park and continue along the tarmac road for 3km until you see the domed roof of the lonely Byzantine **8 Panagia Absinthiotissa Monastery** below. Take the left-hand turn-off to the picnic ground to arrive at the church.

From here drive down into the tidy village of Taşkent, taking the second left-hand turn on the ridge road above the village and continuing on this road as it heads northwest out of the village. From here it's 10km onto **9 Bellapais (Beylerbeyi)** and the beautiful Gothic architecture of Bellapais Abbey.

road to the parking area below the castle. From here it's a steep but gradual walk that takes about 20 minutes. Closed footwear is advised.

Panagia Absinthiotissa Monastery

Located on the flank of the Beşparmak Range, this monastery sits idyllically among juniper trees, taking in the views over the Mesaoria (Mesarya) plain.

Built in the late-Byzantine era, with its colossal 12-windowed drum and dome, the monastery was inhabited by Latin monks during the 15th century who added Gothic vaulting and an unusual narthex with double apses at its end. Across the courtyard, to the north, is the refectory with its shallow ceiling, vaulting and distinctive lancet windows.

Fastidiously restored during the 1960s, the monastery was unfortunately badly vandalised after 1974, with its many frescos either stolen or defaced. The plastered interior, now completely covered with graffiti, and the floor, covered with goat droppings, makes a bizarre and slightly eerie contrast with the still beautiful and soaring architecture.

The monastery is approximately 10 minutes' drive from Buffavento Castle, sitting just above the village of Taşkent. To make this your next stop, simply exit the car park and follow the tarmac road.

Alevkaya Herbarium

On the back road in the Beşparmak (Pentadaktylos) Range, you'll find the forest station between Esentepe (Agios Amvrosios) and Değirmenlik (Kythrea). The **Alevkaya Herbarium** (◷ 8am-4pm) **FREE** here is home to endemic Cypriot flora, including some 1250 native plant species. It displays a range of preserved and live specimens, developed from a collection created by English botanist Deryck Viney, whose book *Illustrated Flora of North Cyprus* documents the country's diverse botanical treasures.

To get to the herbarium, take the signposted forest road, off the southern side of the Beşparmak (Pentadaktylos) Pass. Alternatively, from the northern coastal road, take the road signposted as Karaağaç (Harkia) or Esentepe.

KEEPING THE COAST

The stretch of coast from Kyrenia (Girne) to Yenierenköy (Yiallousa) was once one of the most untouched habitats in the region. Today it's seen many changes. New roadways have caused great swaths of coastline to be paved, and large stretches of undisturbed land have been heavily and quickly developed, with tourism complexes shooting up en masse.

This development began in earnest when the 2004 Annan Plan, which provided a framework for the island's reunification, stipulated that all undeveloped Greek land in the North would be returned to its pre-1974 owners, and that compensation would be awarded in cases where land had already been developed. Ultimately the South rejected the Annan Plan by majority referendum. However, Northern developers ploughed ahead in case an agreement eventuated.

Turkish Cypriot newspaper *Yeni Duzen* stated that, in 2000, new developments covered 607,000 sq metres. In 2005, this area had increased to over 4.4 sq km. Development has affected much natural habitat, regional wildlife and many ancient olive groves. Cultural heritage sites are also at risk. In 2004 the Turkish Cypriot Department of Antiquities and Museums was up in arms after the necropolis of Vounos, near Kyrenia, was damaged: 140 ancient tombs were 'bulldozed, damaged and completely flattened' by a private company building luxury-home complexes. Even after discovery, the company pushed ahead, citing its right to build with government permits.

Politically, these incidents have only added to Greek Cypriot concerns over their rights and land ownership, further complicating the most difficult aspect of any resolution process between North and South. For now, environmentalists on both sides would settle for measured, sustainable and ecofriendly development that would keep certain areas safe while negotiations continue to secure the island's future.

KYRENIA WEST

Lapta (Lapithos)

Surrounded by verdant citrus orchards, the sprawling village of Lapta is a popular day trip from Kyrenia. Although the surrounding area has been gobbled up by bland holiday home complexes, the old district, running up the slope away from the coastline, still boasts green leafy lanes and some traditional charm.

Lapta was one of the original city kingdoms of Cyprus and a regional capital under Roman rule. Its abundant water supply and protected position have made it a favourite choice of foreign rulers and settlers for centuries.

A mixed village pre-1974, Lapta accommodated Greek Cypriots and Turkish Cypriots in harmony, until the skirmishes of the 1960s saw a mosque's bell tower spoiled in the wake of local differences. In the mid-1990s, forest fires devastated much of the region but fortunately missed this town. Today the village is populated by a blend of expats, mainland Turks and Turkish Cypriot villagers.

✖ Eating

Başpınar Restaurant   CYPRIOT €€
(☑ 821 8661; mains 20TL; ☺ 7-11.30pm) Located above Lapta village at the top of the hill, this restaurant sits around an old Roman aqueduct with fantastic views. It serves rabbit stews and the usual meze. Call in advance for a booking.

Hanımeller   CYPRIOT €€
(Fevzi Çakmak Caddesi; mains 18-25TL; ☺ 10.30am-11pm) Grab a table on the shore side to make the most of the sea views, and dine on well-cooked and flavourful kebab dishes as well as all the usual Turkish Cypriot staples.

THE NORTHWEST

The northwest region of the Kyrenia Range includes the Koruçam (Kormakitis) Peninsula. To the south are the agricultural town of Güzelyurt (Morfou) and its bay. The pretty hilled village of Lefke (Lefka) and one-time mining port of Gemikonağı (Karavostasi) are to the west. Further still are the important archaeological sites of Ancient Soloi and Ancient Vouni.

Distances here are relatively short, with the journey best seen in a circular route, returning to North Nicosia (Lefkoşa) via the peninsula and Kyrenia, or vice versa. There is also a border crossing (at the Green Line) to the Republic of Cyprus, at Zodhia, near Güzelyurt.

Beaches

The 12km stretch west of Gemikonağı has a mixture of sand and pebbly beaches, ending at the border with the South.

Yedidalga Beach   BEACH
(Yedidalga Plaji) [FREE] This pebbled public beach with stretches of imported sand has a wooden pier for diving and swimming, a small bar and restaurant, a changing room and toilet facilities. It is well signposted and easily found.

Asmalı Beach   BEACH
[FREE] Asmalı Beach is slap-bang in front of the border village of Yeşilırmak (Limnitis). It's a clean pebbled beach, with a few restaurants surrounding it, catering to those who travel this far.

❶ Getting Around

Regular dolmuşes (minibuses) run from North Nicosia (Lefkoşa) and Kyrenia (Girne) during the day, roughly every half hour to Güzelyurt (Morfou 4TL), and Gemikonağı (5TL) and Lefke (5TL) both via Güzelyurt.

However, getting around is far easier with your own transport, especially if you want to see Ancient Soloi and Ancient Vouni.

Güzelyurt (Morfou)

POP 18, 946

The quiet town of Güzelyurt (Morfou) was once the centre for Cyprus' lucrative citrus industry. The majority of the citrus groves here are still owned by Greek Cypriots, and the area has remained an important point of contention in all reunification talks. The citrus industry here suffered a severe downturn after the 1974 Turkish invasion. The lack of cultivation and maintenance, combined with rising salinity levels in the underground aquifers that water the orchards caused by the level of water reserves falling dramatically, has further hindered the industry.

The vast groves start shortly before the village of Şahinler (Masari), stretching all the way to the sea. During better days, in the early 20th century, this region's oranges were transported by train across the Mesaoria (Mesarya) plain to Famagusta for overseas export. Although this old train route ceased passenger services in 1932, it continued to transport freight until 1951. The line has long since been abandoned and fallen into complete disrepair. You can, however, still see one of the two surviving locomotives, a 1924 Baldwin, out of Philadelphia, at the **Belediye Parki**, just outside town.

Güzelyurt now consists of a few narrow, winding streets, small shops and sputtering agriculture. In the town square, near the

KORUÇAM (KORMAKITIS) PENINSULA

A trip to the exposed northwestern tip of Northern Cyprus, known as **Koruçam Burnu** (Cape Kormakitis), is a fantastic day excursion from Kyrenia, with a number of deserted beaches on the way. Pack a picnic lunch, and enjoy the solitude at the cape and its surrounds. Apart from being the 'land's end', it is also home to one of Cyprus' least-known religious communities, the Maronites.

During the 4th century, Maronites broke away from the prevailing Orthodox religious theory of Christianity, which said God was both man and god. In contrast, they followed the Monophysite religious line, which states that God could only be viewed as one spiritual persona.

Persecuted by Orthodox Christians for their beliefs, they first sought refuge in Lebanon and Syria, before coming to Cyprus in the 12th century in the wake of the crusaders, whom they had helped as auxiliaries in the Holy Land campaign.

Post-1974 the Cypriot Maronites have clung to a tenuous existence in Koruçam village, where they still maintain a church. Over the years, the once-vigorous congregation has gradually left, and now barely 100 remain to keep the old traditions and religion alive. The Maronites, like the Armenians and Latin religious communities, had to choose allegiance with either the Greek or Turkish communities in the 1960s. They chose the Greeks, and since '74 the youth from the village has gradually all but disappeared, crossing over into the South to study in Greek schools. Those who remained in the North have managed to tread the fine line between political and religious allegiances, with some degree of success. Pre-2003 their relatives from the South were even able to visit them on weekends. Since the borders have opened, the South's Maronites visit for longer periods. Many hope that some of the younger generations will return to live here, preserving the village and its people's traditions.

Getting here is pretty simple, with a mostly paved road taking you almost all the way. It's best tackled as a loop starting from the northern end of the Kyrenia–Güzelyurt road, at the junction after the village of Karşıyaka (Vasileia).

From the junction follow the signs to Sadrazamköy (Livera). On your right you will see signs to petite **Horse Shoe Beach** and **Horseshoe Beach Restaurant** (☑861 6664; grills & fish 8TL; ◷11am-8pm), perfect spots for lunch and a swim.

To get to the cape, follow the winding road for 10km past Sadrazamköy; from here you find a 3.5km dirt track, which is easily driven with a conventional car. There are bare rocks, a solar-powered shipping beacon and a small rocky islet just offshore. This is the island's closest point to Turkey, which is a mere 60km across the sea.

For a different and interesting drive back, go via the picturesque inland loop road, through Koruçam village and past the massive Maronite **Church of Agios Georgios**, built in 1940 with funds raised by the villagers.

Koruçam's Maronites have kept their dialect of Aramaic (the forgotten language of Christ) for hundreds of years, interlacing it with Greek, Turkish, French and Italian words, creating a richer version of their own language. While most communicate in this dialect or Turkish, some locals at the small coffee shop in Koruçam village speak Greek.

The final leg back to the Kyrenia–Güzelyurt road is through a Turkish military area, with checkpoints at which you may be stopped. Once past, get on the main highway at Çamlibel (Myrtou) and head back to Kyrenia. From here you can also go south to Güzelyurt or turn southeast toward North Nicosia (Lefkoşa).

impressive modern **mosque**, there are two sights that are worth stopping off for.

⊙ Sights

Agios Mamas Orthodox Church   CHURCH
(Main Square; combined admission with museum adult/student 7/3TL) Dedicated to the island's beloved tax-repelling patron saint, this church was formerly the site of a pagan temple. Before 1974, the faithful used to visit the ancient marble tomb of Saint Mamas here, from which a mysterious liquid is said to have oozed when the Ottomans pierced it looking for treasure.

The liquid, apparently flowing freely at irregular intervals, was supposed to have cured ear aches; as such, ear-shaped offerings can be seen around the tomb.

The church is kept locked, but you can gain access by asking the staff at the Archaeological & Natural History Museum next door.

**Archaeological & Natural
History Museum**   MUSEUM
(Güzelyurt Muzesi; Main Square; combined admission with Agios Mamas Orthodox Church adult/student 7/3TL; ⊙9am-6pm May-Sep, to 3.30pm Oct-Apr) Next door to the Agios Mamas Orthodox Church, this little museum's upper floor displays some extraordinary finds from the archaeological sites of Soli and Toumba tou Skourou as well as an exceptionally beautiful Artemis statue unearthed at Salamis.

The ground floor is given over to a bizarre taxidermy exhibit including a two-headed lamb and (oddly) a bunch of rabbits from New Zealand.

✗ Eating

Nayazi Şah   TURKISH
(☑714 3064; meze 25TL; ⊙11am-10pm) This is one of the best meze houses in the North, located south of the northern roundabout. There is regular live music on weekends and constant platters of meats, including quail and lamb sausages.

Gemikonağı (Karavostasi)

From the calm and secluded rough-pebble beach, you can see the entire coast stretching northeast around Morfou Bay. Although the beaches here are not as visually appealing as the softer, sandy ones found on the north coast, there are far fewer swimmers.

Pre-1974, local villagers from the Troödos foothills came to the bay to swim, and now with the border crossings open, some are coming here again.

The once-flourishing port of Gemikonağı dominates the bay, with its abandoned jetty slowly sagging by the port itself.

East of town, you'll notice the scarred hinterland, heavily mined by a large conglomerate. It ceased mining after 1974 and has left the town with a decidedly backwater appearance.

Nonetheless, the town supports a small local tourist industry, thanks to a few good restaurants and its beaches. Visitors who prefer more rustic and less touristy swimming and dining options should stop here. The nearby **Mardin Restaurant** (☑727 7527; mains 18-25TL; ⊙11am-11pm) has a terrace that overlooks the sea and offers a menu of quality fish dishes, meze and kebabs.

Lefke (Lefka)

POP 11,090

A few kilometres from Gemikonağı, the road runs at a right angle to the hillside village of Lefke. Its position amid limitless greenery and rolling hills gives it a pleasant and fresh feel.

The town's name is derived from the Greek word *lefka* (meaning 'poplar'). Today, with more orange groves and palm trees than poplars, the village is known for its superb citrus fruits.

Although Lefke is home to a large community of British expats, it is also regarded as a stronghold for the Islamic faith. It is the headquarters of the Naqshbandi order of Sufism and their charismatic leader Şeyh Nazım Kıbrısli and his followers. This order follows the principles of Islam dutifully and urges less-strict Turkish Cypriots to do the same.

There is little to do in the village itself, save for taking in the **Piri Osman Pasha Mosque** and its courtyard, walking the windy streets, eating the delicious oranges and spotting pieces of broken aqueducts.

The border crossing at Zodhia is best reached by the main road south from Güzelyurt (Morfou). The crossing has opened up the region again to Tylliria and Pafos Forest, which are only 3km away. The roads through these mountains are buffeted by winds but are an enjoyable drive. There's another border crossing not far from Ancient Vouni, at Limnitis-Yeşilirmak, close to Kato Pyrgos.

Ancient Soloi

One of Cyprus' ancient city kingdoms, **Soloi** (Soli Harabeleri; adult/student 7/3TL; ⊗8am-7pm May-Sep, to 3.30pm Oct-Apr) was originally referred to as Si-il-lu, on an Assyrian tribute list that dates from 700 BC.

The site consists of two main parts: the basilica near the entrance to the site, and the theatre, up the hill and south of the basilica. Most of the site has not yet been excavated but there are also some sparse ruins of a Roman-era Agora north of the entrance, down the hill.

Soloi's grandest period began in 580 BC, when King Philokyprios moved his capital here, from Aepia, on the advice of his mentor, the Athenian philosopher Solon. Philokyprios promptly renamed the citadel Soloi in his honour.

In 498 BC, with the island under Persian rule, Soloi was part of the Ionian revolt, formed by Onesilous, king of Salamis. He had united all the city kingdoms of Cyprus (except Amathous) in an attempt to overthrow the empire, but was ultimately defeated.

Soloi then languished until Roman times, when it flourished once again thanks to its rich copper mines. As was the case in many parts of Cyprus, Soloi and its wealth suffered sacking and looting by Arab raiders in the 7th century AD.

Soloi Basilica   ARCHAEOLOGICAL SITE

St Mark was baptised at Soloi by St Auxibius and its first church is thought to have been built in the 4th century. From what's left today it is difficult to appreciate the size and extent of the church, which by all accounts was impressive.

Most notable are the surviving decorated floors, including the mosaic of a swan with entwined floral patterns and small dolphin nearby.

Roman Theatre   ARCHAEOLOGICAL SITE

The Roman theatre is somewhat restored, after much of its original stonework, taken by the British in the late 19th century, was used to rebuild the dockside at Port Said.

The theatre is said to have been able to accommodate up to 4000 spectators in its day. The famous Roman statuette of Aphrodite of Soli was discovered nearby. It is now on display in the Cyprus Museum in Nicosia (Lefkosia).

Ancient Vouni

The ruins at **Ancient Vouni** (Vouni Sarayı; adult/student 5/3TL; ⊗8am-7pm May-Sep, to 3.30pm Oct-Apr) may be sparse but the views here are truly glorious and well worth the trip. On a superb hilltop location this ancient site originally housed a palace and extensive building complex dating back to the 4th century BC.

The site consists of a discernible megaron (three-part rectangular room with central throne), private rooms and steps leading down to a courtyard and cistern. Here there's a pear-shaped stone believed to have supported a windlass (a machine for raising weights).

Vouni's origins and history are convoluted, but it's speculated that the palace was built by a Persian ruler from the nearby city kingdom of Marion (today's Polis). The intent was to watch over the nearby Greek-aligned city of Soloi. However, this is unconfirmed at best, and based on scant entries by Herodotus, in Book V of his *Histories*. It is true, however, that the stronghold does exhibit Persian palace architecture, which was added to and embellished later under Hellenistic rulers.

The palace was burned down in 380 BC (it's not known why or by whom) and was never re-established. Today the scant remains stand lonely on its hill, commanding excellent panoramic views across the region.

The site is reached by taking the signposted turn from the main road and following a narrow, steeply winding road all the way up the hill until you reach the car park and ticket office.

Famagusta (Mağusa) & the Karpas (Kırpaşa) Peninsula

Best Places to Eat

➡ Petek Confectioner (p186)

➡ Ginkgo (p186)

➡ Oasis Restaurant (p197)

➡ Aspava Restaurant (p187)

Best Places to Stay

➡ Nitovikla Garden (p213)

➡ Seabird (p213)

➡ Oasis at Ayfilon (p214)

➡ Club Malibu (p214)

Why Go?

The thin finger of the Karpas (Kırpaşa) Peninsula is all rolling meadows, craggy cliffs and wild beaches with a handful of snoozy villages thrown in. It's a taste of old-style Cyprus that can't be beaten. Despite new roads and development efforts, it still feels like someone stopped the clocks here a few decades back.

When you've recharged your batteries with the Karpas' serene wilderness, turn back west to visit Ancient Salamis. This enigmatic window into the Hellenic world is the island's most impressive archaeological site.

Just to the south is the fortified city of Famagusta. Climb up to the ramparts to walk the city walls. Then wander through lanes where gently dilapidated houses sit beside crumbling ruins of once majestic churches and breathe in the ambience of faded long-lost grandeur.

Brimming with history and full of mesmerising natural beauty, this is by far the island's most rewarding region to explore.

When to Go

➡ From March to May wild orchids and wildflowers come into bloom on the Karpas Peninsula and a variety of bird life can be spotted in the sky. It's a showcase of Cyprus at it's prettiest – nature-lover's won't want to miss it.

➡ The International Famagusta Art & Culture Festival takes centre stage in the city during June and July with performances held in the Old Town and amid the ancient ruins of Salamis.

➡ During August and September the Karpas' wild beaches are home to both green and loggerhead (*caretta caretta*) turtles that nest and hatch their eggs in the sand along the coast.

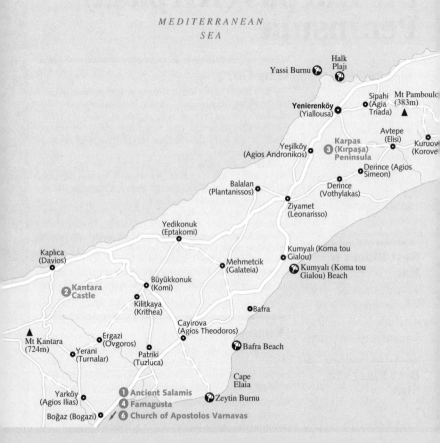

MEDITERRANEAN SEA

Yassi Burnu
Halk Plajı

Sipahi (Agia Triada)
Mt Pamboulo (383m)
Yenierenköy (Yiallousa)

Avtepe (Elisi)
Kuruov (Korove
Karpas (Kırpaşa) Peninsula

Yeşilköy (Agios Andronikos)

Derince (Agios Simeon)
Balalan (Plantanissos)
Derince (Vothylakas)
Ziyamet (Leonarisso)

Yedikonuk (Eptakomi)

Kumyalı (Koma tou Gialou)
Kumyalı (Koma tou Gialou) Beach

Kaplıca (Davios)

Mehmetcik (Galateia)

Kantara Castle
Büyükkonuk (Komi)

Kilitkaya (Krithea)
Bafra

Cayirova (Agios Theodoros)

Mt Kantara (724m)
Ergazi (Ovgoros)
Bafra Beach

Yerani (Turnalar)
Patriki (Tuzluca)

Cape Elaia

Yarköy (Agios Ilias)
Ancient Salamis
Zeytin Burnu
Famagusta
Boğaz (Bogazi)
Church of Apostolos Varnavas

Famagusta & the Karpas Peninsula Highlights

① Exploring one of the most important cities of Cypriot antiquity at **Ancient Salamis** (p188).

② Savouring the spectacular coastal views from the well-

preserved ruins of **Kantara Castle** (p193).

③ Tuning out from the wired world for a couple of days, and enjoying the silence and solitude at one of the remote

rural hotels on the **Karpas (Kırpaşa) Peninsula** (p193).

④ Imagining the glory of days-gone-by while viewing the gated city of **Famagusta** (p182) from its

Zafer Burnu
(Cape Apostolos
Andreas)

Kleides

Monastery of
Apostolos Andreas

Agios Filon
Beach

5 Golden Beach
(Nangomi Bay)

Dipkarpaz
(Rizokarpaso)

Kaleburnu
(Galinopórni)

Skoutari (Üsküdar)

*MEDITERRANEAN
SEA*

N 0 ———————— 10 km
0 ———————— 6 miles

imposing Venetian walls and
commanding bastions.

5 Swimming off one of
the island's finest stretches
of sand at **Golden Beach**
(p193).

6 Admiring the beautiful
architecture and gorgeous
icon collection in the **Church
of Apostolos Varnavas**
(p191).

FAMAGUSTA (MAĞUSA)

POP 40,920

The Old Town of Famagusta (Mağusa) was made for exploration on foot. Winding lanes rimmed with modest houses suddenly give way to ruined Gothic churches where birds nest between the roofless arches and weeds spring from once gloriously intricate mosaic floors. From atop the Venetian walls, the shattered Gothic remnants of once grand churches punctuate the skyline of what was Cyprus' most lavish and important city.

The New Town's large square, Yirmisekiz Ocak Meydanı, is capped by an enormous black statue of Atatürk. It's the major landmark and impossible to miss. Across from the square is the Land Gate, which is the easiest way into the Old Town. There's also a handy car park just to the right as you enter.

Despite this city being one of the island's most intriguing and rewarding to visit, tourism infrastructure remains poor. Most travellers choose to base themselves elsewhere and explore on a day trip.

History

Famagusta and its surroundings have an affluent and complex history. The wide sweep of Famagusta Bay and the sprawling Mesaoria (Mesarya) plain was home to three major settlements over the ages: the Bronze Age city of Ancient Enkomi (Alasia), which existed during the 17th century BC; the Mycenaean settlement and tombs from the 9th century BC, described as a flourishing culture in Homer's *Iliad;* and the illustrious kingdom of Salamis, which prospered through the 6th century BC.

Founded by Ptolemy Philadelphus of Egypt in the 3rd century BC, Famagusta was originally known by its Greek name, Ammochostos, meaning 'buried in the sand'. For many years it was considered the bridesmaid to the famous city kingdom of Salamis, just to its north.

After Salamis was abandoned in AD 648, Famagusta's population greatly increased, but the city didn't truly bloom until the fall of Acre in 1291.

At this point, Christians fleeing the Holy Land took refuge in the city. In the late 13th century it became the region's main shipping stopover, gaining immense wealth almost overnight. A lavish and decadent lifestyle bloomed and more jewels and gold were said to be in Famagusta than in all of Europe's royal courts. This provoked scorn from the pious, who criticised what they felt were the loose morals of its citizens. To counteract this, a great number of churches were quickly built.

The great city's first decline began when the Genoese took control in the 14th century, prompting an exodus of its wealthiest and most illustrious citizens.

Although the town was recaptured by the Venetians 117 years later, its former fortune and decadence never really returned. During this time the huge walls and bastions were constructed, but this belated measure did little to prevent its capture by the Ottomans in 1571. In the bloody 10-month siege that ensued, an estimated 100,000 cannonballs were fired.

Under the Ottomans, Famagusta rotted like a bad tooth. Its ruined buildings were never repaired, leaving it in an almost Gothic time warp. The Old Town, Kaleici, became a Turkish Cypriot stronghold.

The region flourished again in the early 1960s when the renowned, predominantly Greek resort town of Varosia (Maraş; p186), to the south, annually pulled thousands of sun-seeking tourists to its stunning beaches.

However, communal conflicts in 1964 saw more skirmishes in the area, resulting in the Turks essentially barricading themselves within the Old Town's walls and exiling any Greeks left to the confines of Varosia.

The island's invasion by the Turkish army in 1974 forced Famagusta, and more particularly Varosia, into the restricted border zone. Deserted by its Greek population in anticipation of the fast-approaching Turkish military, Varosia remains part of the large, uninhabited buffer zone and is now a ghost town. Haunting, with its gaping dark windows and abandoned tower blocks, and barricaded by oil drums and barbed wire, it is as it was in 1974, save for a few military outposts and occasional UN patrols.

◉ Sights

The eclectic mix of arched lanes, chapel ruins, Turkish baths, Byzantine churches and Knights Templar and medieval quarters are best appreciated on foot. Allow the better part of a day to see the city properly.

★ **Venetian Walls**   HISTORIC SITE

Defining the Old Town, these imposing ramparts were constructed by the Venetians in the early 16th century. Although over 15m high and up to 8m thick, and surrounded by a now waterless moat, the ramparts failed to keep the Ottomans at bay in 1571.

Like their counterpart in Nicosia (Lefkosia), Famagusta's walls comprised 14 bastions and five gates. You can walk almost the entire length of the roughly rectangular layout and enjoy the excellent views of the city below.

Othello's Tower HISTORIC SITE
(The Citadel; Othello Kalesi; adult/student 7/3TL; ⊘ currently closed, when open 9am-8pm Jun-Sep, to 5pm Oct-May) An extension of the Old Town's main walls, Othello's tower was constructed in the 12th century, during Lusignan rule, in order to protect the harbour. In 1492, the Venetians further fortified the citadel and transformed it into an artillery stronghold.

The citadel is currently closed to visitors for extensive restoration work. If it is open again by the time you visit there are various towers and artillery chambers to explore as well as a refectory and living quarters.

The tower's name stems from a vague link to Shakespeare's play *Othello*, which has a modest stage note referring to 'a seaport in Cyprus'. Above the citadel's impressive entrance you'll see the Venetian Lion inscribed by its architect, Nicolò Foscarini. Leonardo da Vinci also apparently advised on the refurbishment of the tower during his visit to Cyprus in 1481.

The gorgeous mix of Venetian and Lusignan architecture inside is a prime highlight of a visit here. The internal courtyard is bordered by the Great Hall, with beautiful vaults and corroded sandstone walls on its far side. Ventilation shafts look out to the border ramparts, leading to Lusignan corridors and sealed chambers. Legend has it that fortunes still lie hidden here, buried by Venetian merchants in the face of the advancing Ottomans.

★**Lala Mustafa Paşa Camii** MOSQUE
(St Nicholas Cathedral; Erenler Sokak; ⊘ outside prayer times) **FREE** The former Cathedral of Agios Nikolaos (St Nicholas) is the finest example of Lusignan Gothic architecture in Cyprus, built between 1298 and 1326. Modelled on France's Cathedral of Reims, it outshines its sister church, the Church of Agia Sofia (now Selimiye Mosque) in North Nicosia (Lefkoşa).

Converted into a mosque (*camii* in Turkish) after 1571's Ottoman invasion, it still dominates the skyline of the Old Town. To enter, time your visit outside of prayer times and dress modestly.

During the Lusignan reign the church was Famagusta's centrepiece. As such, the last Lusignan king of Cyprus, Jacques II, and his infant son (Jacques III) were buried here.

The church was damaged considerably during the Ottoman siege of Famagusta and its twin towers were destroyed. The Ottomans added the minaret, stripped the church's interior of its Christian accoutrements and emptied the floor tombs.

The west-facing facade, now a pedestrian zone, is the most impressive part, with three gracious portals pointing towards a six-paned window, decorated with a circular rose.

Inside, the walls have been whitewashed in Islamic fashion, but the soaring Gothic architectural lines are still easy to follow.

DON'T MISS

WALKING FAMAGUSTA'S WALLS

Start your Famagusta wall tour at the southern end near the **Land Gate** on the **Ravelin (Rivettina) Bastion** (⊘ 9am-6pm Mon-Fri) **FREE**, also known as the 'Akkule' or 'white tower'. It was here that the Ottomans first breached the fortifications, surrendered by the white-flag-waving Venetians. You can enter the warren of rooms within.

From the Ravelin Bastion the walls head north, passing four minor bastions, **Diocare**, **Moratto**, **Pulacazara**, **San Luca** and the steeply pitched **Martinengo Bastion**.

This in turn leads seaward, passing the **Del Mezzo**, **Diamante** and **Signoria Bastions**. Further on is the impressive citadel known as **Othello's Tower**.

The **Sea Gate** on the eastern side originally opened directly onto the sea. Today the wharfs of the modern port have extended the land bridge considerably.

At the southeastern extremity is the **Canbulat Bastion**, in which Ottoman hero General Canbulat Bey died valiantly while attacking the walls on horseback during the bloody siege. From here the walls loop back to the Land Gate via the **Camposanto**, **Andruzzi** and **Santa Napa Bastions**.

Famagusta (Mağusa)

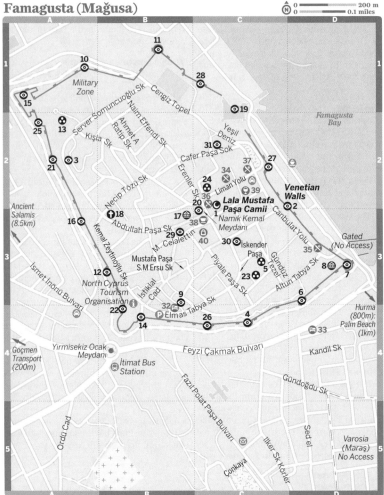

Palazzo del Provveditore HISTORIC SITE
(Venetian Palace; Namık Kemal Meydanı) The ruined arches and supporting columns (taken from Salamis) of the Palazzo del Provveditore sit opposite Lala Mustafa Paşa Mosque. The triple-arched entranceway is the best preserved part.

Namık Kemal Prison MUSEUM
(Namık Kemal Meydanı; adult/child 5/3TL; ⊙9am-2pm Jun-Sep, shorter hours rest of year) This former prison housed Turkish poet, playwright and dissident Namık Kemal (1840–88) for nearly four years after his writings offended the sultan. To be frank, inside there are only a couple of dusty exhibits and portraits and one small room set up with a mannequin of the man himself, so unless you have a particular interest – and read Turkish – you can skip the entrance fee.

Sinan Paşa Camii HISTORIC SITE
(St Peter & St Paul Church; Abdullah Paşa Sokak) Although not open to the public, the magnificent facade of this mammoth 14th-century church, which has survived intact, gives you a good impression of what Famagusta would have looked like before most of its churches and monuments were ruined.

Famagusta (Mağusa)

The church's construction was funded by a local merchant, Simon Nostrano, between 1358 and 1369. During the Ottoman period it served as a mosque and after the British arrived it was used as a wheat store.

Nestorian Church CHURCH
(Abdullah Paşa Sokak) Built between 1360 and 1369 this Nestorian order church has a sublimely well-preserved bell tower and squat golden-stoned facade.

According to local tradition if you take soil from the church grounds and place it in your enemy's house, within one year they'll either die or leave Cyprus (it's probably best not to try out if this works for any enemies you have at home).

Canbulat Museum MUSEUM
(Canbulat Yolu; adult/student 5/3TL; ⊙9am-7pm Jun-Sep, 9am-12.30pm & 1.30-4.45pm Oct-May) During the siege of Famagusta, Ottoman hero Canbulat Bey reportedly charged his horse at a gruesome medieval siege device consisting of a spiked wheel. He destroyed the device, himself and his horse in the process but inspired the Ottomans to conquer the Venetian-held city.

His tomb contains a small museum with a simple collection of pottery and portraits featuring Lala Mustafa Paşa. There's also a historical display detailing the Turkish take on the 1974 events, and the Old Town's enclaves.

St George of the Greeks Church HISTORIC SITE
(Mustafa Paşa S.M Ersu Sokak) The ruins of this once stately Byzantine church are highly picturesque. You can still make out the faint outlines of once rich frescos upon the interior stone walls.

St George of the Latins Church HISTORIC SITE
(Cafer Paşa Sokak) Sitting incongrously amid a traffic intersection, St George of the Latins is one of Famagusta's oldest churches. The remaining walls with their distinctive lancet windows are a good example of early Gothic architecture.

🏖 Beaches

Glapsides BEACH
FREE This sandy public beach is 4km north of Famagusta. Shallow and sheltered by its position in the bay, it's popular with locals and great for kids.

There's a beach bar and restaurant, and you can hire sun loungers and umbrellas. Jet skis, pedal-bikes and canoes are available for

VAROSIA (MARAŞ)

Before 1974, the Varosia (Maraş in Turkish) district was a thriving community of Greek Cypriots. Many owned and ran the large resort hotels in what was considered Famagusta's Riviera, overlooking perhaps the island's most amazing beaches.

In August of that year, with air raids and Turkish military advances in the North, Varosia's residents fled, leaving uncleared breakfast dishes and taking with them little more than the clothes they wore. Many left on the assumption that they would return within a few days, once the emergency was over and a semblance of normality was restored. That didn't happen. The Turkish army marched on the town unimpeded, and to this day Varosia has remained empty.

Now the barricades at Varosia are one of the island's most haunting sights, a lingering reminder of the dark days of 1974. Apartment blocks, shops and houses have remained untouched for 37 years, and are covered in dust and sediment. A looted car dealership still stocks a single 1974 model, entombed in its showroom, frozen in time. The grand hotels of this once booming resort town now have bare windows and shell-fire deposits, and have been left to slowly decay like giant hollow sentinels on the coast.

The city also held Varosia's wealthy Archaeological Museum. No one knows what happened to its vast collection after the initial lootings. This is impossible to verify due to the town's isolation. Historians fear important pieces have been relocated or sold on the black market.

Varosia and the rest of the 'dead zone' are surrounded by barbed-wire fences, and metal drums block the streets, preventing passage within. Visitors cannot enter the area, except for visits to the **Agios Ioannis Church** (admission 4TL; ⊘9am-1pm Mon-Fri), 120m into the restricted area. You will need to pass a checkpoint before you approach – don't be surprised if you're simply turned away.

A very small part of the town is still inhabited, 200m off the main strip of Polat Paşa, where you can drive alongside the fence and peer in. Photography is forbidden.

---

hire, and the conditions are great for snorkelling. The beach is also an avid birdwatching location during migratory seasons.

Glapsides is accessed via the path beside Golden Terrace restaurant, on the main road from Famagusta.

Palm Beach BEACH
The best beach in Famagusta, this strip is located in front of the Palm Beach Hotel & Casino, which is accessible to non-guests. Its amenities are decent but costly. Follow the 'To the Beach Club' signs south of the hotel. Walk southeast along the coast road (Havva Sentürk Caddesi) to get here.

✯ Festivals & Events

**International Famagusta
Art & Culture Festival** CULTURAL
(www.magusa.org/festival) Taking place annually between 20 June and 12 July, this festival has a wide range of music including classical, jazz, hip-hop and reggae, performed by international and local artists. Theatrical performances are staged at Namık Kemal Meydanı, Othello's Tower and the Salamis theatre.

✗ Eating

Famagusta offers a few good restaurants and eateries in and around the Old Town.

★ Petek Confectioner CAFE €
(☑366 7104; Liman Yolu 1; pastries 3-7TL, ice cream 3-8TL; ⊘10am-11pm) Famed throughout North Cyprus, Petek is a temple to all things sugary with towers of *lokum* (Turkish delight), syrupy baklava, and what might be the best *dondurma* (ice cream) on the island. So pull up a pew and watch the world go by from Patek's verandah. Just make sure you've got enough money left over for the dentist bill afterwards.

Ginkgo INTERNATIONAL €€
(☑366 6660; Namık Kemal Meydanı; mains 15-25TL; ⊘11am-10pm) This friendly cafe-restaurant occupies an old *madrasa* (Islamic religious school) and arched Christian building right next to the Lala Mustafa Paşa Mosque. The wide-ranging menu does everything from decent salads and sandwiches to kebabs, pasta and grilled fish. The lunch set-menus are excellent value.

Aspava Restaurant　　　　TURKISH €€
(Liman Yolu 19; kebabs 11-15TL; ⊘11am-11pm) Succulent grilled shish kebabs, mixed grills and meze. Food is served in a vine-covered garden that looks onto the square and mosque.

Desdemona Bar & Restaurant　　TURKISH €€
(Canbulat Yolu 3; mains 17TL; ⊘6pm-midnight) Located in a windowless tower, this place has generous, well-priced meze and an old-world atmosphere. In winter it's almost exclusively a hip music bar for locals.

Hurma　　　　MEDITERRANEAN €€€
(🖉366 9700; Kemal Server Sokak 17; mains 25-30TL; ⊘6.30-11pm) Practically next door to the Palm Beach Hotel & Casino, this stylish hacienda-styled restaurant with palm trees and tranquil terrace overlooking the sea serves swank international cuisine such as escargot and fresh fish with lemon-garlic herbs.

🍸 Drinking & Nightlife

Famagusta is pretty light on drinking and entertainment. The road heading past the university towards Salamis is usually your best bet, with a string of clone-like bars and cafes.

D&B　　　　CAFE
(Namık Kemal Meydanı; ⊘10am-11.30pm) This place is great for a drink right in the heart of town, directly opposite the main mosque. Everyone from local students to travellers fills the seats here and it's the perfect spot to rest up after some serious ruin-treading.

Monks Inn　　　　BAR
(⊘5pm-late) Inside a medieval house, this bar is all about chilling out and sampling the cocktails. It's tucked away in a side street just east of Lala Mustafa Paşa Camii.

🛍 Shopping

Famagusta is very limited when it comes to shopping. Be aware that certain products are most likely counterfeits from Turkey, including items such as brand-name watches, sneakers and apparel.

Hoşgör　　　　ANTIQUES
(Mahmut Celalettin Sokak 24/1; ⊘10am-2pm Mon-Sat) In this interesting antiques trove you can find traditional Cypriot ceramics, engravings, embroidery and gifts.

ℹ Information

There are ATMs and a bank on Namık Kemal Meydanı, opposite Lala Mustafa Paşa Mosque.

Money-Exchange Office (İstiklal Caddesi; ⊘8am-5.30pm Mon-Fri)

North Cyprus Tourism Organisation (NCTO; 🖉366 2864; Ravelin Bastion; ⊘8am-5pm) Just inside the Land Gate. English-speaking staff. Good free maps of the Old Town in English and Turkish.

Police Station (🖉366 5310; İlker Sokak Körler) Located just to the south of the old city along İlker Sokak Körler.

Yaşam Hastanesi (🖉366 2876; Gazi Mustafa Kemal Bulvarı) Five minutes south of the Old Town.

ℹ Getting There & Away

BUS

Famagusta is well connected with both North Nicosia (Lefkoşa) and Kyrenia by bus.

From the **İtimat bus station** (İtimat Otogar; 🖉366 6666; Onbeş Ağustos Caddesi), buses to North Nicosia (8TL, one hour) leave half-hourly between 7am and 5.30pm.

Also from the bus station, buses to Kyrenia (Girne; 8TL; 1¼ hour) leave hourly at 20 minutes past the hour between 6.20am and 17.20am. The Girne-bound buses also stop at the Goçmen Transport office 10 minutes later.

If you're coming from Kyrenia, the buses terminate at the **Goçmen Transport office** (🖉366 4313; www.gocmentransport.com; Gazi Mustafa Kemal Bulvarı) rather than at the bus station.

MINIBUS

There are dolmuşes (minibuses) to Yenierenköy (Yiallousa; 7TL, one hour) and Dipkarpaz (Rizokarpaso; 7TL, one hour) on the Karpas Peninsula at 1pm and 5pm Monday to Saturday. They leave from just behind the İtimat bus station.

ℹ Getting Around

There are no public buses within the city as most major sights and services are within walking distance.

Taxi stands are dotted around the central town. **Kale Taksi** (Liman Yolu) and **Ada Taksi** (İsmet İnönü Caddesi) both operate in and around Famagusta as well as further afield. Tariffs are generally fixed but check before accepting a ride.

A taxi to Salamis should cost 25TL one way.

FAMAGUSTA & THE KARPAS PENINSULA FAMAGUSTA

AROUND FAMAGUSTA

The main sites and beaches of the region are 9km to 10km north of Famagusta and around its bay.

If you're driving you can check out some of the less-frequented inland villages like Geçitkale (Lefkoniko) and İskele (Trikomo) of the Mesaoria (Mesarya).

🏊 Beaches

Great stretches of beach can be found from Ancient Salamis, north of Famagusta, right around Famagusta Bay. The sea is knee deep to about 70m out and can be quite choppy on windy days.

Silver Beach   BEACH
North of Famagusta before Salamis, this shallow sandy beach is perfect for swimming and snorkelling, whereby you can explore the submerged harbour of the ancient city.

Bediz Beach   BEACH
Just past Salamis, this soft-sand beach offers all amenities, including sunbeds, umbrellas, showers and a restaurant-bar. If it's hot and you plan to see the ruins, take a swim here afterwards.

Bafra Beach   BEACH
This signposted public beach is 10km beyond Boğaz (Bogazi); turn right towards Bafra Bay. The beach is sandy with clear water and basic facilities.

ℹ️ Getting Around

The area is best seen with your own car, but most sites are close enough together for taxis to be affordable.

Cycling is another good option, but you will need your own bike as there aren't any good bike-hire places in Famagusta.

Minibuses between Famagusta and Yenierenköy (Yiallousa) can drop you off at the Salamis turn off and at Boğaz, but they run infrequently.

Ancient Salamis

According to legend, **Salamis** (Salamis Yolu; adult/student 9/3TL; ⊙ 9am-8pm Apr-Oct, to 5pm Nov-Mar) was founded around 1180 BC by Teucer (Teukros), son of Telamon, King of Salamina, on the Greek mainland. Brother to the hero Ajax, he was unable to return home from the Trojan War after failing to avenge his brother's death.

Today the vast, scattered remnants of this ancient kingdom, 9km north of Famagusta on the seaward side of the Famagusta–Boğaz

Around Famagusta (Mağusa)

highway, are one of the island's premier archaeological sites.

After its legendary beginnings, Salamis later came under Assyrian rule; the first recorded mention of it is on an Assyrian stele dated to 709 BC.

After a land and sea battle between the Greeks and the Persians in 450 BC the city (and island) submitted. The city remained under Persian control until the great patriot king Evagoras fought for and obtained independence. During his reign Salamis flourished. It issued its own money and nurtured a thriving philosophical and literary scene, receiving noted Greek thinkers and poets.

Later, after Alexander the Great put an end to Persian domination across the island, the city saw a short period of peace. Nicocreon (the last king of Salamis) submitted to Alexander's rule and after Alexander's death, continued to cooperate with the subsequent Ptolemaic rulers; quelling uprisings in other Cypriot kingdoms. Nicocreon's death in 311 BC remains a mystery. Some texts says that he committed suicide while others hold that he was murdered. What is clear is that despite Ptolemy rule over Salamis lasting until 58 BC, the city began to flounder after Nicocreon's death.

It wasn't until Cyprus became a Roman colony that the city prospered again, through rebuilding and public works. It went on to suffer two earthquakes and a tidal wave, requiring rebuilding once more, courtesy of Emperor Constantine II. In AD 350 the city was renamed Constantia and declared Episcopal.

Constantia suffered similar problems to its predecessor and in the 7th and 8th centuries it suffered Saracen Arab raids.

Its silted-over harbour became unusable and the city was essentially forgotten. Many of its stones were later used to build Famagusta.

Gymnasium
ARCHAEOLOGICAL SITE

The remains of the city's gymnasium, with columned courtyard and adjacent pools, used for exercise and pampering, allude to Salamis' original grandeur. Its northerly portico is surrounded by headless statues despoiled by Christian zealots as symbols of pagan worship. Many that had survived numerous raids have disappeared since 1974. Fortunately, some made it to Nicosia's Cyprus Museum and are now prized exhibits.

ℹ️ SALAMIS TIPS

➡ Allow at least half a day for your visit. There is about 7km of rambling to see it all.

➡ Once you pass the main entrance, stick to the site map so that you don't retrace your steps too much.

➡ On hot days take a hat and bottles of water with you as there's no shade.

➡ Be wary of snakes, especially in the more overgrown parts of the site.

➡ The adjacent beach is perfect for a swim after a day's exploring. There's a good patch of sand right by the entrance car park or, for a mid-exploration dip, take the short trail down to the beach from the Kambanopetra Basilica.

➡ The handy restaurant at the site entrance car park dishes up excellent meze and grills. It's a top spot for lunch.

Baths
ARCHAEOLOGICAL SITE

East of the portico are the Hellenistic and Roman baths, where you can see the exposed under-floor heating system. The southern entrance has a fresco of two faces, and in the south hall are two of the site's finest mosaics, dating from the 3rd and 4th centuries AD.

One mosaic depicts Leda and the swan, the other Apollo and Artemis combating the Niobids. Some believe that the latter is a scene of a battle between warriors and Amazons.

Theatre
ARCHAEOLOGICAL SITE

Dating from the time of Augustus (31 BC to AD 14), the theatre once held 15,000 spectators. Much of it was destroyed by earthquakes, leaving stone raiders to seize its blocks for building projects elsewhere. Since then, it has been partially restored and occasionally hosts outdoor events (look out for advertisements in Famagusta).

Roman Villa
ARCHAEOLOGICAL SITE

South of the theatre, the villa was originally a two-storey structure made up of a reception hall and an inner courtyard with columned portico. The villa was utilised long after the city was finally abandoned and used as an olive oil mill. The grinding stone can still be seen today.

FAMAGUSTA (MAĞUSA) & THE KARPAS (KIRPAŞA) PENINSULA ANCIENT SALAMIS

Ancient Salamis

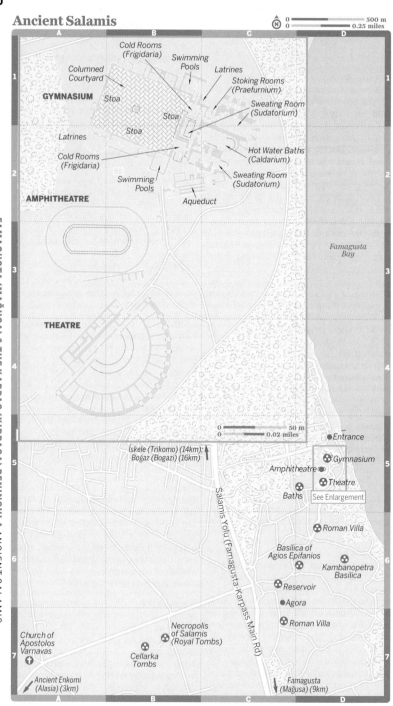

Kambanopetra Basilica ARCHAEOLOGICAL SITE
The vast remains of this 4th-century basilica are an entrancing spot with lonely columns backed by the sea. Originally it would have been an impressive church with three apses. In the complex behind the church (believed to have contained a bathhouse) there is an intricate, well-preserved mosaic floor.

Basilica of Agios Epifanios ARCHAEOLOGICAL SITE
Once the largest basilica in Cyprus, this church was built during the episcopacy of Epifanios (AD 386–403) and completely destroyed during Arab raids in the 7th century.

Reservoir ARCHAEOLOGICAL SITE
At the southern end of the site you come to the Roman-era reservoir, which stored the water brought to Salamis by a 50km aqueduct.

Agora & Temple of Zeus ARCHAEOLOGICAL SITE
Just behind the reservoir are the sparse remains of **Agora** – the city's place of assembly during the Roman era – and the **Temple of Zeus** which the Romans built over an earlier Hellenistic temple. Not much remains from either complex; the stones having long been pilfered for other building projects.

Necropolis of Salamis

This ancient **cemetery** (Royal Tombs, Salamis Mezarlık Alanı; ☑ 378 8331; adult/student 7/3TL; ⊙ 9am-5pm) dates back to the 7th and 8th centuries BC and consists of a scattering of 150 graves spread out over the wide field.

The arrangement of the burial chambers closely matches descriptions of Mycenaean tombs in Homer's *Iliad*. Kings and nobles were buried here with their favoured worldly possessions, food, drink, and even their sacrificed slaves.

The tombs are prominently signposted, south of the Salamis turn-off, along the road to the Church of Apostolos Varnavas.

Further south on the site, marked by a lone eucalyptus tree, are the Cellarka tombs. These smaller rock-cut tombs were used for less important members of the royal community. The tombs have steep steps leading to the underground chambers where stone urns were placed pending the decomposition of their contents. Thereafter the bones were removed and the chambers reused.

Most tombs have been looted over the years, though at least three have yielded treasure and antiquities that are now in Nicosia's Cyprus Museum.

Church of Apostolos Varnavas

This beautiful Orthodox **church** (☑ 378 8331; adult/student 7/3TL; ⊙ 9am-7pm Jun-Sep, to 3.30pm Oct-Apr) is dedicated to St Paul's good friend Varnavas (Barnabas), who was born in Cyprus and carried out his missionary work here. Although his name and work are listed in the Bible's 'Acts of the Apostles', he was never officially one of them.

Today the church is an icon museum with a wide selection of Greek Orthodox icons and some frescos on display but its the stunningly well-preserved architecture of the building that is the true star.

Three monks (who were also brothers) called Barnabas, Stefanos and Khariton governed the church from 1917. They attempted to remain after 1974 but ultimately left in 1976, following constant searches of the premises and travel restrictions imposed by the Turkish authorities. They lived out their days at Stavrovouni Monastery.

The church was spared from the destruction and looting that befell many churches in the North when Turkish authorities turned it into a museum. Although many Greek Cypriots have objected to the site's use for monetary gain and not for worship, they are pleased the church has survived.

The original church was built in AD 477, over the site of Varnavas' tomb. It was discovered by Anthemios, the bishop of Constantia (Salamis), following a revelation in a dream. The current structure was built by Archbishop Philotheos in 1756 and incorporates much of the original church.

In the courtyard there is also a small archaeological museum, which contains some excellent finds from Salamis and nearby Enkomi. Some of its contents may have been moved from Varosia's now defunct Archaeological Museum.

The artefacts and the rooms are not well signed. Clockwise from the entrance, the first room houses Bronze Age objects, the next has exhibits from the Venetian period, and there's a mixture of Ottoman and Classical periods in the final room. The most interesting exhibit is the statue of a woman holding a poppy, believed to be the goddess Demeter.

The church is 9km northwest of Famagusta, 2km down the well signposted turn-off just south of Salamis.

Ancient Enkomi (Alasia)

The Bronze Age city of **Enkomi** (Enkomi Ören Yeni; adult/student 5/3TL; ⊘ 9am-7pm May-Sep, to 3.30pm Oct-Apr) dates back as far as 1800 BC. It rose to prominence when it became a large copper-producing centre during the late Bronze Age (1650–1050 BC).

What remains of the present site dates from around 1200 BC. The rectangular grid layout was established then, and its fine public buildings were erected.

The site is a two kilometres west, along the same road, from the Church of Apostolos Varnavas. The site itself is widespread and requires a lot of walking to get around. Pick up a leaflet with map at the ticket office to help with navigation.

Enkomi was known for its high standard of living and its wealthy merchants who conducted trade as agents of the Mycenaeans.

Akkadian cuneiform slabs found in Tel el-Amarna, Egypt, contain promises of copper to the pharaoh from the king of Alasia, in return for silver and luxury items. It's still unclear whether the name Alasia referred to Cyprus as a whole or just Enkomi itself.

A fire and at least two earthquakes led to Enkomi's decline, and then its inland harbour silted up. Some speculate that its last residents headed to the coast and founded Salamis. Much of the site has been looted, but many of its tombs were said to have held gold, ivory and exquisite Mycenaean pottery.

Southern Site   ARCHAEOLOGICAL SITE

The southern end of the site (nearest the ticket office) is where excavations in the early 20th century unearthed some of Enkomi's most important finds.

From south to north you see the **House of Bronzes**, where bronze accoutrements were unearthed in 1934, the **House of Pillar**, a public building, the **Sanctuary of the Horned God**, where a 60cm-tall bronze statue (now in the Cyprus Museum) was found, and **Tomb 18**, where most of the site's treasure was recovered.

Cenotaph Mound   ARCHAEOLOGICAL SITE

The cenotaph mound, built on a rocky outpost, escaped much of the looting the rest of Enkomi suffered with its funeral pyre concealing much of its contents from tomb-robbers. Limestone statues, amphorae from Rhodes, an archaic bronze shield and clay effigies have all been recovered from here.

Archaeologists now contend that this probable tomb may have belonged to Nicocreon and that the plain between Enkomi and Salamis was once a significant connection between the two cities.

İskele (Trikomo)

The crossroads village of İskele, birthplace of Ethniki Organosi tou Kypriakou Agona (EOKA; National Organisation for the Cypriot Struggle) leader Georgios Grivas, is noteworthy for its 12th-century church **Panagia Theotokos** (Church of the Blessed Virgin Mary) which is now an **icon museum** (İskele İkon Müzesi; adult/student 5/3TL; ⊘ 9am-5pm Jun-Sep, to 3.30pm Oct-May).

The domed building, with arched recesses in its side walls, has fine paintings of the Virgin Mary of the Annunciation and the Prayer of Joachim and Anna, in which the couple are seen embracing while a young girl peers from behind a window. The marble inlay from the church's original iconostasis is in the belfry.

Panagia Theotokos is easy to spot on the western edge of the village.

Boğaz (Bogazi)

This small fishing village, about 24km north of Famagusta, is the last beach stop before the road takes you inland to the Karpas (Kırpaşa) Peninsula proper. The small harbour still has a quaint, yesteryear ambience, filled with local fishing boats while just to the south is a stretch of developed beach with straw umbrellas and sun loungers.

Many Russian, German and British visitors rent villas here during the summer and the coastline is packed with modern identikit holiday-home developments. To cater for this seasonal influx the seafront is filled with pricy fish taverns. Located on the sea walk, with great views, reasonably priced **Kiyi** (Boğaz; mains 25-30TL; ⊘ 11am-11pm) serves fresh fish (caught daily) with large portions of chips.

KARPAS (KIRPAŞA) PENINSULA

A far cry from urban activity, the Karpas Peninsula (also known as Karpasia and Kırpaşa in Turkish) offers miles of rolling fields, wildlife, olive groves, carob trees, endless beaches with fantastic swimming, forgotten archaeological sites and the remains of broken Christian churches. The area is bliss for cyclists and ramblers, with mesmerising wildflowers that burst into colour every spring.

The peninsula has remained virtually untouched by development, its smattering of villages almost lost in time. The region somewhat sidestepped the events of 1974 as its isolated Turks and Greeks ignored the call to segregate themselves and continued to live alongside each other.

The village of Dipkarpaz (Rizokarpaso) remains home to some elderly Greek Cypriots, but most villages are now populated by mainland Turkish settlers, which is more apparent the further north you go.

The most sizeable village is Yenierenköy (Yiallousa), with its small square and village centre. It has a good tourist office, set up with the intention of increasing interest in the region. With access from the Republic of Cyprus now essentially a non-issue, more travellers are beginning to visit the Karpas, and prices are beginning to reflect this.

Many Greek Cypriots make the twice-yearly pilgrimage from the south to the very tip of the island to visit the revered Monastery of Apostolos Andreas.

Developers are starting to encroach further up the peninsula, and you may notice some gaudy out-of-place concrete stuccoes cropping up. Thankfully, the entire cape from Dipkarpaz upwards has been declared a national park, and it's hoped that this will preserve the area's wildlife and ecology for years to come.

🏖 Beaches

Kumyalı Beach   BEACH
(Koma tou Gialou) This little beach–fishing harbour, just outside the village of Kumyalı, is ideal for a last stop and swim as you drive up the western flank of the peninsula to the more exquisite beaches.

Golden Beach   BEACH
(Nangomi Bay) Possibly the best on the island, Golden Beach is worth the trip to the Karpas in itself. Its white sand dunes and gentle curves meet the calm, clear sea, and wild donkeys graze nonchalantly on the hills while you soak up the tranquility. It's truly enchanting, with little development.

The beach is 5km before Zafer Burnu (Cape Apostolos Andreas). Situated between scrubby headlands and stretching for several kilometres with some basic restaurants and accommodation options.

Now part of a national park and also prime turtle-nesting ground. If you're visiting in September, contact the certified volunteers (www.cyprusturtles.org) who monitor the progress of the turtles and you may even be lucky enough to witness baby turtles hatching.

Agios Filon Beach   BEACH
With its soft sand and big, flat sea rocks, this is another fantastic beach, near the Oasis

---

PROTECTING THE WILDERNESS

In 1983, 150 sq km of the Karpas region, from the municipality of Dipkarpaz (Rizokarpaso) to Zafer Burnu (Cape Apostolos Andreas), was declared a national park by Turkish Cypriot authorities. Since then, encroaching development and the building boom of 2004, in anticipation of the island's unification, saw nearby places like Bafra and Yenierenköy (Yiallousa) build new hotels and resort complexes. This rapid development has conservationists deeply concerned about the sustainability of the region's greater environment, particularly its unique wildlife, plant life, undiscovered archaeological sites and rugged beaches.

Now lobby groups, biologists and environmentalists are banding together and pushing for an extension to the park's boundaries to include Ronas Bay (north of Dipkarpaz). They want a commitment to adhere to stricter guidelines regarding the peninsula's use and further development. Most pressing are concerns over the building of new roadways and the scope of electrification plans for remote areas of the cape. It's clear that declaring the area a national park is a step in the right direction, but more needs to be done to protect one of the island's last unspoilt habitats.

Karpas (Kirpasa) Peninsula

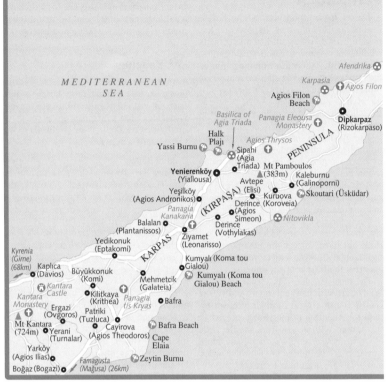

at Ayfilon hotel and restaurant. It's also a turtle-hatching beach and a great place to watch the sunset.

ⓘ Getting Around

The only public transport in the area is the bus from Famagusta to Yenierenköy (6TL, 1¼ hours). Thus your own transport is necessary to explore this region properly. Taxis can be arranged locally.

The main road to the peninsula is first-rate, though signs to some of the sites lack clarity and prominence, so bring your own map.

Kantara Castle

The best vantage point on the Karpas is from this Lusignan Gothic **castle** (Kantara Kalesi; adult/student 6/3TL; ⊘ 9am-5pm Jun-Sep, to 3.30pm Oct–May), one of three in Cyprus. Kantara Castle, is the furthest east and the lowest in elevation at 690m. It has a 360-degree view of the region and a clear day, you can see the coast of Turkey and even Syria. The castle's documented history dates back to 1191 when Richard the Lionheart seized it from Isaak Komninos, the Byzantine emperor of Cyprus.

Kantara was used as a beacon station to communicate with Buffavento Castle to the west. Its significance faded in the 16th century when Venetian military strategists began to depend more on firepower than elevation for protection. In 1521 they relocated their garrison from here and the castle was left open to raiders searching for the treasures told of in legends about Kantara.

Today you can see the castle's well-preserved northern section, its towers and walls still resolutely standing. The outer entrance leads into the now somewhat overgrown barbican. The north and south towers guard the inner entrance, where you

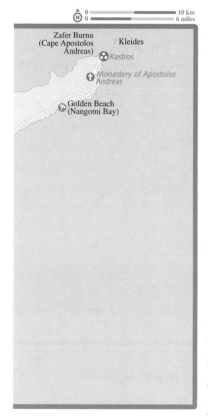

Zafer Burnu
(Cape Apostolos Andreas)

Kleides

Kastros

Monastery of Apostolos Andreas

Golden Beach (Nangomi Bay)

0 — 10 km
0 — 6 miles

Yenierenköy (Yiallousa)

Formerly a predominantly Greek village, Yenierenköy was resettled by Turkish Cypriot residents of Erenköy (Kokkina) in the South. It's the peninsula's second-largest village, with the new €15-million **Karpaz Gate Marina** (www.karpazbay.com), which is home to a couple of good restaurants, just to the north.

At the **tourist information office** (☑374 4984; Yenierenköy; ☺10am-6pm Jun-Sep, 9am-3pm Oct-May) the staff speak English and have lots of information on the peninsula. Sites in the region include the colossal **cave tombs** at Derince (Vothylakas) and some smaller versions between Avtepe (Elisi) and Kuruova (Koroveia). This area is largely unexplored. The many rough tracks here head south, toward the sea, leading you to the ruins of the ancient Bronze Age fort of **Nitovikla**.

Further east along the coast are some **sandstone caves** near Kaleburnu (Galinoporni). If you intend to drive these tracks, a 4WD is recommended. Take a good map with you, and ask at the information office (or in the local village) about how to best go about finding these unmarked sites before setting out.

Sipahi (Agia Triada)

The small village of Sipahi is home to many mainland Bulgarian Turkish settlers and a tiny community of Karpas Greeks. Like the equally small group in Dipkarpaz, they refused to leave their homes in the North and have continued to live on the peninsula despite the political situation.

The village has some superb mosaics in the now-ruined **Basilica of Agia Triada** (Sipahi; adult/student 5/3TL; ☺9am-5pm), dating from the 5th century.

While little is left of the main structure, the basilica has extensive flooring, intricately patterned with geometric and abstract mosaics. Greek inscriptions at both the northern and southern ends of the former nave reveal that the church's construction was partly financed by Deacon Iraklios on a personal vow of dedication.

The site is at the eastern end of the village and is best approached from the Dipkarpaz end of Sipahi.

enter the castle proper. Inside you'll find the garrison, latrines and a cistern.

The highest point of the complex is the lookout tower, from where flares were lit to warn of impending danger. At the castle's southwestern end are further garrisons and the postern gate, used to unleash troops and catch would-be attackers off-guard. The roof of the north tower is narrow, unfenced and vertiginous, but the views are incredible.

A free map is provided; you'll need about an hour to see everything. Children should be accompanied by an adult at all times, as there are some unfenced drops, rough tracks and uncapped holes on the site.

From Kyrenia it takes about two hours to reach the castle. You turn off the coastal highway at Kaplıca and take the narrow, winding (but easily driveable) road upwards to the car park.

FAMAGUSTA (MAĞUSA) & THE KARPAS (KIRPAŞA) PENINSULA YENIERENKÖY

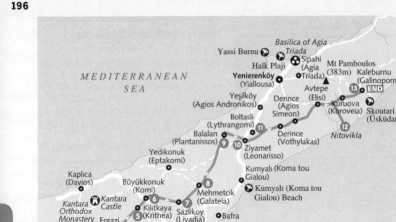

🏃 Driving Tour
Remote Rural Villages of the Karpas

START İSKELE (TRIKOMO)
FINISH KALEBURNU (GALINOPORNI)
DISTANCE 85KM; FIVE TO SIX HOURS

After perusing the church and museum at **1 İskele**, head north past Ardahan (Ardana), swinging east along 12km of zigzagging road past cliffs, hills and the hidden medieval **2 Kantara Orthodox monastery**. Take the main road leading south to the village of **3 Yerani** (Turnalar), where you can check out the church of Panagia Evangelistria, 1km to the town's west. From here go east (via Kutulus Turnalar Yolu) through the traditional village of **4 Ergazi** (Ovgoros), then a further 9km northeast to **5 Kilitkaya** (Krithea). Another 2.5km along this road is the settlement of **6 Büyükkonuk** (Komi), Cyprus' first eco village, with restored traditional buildings and an old olive mill. After you've tried some local almonds and figs, take the old road east to the village of **7 Sazlikoy** (Livadia) and the 6th-century ruins of Panagias tis Kryas church. The road northeast takes you to the

vineyards of **8 Mehmetcik** (Galateia) village and its 95-proof *zivania*. Leave via the main northeasterly road (not the stadium road) through the centre of the Karpas, and travel 16km through fields and groves to reach **9 Balalan** (Plantanissos). Continue southwest another 3km to **10 Ziyamet** (Leonarisso). Carry on past the crossroads in Karpas Anaylou and past Gelincik (Vasili) to the village of **11 Boltasli** (Lythrangomi). Here you'll find the 6th-century church of Panagia Kanakaria. It's kept locked but the village *muhtar* (elected leader) has the key. Ask around to find him. From here a road joins a string of small villages, Derince, Avtepe and Kuruova, with a series of unmarked tracks that lead to ancient cliff-tombs and the Bronze Age stronghold of **12 Nitovikla** (3km away) on the southern coast. Ask at the villages for the best paths to hike. Hop back in the car and go east to **13 Kaleburnu** (Galinoporni), where you can grab a bite and take the beach track to Skoutari (Üsküdar) for a refreshing swim.

Dipkarpaz (Rizokarpaso)

POP 3500

This is the peninsula's largest and most remote village, where a large contemporary mosque sits next to an old Orthodox church. The church is a silent companion, as its bell is no longer tolled, although a small number of Greek Cypriots still live in the village. The once thriving town is now mostly populated by mainland Turks and Kurds, who work the land and live in difficult rural conditions.

A small ring of shops and a petrol station are the only real facilities and the last chance to fill up. **Manolyam Restaurant** (mains 20-30TL) sits right next to the Karpaz Arch Houses, 500m from the village centre. It serves traditional Turkish-style food and a small but filling array of mixed meze.

Agios Filon & Afendrika

The 12th-century **Agios Filon Church** stands silently on the sparse coastline some 5km north of Dipkarpaz. Located right next to the Oasis at Ayfilon hotel, its well-preserved outside walls were built over an earlier 5th-century Christian basilica. The conceptual mosaics from the basilica can be seen outside the walls of the later church. This area was once the ancient site of **Karpasia**, prominent during the Hellenistic period and the Middle Ages. A Roman harbour was also situated here, and the remains of the breakwater can still be seen in the sea.

Bordering is the idyllic Agios Filon Beach and the **Oasis Restaurant** (Oasis at Ayfilon; mains 20-30TL; ⊙11am-3pm & 6-11pm; 🖉), serving chargrills and the peninsula's best freshly caught fish, marinated in olive oil.

A further 7km east is **Afendrika**, a major city in the 2nd century BC. What remains is a set of contiguous ruins comprising three churches: 6th-century **Agios Georgios**, **Panagia Khrysiotissa** and 10th-century **Panagia Asomatos**. Nearby are the necropolis and what remains of the citadel.

Monastery of Apostolos Andreas

On 15 August and 30 November, coachloads of Greek Cypriots make the long trek to this **monastery** (donations accepted), near the tip of the Karpas Peninsula. The object of their pilgrimage is to visit this site where miracles are reputed to take place.

Long-awaited restoration began on the monastery in 2013 and it may be closed when you visit. Ask at the Yenierenköy tourist information office. If it's open, travellers are welcome at the monastery throughout the year.

The monastery's reputation for miracles was obtained during the time of St Andrew (the patron saint of sailors), who reputedly restored the sight of a ship's captain when he arrived from Palestine. Since then attested-to miracles range from curing blindness and epilepsy to healing the crippled and granting extraordinary wishes.

Before 1974 the monastery was well supported by its devotees and pilgrims but since then – isolated from its patrons and with only a few Greek Cypriot caretakers – the great monastery began a slow and steady deterioration. Turkish Cypriot authorities began to allow a small number of pilgrims to enter the North on organised visits to the monastery from 1996. Today, with the border crossings opened, the pilgrimage is far simpler and the faithful can visit this site of holy miracles unescorted.

Zafer Burnu (Cape Apostolos Andreas)

A mere 3km from Apostolos Andreas monastery, along a dirt track, is the easternmost tip of Cyprus. From here you can see the cluster of rocky isles known collectively as the **Kleides** (The Keys).

The neolithic site of **Kastros** was once located here. Later, the ancient Greeks built a temple to Aphrodite, of which nothing remains. If you happen to have a 4WD, you can take the rougher northern track back to Dipkarpaz, though it can be particularly difficult in wet weather.

Accommodation

Best Places to Stay

➡ Bellapais Gardens (p212)

➡ Linos Inn (p204)

➡ Elyssia (p203)

Best Budget Hotels

➡ Pyramos Hotel (p204)

➡ Petrou Bros (p207)

➡ Bunch of Grapes Inn (p201)

Best Agrotourism Options

➡ Nitovikla Garden (p213)

➡ Gabriel House (p208)

➡ To Spitiko tou Arhonta (p202)

Where to Stay

Part of the charm of Cyprus is that each region has a distinctive character, so deciding on *what* you want from your holiday experience is the first priority. In the south, Larnaka is at the centre of the most tourist-driven part of the island, with nearby Agia Napa still the clubbing capital. To the west, sophisticated Lemesos is the restaurant hot spot and is an ideal central base for exploring inland and further afield. Still due west, Pafos is a favourite with families, and tour groups, but also provides easy access to the unspoilt west-coast beaches and the Troödos Mountains. The urban flip side is the capital, cultural Nicosia (Lefkosia), with fantastic museums, galleries and historic sights. In North Cyprus, Kyrenia has some superb hotels overlooking the harbour while, to the west, the Karpas (Kirpaşa) Peninsula is perfect for those who want to get away from it all, surrounded by stunning scenery, pristine beaches and coves.

Pricing

The following price ranges refer to the cost of a double room, including private bathroom and excluding breakfast. Prices ranges are for the low (winter) and high (summer) seasons.

In the budget category you may have to share a bathroom and facilities will be limited. Midrange choices often include satellite TV, private balconies and wi-fi, while the top end offers all this and more, with the accommodation generally housed in a sumptuous historic (or cutting-edge contemporary) building.

CATEGORY	COST
€	less than €60 (Republic of Cyprus), less than €40 (Northern Cyprus)
€€	€60-90 (Republic of Cyprus), €40-70 (Northern Cyprus)
€€€	more than €90 (Republic of Cyprus), more than €70 (Northern Cyprus)

Types of Accommodation

Cyprus runs the gamut of places to unpack your suitcase, ranging from beach huts to super-luxurious hotels. The rates listed in the *Cyprus Hotel Guide*, issued free by the Cyprus Tourism Organisation (CTO), are the maximum prices (normally applicable in mid-summer) and are regulated by the CTO.

Agrotourism

There is a good range of agrotourism places to stay in the South. Some are self-contained houses with gardens that are ideal for large families or groups of friends, while couples may prefer a self-contained apartment in a historic stone-clad complex. All are fully equipped, and many have extras like swimming pools and wi-fi. This is also a superb and often very economical way for independent travellers to see the country. Rates are about €40 for a single room, €55 to €70 for a double and €100 for a luxury studio.

Most properties are situated away from major centres, so you'll need your own transport to get around, or you'll have to rely on sometimes sketchy public transport.

Camping

In the South there are only four licensed camping grounds, all with seasonal opening times: two in Pafos, one in Lemesos and one in Troödos. All have hot showers, a mini market and a snack bar. The North has even fewer camping grounds, and facilities aren't as good as in the South. Costs are similar, however.

Private Rooms

Domatia (private rooms for rent), advertised by the word *camere,* are not common in Cyprus; in fact, the practice is officially discouraged by the CTO. However, in Agia Napa you'll see signs advertising rooms, and occasionally come across them in the more popular mountain resorts such as the Troödos Mountains and the Pafos district in the South. Unsurprisingly, the rooms are exceedingly cheap, generally hovering around €15 to €20, and meals can often be provided. If you don't see any obvious signs, consider asking in the local taverna or bar.

Hotels

In the main southern resorts, many hotels deal primarily with package-tour groups. However, individual travellers can usually still find a room even in 'resort' hotels. Quality varies markedly, though prices are strictly controlled by the CTO. In general, hotels will have good facilities, mainly geared for families; most include breakfast in the price.

The quality of hotels in the North is generally good at the top end of the scale. Package-tour visitors constitute the bulk of guests, but as in the South, there will usually be a room available for walk-ins. The *North Cyprus Hotel Guide* is available from the North Cyprus Tourism Organisation (NCTO) and tourist offices in the main towns, while the **North Cyprus Hotels** (www.northcyprushotels.co.uk) website provides a comprehensive guide to hotels in Northern Cyprus.

Throughout Cyprus (as with anywhere in the world) you can often save money by booking hotels online.

Apartment Hotels

Apartment hotels are becoming increasingly popular and are prevalent in the main southern resorts of Pafos, Lemesos and Larnaka, as well as in and around Kyrenia in Northern Cyprus. Most have well-equipped kitchens. They are particularly ideal for families with young children (or fussy eaters!).

Costs typically start at around €35 for a studio apartment and €40 for a double room (both including kitchenette).

ECOFRIENDLY ACCOMMODATION

In 2014 the Cyprus Tourism Organisation (CTO) determined minimum mandatory sustainability standards for hotels located throughout the Republic. These included supporting local agriculture, using Cypriot products and services (as far as possible) and reducing energy and waste use. This is another giant eco-stride for a country already recognised for its unequalled commitment to solar power in Europe.

LEMESOS & THE SOUTH

Lemesos (Limassol)

The good news is that there are plenty of hotels in Lemesos. The bad news is that they are mostly along a 9km tourist strip to the northeast of the old city, and are often crowded and overpriced. The old city doesn't feature many high-quality establishments, but hotels in this area are more used to walk-in travellers and are likely to have rooms vacant.

The cheapest hotels are clustered to the east of the castle, while the more luxurious hotels are located at the far northeastern end of the tourist centre.

Metropole　　　　　　　　　　　HOTEL €
(Map p49; ☑ 2536 2686; Ifigenias 6; s/d €45/55; ✳🛜) A sound budget option in the heart of the historic centre. This comfortable place has decent-sized, slightly dimly lit rooms sporting soothing pale peach and cream decor with pleasant prints of local scenes on the walls, and balconies made for pint-sized people.

Lordos Hotel Apts　　　　APARTMENTS €
(☑ 2558 2850; www.lordoshotelapts.com; Andrea Zaimi 13; 2-person apt from €55; ✳🛜) These basic, no-nonsense but squeaky-clean apartments with kitchenettes offer good value for self-caterers. Rooms can verge on the noisy side – light sleepers should ask for one away from the road. It's a block away from Debenhams department store (an excellent directional landmark) with the historic centre a 2km walk away.

Luxor Guest House　　　　　　　INN €
(Map p49; ☑ 2536 2265; Agiou Andreou 101; s/d €20/40) This long-time backpacker haunt is looking rough around the edges these days but manager Serg is as welcoming as ever. The airy rooms with painted wood-board ceilings and dinky balconies (all shared bathrooms) brim with creaky, faded glory. If you prefer character over amenities, and need a cheap sleep, it's still fine for a night.

★Chrielka　　　　　　　　APARTMENTS €€
(☑2535 8366; Olympion 7; low-high studio €60-70, apt €85-110; ✳🛜🌊) The common areas are festooned with elegant Asian ceramics and artefacts collected by owner Mr Nikitas during his travels. The 33 apartments and studios here are tastefully decorated and include balcony and kitchenette. There's a cute bar and a little pool, and the location beside the Municipal Gardens is refreshingly peaceful.

Estella Hotel Apartments　　APARTMENTS €€
(☑2532 1922; www.estellacyprus.com; Christaki Kranou 3, Germasogeia; low-high r €45-60; 🅿✳🛜🌊) This tidy option has good-sized and light-filled rather colourful rooms as well as slightly squashy studios with kitchenettes. It's all shipshape, kept scrupulously clean and has a homely vibe with staff that go out of their way to help. It's in the tourist area, about 4km east of the historic centre.

VILLA RENTALS

Renting a villa is a very common practice in Cyprus, since it's cheaper for a week or 10-day stay than a hotel room. You'll be able to find good villas, with or without pools, in the tourist centres or in the middle of nowhere. Real estate agencies can often help. Alternatively, check the classified sections in the local English-language newspapers. Expect to pay from €40 per person per night. There's usually a minimum stay of at least two weeks.

A number of websites also offer villa rentals:

Rent Cyprus Villas (www.rentcyprusvillas.com) Luxury villas for rent.

Cyprus Apartments (www.cyprus-apartments.net) Self-catering apartments throughout the main southern resorts.

Owners Direct (www.ownersdirect.co.uk/cyprus.htm) Long-time respected source of privately owned accommodation to let.

Rent Villa Cyprus (www.rentvillacyprus.net) Large choice of villas, most with a minimum of one-week rental.

Londa
BOUTIQUE HOTEL €€€

(☎2586 5555; www.londahotel.com; George A 72, Potamos Germasogeia; low-high r incl breakfast €119-180; P❄🖥🏊) The island's first couture hotel oozes casual glamour with rooms filled with lashings of white linen, cool earthy colours and contemporary custom-made furnishings. Extensive facilities include spa, infinity pool and the Caprice Bar, which flips to a smoochy club in the evening when the resident DJ takes centre stage. Located 550m east of the historic centre.

Curium Palace
HOTEL €€€

(☎2536 3121; www.curiumpalacehotel.com.cy; Vyronos 2; low-high incl breakfast s €75-90, d €90-115; P❄🖥🏊) All snazzy chandeliers and white marble in the foyer, this long-standing hotel is one of Lemesos' classiest choices. Expect spacious rooms fitted out in soothing neutrals with large gleaming bathrooms and a host of added trimmings for a comfortable stay, including a fitness centre, tennis court and a choice of restaurants and bars.

Le Meridien Limassol
HOTEL €€€

(☎2586 2000; www.lemeridien-cyprus.com; Lefkosia-Lemesos Hwy; low-high s €101-170, d €120-292; P❄🖥🏊) This luxury beach-side giant has all the bells and whistles you'd expect, from sumptuous spa to a myriad of dining and entertainment choices. Rooms are bright and contemporary with a suitably 'beachy' feel and there are also rooms for those with accessibility needs. The hotel is located around 13km east of the Municipal Gardens, following the coastal road.

Around Lemesos

Bunch of Grapes Inn
HOTEL €

(☎2522 1275; Ioannou Erotokritou 9, Pissouri; s/d/tr €30/50/60; 🖥) This atmospheric old mansion (with popular restaurant) dates back some 200 years and was once home to a wealthy Pissourian. Located in the centre of the village, it has nine basic rooms (fan only) with bags of simple country character that look out onto a central courtyard perfumed by jasmine and honeysuckle.

Art by Praxis
APARTMENTS €€

(☎9989 4737; www.artbypraxis.com; Governor's Beach; low-high studio €45-55, apt €55-75; P❄🖥) 🖋 These ultra-modern apartments, situated within walking distance of Governor's Beach, have striking contemporary artwork

and sleek minimalist style. Rentals usually have to be booked for a minimum of three nights. Praxis is a Lemesos-based architectural and design company that focuses on bioclimatic design. Consequently, the apartments are built with recyclable materials, the energy is exclusively solar and irrigation is supplied by recycled water.

Vouni Lodge
AGROTOURISM €€

(☎9968 5395; www.agrotourism.com.cy; Vouni; 2-/4-person apt €65-85; P🖥) Located on the main street in the village, this 200-year-old building has three apartments, decorated in rustic traditional style with beamed roofs, wrought-iron furniture and lacy bed covers, and outside tables under the olive trees. The top-storey apartment has distant sea views. There's a minimum three-night stay.

★ Apokryfo
BOUTIQUE HOTEL €€€

(☎2581 3777; www.apokryfo.com; Lofou; r incl breakfast from €150; P❄🖥🏊) A piece of rural-chic on the edge of Lofou village; Apokryfo means 'hidden away' in Greek and it's certainly appropriate for this charming boutique hotel. Restored by architect Vakis Hadjikyriacou and his interior-decorator wife, rooms effortlessly blend rustic character with modern luxury, utilising earthy colours, limed wood and local textiles. This is one hideaway you won't want to leave.

Baby baths, cots and highchairs can be arranged. The hotel's Agrino restaurant is also top notch.

ACCOMMODATION AROUND LEMESOS

TROÖDOS MOUNTAINS

Troödos

Troödos Forest Park has four campgrounds. The Troödos campground is best for longer stays. The other three sites, Platania, Kampi tou Kalogyrou and Prodromos dam, are also good but are designed for shorter stays or weekenders and have more basic facilities.

Troödos CAMPGROUND €
(☑ 2242 1624; camp sites per tent €6; ⊙ May-Oct; 🅿) Situated 500m east of Central Troödos, with cooking facilities, showers, toilets and water. Tent included in the price.

Jubilee HOTEL €€
(☑ 2542 0107; www.jubileehotel.com; low-high s €35-50, d €70-95; 🅿 ✳ @ 🛜) This long established hotel is 350m from the village on the Prodromos road. It's the best place to stay during the snow season for access to the slopes; the sitting rooms are suitably cosy with fireplaces, warm colour schemes and card tables. The hotel is undergoing considerable renovation that should be completed by spring 2015; prices may alter slightly.

Platres

Colonial Britain still lingers in the mountain hotels: most have a very old-world feel to them and are full of character. Agrotourism is becoming more and more popular throughout the villages, with some great options now available.

Petit Palais HOTEL €
(☑ 2542 2723; www.petitpalaishotel.com; Platres; s/d €35/50; 🛜) Located right on the main crossroad in town and impossible to miss, this Alpine-style hotel is very good value. The rooms are spacious and comfortable with parquet floors and a play-it-safe cream colour scheme. All have balconies; the corner rooms have two (No 100 is a good choice). There's a large sun terrace and a downstairs restaurant and bar.

★ **New Helvetia** HOTEL €€
(☑ 2542 1348; www.newhelvetiahotel.com; Elvetias 6; s/d incl breakfast €45/70; 🅿 ✳ @) Situated in an isolated and peaceful location at the northeastern end of the village, this

hotel, founded in 1929, has an evocative old-fashioned feel of luxury and comfort. The rooms have a fresher, albeit still rustic, look with parquet floors and wooden balconies overlooking the pines.

Semiramis HOTEL €€
(☑ 9979 2331; www.semiramishotelcyprus.com; Spyrou Kyprianou 55; low-high r incl breakfast €45-75; 🅿 ✳) Great little family-run hotel among the pines, with 1900s charm and just 10 cosy rooms. Staying here feels a lot like your own private getaway, with catered breakfast, a relaxed atmosphere and personable staff.

Forest Park HOTEL €€€
(☑ 2542 1751; www.forestparkhotel.com.cy; Spyrou Kyprianou 62; s/d incl breakfast €70-95; 🅿 ✳ @ 🏊) This large hotel is dripping with history, having played host to Greek, Egyptian and British royalty. Its appeal has faded somewhat over the years, although the old-world glamour still echoes in its sumptuous bar. There are two pools, gym, massage parlour and sauna, and the rooms are fully equipped. It is frequented by wealthy Cypriots.

Around Platres

To Spiti tou Xeni AGROTOURISM €
(☑ 9941 9251; Galata; studio €40-50; 🅿 ✳) This well-maintained traditional house in the village of Galata is completely self-catering. It has good-size beds, a fireplace and clay ovens. The views of the surrounding hills and valley are wonderful, and there's a sense of serenity about the whole place. Call Mrs Vathoulla directly for access and group rates.

★ **To Spitiko tou Arhonta** AGROTOURISM €€
(☑ 2546 2120; www.spitiko3elies.com; 2-/4-person apt €75/130; 🅿 ✳ 🛜) Perched above the village of Treis Elies, with a shady garden, the house has two one-bedroom apartments and one two-bedroom apartment, all self-catering and decorated like a rustic paradise. Friendly owner Androulla may even give you a lesson in cooking *kleftiko* (oven-baked lamb), as she prepares meals on request. If you're exploring the E4 route, this is an ideal base.

Airport transfers available, along with bicycle rental. There's a minimum two-night stay.

RURAL ACCOMMODATION

Agrotourism (accommodation in rural properties) dates back to the 1990s when the Cyprus Agrotourism Company (CAC), concerned at the continuing local exodus, sought to protect the heritage of traditional homes by supporting their conversion into atmospheric accommodation for tourists. Aside from hiking, cycling and winter skiing, other promoted activities may include haloumi cheese making, olive picking, horse riding and organised excursions to Byzantine churches. There are around 100 properties, located primarily in the foothills of the Troödos Mountains, as well as throughout the districts of Nicosia, Larnaka, Lemesos and Pafos. For an excellent colour brochure listing agrotourism places to stay, contact the **Cyprus Agrotourism Company** (☎2233 7715; www.agrotourism.com.cy; PO Box 4535, CY-1390 Lefkosia) or check the online listings.

Stou Kir Yianni HOTEL €€

(www.omodosvillagecottage.com; Aivou 15, Omodos; r incl breakfast €70; ☎) This pleasant small hotel is located down a narrow side street in the centre of the village. Rooms have dark-wood furniture, colourful paintwork and canopy beds, as well as small kitchenettes; make sure you go for one with a balcony overlooking the street. The restaurant here is one of the best in town.

Marathasa Valley

The sleeping options in Pedoulas are respectable; you can expect the basics of simple decor and comfort.

★ Elyssia HOTEL €

(☎9975 3573; Filoxenias 47, Pedoulas; low-high r incl breakfast €40-60; P ✱ ✲) These spacious, pretty rooms all have balconies that overlook the valley. The hotel is obviously well cared for by the owner, who is charming and eager to please. Three of the rooms have Jacuzzis at no extra cost. The rooftop terrace is a wonderful alternative to the swimming pool, and the excellent downstairs restaurant offers breakfast, and traditional Cypriot food later in the day.

Christys Hotel HOTEL €

(☎2295 2655; anchristys@cytanet.com.cy; Filoxenias 45; r €21; ☎) This family-owned hotel is a little scuffed but the rooms are perfectly acceptable and clean, though bathrooms are small. There's a large terrace where you can enjoy breakfast under the grapevines admiring the view over the rooftops. All in an all, a cheap sleep winner.

Two Flowers HOTEL €

(☎2295 2372; Filoxenias 26, Pedoulas; low-high r incl breakfast €40-60; P ☎) An attractive little B&B that offers individualised rooms – red curtains and a matching red quilt in one, a simple, white rustic look in another – some with a view of the valley. It's very family friendly and great value.

Olga's Katoï AGROTOURISM €€

(☎2235 0283; Kalopanayiotis; d incl breakfast €70; P ✱ @ ☎ ✲) This two-storey traditional stone house has been meticulously maintained for over 300 years. It consists of a main house with sitting room, kitchen and two of the 12 bedrooms located upstairs; the 10 other bedrooms are built in a row separately, and all have fantastic views of the surrounding valley. Breakfast is served on the terrace.

To Spiti tis Polyxenis AGROTOURISM €€

(☎2249 7509; 2-/4-person house €70/145; P ✱) This two-bedroom house is on the Nicosia side of Kalopanayiotis village. The house is decorated with traditional furniture, with large wooden doors opening onto a peaceful, sun-filled courtyard. There's also a kitchenette and a large bathroom.

Solea Valley

Kakopetria has one of the best choices of quality accommodation in the mountains.

Ekali HOTEL €

(☎2292 2501; www.ekali-hotel.com; Grigoriou Digeni 22, Kakopetria; s/d €40/55; P ✱) A straightforward, tidy and clean option, with decent rooms decorated in dark-red hues, and laminated-wood flooring. It's a good hotel for families with young children, as the rooms have baby-monitoring facilities. Can be overpriced without a booking.

Mill Hotel
HOTEL €€

(☎ 2292 2536; www.cymillhotel.com; Mylou 8, Kakopetria; r incl breakfast €90; ☻ closed 20 Nov–20 Dec; P❄ 🛜) Situated at the old mill site, on the hill side of the river, this historic hotel offers a range of well-sized, comfortable rooms decorated in a plush neocolonial style. Bright and airy, with big bathrooms (all with Jacuzzi), it's ideally located two minutes from the town square.

★ Linos Inn
HOTEL €€€

(☎ 2292 3161; www.linosinn.com; Palea Kakopetria 34, Kakopetria; low-high r €80-95; P❄@) The captivating original architecture has been retained here wherever possible. The inn is laden with antique furniture, rustic rooms, four-poster beds covered in woven white linen, and fireplaces. In the top-end suites and studios are plasma-screen TVs and Jacuzzis and there's a separate sauna. Book in advance if you're visiting on a weekend. The restaurant serves high-quality traditional food.

Agros

Archontiko Rousias
AGROTOURISM €€

(☎ 2275 0605; Palichori; 2-/4-person house €70/140; P❄) This replete old house offers agrotourism at its finest in the village of Palichori (14km east of Agros). The house has deluxe rooms with modern facilities, but retains all its original characteristics. Great for self-catering families or romantics looking for a mountain escape. The balconies have unparalleled views over the village.

Rodon
HOTEL €€

(☎ 2552 1201; www.rodonhotel.com; Agros; r incl breakfast €55-70; P❄@🏊) This sweeping modern hotel, with views of the rooftops and mountain ranges beyond, is smart and swish, catering to large groups and package tourists. There are excellent facilities like the restaurant, bar, two pools and tennis courts that are worth a visit on their own. Ideal base for the area's many walking paths.

PAFOS & THE WEST

Pafos

Accommodation in Pafos is mainly designed for package-tour groups, with only a handful of good budget places. Although most standard hotels aren't used to independent travellers, they will accommodate you if there is space, which outside July and August is generally not a problem. Consider an apartment hotel, which keeps the costs down and usually equals considerably more living space than a standard hotel. Most hotels are in Kato Pafos.

★ Pyramos Hotel
HOTEL €

(Map p85; ☎ 2693 0222; www.pyramos-hotel. com; Agias Anastasias 4, Kato Pafos; low-high incl breakfast s €35-40, d €45-50; P❄🛜) For something different, grab a room overlooking the fascinating adjacent archaeological site of Hrysopolitissa Basilica. Soothingly decked out with cream walls, orange throws and classy mosaic-tiled bathrooms, this is one of the better small hotels in Kato Pafos. The hotel is fronted by a small bar, which also offers complimentary wi-fi to guests.

Crystallo Apartments
APARTMENTS €

(Map p85; ☎ 2695 4233; crystallo@cytanet.com. cy; Ikarou 2, Kato Pafos; low-high 2-person studio €40-50; @🏊) These spacious studio apartments in Kato Pafos are well equipped with kitchenettes (including plenty of pots and plates), dining table and chairs, sofa, comfy chairs, TV and small terraces. Some overlook the adjacent historic Ayia Marina church while others front the swimming pool. The whole place was updated in 2013, which is thankfully not reflected in the price.

There are a couple of internet terminals in the lobby and an adjacent bar-cafe. Owner George will give you a warm welcome.

★ Axiothea Hotel
HOTEL €€

(Map p88; ☎ 2693 2866; www.axiotheahotel.com; Ivis Malliotis 2, Kato Pafos; low-high s €35-40, d €45-65; P❄🛜) This dusky pink hotel has been tastefully renovated. Carpets have been replaced with cool stone tiles and the colour scheme throughout is all soothing blue greys and soft greens. Sweeping panoramic sea views can be seen from the elegant reception area and bar as well as many of the rooms.

Those on the first floor have large private balconies.

Take a look at the art work, much of it is by well-known Cypriot artist Christos Christou, a childhood friend of the owner.

Kiniras HOTEL €€
(Map p88; ☑ 2694 1604; www.kiniras.cy.net; Leoforos Archiepiskopou Makariou III 91, Ktima; low-high incl breakfast s €40-60, d €65-80; ❄ ⓢ) Central Kiniras is passionately run by charismatic owner Georgios, who also painted the colourful frescos and paintings here. Rooms vary in size and some have balconies, but they all exude a homey, historic feel with high ceilings, muted colours and all the essentials, including telephone, radio, TV and fridge. A spa is set to open late 2014.

The hot and cold breakfast buffet is superb and the restaurant, Kiniras Garden (p90), is a great place to eat.

Agapinor Hotel HOTEL €€
(Map p88; ☑ 2693 3926; www.agapinorhotel.com. cy; Nikodimou Mylona 24-25, Ktima; low-high incl breakfast s €45-65, d €65-90; ⓟ ❄ ⓢ) This Ktima hotel is popular with tour groups and has excellent facilities, with two pools, a sun terrace, airy recently re-carpeted rooms and an evening restaurant that specialises in Cypriot cuisine, but also produces a particularly tasty Brit-style cottage pie.

Dionysos HOTEL €€
(Map p85; ☑ 2693 3414; www.dionysoshotel paphos.com; Dionysou 1, Kato Pafos; low-high incl breakfast s €55-60, d €60-70; ❄ @ ⓢ ⓢ) Off the main Posidonos avenue in Kato Pafos, the Dionysos is a solid midrange choice with a shady courtyard, a small pool and solarium area, and a warm colour scheme throughout with plenty of natural timber and limestone. The rooms have benefited from a revamp and have a slick contemporary look with a paint palette of dark browns, charcoal greys and soothing cream.

There are private balconies, fridges and satellite TV. You pay a few euros extra for a pool view. Free wi-fi is available in reception and public areas.

Daphne APARTMENTS €€
(Map p85; ☑ 2693 3500; www.daphne-hotel.com; Alkminis 3, Kato Pafos; low-high s €30-60, d €50-75; ❄ ⓢ) An apartment complex off the main tourist beat, Daphne is a good self-catering choice. The apartments are fully equipped and neat, and there is a slightly exposed (to the street) pool at the front. There's a chil-

dren's area, free cots and good concessions for kids. The Kato Pafos location is very central and the service friendly.

★**Annabelle** HOTEL €€€
(Map p85; ☑ 2693 8333; www.annabelle.com. cy; Posidonos; low-high r incl breakfast €180-230; ⓟ ❄ ⓢ ⓢ) A fabulous Kato Pafos hotel with luxurious rooms, some with private pools (oh, the decadence). The large hotel pool snakes through the site and the deck chairs that sit on the pool's edge are shaded by lofty palm trees. There are several restaurants and bars, plus a spa and yoga classes. Families can also enjoy excellent children's facilities.

At the very least, drop by here for a classic English tea (€13) with homemade scones and cream, plus finger sandwiches and cake.

Alexander the Great HOTEL €€€
(Map p85; ☑ 2696 5000; www.kanikahotels.com; Posidonos; low-high r incl breakfast €100-140; ⓟ ❄ ⓢ ⓢ) A stylish Kato Pafos hotel that caters mainly to a well-heeled package-tour crowd. The rooms are plush and carpeted with an elegant blue-and-gold colour scheme and tasteful artwork on the walls. It has everything you need if you don't want to leave the hotel – tennis, gymnasium, children's area, indoor and outdoor pools, restaurant and bar – and it's right on the beach.

Around Pafos

Camping Feggari CAMPGROUND €
(☑ 2662 1534; Coral Bay; camp sites per adult/ child €7/4; ⓢ Apr-Oct; ⓟ) Surrounded by cypress trees, just a couple of minutes' stroll from Coral Bay beach and close to plenty of shops and restaurants, this is a pleasant campground with good facilities, including a snack bar. Prices include a tent.

Akamas Heights

Makriniari AGROTOURISM €
(☑ 2693 2931; www.agrotourism.com.cy; Kritou Terra; 1-bedroom apt from €40) This single-storey stone-clad rural house is perfect for passing a relaxing few days. The one-bedroom apartments surround a central courtyard and garden, complete with traditional oven and overlooking a green gorge.

Amarakos Inn AGROTOURISM €€

(☑ 2663 3117; www.amarakos.com; low-high studio €70-75, 1-bedroom apt €80-100; ✳ @ ⍾ ☀) This attractive place has spacious air-con apartments in a wood-and-stone complex of buildings surrounding a flower-filled central courtyard with fragrant honeysuckle and jasmine and an original grape press. Two of the apartments have fireplaces. The family owners can organise cultural minibus excursions and horse riding. There is a pool, children's facilities and an excellent in-house restaurant.

Droushia Heights Hotel HOTEL €€

(☑ 2633 2200; www.droushiaheightshotel.com; Droushia; s/d incl breakfast €45/90; P ⍾ ☀) Located on the fringe of the village so it doesn't detract from the historic quaintness of the place, this eminently comfortable hotel has a fashionable contemporary interior and luxurious extras like a gym and an infinity pool with panoramic views stretching to the sea. Rooms are decked out in soothing shades of pale grey, olive green, cream and taupe.

Sapho Manor House AGROTOURISM €€

(☑ 2633 2650; www.agrotourism.com.cy; Dhrousia; studio from €55, 2-bedroom apt €70; ⊙ May-Oct; ⍾ ☀) This aesthetically restored mansion dates back to 1912 and is located within confessional distance of the pretty village church. There are several studios and apartments, all decorated in the traditional rustic style. You can pay €10 more for a private studio terrace. There's a communal garden, a swimming pool and a laundry room (€6 per load).

★**Ayii Anargyri Natural Healing Spa Resort** HOTEL €€€

(☑ 2681 4000; www.aasparesort.com; Miliou; r from €105; P ✳ ⍾ ☀) Situated just outside the unspoilt village of Miliou, in a valley surrounded by thickly wooded slopes, this gorgeous place is set in a former monastery (18 of the rooms are former monks' cells). There is little that's monastic about the adjacent luxurious spa, all glossy marble and offering traditional healing treatments like a sea mineral wrap (€70) or the tempting Goddess Bath (€100), combined with the latest therapeutic techniques. The mineral-rich spa water gurgles forth from the 17th-century Ayi Anargyri springs.

Akamas Peninsula

★**Bougainvillea Hotel Apartments** APARTMENTS €

(Map p99; ☑ 2681 2250; www.bougainvillea.com. cy; Verginas 13, Polis; studio €50, 1-bedroom apt €65; ⊙ Apr-Oct; ✳ ☀) Positively the best place to stay in Polis. A flowery path runs alongside the apartments, which have a bedroom, living room, and balcony with views of peaceful olive groves. The whole place has an intimate, homey feel, with a swimming pool, plus lawn and a small playground for children.

Polis Camp Site CAMPGROUND €

(☑ 2681 5080; camp site per adult/child/tent €2.50/1/3; ⊙ Apr-Oct; P) Surrounded by fragrant eucalyptus trees that offer good, thick shade, this lovely camp site has its own quality beach, plenty of space and good facilities. Located about 2km north of Polis, it's signposted from the town centre. Concerts are regularly staged here during the summer months.

Stephanos Hotel Apartments APARTMENTS €

(☑ 2632 2411; www.stephanos-hotel.com; Leoforos Arsinois, Polis; 2-person apt €50; ⊙ Apr-Nov; P ✳ ⍾ ☀) Comprising two apartment blocks surrounding a central pool, this Polis option is well maintained and sparkling with light pine-and-cream decor, well-equipped kitchenettes and private balconies. It's popular with walkers from the UK and Germany. The sprawling downstairs restaurant serves decent, if unexceptional, Cypriot food.

★**Paradisos Hills** BOUTIQUE HOTEL €€

(☑ 2632 2287; www.paradisoshills.com; Lysos; s/d incl breakfast €70; P ✳ ⍾ ☀) Located 13km southwest of Polis overlooking the pretty village of Lysos, this hotel has superb facilities, including an infinity pool with fabulous panoramic views and an excellent restaurant – cookery classes are regularly organised (one day, €140). The rooms are tastefully furnished with terracotta tiles, dark-wood furniture and lashings of white linen. Private terraces have sea or mountain views.

Nicki Holiday Resort APARTMENTS €€

(☑ 2632 2226; www.nickiresort.com; Polis; low-high studio apt €45-70; ⊙ Apr-Nov; P ✳ ☀) A family-run apartment hotel situated a kilometre south of the centre, on the way to

Latsi. The 10 low-rise apartments are sur-rounded by landscaped gardens and three swimming pools, including a paddling pool for tots. When it's time to flop at the end of the day, you won't be disappointed: the rooms are just fine, with well-equipped kitchenettes and satellite channels for that favourite soap. Additional facilities include restaurant, snack bar and tennis courts.

Tylliria

Tylos Beach Hotel   HOTEL €
(✆2652 2348; www.tyloshotel.com.cy; Nikolaou Papageorgiou 40, Kato Pyrgos; s/d incl breakfast €30/60; ❀❈) Decorated in modern (rath-er than contemporary) style, Tylos has tidy, small rooms with chipped marble floors, pine-and-pale-blue decor and small balco-nies, most overlooking the harbour. The downstairs restaurant is vast both inside and out and seems more suited to huge tour groups than the normal smattering of diners.

Western Troödos

Stelios House   AGROTOURISM €
(✆2672 2343; www.agrotourism.com.cy; Pano Pa-nagia; 2-person apt from €50; P) Stelios is one of several traditional stone houses in the region that have been converted into apart-ments for tourists. There is little to choose between them, with their warm rustic col-our scheme, wooden shutters and private balconies. Stelios has the advantage of a lovely large courtyard.

LARNAKA & THE EAST

Larnaka

In town there's a good choice of small mid-range hotels (some in restored houses) and self-catering apartments that are ideal for independent travellers exploring the island from a single base. East of town the luxu-ry hotel complexes roll out along Dekelia beach, centring on beach holiday fun. As they cater mainly to package holidaymakers, you're more likely to get a good deal through the internet than by just walking in. Ad-vance bookings for all of Larnaka's accom-modation is generally a good idea during the summer months.

Alkisti City   HOTEL €
(Map p107; ✆2481 5140; www.cityalkisti.com; Agiou Lazarou; s/d €35/45; P❀❈) This tradi-tional stone house was completely renovat-ed in 2006 and converted into a charming eight-room hotel. The compact rooms have jazzy modern furnishings and are comforta-bly set up. Downstairs there's a grassy court-yard for sunbathing. Situated just across from Agios Lazaros, the location is perfect. Reception isn't staffed 24/7 so it won't suit everyone.

Eleonora   APARTMENTS €
(Map p107; ✆2462 6222; www.eleonorahotelapts. com; Ermou 55; low-high studio €40-55, suite €50-75; P❀❈) Right in the heart of town, Eleonora has spacious, clean studios all with kitchenettes that offer excellent value for money. The larger suites are a safe bet for families and can easily sleep up to four people.

★Hotel Opera   HOTEL €€
(Map p107; ✆2440 0110; www.hoteloperalarn aca.com; Leoforos Faneromenis 11; s/d €50/60; P❀❈) All hazy Mediterranean blues and whites, Hotel Opera is a cosy home-from-home with breezy, fresh-feeling rooms, a sweet little sun terrace, lots of quirky art and nice touches like complimentary cof-fee, fruit and cakes. The friendly manage-ment go out of their way to help and its great position, next to the Agios Lazaros, tops it off.

Livadhiotis City   HOTEL €€
(Map p107; ✆2462 6222; www.livadhiotis.com; Nikolaou Rossou 50; s/d €65/85; P❀@) A stone's throw from both the Agios Lazaros and the beach, this snazzy hotel offers slight-ly snug rooms with rather hip late-retro decor. The cool coffee shop downstairs is a summer hot spot.

Petrou Bros   APARTMENTS €€
(Map p107; ✆2465 0600; http://petrouapartho tel.com; Armenikis Eklisias; low-high apt €34-65; P❀❈) Good value, light-filled and central, these apartments have sizeable kitchenettes equipped with a fridge, two hot plates and plenty of pots and pans, and all the basic furniture you need.

E-Hotel
HOTEL €€€

(🖉 2474 7000; www.hotel-e.com; Faros 1, Pervolia; s/d €70/140; P ❄ @ 🛜 🌊) Near quiet Faros Beach, this swish complex and spa is located 20 minutes west of town by car. Luxurious, modern rooms are well equipped with plasma TVs, sparkling bathrooms and neutral colourings, while the spa has a host of treatments to choose from. If you have a car (there are no amenities nearby), it's a lovely serene choice.

Sun Hall
HOTEL €€€

(Map p107; 🖉 2465 3341; www.aquasolhotels.com. cy; Leoforos Athinon 6; low-high incl breakfast s €76-124, d €90-147; P ❄ @ 🌊) Right on the seafront, this plush hotel has slick service and contemporary-style rooms all with balconies and good-sized modern bathrooms. Ask for a seafront room for the full Finikoudes coastal experience.

Golden Bay
HOTEL €€€

(🖉 2464 5444; www.goldenbay.com.cy; Dhekelia; s/d from €90/120; P ❄ @ 🛜 🌊) Larnaka's luxury giant leads the list of beachfront hotels on the coastal-strip 8km north of the city centre. It has all the bells and whistles you expect from a top-end establishment with airy and supremely comfortable rooms and all the pools, bars, restaurants, and family-friendly facilities you could need. Guests with accessibility needs are catered for as well.

Around Larnaka

The villages in the hills to the west of Larnaka provide excellent alternative accommodation options for those who want to dig a little deeper into Cypriot life. Because of irregular public transport in this region, hotels are only really suitable for those with their own transport.

Iosiphis House
AGROTOURISM €

(🖉 9979 0780; www.iosiphishouse.com; 1 Apriliou 19, Lefkara; apt €45-55, family apt €55-90; ❄ 🛜) In picturesque Lefkara, these dinky apartments, with full kitchenette, are just the ticket if you want a village experience. Just five apartments are here, with two of them boasting ample enough space for families. Full of rustic charm inside, they open out onto a cute stone inner-courtyard that's great for relaxing after a day of exploring.

★ Gabriel House
AGROTOURISM €€

(🖉 9945 1250; www.gabrielhouse-cy.com; Kato Drys; apt €70; ❄ 🛜) With a cosy village-style aesthetic, Gabriel House is a tranquil place with welcoming and friendly management. The two apartments, with kitchenette, are brim full with character with local stone walls, lacy bedspreads and nooks and crannies filled with local ceramics. A fantastic choice for those looking for a peaceful hideaway packed with local charm.

Lefkara Hotel
AGROTOURISM €€

(🖉 2434 2154; www.lefkarahotels.com; Lefkara; s/d incl breakfast €60/70) Right in the centre of Lefkara village, this characterful hotel is loaded with old-world charm with simply decorated, decent-sized rooms. The restaurant downstairs is a good spot for dinner or lunch if you're just passing through.

Agia Napa

Between mid-June and mid-August you will need to pre-book. Being a resort town, Napa offers a plethora of accommodation, with everything from unlicensed rooms to top-end hotels. Rooms generally reflect the fact that many visitors only use them to sleep in (or sleep it off in). Most are clean but plain (sometimes dated), with prices somewhat inflated across the board. Independent travellers will be welcomed if there is space (or shuffled off to a buddy hotel), but expect another price hike for just rolling up. Many hotels along the coast only operate from March to October.

Green Bungalows
APARTMENTS €

(Map p118; 🖉 2372 1511; www.greenbungalows .com; Katalymata 19; low-high studio €32-50, apt €40-60; ☉ Apr-Oct; P ❄ @ 🌊) This reveller hang-out has basic studios and apartments with tiled floors, balconies and small kitchenettes. You don't get much (air-con and wi-fi are extra) and it's looking a tad weary, but it's a cheap place to rest your head after partying.

Napa Prince
APARTMENTS €€

(Map p118; 🖉 2372 1483; www.napaprince.com; Tefkrou Anthia 65; low-high r €40-80; P ❄ 🛜 🌊) Although a little dated, this family-owned and run hotel has a friendly atmosphere and good-value, clean rooms that are only a hop, skip and jump from the Square. It has an excellent pool with a refurbished bar, and staff who are happy to help with anything. Air-con is an extra €6 per day.

Okeanos Beach HOTEL €€
(Map p118; ✆2372 4440; www.okeanoshotel.com.cy; 1 Oktovriou; low-high r €70-112; P❋@❄) The Okeanos has a great location, within walking distance to everything, and its clean, bright rooms have nice little balconies overlooking the pool and beach.

Limanaki Beach HOTEL €€
(Map p118; ✆2372 1600; www.limanakibeach.com; 1 Oktovriou 18; low-high r €65-130; P❋@❄) Apart from the weird coloured lighting in the foyer and the fact that wi-fi isn't free, this hotel is a decent choice with an excellent location near the port. The smallish, modern rooms are spotless with balconies overlooking the inviting pool.

Florence Hotel APARTMENTS €€
(✆2372 2088; Leoforos Nisiou; low-high apt €50-70; P❋❄) Just out of the town centre, Florence has cosy and quiet apartments, with old-fashioned furniture, set around a well-maintained pool area. Good value and friendly, it's popular with families who prefer to be outside of the central hustle. Air-con is extra.

Napa Mermaid HOTEL €€€
(✆2372 1606; www.napamermaidhotel.com; Leoforos Kryou Nerou 45; r €90-150; P❋❄) This swish hotel, near the beach but still within walking distance to town, is a quiet option in Agia Napa. Modern rooms are elegantly appointed in cool neutral tones, while the facilities – pool, tennis court, bars and restaurants – provide everything you need if you want a holiday centred on the sun and sand.

Atlantica Aeneas HOTEL €€€
(✆2372 4000; www.atlanticahotels.com; Leoforos Nisiou 100; low-high s €65-110, d €105-150; P❋@❄) For those wanting something a little more upmarket, the Aeneas is the way to go. It boasts contemporary 'inland' rooms, which open onto one of the biggest pools in the Med. This place is an opulent haven dedicated to water, with all the trimmings. It is also ideally situated opposite Nissi Beach.

Around Agia Napa

The majority of hotel options are clustered along the Protaras–Pernera road, with most geared to package-holiday visitors. There is little in the way of budget accommodation, but an array of choice otherwise. Bookings are recommended in the high season.

Brilliant APARTMENTS €€
(✆2383 2211; www.brillianthotelapts.com; Kavo Greco, Protaras; studio/apt €100/120; P❋❄) These clean and bright, open-plan style apartments with kitchenettes and terraces are a great deal. The complex has excellent facilities with pool, bar and a good restaurant. A minimum one-week stay is usually required.

Seagull APARTMENTS €€
(✆2383 1270; www.seagullhotelapts.com; Hifastios 2; low-high studio €40-63, apt €48-65; P❋❄) Located close to the beach in Pernera, 2km further along the coast from Protaras, Seagull has very bright and spacious, minimally furnished apartments with balconies. The pool is an excellent size, so it's great for families. Open May through October.

Cavo Maris Beach HOTEL €€€
(✆2383 2043; www.cavomaris.com; Protaras; low-high r €65-120; P❋@❄) Straddling its own strip of beach, this large family-friendly hotel has all the pools, restaurants, bars and entertainment for a holiday that's about sun, sand and the sea. The spacious rooms are kind of bland but are light-filled and have good-sized balconies. Open April through October.

NICOSIA (LEFKOSIA) & AROUND

Nicosia (Lefkosia)

Budget accommodation is quite poor in Nicosia. Most of what once existed has either closed down or been upgraded to a midrange category. Nicosia's top-end hotels include all the usual suspects, with luxurious comfort and design. But with a couple of exceptions, there's a lamentable lack of imaginative and original establishments here.

ACCOMMODATION AROUND AGIA NAPA

Sky Hotel
HOTEL €

(Map p130; ☎ 2266 6880; www.skyhotel.ws; Solonos 7c; s/d incl breakfast €40/50; ※ �) The best budget place in Nicosia, Sky is bang in the middle of the historic centre, surrounded by souvenir shops and cafes. Rooms are large, plain and a tad gloomy, but the breakfast buffet is more generous than most and service is always with a smile.

Averof
HOTEL €

(☎ 2277 3447; www.averof.com.cy; Averof 19; s/d incl breakfast €45/65; ※ 奈) Close to the historic centre, near the British High Commission and in a quiet residential part of Nicosia, this place prides itself on its rather kitsch rustic decor and attentive service. The mock-traditional rooms are spacious, clean and bright. Excellent cut-price deals are available for longer stays.

Classic Hotel
HOTEL €€

(Map p130; ☎ 2266 4006; www.classic.com.cy; Rigenis 94; s/d €77/90; P ※ 奈) This hotel, close to Pafos Gate, is a member of the 'Small Luxury Hotels of the World' group, and you can see why. From the reception to the rooms, everywhere is done up in relaxing colours of creams and woods; the design is minimalist and the rooms are smart and comfortable. The 59 Knives restaurant, part of the hotel, specialises in haute cuisine, adding its own contribution to the Classic's luxuries – together with the rooftop gym.

Centrum
HOTEL €€

(Map p130; ☎ 2245 6444; www.centrumhotel.net; Pasikratous 15; low-high incl breakfast s €60-70, d €70-80; ※ @ 奈) A fairly stylish place that's a cross between a boutique and a business hotel, the Centrum offers spacious rooms, some with balconies, decked out in blush and salmon colours; some have baths, too, so state your preference when booking. The Byzantine wing sports more traditionally furnished rooms. The hotel is within seconds of Plateia Eleftherias. The business facilities are excellent, and the restaurant is known for its Cypriot cuisine.

★ Royiatiko
HOTEL €€€

(Map p130; ☎ 2244 5445; www.royiatikohotel. com.cy; Apollonos 27; s/d incl breakfast €75/100; P ※ 奈 ⊠) Rooms here are elegantly decorated in tones of brown and cream, with large marshmallow-soft cushions on the beds. There are fridges, kettles, fresh flowers and stylish bathrooms with steely grey floor tiles, plus a well-equipped gym and heated pool (in winter). The location is perfect, in the heart of the historic centre.

Cyprus Hilton
HOTEL €€€

(☎ 2237 7777; www.hilton.com; Leoforos Archiepiskopou Makariou III; low-high incl breakfast s €173-218, d €207-252; P @ 奈 ⊠) This premier hotel was apparently the gathering ground for Eastern and Western spies during the Cold War, when Cyprus' strategic position was invaluable. Who knows what political manoeuvring went on in its luxurious rooms, indoor and outdoor pool, tennis and squash courts, and in-house restaurants? Check the website for special cut-price deals.

Around Nicosia

★ Avli House
AGROTOURISM €

(☎ 2254 3236; www.avli.net; Markou Drakou 3, Lythrodontas; low-high d €45-52, family ste €75-86, house €240-268; P) Situated close to the Maheras Forest, this delightful rural accommodation is in the village of Lythrodontas. It can sleep up to 14 people in self-contained rooms and has a pretty plant-filled central courtyard surrounded by the apartments and house, all of which have benefited by the fact that the owner is an accomplished artist. A two-night minimum stay is required.

The rooms have paintings and (tasteful) etchings on the walls, plenty of warm woodwork, colourful fabrics and rugs, and some eye-catching traditional architectural features.

NORTH NICOSIA (LEFKOŞA)

North Nicosia has a fairly bleak range of accommodation. The budget 'hotels' are around the Selimiye Mosque area and in the streets east of Girne Caddesi. They all have dorm-style rooms where a bed costs around €7, but we don't recommend any of them. Apart from that, there's a handful of midrange to top-end hotels that, despite the presence of casinos, are reputable.

City Royal
HOTEL €€

(☎ 228 7621; www.city-royal.com; Gazeteci Kemal Aşik Caddesi; s/d €50/70; ※ 奈 ⊠) A popular choice with travellers on business and casino lovers. Rooms are carpeted and spacious with minibar, phone, satellite TV, and even a phone in the bathroom. There is also a swimming pool, a gym and the inevitable casino. To reach here, head northeast of the Kyrenia Gate for around 300m.

Saray
HOTEL €€

(Map p152; ✆ 228 3115; saray@northcyprus.net; Atatürk Meydanı; s/d/tr €45/77/88; ❋ @ ⏰) This hotel has seriously kitsch decor: gold lacquered headboards and swirling patterned carpets. But it is comfortable and central and there's a '70s-style casino in the basement – although it's more Blackpool Pleasure Beach than Caesar's Palace. Breakfast is on the 8th floor accompanied by stunning panoramic views.

Interestingly, the hotel was the first ever Turkish-Cypriot hotel, built in 1962 by the members of the Vakif, an ancient Ottoman religious order.

Golden Tulip
HOTEL €€€

(✆ 610 5050; www.goldentulipnicosia.com; Dereboyu 1; s/d €85/135; ℗ ❋ ⏰ ⏰) One of the latest hotels to open here, the Golden Tulip looks more like an upended glass canister than anything more floral. Within there's a glossy corporate look and a comprehensive list of facilities, including health club and spa, children's nursery and, yes, yet another casino if you fancy a flutter. The standard is high and the service is top notch, but the atmosphere is international – and anonymous. The hotel is located in the New City, just west of the northern end of Mehmet Akif Caddesi.

KYRENIA (GIRNE) & THE NORTH

Kyrenia (Girne)

There are accommodation options in or near the old town area, surrounding the harbour, and plenty of megalithic resort options (catering mainly for package holidays) on the outskirts of town.

★ Nostalgia
HOTEL €

(Map p162; ✆ 815 3079; www.nostalgiaboutique hotel.com; Cafer Paşa Sokak 7; dm/s/d incl breakfast €12/20/35, annexe s/d €30/50; ❋ ⏰ ⏰) Amid the old town's lane labyrinth, Nostalgia is an atmospheric place, decorated with higgledy-piggledy old-fashioned clutter. The small rooms are a tad dark but have bags of rustic charm with touches like wooden ceilings and four-poster beds. There's also a dorm for those watching their pennies. Around the corner the annexe has more expensive rooms set around a pool.

Due to its location, and the age of the building, noise can be an issue for light sleepers.

Cyprus Dorms
HOSTEL €

(Map p162; www.cyprusdorms.com; Bozoklar Sokak; low-high dm €10-12, s €25-30, d €30-35, tr €39-46; ❋ ⏰) Decent dorms and good-sized private rooms make Cyprus Dorms a budget haven. Service can be haphazard but it's clean, the hot water works and the location – steps from the harbour – can't be beaten.

White Pearl Hotel
HOTEL €€

(Map p162; ✆ 815 0429; www.whitepearlhotel.com; Efdal Akca Sokak 26; s/d €50-68; ❋ ⏰) It's all about those gorgeous sea views at this mid-range winner, slap-bang on the harbour. The nine cosy rooms are simple but super-clean and nearly all boast balconies looking over the Mediterranean. Further bonuses are helpful management and a roof terrace with bar and Indian restaurant; good for a visit even if you're not staying here.

Dome Hotel
HOTEL €€

(Map p162; ✆ 815 2453; www.hoteldome.com; Kordon Boyu Caddesi; s/d/ste €50/68/80; ℗ ❋ ⏰ ⏰) Famously mentioned in Lawrence Durrell's *Bitter Lemons of Cyprus,* the Dome has been in business since 1928. Yes its showing its age, but for days-gone-by ambience this grand dame of the Kyrenia scene can't be beaten. Grab one of the quiet and spacious seafront rooms, with balcony overhanging the waves, to make the most of the experience.

The Colony
HOTEL €€€

(Map p162; ✆ 815 1518; www.thecolonycyprus.com; Ecevit Caddesi; s/d/ste €110/130/160; ℗ ❋ ⏰ ⏰) By far Kyrenia's most luxurious hotel, The Colony's rooms are packed full of plush fabrics and nice artwork with lovely touches of old-school style. The downside is you don't get sea views from the rooms, but the rooftop terrace with glamour-puss pool area, and sweeping panoramas, more than makes up for it.

ACCOMMODATION KYRENIA (GIRNE)

Rocks Hotel & Casino HOTEL €€€
(Map p162; ☑650 0400; www.rockshotel.com;
Kordon Boyu Caddesi; s/d/ste €145/195/350;
P❄☎♨) This hotel-casino giant offers
large elegantly styled rooms and a whole
bundle of amenities with gym, spa, Turkish
bath and attractive shore-side pool area.
Booking a package via a travel agent will
get you a substantial discount on the rack
rate.

Around Kyrenia & the Ranges

The coast both west and east of Kyrenia
is where you'll find most of North Cyprus'
resorts aimed at package tourists. Bellapais
has some excellent alternative places to stay.
It's close enough to Kyrenia to be easily accessible, but far enough (and high enough)
away to feel peacefully distant.

Lapida Garden HOTEL €€
(☑862 1500; www.lapidahotel.com; Ibrahim Nidai
Caddesi, Lapta; s/d/tr €36/40/56, with sea view
s/d €40/48; P❄☎♨) This family-run hotel
is set between fields of lemon trees, with a
wonderful lush garden and pool at the back.
The bright, clean, spacious rooms are simple but homely with touches of purple for
some extra pizazz. The restaurant – full of
ornament clutter and plants – is very sweet
and the meals (set menus 20TL to 25TL) are
great value.

Gardens of Irini B&B €€
(☑815 2820; www.gardensofirini.com; Bellapais;
r from €40, per week €300) At the top of Bellapais village, Gardens of Irini has two art-
fully ramshackle self-catering cottages with
private courtyards surrounded by a verdant
garden. Owner Deirdre cooks up breakfasts
(and dinners by request) served amid the
leafy surroundings. You must love animals
to stay here as the gardens have become a
sanctuary for cats and placid stray mutts.

Olive Paradise Village HOTEL €€
(☑821 3390; www.oliveparadisevillage.com; Ibrahim Nidai Caddesi, Lapta; s/d €25/50; P❄☎♨)
The chalets here are set back from the
road, surrounding an inviting pool area
giving the entire place a tranquil feel. The
split-level cabins are quite drab, but the
suites, with their alpine-overload of pine
cladding, are lovely, light and fresh-feeling

with glorious views to boot. It's open from
April to November.

★**Bellapais Gardens** BOUTIQUE HOTEL €€€
(☑815 6066; www.bellapaisgardens.com; Bellapais; low-high studio s €63-130, d €75-170, cottage
s €85-155, d €115-205; P❄☎♨) Just beneath
Bellapais Abbey, this lovely resort, amid
lush gardens, is a tranquil hideaway well
worth splashing out for. Rooms ooze casual
luxury with fresh, modern decor and contemporary bathrooms. The split-level cottages, with expansive sea views from the
balcony, are particularly inviting. Sip your
drink poolside, while admiring the abbey's
architecture above, and you may decide to
never leave.

Hideaway Club HOTEL €€€
(☑822 2620; www.hideawayclub.com; Edremit
Caddesi, Karaoğlanoğlu; r low-high from €70-80;
P❄@☎♨) Hideaway has a brilliant white
theme, with pools and patios, backed by the
grandeur of the mountains. The spotless
sea-view cottages are dressed with fresh
flowers and lace. This is a serene getaway
for couples and romantics, as the hotel has
a child-free policy. It's about 4km west of
Kyrenia, heading toward Lapta.

Bella View HOTEL €€€
(☑816 1155; www.bellaview.net; Bellapais Yolu, Bellapais; low-high s €40-50, d €60-85; P❄☎♨) If
you've got your own transport, this friendly hotel on the main road between Girne
and Bellapais is a great choice. Rooms are
packed with old-world character with dark
wood, antiques, Turkish carpets and soothing caramel-toned fabrics. The large pool
terrace has great views up to Bellapais Abbey (20 minutes' walk uphill).

The Northwest

Lefke Gardens HOTEL €€
(☑7288 223; www.lefkegardenshotel.org; Lefke;
s/d/tr incl breakfast €32/49/65; ❄☎♨) This
little hotel should be your first port of call
if you're looking for a room for the night in
the northwest. Housed in a traditional Ottoman-style building, the rooms are decorated
in simple Turkish style and open out onto a
central courtyard.

Güzelyurt Otel HOTEL €€
(☑714 3412; Bahçelievler Bulvarı; s/d €30-50;
❄♨) If you should find yourself stuck in

Güzelyurt for the night, this basic hotel on the edge of town is the only decent accommodation around. Rooms are a tad drab but clean and there's a swimming pool and bar to keep you entertained.

Soli Inn   HOTEL €€

(☎727 7575; soliinn@northcyprus.net; Gemikonaği; s/d incl breakfast €30-50; P☀) West of Güzelyurt at Gemikonaği, this midrange hotel is right by the sea and caters mostly for tourists from mainland Turkey. It has simple doubles and (better-equipped) suites. There's a decent pool and golf course nearby.

FAMAGUSTA (MAĞUSA) & THE KARPAS (KIRPAŞA) PENINSULA

Famagusta (Mağusa)

Famagusta's hotels are generally an either-or equation: either ultra-swanky or basic, with very little in between. Due to the lack of accommodation options in the city, most travellers choose to visit on a day trip rather than stay overnight.

Altun Tabya   HOTEL €

(Map p184; ☎366 2585; altuntabyahotel@hotmail.com; Kızılkule Sokak, Old Town; s/d/tr €25/30/35, d with air-con €35) Look, it's as basic as they come (only one room has air-con), but it's clean, every room has a dinky balcony, there's a decent supply of hot water and owner Halil is a fun and friendly guy who really endeavours to please. If you want to be right in the Old Town, this is a great choice.

Portofino   HOTEL €

(Map p184; ☎366 4393; www.portofinohotel-cyprus.com; Feyzi Çakmak Bulvarı 9; s/d/tr €25/35/50; P☀) Just outside of the Old Town walls, near the port, Portofino has large, dated rooms that could do with a serious refurbishment but are a fine place to rest your head for the night. It does have a decent pool.

Crystal Rocks   BUNGALOWS €€

(☎378 9400; www.cypruscrystalrocks.com; Salamis Yolu; r €57-70; P☀) Over 60 bungalows, 10km north of Famagusta, next to the beach and not far from Salamis. Very popular with European travellers, the modern, bright split-level cabins have a bit of a 1980s vibe going on and are all spotlessly clean. The swimming pool and aqua-slides are a hit with children.

Salamis Bay Conti   HOTEL €€€

(☎378 8201; www.salamisbayconti.com; Salamis Yolu; r €60-90; ☀) Located 8km north of Famagusta, this good-value giant has a large attractive pool area and its own expansive sandy beach. Rooms are suitably big and elegant to match the spa, casino and numerous bars and restaurants all offered. Rooms without sea view are more cost effective.

Karpas (Kirpaşa) Peninsula

The peninsula offers some remarkable alternative accommodation not found elsewhere on the island. If you're a nature lover, this is the place to head for get-away-from-it-all bliss where you can unplug from the world for a while.

★**Nitovikla Garden**   AGROTOURISM €€

(☎375 6120; www.nitovikla.com; Kumyalı; s/d €25/50; P☀) Full of character and antique agricultural clutter, Nitovikla is a cosy home away from home. There are 10 rooms, all decorated in traditional style with carved wooden furniture and embroidered textiles, and lots of lovely cushion-strewn nooks and crannies where you can chill out. A top-spot for walkers, cyclists and anyone who wants to enjoy the Karpas' incredible natural beauty.

Owner Zekai has put mammoth amounts of effort into imparting his expertise and general love of food and life into his hotel and restaurant. There are bikes to rent and tonnes of local walking information is available. It's right in the centre of Kumyalı village, near the church, with the beach an easy stroll away.

Seabird   BUNGALOWS €€

(☎372 2012; Golden Beach, Dipkarpaz; s/d/tr half-board €45/60/80; ☉Mar-Nov; P) Barely 1km past the Monastery of Apostolos Andreas, this charmingly rustic hotel is low-key living at its best. The handful of wood and stone huts are right on the beach with bed, mosquito net and plentiful hot water. The restaurant serves up tasty meals including fish bought from local fishermen and during the evening the peaceful ambience is priceless.

Oasis at Ayfilon
BUNGALOWS €€

(☎ 0533 840 5082; www.oasishotelkarpas.com; Agios Filon Beach, Dipkarpaz; low-high d €35-50; P) Ideal for travellers looking for a slice of simple life, the minimalist cabins here are built right on the cliff with waves crashing into the rocks below. Each has comfortable beds with mosquito net and five-star views over the sea. There's a good restaurant here too.

Blue Sea
HOTEL €€

(☎ 372 2393; www.blueseahotelkarpaz.com; Golden Beach, Dipkarpaz; low-high s €25-35, d €35-50; P ✲) Family run, quiet and basic, Blue Sea is near Golden Beach, on the peninsula's south side, and built on a rocky spur shaded by shoreline trees. Fresh fish are caught daily and served by the hotel's owner.

Club Malibu
HOTEL €€

(☎ 374 4264; www.clubmalibucy.com; Yenierenköy; low-high s €40-47, d €50-60; P ✲ 🛜) The simple, bright rooms at this low-rise hotel and restaurant are right on a lovely patch of

BOOK YOUR STAY ONLINE

For more accommodation reviews by Lonely Planet authors, check out hotels. lonelyplanet.com. You'll find independent reviews, as well as recommendations on the best places to stay. Best of all, you can book online.

beach and have balconies with either sea or garden views.

Karpaz Arch Houses
HOTEL €

(☎ 372 2009; www.karpazarchhouses.com; Dipkarpaz; r €45; P ✲ 🛜) Approximately 500m from the centre of Dipkarpaz village, this traditional stone house is home to 12 decent-sized rooms with cooking facilities making it a good choice for self-caterers.

Kaplıca Beach Hotel
HOTEL €€

(☎ 387 2031; www.kaplicabeach.com; Main Rd, Kaplıca; r from €50; P 🛜) Across the road from Kaplıca Beach, these chalets have massive, sparsely furnished rooms. A good option if you're looking for a get-away-from-it-all just steps from the beach.

Understand Cyprus

Cyprus Today

In the Republic of Cyprus, a new centre-right president has been elected and a banking crisis has attracted worldwide attention, leading to stringent austerity measures that have been met with overall calm by these resilient people. Peace talks are on course again and the discovery of oil and natural gas reserves are a real cause for optimism on both sides of the Green Line.

Best in Print

Bitter Lemons of Cyprus (Lawrence Durrell) Memoir set in the 1950s.
A Traveller's History of Cyprus (Tim Boatswain) A concise history.
Journey into Cyprus (Colin Thubron) Chronicles a 600-mile walk through Cyprus in 1972.

Best Online

Talk Cyprus (www.cyprus-forum.com) Where Cypriots discuss politics.
Cyprus Tourism Organisation (www.visitcyprus.com) CTO's official website packed full of useful information.
Cypriot Food (www.flavoursofcyprus.com) Classic and modern recipes for authentic cuisine.
Cyprus Business Directory (www.cyprusbestcompanies.com) An up-to-date and far-reaching business directory.

Etiquette

Driving Cypriots love to talk on mobile phones and not use indicators while driving. Make eye contact at intersections before you pull out.
Tact Use it when discussing politics, division and the Green Line.
Eating out If you're invited out for a meal, the bill is paid by the host and not split. Offer to contribute, knowing you'll most likely be scoffed at.

Peace Talks Gain Momentum

Since its division in 1974, talks to reunite Cyprus have taken place sporadically with little success. Many had hoped Cyprus' EU membership would increase the chances of reunification but, sadly, it seemed to have only muddied the waters, with the larger EU nations weighing in on the debate. Peace talks were revived in 2008, however, when the Republic's president Demetris Christofias promised to work with the then Turkish Cypriot leader Mehmet Ali Talat, generating over 100 meetings. Their attempts at camaraderie, aimed at creating a 'climate of peace', began to worry officials on the Turkish mainland. The situation was quickly blunted when the pro-Turkish Dervis Eroglu came to power in 2010.

For the following few years there was the usual rhetoric regarding talks with UN mediators. However, in February 2014 it seemed a corner was turned when, for the first time in 55 years, talks took place in Athens and Ankara simultaneously by negotiators Kudret Özersay for the Turkish Cypriots and Andreas Mavroyiannis for the Greek Cypriots. Then, in the same month (and after close to a two-year hiatus), Greek Cypriot and Turkish Cypriot leaders issued a joint declaration outlining a peace plan to bring an end to the crisis. At the time of writing, these peace talks were in their second phase with the Turkish Cypriot side predicting that a settlement could be reached within months, while the Greek Cypriots were more cautious, professing that there remained a considerable distance between the two sides.

Ties have also been strengthened with the US with a visit to both the Greek Cypriot and Turkish Cypriot communities in May 2014 by Vice President Joe Biden who vouched US support in providing assistance to resolving the island's 40-year old stalemate.

The EU & the Economy in the Republic

EU succession (2004) changed the landscape in the Republic of Cyprus in a variety of areas. Fees and charges increased for prospective home- or landowners and the cost of water and electricity concurrently skyrocketed. The price of food, local produce and the cost of a cup of coffee also increased. There have also been considerable changes in demographics over the past decade with foreign workers from Eastern Europe, Asia, Africa and India filling the labour markets. This has created cheap labour and now restaurants and shops are predominantly staffed by Eastern-bloc waiters and sales staff, and many families have Sri Lankan or Philippine maids and nannies.

A combination of joining the eurozone and sharing close financial ties with Greece had a severe and negative impact on Cypriot banks (who were major holders of Greek government and corporate bonds) between 2012 and 2013. In March 2013 banks closed for 12 days while a deal was struck for a €10 billion bailout by the International Monetary Fund and the EU. The loan was conditional on Cyprus raising €5.8 billion through various austerity measures.

A year later witnessed cautious signs of recovery. The economy shrunk by just 5.4% (as opposed to the 20% predicted), the financial sector showed signs of stabilisation and tourism remained solid, particularly among big-spending Russians. The discovery of oil and natural gas deposits in the waters off Cyprus could also mark an end to the island's financial woes, as well as speed up the possibility of reunification with the North, as oil companies signal that they, too, want a solution as soon as possible before investing huge sums in offshore oil exploration.

Russians in the Republic

Cyprus' Russian-speaking population in the Republic is a considerable 40,000 (out of a total population of around 800,000). The majority live in and around Lemesos, leading to its nickname of Limassolgrad, where menus and shop signs in Russian are common, especially around the main coastal promenade. There are three local Russian newspapers, as well as at least one Russian school. Lemesos is also home to the annual two-day Cyprus-Russian Festival in June, which kicked off in 2004, and includes concerts by top names in the Russian music scene, as well as the Russian food exhibitions and fireworks. Furthermore, on a more sobering monetary note, Cyprus is the beneficiary of considerable funds from Russia – some 25% of the total bank deposits in the Republic, along with a whopping one-third of all foreign investment.

POPULATION: **1,120,500 (295,000 ESTIMATED NORTHERN CYPRUS)**

AREA: **9251 SQ KM (3355 SQ KM NORTHERN CYPRUS)**

GDP: **REPUBLIC OF CYPRUS US$21.827 BILLION (NORTHERN CYPRUS US$4.3 BILLION)**

if Cyprus were 100 people

71 would live in towns
29 would live in the country

belief systems
(% of population)

78
Greek Orthodox

18
Muslim

4
Others

population per sq km

CYPRUS   UK   GREECE

= 86 people

History

Although the last few decades have seen their share of troubles, Cyprus' position, at the nautical crossroads of the eastern Mediterranean basin has meant an equally complex and turbulent history that stretches way back over the centuries, with various waves of invaders who have influenced and left their mark on the island. Naturally, the following is not an exhaustive history of the island; rather it is aimed at forming a framework and background to the current political, economic and territorial situation.

Ancient Cyprus

City Kingdoms of Cyprus

In the 1st century BC, tin was imported from Lebanon to Cyprus and mixed with copper to make bronze. This composition was stronger and more durable, creating better tools and weapons.

Visitors to Cyprus today can see extraordinary remains of ancient city kingdoms, which excavations have revealed were both highly prosperous and influential during the Hellenistic period. These city kingdoms were established at Kourion, Pafos, Marion (now Polis), Soloi, Lapithos, Tamassos and Salamis, with two more later established at Kition and Amathous. The Phoenicians, great traders from across the sea in Lebanon, also settled here around this time in Kition (Larnaka) and introduced the Greek alphabet to Cyprus (the Phoenician phonetic alphabet is believed to be the ancestor of virtually all modern alphabets).

Between 1400 and 1200 BC, Mycenaean and Achaean Greek settlers began to arrive en masse, bringing with them language, culture, art and gods. The Cypriots found a particular affinity with the fertility goddess Aphrodite, and Cyprus remains the legendary birthplace; the rock near Pafos marking her place of birth remains firmly on the tourist trail to this day.

Thereafter, from 750 BC to 475 BC, the city kingdoms oversaw a period of advancement and increasing prosperity as demonstrated by the spectacular Royal Tombs near Salamis, which contain extravagant examples of wealth and closely match Homer's descriptions of Mycenaean burials in *The Iliad*. Ancient Salamis is the most significant of the ancient city kingdoms' archaeological sites that can be visited today; don't miss it!

During this time, Greek influence spread throughout the island, and Cyprus attracted a string of foreign rulers including the Assyrians, the Egyptians and then the Persians. These powers sought control through

TIMELINE	Millions of years ago	10,000–8000 BC	6000 BC
	The island is forced to the surface from the Mediterranean ocean floor, revealing the Troödos Mountains, Kyrenia mountain ranges and Mesaoria plain. Scientists now study the sea bed here.	Hunter-gatherers develop the first settlements. The world's earliest water wells are made and domesticated animals are introduced.	Stone buildings, like those of Choirokoitia, are built in small enclosed villages. Inhabitants begin to form working societies with organised crops, stonework and domestic pets.

tribute more than settlement, essentially leaving the city kingdoms to self-govern.

In 498 BC, under King Onesilos of Salamis, the city kingdoms joined in the Ionian revolt against Persian rule, with the exception of Amathous, which aligned itself with the Phoenicians. The Persians landed their army just off Salamis, and a battle raged. Ultimately the King of Kourion, Stesenor, betrayed the Greeks. Onesilos was killed and the revolt was crushed.

The island maintained its strong links with Hellenism, despite Persian hegemony. In 381 BC, King Evagoras of Salamis tried to unite the city kingdoms with the Greek states, and attempted to overcome the Persians once more. He was defeated and assassinated seven years later, effectively ending the classical age of Greek influence (the remains of which are prevalent on the island to this day).

If you love ancient Cypriot pottery and sculpture, as displayed in museums and often emulated by local artists, get more information at www.thebritish museum.org.

Hellenistic Cyprus

Alexander the Great's emphatic victory over Persian ruler Darius III at Issus in 333 BC released the island from the Persian Empire. However, Alexander's control of Cyprus, as a part of the Greek Empire, was fleeting. He asserted his authority by giving the city kingdoms autonomy but refusing to allow them to make their own coins. After his death in 323 BC and after some quarrelling among his successors, the city kingdoms were subjugated by Ptolemy I of Egypt, who took over the island as a part of Hellenistic Egypt.

HOUSE OF STONE

Human habitation of the island began around 10,000 BC, when hunter-gatherers roamed the coastal caves of Akrotiri Aetokremnou (Vulture Cliff) and its peninsula in the South. These people may have brought about the extinction, via hunting, of the Pleistocene-era pygmy hippopotamus and dwarf elephant (a skeleton of the latter was discovered in a cave near Kyrenia in 1902).

Eventually, in around 6000 BC, these nomads built stone villages like the Aceramic neolithic settlement of Choirokoitia, a fascinating site near Larnaka that can be visited today.

Built on the side of a hill, beside the banks of a river, its more than 300 inhabitants lived in round, flat-roofed *tholoi* (huts) made of stones and mud. They were similar to the contemporary buildings found in Crete and Mesopotamia. The huts were organised within a protective rock wall, around a central courtyard, with some chambers dedicated to cooking and eating, and others to sleeping and storage.

Evidence shows the inhabitants produced stoneware tools, weapons, containers and jewellery. They picked fruit, fished and kept sheep and goats. They even kept pets. The oldest known feline–human connection – a domesticated cat buried with its owner – was unearthed here, far pre-dating similar ancient Egyptian finds.

2500 BC	2300–1950 BC	1950–1650 BC	1650–1050 BC
Levantine immigrants bring new technologies and styles. Artistic achievements include the production of cross-shaped human figurines made from picrolite, a local Cypriot stone.	The early Bronze Age; objects are cast using imported tin and imaginative pottery designs flourish, drawing noticeably on human and animal life in and around the villages.	Middle Bronze Age; sustained copper mining and the beginning of trading relationships with the Aegean. Settlements keep to the foothills and plains in largely agrarian communities.	Writing in the form of a linear script known as Cypro-Minoan is adapted from Crete. Extensive foreign trade coincides with production of fine jewellery, carving and pottery.

The island's capital was moved from Salamis to Pafos, which was easily accessible by sea from Alexandria in Egypt. From this time, unsurprisingly, Egyptian influences prevailed with local cults being introduced and assimilated with Egyptian gods and goddesses. Cyprus also grew to become an intermediary between the Greek world and the near East, with craftsmen, sculptors and merchants from throughout the eastern Mediterranean introducing ceramics, sculpture and jewelery.

Nicocreon, the last king of Salamis, assisted Ptolemy in centralising power away from the city kingdoms to a single appointed governor-general in Pafos. Later suspected of betrayal, he burnt his opulent Salamis palace to the ground before committing suicide.

A *demos* (house and senate) version of parliament was subsequently established on the island and it remained a Ptolemaic colony for a further 200 years, languishing under the rule of an appointed governor-general.

> Cyprus is one of the five richest copper-deposit areas in the world, and during the Copper and Bronze Ages, Cyprus was one of the world's richest countries.

Romans & Rising Christianity

Cyprus was annexed by the expanding Roman Empire in 58 BC, with orator and writer Cicero becoming one of its first proconsuls. Despite being briefly given to Cleopatra VII of Egypt by Mark Anthony (her lover) and subsequently handed back to Roman control, Cyprus enjoyed some 600 years of relative peace and prosperity under Roman rule, and many public buildings, aqueducts, harbours and roads date from this time; noteworthy among them were the theatre at Kourion, the colonnaded gymnasium at Salamis and the Sanctuary of Apollon Ylatis. Many of these ancient ruins can still be seen today, along with the many mosaic floors depicting scenes from Greek mythology. Trade also flourished with exports including decorative pottery, copper and glassware.

COPPER ISLAND

Once copper was discovered in around 2600 BC, it progressively replaced the old stone repertory and led to the excavation of abundant copper deposits in the Troödos Mountains. The country's production and export of copper became highly organised, and trade with Mediterranean islands and Egypt began in earnest. This gave Cyprus great commercial importance in the civilised Mediterranean world.

During the island's transition to the Bronze Age, around 2000 BC, a wave of foreign influence, from immigrants like the Hittites, brought new technologies and styles. This age also saw new towns established around the coast, with overseas trade of pottery containers and copper ingots (shaped like oxhide) expanded further.

Cyprus enjoyed an unprecedented level of prosperity, accompanied by the movement of foreign goods and people into the island. It became a meeting point of Western and Eastern civilisations thanks to its location and natural wealth.

1200 BC	1200–1100 BC	1200–1000 BC	11th century BC
The island enjoys an unprecedented level of prosperity and immigration. The first Greeks settle on the island, introducing new language, art, gods and culture.	Cities are built (or rebuilt) in a rectangular grid plan. Town gates and important buildings correspond to street systems. Increased social hierarchy and order are introduced.	The great Greek city kingdoms of Salamis, Kourion, Pafos, Marion, Soloi, Lapithos and Tamassos flourish. And the island enjoys a period of rapidly increasing advancement and prosperity.	Classical authors credit Greek heroes returning from the Trojan War with founding influential towns: Salamis is said to have been established by Teucer, and Pafos by Agapenor (of Tegea).

Island of Saints

Christianity made its early appearance on the island in AD 45. It was during this period that the apostle Paul began spreading the new religion on the island, accompanied by Barnabas, a Greek Jewish native of Salamis. He was later canonised St Barnabas (Agios Varnavas in Greek). The missionaries travelled across the island preaching the word of God and converting many locals. Once they reached Pafos, the Roman proconsul Sergius Paulus granted them an audience. A court magician mocked the apostles upon their speech about Jesus, angering Paul, who is said to have temporarily blinded the sorcerer for his disbelief. The proconsul was so struck by this act that he was among the first to convert to Christianity. Cyprus became the first country in the world to be ruled by a Christian and Christianity flourished on the island.

The apostles set up the Church of Cyprus, one of the oldest independent churches in the world, and the island quickly became known as 'The Island of Saints'.

A number of those involved in the early development of Christianity were sanctified, including Lazarus, raised from the dead by Jesus, who became the archbishop of Kition. St Helena also visited the island with pieces of the 'Holy Cross' that she left in the protection of Stavrovouni Monastery and at Tochni, where they can still be found today.

By the time of Constantine the Great, Christianity had almost completely supplanted paganism.

> Greek Cypriots are mainly the descendants of early Mycenaean and Achaean settlers, who intermingled with the indigenous population around 1100 BC, and subsequent settlers up to the 16th century.

Byzantine Cyprus
Constantinople Calling

The Roman Empire was divided in AD 395 and Cyprus fell under its eastern half, the Byzantine Empire, with its capital in Constantinople. Byzantine rulers were sent to Cyprus to govern the island.

The island was able to keep a considerable degree of ecclesiastical autonomy when the Archbishop of Cyprus convinced the Byzantine emperor that the Church of Cyprus had been founded by the apostles. In AD 488 the archbishop was granted the right to carry a sceptre instead of an archbishop's crosier. He was also given authority to write his signature in imperial purple ink, a practice that continues to this day.

During this period, many of the stunning churches of the island were built, with frescoed walls, mosaics and domed roofs, including the church of St Barnabas, built over his grave in Famagusta.

This relative stability would not last long, as the island would soon be at the forefront of clashes between the Byzantines and the growing Islamic empire.

> For more insight into the archaeology of Cyprus, check the excellent website www.cyprus-archaeology.org.uk.

8th–3rd Centuries BC	560–525 BC	499–450 BC	411–325 BC
The Assyrians become the first of a series of conquerors to control Cyprus, followed by the Egyptians under emperor Amasis (568–525 BC), and the Persians under King Cyrus (525–333 BC).	The first Cypriot coins appear under the auspices of the King of Salamis. They are created out of base metals, using the Persian weight system.	The city kingdoms of Cyprus join the Ionian revolt against the Persians. Salamis is punished for its role as the revolt is crushed. Kition becomes an important Phoenician trading post.	The Classical Age; Alexander the Great releases Cyprus from the Persians (351 BC). Cypriot art develops under strong Attic influence. Zenon the philosopher is born in Cyprus (334 BC).

Arab Raids

Islamic expansion in the 7th century had a profound effect on the island. The lands of the Byzantine Empire were attacked by Muslim Arabs. Fleets of ships began a series of bloody raids starting in 647, killing many and destroying coastal cities. Salamis (Constantia) was ravaged and sacked heavily, never quite recovering. The city kingdom of Kourion declined dramatically, and coastal settlers moved inland.

In response, fortifications and castles were built, the three grandest being those of St Hilarion, Buffavento and Kantara in the Kyrenia mountains, defending the north coast.

During one such raid in Kition, Umm Haram, the wife of an Arab commander and the aunt of the Prophet Mohammed, fell from her mule and died. The mosque at Hala Sultan Tekke was built at the site of her fall on the edge of Larnaka's salt lake. It is among the holiest places in the Muslim world.

In 688 a truce was called when Justinian II and the Arab caliph Abd-al-Malik signed an agreement for the joint rule of Cyprus. This agreement remained until 965, when Emperor Nikiforos Fokas sent an army of men to the island to regain complete control for the Byzantines.

New governors were sent to Cyprus as dukes. Due to the devastation of the coastal cities, the capital was moved inland to Nicosia (Lefkosia) and built on the remains of the old city of Ledra.

The Stones of Famagusta is a 2008 documentary that traces the historical remains of Famagusta's beautiful, ruined architecture. A labour of love by two British expats, it's treasured by the local population.

The Crusades

Byzantine rule may well have continued had it not been for renegade governor Isaak Komninos, who proclaimed himself emperor of Cyprus in 1184.

On his way to the Holy Land as part of the Third Crusade, King Richard the Lionheart's fleet met with inclement weather and was forced to dock in Lemesos. The first ship to make port was that of the recently widowed Queen Joan of Sicily, Richard's sister, and his fiancée, Berengaria of Navarre.

Komninos attempted to capture the royal party and hold them to ransom. King Richard was outraged at this news and marched on Lemesos, overthrowing Komninos and seizing control of the island. This effectively brought an end to Byzantine rule.

Komninos fled to Kantara Castle in the north, and King Richard married his queen in Lemesos Castle in 1191. To this day Cyprus is the only foreign country to have held an English royal wedding.

Richard fell ill and stayed in Cyprus, postponing his campaign to the Holy Land. He was joined by the French knight Guy de Lusignan, who assisted him in finishing off Komninos. Upon Komninos' capture, he was chained in silver, instead of iron, at his pleading.

323 BC	323–58 BC	300 BC	289 BC
After the death of Alexander, Cypriot kings side with Ptolemy I against Antigonos. Ptolemy becomes ruler of Egypt, Syria, Pentapolis (Libya) and Cyprus (323–283 BC).	Strong commercial relationships with Athens and Alexandria maintain Hellenistic influence on the island. Carried out by administrators from Egypt, Ptolemaic rule continues until 58 BC.	Zenon's Stoic school of philosophy becomes dominant in Athens. Based on logic and formal ethics, it flourishes during the Hellenistic period through to the Roman era.	Ptolemy II becomes co-regent of Egypt, Cyprus and the outlying areas. The important trade port of Famagusta (near Salamis) is founded during his reign (285–247 BC).

Richard went on to conquer the entire island and stayed for a year until he was well enough to travel. He then sold Cyprus to the Knights Templar to boost his coffers. The Knights ultimately were unable to afford the upkeep and, in turn, sold it to the dispossessed king of Jerusalem, Guy de Lusignan, in 1192.

Lusignan Dynasties

The French-speaking lord of Cyprus, Guy de Lusignan, established a lengthy dynasty that brought mixed fortunes to the island. He died in 1194 and was buried at the Church of the Templars in Nicosia and succeeded by his brother, Amalric.

Guy had invited Christian families who had lost property in the Holy Land to settle in Cyprus, many of whom were still concerned with the territorial affairs and disputes in Jerusalem. This proved to be a great economic strain on Cyprus, until the fall of Acre (Akko) in 1291.

For 100 years or so thereafter, Cyprus enjoyed a period of immense wealth and prosperity, with current-day Famagusta (Mağusa) the centre of unrivalled commercial activity and trade. Many of the Byzantine castles were added to in grandiose style, and fine buildings and churches were erected. The Church of Agia Sofia in North Nicosia (Lefkoşa), Bellapais Abbey in Kyrenia (Girne) and Kolossi Castle, near Lemesos, were completed during this period.

Lusignan descendants continued to rule the Kingdom of Cyprus until 1474. The island's prosperity reached its zenith under King Peter I (r 1359–69), who spent much of his time overseas at war. He quashed many attempts at Turkish piracy raids, before mounting a counter-attack in 1365. During this unsuccessful crusade, he only managed to sack the city of Alexandria. Upon his assassination at the hands of his nobles, the fortunes of the Lusignans took a turn for the worse.

Eyeing Cyprus' wealth and strategic position as an entrepôt, Genoa and Venice jostled for control. Genoa ultimately seized Famagusta and held it for 100 years; the fortunes of both Famagusta and the island declined as a result. The last Lusignan king was James II (r 1460–73), who managed to expel the Genoese from Famagusta. He married Caterina Cornaro, a Venetian noblewoman, who went on to succeed James. She was the last queen of Cyprus and the last royal personage from the Lusignan dynasty. Under pressure, she eventually ceded Cyprus to Venice.

Venetian Forts

The Venetians ruled Cyprus from 1489 to 1571. Their control was characterised by indifference to the Greek population, who fared no better under their new overlords than they had under the Genoese.

The citizens of Famagusta (Mağusa) were so rich and so debauched that a merchant once ground a large diamond to season his food, in front of all his guests.

60 BC	58 BC–AD 395	45	115–16
Noted Cypriot physician Apollonios of Kition is born. He would write several important medical books of antiquity. *Peri Arthron* (On Joints), with hand-painted sketches, is the only one to survive.	Romans take over from the Ptolemaic dynasty. Important public buildings are constructed, such as theatres and gymnasiums. Roads and vital aqueducts are built, bringing water to settlements.	Christianity is brought to the island by St Paul and St Barnabas. The Church of Cyprus is established. Cyprus is the first country to be ruled by a Christian.	A major Jewish revolt throughout Mesopotamia spreads to Cyprus and leaves thousands massacred. Roman emperor Trajan intervenes to restore peace and expels the Jews from Cyprus.

As excellent traders, the Venetians' chief concern was the expansion of their maritime empire. They used the island for its position along the vital Silk Route to China and as a defence against the growing Ottoman threat. They built heavy fortifications around the cities of Nicosia and Famagusta, believing the Ottomans would attempt to strike there.

Most Turkish Cypriots are descendants of Ottoman settlers who arrived in Cyprus from 1570, following their conquest of the island over the ruling Venetians.

The Ottomans did so, first attacking Nicosia, defeating it swiftly and slaughtering the garrison. They then turned their attentions to Famagusta. The severed head of Nicosia's governor was sent as a grim message to Famagusta's Venetian captain-general Marcantonio Bragadino. He quickly prepared for the assault, with some 8000 men at the ready.

The Ottomans laid siege to the city with over 200,000 men and 2000 cannon. Bragadino held out for nearly a year, completely surrounded, with Famagusta bay filled with Ottoman ships.

Upon his capture, Bragadino was tortured horrifically for his defiance. His ears and nose were cut off before he was skinned alive.

The fall of Famagusta signalled the end of a Western presence and Christian outpost in the Levant for the next 300 years.

Ottoman Rule

Over 20,000 Turks settled in Cyprus following its capture from the Venetians in 1571, but the island was not a high priority for the Ottomans. The ruling sultan sent Turkish governors to rule the island, who quickly suppressed the Latin church. They abolished serfdom and restored the Orthodox hierarchy and Church of Cyprus to better appease and control the population.

From then on, taxes were arbitrarily increased for the Greek Cypriot population, and the Orthodox archbishop (considered the leader) was made responsible for their collection. In the wake of huge taxes, some Greeks converted to Islam to avoid oppression.

The Ottomans appointed a Dragoman of the Serai (translator to the governor's palace) to each town. They resided in opulent stone houses and acted as arbitrators for all business with Greek Cypriots.

In 1821 Greeks from the mainland were fighting the great war of liberation against the Ottomans. Cypriot Orthodox Archbishop Kyprianos sent money and support to Greece, in the hope that it would help to free Cyprus also. When the *paşa* (lord) Mehmed Silashor found out, he had the archbishop hanged in the public square in front of the *serai* (palace). Any support for the growing Greek revolution was quickly crushed. Another three bishops were beheaded on similar suspicions, and several priests, including the Abbot of Kykkos, were also put to death.

The Ottomans remained in control of the island until 1878, when the British sought authority in the region.

4th century	350	395–647	647
A series of powerful earthquakes rocks the island and many coastal cities are badly damaged or destroyed, including the prized city of Salamis. Drought and famine also result.	Salamis is rebuilt by Constantius II, son of Constantine the Great. The site is lavishly decorated and renamed Constantia.	The island comes under Byzantine rule after the Roman Empire splits. The Church of Cyprus receives unprecedented ecclesiastical autonomy from Constantinople, a practice that continues today.	The first of the Arab raids causes great destruction and suffering. Salamis is destroyed and Kourion fades. Coastal inhabitants migrate inland to avoid constant pillaging and attacks.

Modern Cyprus
Civil Struggle

In 1878 Turkey and Britain signed an agreement whereby Turkey would retain sovereignty of the languishing colony, while Britain would shoulder the responsibility for administering the island. Britain's aim was to secure a strategic outpost in the Middle East, from where it could monitor military and commercial movements in the Levant and the Caucasus. As part of the agreement, Britain would protect the sultan's Asian territories from threat by Russia. In 1914 the start of WWI meant the parties were at war. Britain assumed outright sovereignty of the island, but Turkey did not recognise the annexation of its territory until the 1923 Treaty of Lausanne. This treaty also included territorial claims with the newly independent Greece.

British control of Cyprus was initially welcomed by its mostly Greek population, since it was assumed that Britain would ultimately work with the Greeks to achieve *enosis* (union) with Greece. Turkish Cypriots, a 17% minority of the population, were less than enthusiastic at the prospect, fearing they would be ostracised.

Between 1955 and 1958 a Cypriot lieutenant colonel, Georgios 'Digenis' Grivas, founded the Ethniki Organosi tou Kypriakou Agona (EOKA; National Organisation for the Cypriot Struggle) and launched a series of covert attacks on the British military and administration. EOKA began these attacks to show their frustration with the British for not helping to

Colin Thubron's *Journey into Cyprus* is a classic travel tale. In 1974, just before the Turkish invasion of the island, the author crossed almost 1000km on foot, and his story weaves myth, history and personal anecdotes.

HISTORY MODERN CYPRUS

THE CASE OF THE KANAKARIA MOSAICS

Resembling some Raymond Chandler crime thriller, one of the most famous cases of looting concerned the Kanakaria mosaics that were stolen, sometime between 1974 and 1979, from the Panagia Kanakaria church in the Karpas Peninsula. The priceless mosaics later turned up in Indianapolis where an art dealer was hawking them around museums and galleries for a hefty $20 million or so. The wised-up curator at the J Paul Getty Museum in California became suspicious and contacted the Greek Cypriot authorities who confirmed that these were, indeed, the stolen mosaics from the Panagia Kanakaria church. They were duly returned in 1991 and can be seen today at the Byzantine Museum in Nicosia.

The Turkish art dealer, who was later identified as Aydin Dikmen, was eventually located in Munich in 1997 after an eight-month sting operation. His apartment was raided by police who discovered a further priceless collection of some 5000 Cypriot icons, frescos and other treasures concealed inside the walls and under the floorboards at his apartment. These included two priceless icons stolen from the monastery of St Chrysostomos.

The art treasures were eventually returned to Cyprus in 2010, after more than a decade of legal wrangling in the Bavarian courts.

688–965	1191	1191–92	1192
Justinian II and the Arab Caliph Abd-al-Malik agree to jointly rule Cyprus. Their agreement is broken in 965 and the Byzantines once again take over the island.	Richard the Lionheart is shipwrecked at Lemesos on his way to Acre; the English king conquers Cyprus and weds Princess Berengaria at Agios Georgios chapel in the town.	Richard falls ill amid concerns for his coffers. After finishing off Lemesos governor Isaak Komninos, he sells Cyprus to the Knights Templar to raise funds for a third Holy Crusade.	Guy de Lusignan takes Cyprus from the Knights Templar. Splendid churches and castles are built.

further their ultimate goal of *enosis*. Find out more about this tumultuous period by visiting the Agios Georgios Museum in Pafos.

The British came up with various proposals for limited home rule, but Turkish Cypriots began to demand *taksim* (partition), whereby the island would be divided between Greece and Turkey.

In 1959, Greek Cypriot ethnarch Archbishop (and president) Makarios III and Turkish Cypriot leader Faisal Küçük met in Zurich. They came to ratify a previously agreed plan whereby independence would be granted to Cyprus, under conditions that would satisfy all sides.

The British were to retain two military bases and a number of other sites as part of the agreement. Cyprus also agreed not to enter into any political or economic unions with Turkey or Greece, or to be partitioned. Political power was to be shared on a proportional basis of 70% Greek and 30% Turkish. Britain, Turkey and Greece were named as the 'guarantor powers' of the island.

> Turkey cannot join the EU without a settlement in Cyprus, and that would mean recognising the Greek Cypriot government.

RAUF DENKTAŞ: PORTRAIT OF A RENEGADE

Viewed as the bane of Cypriot society by Greeks, and saviour of the nation by many Turks, Rauf Denktaş still provokes strong feelings among Cypriots. Before he stepped down as president of the self-proclaimed independent republic in 2005, this one-time lawyer was matched in resilience and political longevity by few neighbouring Middle Eastern political leaders. He used charm and tenacity to lead the Turkish Cypriot community from well before the forced division of Cyprus in 1974. Until Mehmet Ali Talat won the 2005 election, he had been leader for 31 years.

A mercurial character, Denktaş was born near Pafos on the island's southern coast and trained as a barrister in London before commencing his long political career. As leader of the Turkish Communal Chamber from 1960, he was in and out of the spotlight – and trouble – until 1974, when he became leader of the partitioned Turkish Cypriots.

Denktaş was known for his persistence and perceived intransigence in seeking a solution for reuniting Cyprus. His drive to seek a mutually acceptable solution to the political impasse was compromised by a steadfastness and unwillingness to deviate from the long-held party line. At thrice-weekly talks held in the UN buffer zone during the spring and summer of 2002, Denktaş refused to concede any ground from the position of his Turkish-mainland backers. They insisted on a bizonal, bicommunal state, with a large degree of autonomy and separation between the two communities. These talks sputtered on into 2003 without any progress.

During that year, Denktaş made the surprise announcement that he would ease border controls between the two parts of the island, thus allowing Cypriots from both sides to cross with immediate effect. This decision marked a major point in Cyprus' history, and was a crucial step towards a different future for the island.

1194	1478	1571	1625–1700
The feudal system is introduced to the island by Amalric Lusignan upon the death of his younger brother Guy. He becomes King of Cyprus as Amalric I.	The last Lusignan king, James II, weds Venetian noblewoman Caterina Cornaro, who becomes the last queen of Cyprus. In 1489 she cedes Cyprus to Venice.	The Ottoman Empire crushes the Venetians and takes over Cyprus. Orthodox hierarchy is restored to assist in local taxation. Some 20,000 Turks settle on the island.	Plague wipes out over 50% of the estimated population on the island. A string of bloody insurgencies against oppressive Ottoman rule are savagely quashed. The plague ends in 1700.

New Republic

The independent Republic of Cyprus was realised on 16 August 1960. Transition from colony to independent nation was difficult, with sporadic violence and protest, as extremists from both sides pushed opposing agendas.

Serious sectarian violence broke out in 1963, further dividing the Greek and Turkish communities. Turkish Cypriots withdrew from government, claiming that President Archbishop Makarios was pro-*enosis*, and wasn't doing enough to control radicals.

In 1964 the UN sent a peacekeeping force to the island headed by British Major General Peter Young. The general drew a green line on a map of Nicosia separating the Greek and Turkish areas of the capital, thus forming the 'Green Line' that would go on to divide the entire island. Many Turkish Cypriots moved to enclaves around the island, separating themselves from the Greeks.

With the Cold War at its peak, Cyprus had strategic value for the British and Americans in monitoring Soviet activity. Makarios sought a position of political nonalignment, and was suspected of being a communist. The Americans and their British allies feared another Cuban crisis – only in the Mediterranean – which added urgency to their interference.

While the island was still politically unstable, the situation on the ground quietened between 1964 and 1967, as Turkish Cypriots withdrew to consolidated areas. This included setting up a provisional government in North Nicosia (Lefkoşa).

Coup d'État & Invasion

Discussion of segregating the Greek and Turkish Cypriot communities stepped up again in 1967. A coup in Greece installed a right-wing military junta, and Greece's relations with Cyprus cooled. Makarios had a number of diplomatic meetings with the Soviets, in keeping with his policy of nonalignment. Both the Greek junta and the Americans were suspicious of this, and were fearful that the island would lean towards communism.

In July 1974 the CIA sponsored a Greek junta–organised coup in Cyprus, with the intention of installing a more pro-Western government.

On 15 July a renegade detachment of the National Guard (numbering a mere 180), led by officers from mainland Greece, launched an attempt to assassinate Makarios and establish *enosis*. Makarios narrowly escaped. Cypriot Nikos Sampson, a former EOKA member with ties to the Greek junta, was proclaimed president of Cyprus.

Five days later, Turkish forces landed troops close to Kyrenia (Girne), using the right to restore a legal government as the pretext.

The regular Greek Cypriot army tried to resist the Turkish advance. However, once the Turks established the bridgehead around Kyrenia, they quickly linked with the Turkish sector of North Nicosia. From this

While Turkish Cypriots and Greek Cypriots may be separated by physical barriers, they share the notion of a single god – even though they worship in two different religions, Sunni Islam and Eastern Orthodoxy.

HISTORY MODERN CYPRUS

Even with its increasing economic expansion, the North is heavily dependent financially (and politically) on Ankara – to the tune of more than US$600 million a year.

1821	1878–1923	1914–15	1923–25
Greek Cypriots side with Greece in a revolt against Turkish rule. The island's leading Orthodox clergy are executed as punishment, and 20,000 Christians flee the island.	Britain leases Cyprus from Turkey, as the administrator of the island. The British formally annex Cyprus in 1914. Turkey does not recognise the annexation until 1923.	Turkey sides with Germany in WWI. Britain offers Cyprus to Greece as incentive to support the British. King Constantine declines in an attempt to remain neutral.	Turkey is compensated by the British for its loss of the island. Cyprus becomes a Crown Colony (1925) and is governed by the British High Commissioner.

point the Greek Cypriot army was outnumbered and could not stop the crushing Turkish assault. On 23 July 1974 Greece's junta on the mainland fell and was replaced by a democratic government under Konstantinos Karamanlis. At the same time, the Cypriots removed Sampson and replaced him with Glafkos Clerides, president of the House of Representatives and a member of the democratic government.

The three guarantor powers – Britain, Greece and Turkey – met for discussions in Geneva, as required by the treaty, but it proved impossible to make the Turkish halt their advance. They pressed on for over three weeks, until 16 August 1974. At that time Turkey controlled 37% of the northern part of the island. By the time Makarios returned to resume his presidency, having escaped the assassination attempt, Cyprus was divided.

A total of 190,000 Greek Cypriots who then lived in the northern third of Cyprus were displaced, losing their homes, land and businesses. Many were caught in the onslaught and killed; the rest fled south for safety. At the same time around 50,000 Turkish Cypriots moved from the South to the Turkish-controlled areas in the North.

The human and economic cost to the island was catastrophic. The now-truncated Republic of Cyprus was deprived of some of its best land, two major cities, its lucrative citrus industry and the bulk of its tourist infrastructure. There was also widespread looting.

The invasion and forced division of Cyprus served convoluted political and military purposes. Reinstatement of the rightful government and dissipation of the military junta did not alter the Turkish government's

A GREEN LIGHT ON THE GREEN LINE

It all happened in a matter of hours. On 23 April 2003 Rauf Denktaş, then leader of the Turkish Cypriots, made the surprise announcement that the Green Line would open that day for all Cypriots to cross from 9am to midnight. The Greek Cypriot government, gobsmacked by the news, was silent. No on knew how the Cypriot people would react and what the consequences of this decision would be.

Starting with a few eager early-morning visitors, thousands of people crossed the border over the coming days. Friends and family met, and many tears were shed. Greeks and Turks visited their former homes and were welcomed by the current inhabitants. The two peoples treated each other with civility and kindness and, more than a decade after the checkpoints' opening, no major incidents have been reported.

Many Turkish Cypriots now cross the line every day on their way to work in the southern part of the island. Serdar Denktaş, the son of Rauf and the man behind the realisation of the border opening, dubbed the events 'a quiet revolution'. Many compared it to the the fall of the Berline Wall in 1989, minus the dramatic knocking down of the buffer zone, an event still to take place.

1955–60	1963–64	1974	1975
Ethniki Organosi tou Kypriakou Agona (EOKA; National Organisation for the Cypriot Struggle) is founded. Guerrilla warfare is directed at the British. Makarios is first president of an independent Cyprus.	President Makarios proposes constitutional changes; inter-communal fighting ensues. Turkish Cypriots withdraw and UN peacekeeping forces arrive. The Green Line is first drawn across Nicosia.	Greek junta organises a coup. Turkish army invades, taking a third of the island. Archbishop's Palace is the scene of much fighting. Makarios resumes presidency. Cyprus is divided thereafter.	Turkish Cypriots establish an independent administration, naming Rauf Denktaş as its leader. Denktaş and Clerides then agree on a population exchange between North and South.

stance. It forcibly continued its illegal occupation of the North and the Turkish troops remained.

The UN has maintained a peacekeeping force along the Green Line and the border that runs the length of the island ever since. They oversee the buffer zone that runs parallel to the Green Line with barbed wire and regular patrols. This no-man's land with its bombed-out buildings is a poignant reminder of the brutality of the conflict.

The declaration of a separate Turkish Republic of Northern Cyprus (TRNC), by President Rauf Denktaş, came in 1983. It is only officially recognised by Turkey.

Unification Attempts

In the years since division, talks to reunite the island have taken place sporadically, with both sides presenting entrenched and uncompromising points of view. During the spring and summer of 2002, Cyprus and Turkey were seeking entry into the EU and the leaders of both the North and the South had thrice-weekly talks aimed at reunification. Again discussions got bogged down by the intricacies of land ownership and the real number of Turkish mainland settlers.

In April 2003, TRNC President Rauf Denktaş made the surprise announcement that travel restrictions across the border would be eased, thus allowing Greek Cypriots daily access to visit the northern parts of the island. Since then seven checkpoints have been opened and visiting periods have gone from daily restrictions to up to three months.

During this period former UN secretary general Kofi Annan brokered an agreement allowing separate island-wide referenda on a reunification plan. The 'Annan Plan', as it was known, was designed to make Cyprus a federation of two constituent states, with shared proportional power. Political leaders on both sides campaigned for a 'no' vote. Greek Cypriots rejected the plan (76%), while Turkish Cypriots endorsed it (65%).

In 2013 right-wing, pro-austerity Nicos Anastastiades was elected as the new President in the Repubic and a peace plan was, once again, on the agenda. High-level talks took place between leaders from both sides and, at the time of writing, there is a sense of cautious optimism in the air and the belief that there will be a different, united future for the island, sooner rather than later.

Repairing the Damage

Many Greek Cypriots quickly regrouped after 1974, putting their energies into rebuilding their shattered nation. Within a few years the economy was on the mend and the Republic of Cyprus was recognised internationally as the only legitimate representative of the island. The

Echoes from the Dead Zone: Across the Cyprus Divide by Yiannis Papadakis is about the author's journey from the Greek to the Turkish side of the border, overcoming prejudices and finding understanding.

Cyprus: A Modern History by William Mallinson explores Cypriot history with a focus on the post-1974 period. It examines the great importance of EU membership for both Cyprus and Turkey.

HISTORY MODERN CYPRUS

1977	1983	1999	2002
The first president of Cyprus, Archbishop Makarios III, dies suddenly at 63. Over 250,000 mourners pay respects during the funeral service. He is succeeded by Spyros Kyprianou.	Turkish Republic of Northern Cyprus is proclaimed by its leader. Its sovereignty is only recognised by Turkey. Thousands of mainland Turks settle in the North of the island.	The Republic of Cyprus starts to prosper economically and the standard of living booms. Northern Cyprus is supported largely by Turkey in the wake of international economic sanctions.	Cyprus and Turkey both seek entry to the EU. The leaders of the Republic and the North attend intense talks, aimed at reunification. Talks stall and no agreement is reached.

BORDER BLOODSHED

On 11 August 1996, a Berlin-to-Cyprus peace ride by motorcyclists from around Europe ended at the Greek Cypriot village of Deryneia. The village adjoins the Green Line that divides Northern Cyprus from the Republic of Cyprus. Among the riders that day was a young Greek Cypriot from Protaras by the name of Tasos Isaak.

The riders protested at the border to show their ongoing frustration at the continuing occupation of the North by Turkish forces, and a melee ensued. Clashes between Greek Cypriots and Turkish Cypriots broke out in the UN buffer zone separating the two communities.

In the chaos, Tasos Isaak was cut off from his fellow demonstrators, and surrounded by Turks. Despite the fact that he was unarmed, he was set upon and beaten to death. Isaak's body was later recovered by UN personnel.

Three days later, a crowd once more gathered at the Deryneia checkpoint to protest against the death. Among the protesters was Solomos Solomou, a 26-year-old who was enraged at the death of his friend, Isaak. Despite attempts to hold him back, Solomos eluded the UN peacekeepers and slipped across no-man's land to one of the flagpoles carrying the Turkish Cypriot flag. Cigarette in mouth, he managed to climb halfway up the flagpole, before being struck by five bullets. The shots came from the nearby Turkish Cypriot guard post, and possibly from bushes sheltering armed soldiers. Solomos' death was captured on video, and is replayed at the viewing points that overlook the site of the Deryneia deaths.

economy pushed ahead through the 1980s. The opening of the Cyprus Stock Exchange, in 1999, initially absorbed vast amounts of private funds. In the early 2000s the stock exchange took a full-size nose dive and many Cypriots lost huge amounts of money. Similar financial losses were endured in 2013 as a result of the deepening recession, banking crisis and ensuing EU bailout (on the condition that strict austerity measures were taken).

Tourism has remained buoyant, however; British visitors remain the largest group, but there has a marked increase in Russian tourists.

North of the Green Line is known by most foreigners simply as 'Northern Cyprus' and by the Greeks as the 'Occupied Territories' *(ta katehomena)*. This area, by comparison to the South, has developed at a snail's pace. An influx of Turkish mainlanders and international economic sanctions against the unrecognised Northern government has made progress difficult. It remains largely supported by its client and sponsor nation, Turkey, through direct funding and its use as a Turkish military outpost.

Numerous mainland Turkish settlers have married Turkish Cypriots. These relationships are somewhat frowned upon by middle-class Turkish Cypriots, who see themselves as different from the mainlanders.

2003	2004	2012	2013
The North's leader, Rauf Denktaş, announces a surprise decision to allow Cypriots from both sides to visit the opposing parts of the island. The first crossings in 29 years are peaceful.	Republic of Cyprus joins the EU.	Pavlos Kontides wins a silver medal in the Laser sailing event at the London Olympics, Cyprus' first ever Olympic medal.	Veteran right-winger Nicos Anastasiades is elected president in the Republic of Cyprus.

The Cypriot Way of Life

Cypriot culture is a unique blend of Mediterranean and Middle Eastern, moulded by centuries of rule by different nations that have coveted, fought over and possessed the island. Family life is considered of paramount importance and respect for the older generation remains strong. Despite an outwardly relaxed attitude towards religion, the traditions and values of the Orthodox church (in the South) and Islam (in the North) still play a key role in society as a whole.

The Great Divide

The daily lives of Cypriots are still largely dominated by the domestic and international focus on the division that scores the island. Over the last 40 years, nearly two generations have grown up with partition and the incessant political news and discussions on both sides of the Green Line regarding the 'Cyprus problem'. Nowadays, although there remains some allegiance to mainland Greece or Turkey, most people see themselves as Cypriot first and Greek or Turkish second. In recent years a significant number of the younger population on both sides of the divide, who were born after the island was split in two, have become increasingly tired of the political manoeuvring that dominates Cypriot headlines and are pressing for a final resolution.

When the first border crossings between North and South opened in 2003, no one knew how the Cypriot people would react and what the consequences would be. Would there be riots or civil unrest? After all, no one had crossed the Green Line for 29 years, save for diplomatic reasons. Many still had friends, relatives and homes they missed on the 'other side'.

The newly opened checkpoints swelled with thousands of people crossing the border. Many Turkish Cypriots who came south were enchanted by the comparative wealth and the elegant shops and restaurants in the streets of Nicosia (Lefkosia), while many Greek Cypriots wandered the streets of North Nicosia (Lefkoşa), surprised at the way time had stood still for 30 years. Old acquaintances met and tears were shed. Some Greeks visited their former homes and properties in the North, and in some cases existing inhabitants reportedly welcomed visitors cordially and even invited them in for coffee and gave them gifts of citrus fruit and flowers. It is estimated that more than 35% of Cyprus' population crossed in the first two weeks, and over 25,000 Turkish Cypriots applied for a Cypriot passport (from the Republic of Cyprus) in that year alone.

The people have treated each other with studied civility and kindness, and even now, years after the openings, no major incidents have been reported. Since the attitude to crossing the border has normalised, over 20 million crossings have been recorded, with around 70% of those North to South. Indeed, many Turkish Cypriots now cross the Green Line daily to shop or work in the southern part of the island. While Greek Cypriots make up less of the border traffic, many do head over for Easter holidays

Fast Facts

The sun shines 326 days a year on average.

The highest point is Mt Olympus at 1952m.

Cyprus is an ophiolite that rose from the sea 20 million years ago.

Using first names alone is considered too familiar and is only done among friends. People greet each other with the title *kyrie* or *kyria* ('Mr' and 'Mrs' in Greek) before the person's name. In Turkish *bey* and *hanım* are used the same way, after naming the person.

and in particular to visit Apostolos Andreas church and for shopping bargains and casino visits.

While politics are discussed openly on both sides, travellers should always approach the subject with tact. Both Greek Cypriots and Turkish Cypriots may be forthright in discussing the issue, but it's still better to let them initiate the discussion. There are pockets of hard-liners still on both sides of the island and for the older generation, especially who experienced the trauma of partition first-hand, the sensitivity they feel in relation to this subject cannot be overstated.

Multiculturalism

Traditionally, ultimate relaxation for a Cypriot man in his courtyard or garden requires the use of seven time-honoured wooden chairs. One for his stick, one for his coffee, one for each arm, one for each leg and of course one to sit on.

Although immensely hospitable people by nature, some Cypriots regard outsiders with a slight caution and wariness, perhaps understandably so given the island's long history of occupation and struggle for independence.

Patriotism is a strong force in people's identity. In the North, some Turkish Cypriots define settlers from mainland Turkey as outsiders and make a clear definition between the two. Similarly in the South, for a small number of locals, especially those who have never left the island, even expatriates and second-generation Cypriots from the UK, US, Canada and Australia are considered to be *xeni* (foreigners).

Both sides of the island have had an influx of foreign migrants over the past decade. North Cyprus' universities have attracted a large number of foreign students, many of which have stayed on to work afterwards, while in the South a growing number of manual and service jobs are filled by migrant workers. This swift multicultural transformation has greatly changed the face of the island's population. Combine this with the lasting 'Britishness' that remains from the island's colonial past and from its present-day reliance on tourism and, rightly or wrongly, many locals feel bombarded by outsiders.

Much of the worry stems from the gradual loss of traditional lifestyle and culture. While this has caused some consternation and resentment, this expanded diversity has been welcomed by others, especially those Cypriots who have travelled and studied abroad.

Gradually most Cypriots are recognising the trend in their society towards greater multiculturalism. Indeed, this is reflected in the increasing number of Cypriots who are marrying foreigners (14% of marriages), particularly Europeans and Russians (many of whom belong to the Orthodox Church), creating a new generation of multicultural Cypriots. This phenomenon suggests that if racial and cultural barriers do linger – as some suspect they do – then their influence is diminishing.

THE KAFENEIO & THE TEAHOUSE

In South Cyprus' villages, the local *kafeneio* (coffee shop) is the central meeting point. Most will have two such places, distinguished by their political alignment (socialist or nationalist). In the North the village hub is the local teahouse. Both South and North, these cafes are filled with men of all generations, sitting, serving or flipping beads. Many come and go on their way to and from work. The older men sit quietly, spread across chairs, waiting out the days like oracles, eating haloumi and olives or drinking coffee, tea and (in the South) *zivania* (fermented grape pomace). Good friends sit in pairs, smoking cigarettes and playing *tavli* (backgammon) in the shade of the vine leaves. Their dice rattle, while moves are counted and strategies are shaped in whispers. And come lunchtime, only the lingering smoke remains, as the men stampede home for their midday meal and siesta, returning in the evening to do it all again.

SUMMER SOUVLA

A favourite Cypriot pastime is enjoying a *souvla* (spit-roast) that's been cooking for hours over burning coals. It's especially fine on the beach. There's the joke that a Cypriot's favourite vehicle is a pick-up truck, because 20 chairs, a table and all the barbecue equipment can fit into the tray when the family heads out for the weekend. Indeed, part of the summer holidays for many Cypriots is often spent camping on beaches, where the sound of rotating skewers and the smell of soft lamb with herbs permeates the sea air.

This hangover of insularity is more than balanced by a natural tendency of hospitality towards guests. Most visitors to the island will find the Cypriots they meet to be amazingly friendly, welcoming and kind, regardless of whether they live in cities, villages or less-developed areas.

Orthodoxy & Islam

Almost 78% of Cypriots are Greek Orthodox, 18% are Muslims and the remaining 4% are Maronite, Armenian Apostolic and other Christian denominations. Due to the island's division, Muslims predominantly live in the North, while the Greek Orthodox live in the South.

The recent increase in asylum seekers from the Middle East, Africa and Central and South Asia has increased the number of practising Muslims living in the Republic, particularly in the centres of Larnaka, Nicosia and Lemesos, which all have mosques.

The presence of the Orthodox Church is ingrained in both politics and daily life in the South, with the Cypriot year centred on the festivals, celebrations and Saints days of the Orthodox calendar. Sundays in particular are popular for visiting monasteries and the Byzantine churches in the Troödos Mountains.

In the North, Turkish Cypriots are mostly secular Sunni Muslims. While religion plays an important part in Turkish Cypriot culture, the more conservative Islamic tradition practised elsewhere in the Middle East is not so obvious in Cyprus. Alcohol, for example, is widely available and frequently consumed by Turkish Cypriots, and women dress far more casually than their counterparts in other countries where Islam is the main religion.

Topless sunbathing is generally OK in the Republic; baring all is not. There are no nudist beaches in Cyprus. In North Cyprus sunbathe topless only on private resort beaches (and check first if it's OK). Anywhere on the island, once you leave the sand remember that Cyprus is a traditional country, so best to put on a T-shirt.

Changing Roles

Traditional ideas about the proper role of women – cooking, cleaning and tending to house and family – persist in some sectors of Cypriot society. However, modern Cypriot women, particularly those who live in cities, like to dress in designer labels, frequent beaches in bikinis, have careers and go out on the town.

Cypriot women have freedom and independence in many areas, but more needs to be done, especially when it comes to employment, as professional positions are still very much male dominated.

Attitudes towards homosexuality have relaxed somewhat over the years, although open displays of affection are still frowned upon by many. Several gay bars and clubs can be found in cities like Nicosia, Lemesos, Larnaka and Pafos, offering diverse and comfortable atmospheres. On the Turkish side of the island it is still advisable to be discreet, particularly once away from the heavily touristed coast around Kyrenia (Girne).

Landscapes & Wildlife

For a growing number of visitors, Cyprus' one-of-a-kind flora and fauna is the number-one reason for travelling. Tiny rare orchids bloom amid the hillside wildflowers in early spring. Turtles nest on the beaches in their thousands during summer. Endemic bird species, along with seasonal visitors, can be spotted in the high forests and lowland salt lakes. This rich biodiversity makes it a nature-lover's paradise.

Lie of the Land

Shaped like a swordfish surfacing from the sea with its sharp tip and flared fins, Cyprus is the third-largest island in the Mediterranean.

In the North, the 170km-long Kyrenia (Girne) Range was formed by upward-thrust masses of Mesozoic limestone. It's most famous feature is the five-ridged peak known as Five-Fingers Mountain (Beşparmak,

Above Kotschy's bee orchid

in Turkish; Pentadaktylos, in Greek) that runs practically parallel to the northern coastline.

Directly south of this mountain range is the vast Mesaoria plain (whose name means 'in between mountains' in Greek), which stretches from Güzelyurt (Morfou) in the west to Famagusta (Mağusa) in the east, with the divided capital of Nicosia (Lefkosia) situated at its middle. The plain has over 1900 sq km of irrigation and is the island's primary grain-growing area.

Further south, the island is dominated by the vast range of the Troödos Mountains, created millions of years ago by rising molten rock in the deep ocean. It features the imposing Mt Olympus and its lower plateaus to the east. This area is rich in minerals and natural resources like chromite, gypsum, iron pyrite, marble and copper. Mined for thousands of years, it was instrumental in the island's development during ancient times.

National Parks & Reserves

The upgrading of natural areas to national-park status has steadily increased. The declared list of parks in South Cyprus includes Akamas National Forest Park, Pafos region; Troödos National Park, declared in 1992; Cape Greco and the Peninsula Bay, east of Agia Napa; Athalassa National Forest Park, west of Nicosia; Polemidia National Forest Park, near Lemesos; Rizoelia National Forest Park, near Larnaka; and Tripylos Natural Reserve, east of Pafos, which includes the wonderful Cedar Valley.

There's also one marine reserve: Lara Toxeftra Reserve, off the west coast near Lara, Pafos region, established to protect marine turtles and their nesting beaches.

In North Cyprus, 150 sq km of the Karpas (Kırpaşa) Peninsula has been declared a national park. Environmentalists were successful in having the vulnerable and precious area protected from development. Rare

A handy field companion is *Butterflies of North Cyprus* by Dr Daniel H Haines and Dr Hilary M Haines. It's a comprehensive guide available in paperback.

Check out *The Floral Charm of Cyprus*, by Valerie Sinclair, for further information about the range of flora on the island.

LANDSCAPES & WILDLIFE LIE OF THE LAND

FLOWER POWER

For the best flower-spotting, enthusiasts will need to spend plenty of time trekking and searching, as many species are limited to small geographical areas. You'll need to enjoy a ramble and be patient.

Casey's larkspur This is a late-flowering species that carries a dozen or more deep-violet, long-spurred flowers atop a slender stem. Its habitat is limited to the rocky peaks 1.5km southwest of St Hilarion.

Cyprus crocus This is a delicate white and yellow flower from the iris family. An endangered species, it's protected by law and is generally found at high altitudes in the Troödos Mountains.

Cyprus tulip Delicate and dark red, this is another rare, protected species found in the Akamas Peninsula, the Koruçam (Kormakitis) Peninsula and remote parts of the Beşparmak (Pentadaktylos) Range.

Orchids The most popular wildflowers for enthusiasts, its varieties include the one endemic orchid, Kotschy's bee orchid, an exquisite species that resembles a bee, both in its shape and patterning. While fairly rare, it's found in habitats all over the island. Other varieties found on the slopes of Mt Olympus include the slender, pink Troödos Anatolian orchid, the cone-shaped pyramidal orchid, the giant orchid and the colourful woodcock orchid.

St Hilarion cabbage This unlikely sounding beauty grows in the North, mainly on rocky outcrops near St Hilarion Castle. This large endemic cabbage flower grows to 1m in height and has spikes of creamy white flowers.

Troödos golden drop A member of the borage family, this is an endemic yellow bell-shaped flower appearing in leafy clusters. Another endangered species, it's confined to the highest peaks of the Troödos Mountains.

Cyprus has 140 unique flowering plants only found in the Troödos Mountains, 390 different migratory bird species during spring and autumn, and over 80 nesting sites for rare and protected turtles.

Landscape near Latsi (p98) on the Akamas Peninsula

marine turtles that nest in the beaches on both sides of the peninsula are now benefiting from this decision.

A Plethora of Plant Life

The diversity of Cyprus' flora is not immediately obvious to first-time visitors. After the explosion of colour from endemic flora and wildflowers in spring, summer sees the island assume an arid appearance, with only a few hardy flowers and thistles.

For those wanting to be immersed in the natural habitat, a growing choice of rural accommodation in the mountains and traditional villages is now available. Visit www.agrotourism.com.cy.

The island is home to some 1800 species and subspecies of plants, of which about 7% are indigenous to Cyprus. Five major habitats characterise Cyprus' flora profile: pine forests, garigue and maquis (underbrush found in the Mediterranean), rocky areas, coastal areas and wetlands. One of the main places for indigenous plant species is the Troödos Mountains, where around 45 endemic species can be found.

The Karpas (Kırpaşa) Peninsula has a further 19 endemic species that are found only in the North.

Over 40 species of orchids can be found on the island; many of these, such as the rare Punctate orchid, can be spotted in the lap of the Kyrenia Range. The best time to see Cyprus' wildflowers is in early spring (February to March) or in late autumn (October to November), when most of the species blossom, taking advantage of the moister climate.

Environmental Awareness

This beautiful island is unfortunately beset with environmental issues. True, some of its environmental concerns stem from tourism, but there is also the much deeper issue of littering on streets and beaches, and garbage dumping on roadsides. Industrial waste, fridges, rubble and all sorts of debris are often dumped in forests and near natural salt lakes.

Sea caves (p123) near Agia Napa

In an attempt to remedy this situation, the government has responded with advertisements encouraging people to put rubbish in bins and stop discarding cigarette butts on beaches. There are new recycling points across the island. On a more grassroots level, educational programs have been launched in primary schools to encourage the next generation to be more aware of their environment and the benefits of recycling. Local councils have joined in, providing skips near and around natural habitats where dumping regularly occurs. Positive actions like these are providing new hope and putting a much-needed focus on the issue.

Water, Water, Everywhere...

A significant ongoing issue for the island is the shortage of water. Population growth, mismanagement of underground aquifers and years of drought, which depleted water reserves in dams and reservoirs, have all added to Cyprus suffering a severe water crisis.

Looking for a permanent and sustainable solution, the South opted to begin building desalination plants in the 1990s. There are now four installations (which each produce 40,000 cubic metres of water per day) already supplying over 50% of domestic water and another being built.

In North Cyprus an ambitious plan to build an underwater pipeline from mainland Turkey to North Cyprus has begun construction in 2013. The project – which has an estimated cost of US$484 million – plans to carry a steady supply of water from Turkey to the North. When completed, it will be the longest undersea water pipeline in the world. While detractors claim the project is economically unsustainable, others believe that the water pipeline could not only solve the North's water woes but also be key in finally reuniting the island by setting up water-sharing plans between North and South.

Although years of meagre rainfall is the main cause of Cyprus' water woes, the influx of nearly three million tourists every year has also added to the problem. Travellers should endeavour to be extra aware of their water usage while here.

Island Animals

Bird Life

Cyprus is a major overwintering stop on the north–south migration routes and is also home to two endemic bird species. The Cyprus warbler and Cyprus wheatear are found nowhere else in the world and many bird enthusiasts come to the island solely to tick them off their spotting list.

Although only approximately 50 species of birds are resident in Cyprus year-round, during the major Mediterranean migration period over 200 species utilise the island as one of their stops along the route.

October through to April are all good birding months but the spring, particularly April, is peak time for birdwatching.

Mammals

While the most famous Cypriot wild animal is still the mouflon, a scattering of twitchy wild donkeys can be seen on the Karpas (Kırpaşa) Peninsula. They are believed to have evolved from the domesticated donkeys that escaped or were abandoned in 1974.

In the island's differing forest environs you may also see smaller animals such as foxes, rabbits, hares, hedgehogs, squirrels and fruit bats.

Reptiles

The island's dry, hot summer landscape is a natural home for lizards, geckos, chameleons and snakes, of which only the Montpellier snake and blunt-nosed viper are poisonous. Lizards, in particular, pop up everywhere, sunbathing on rocks, ruins and concrete walls. If you stay in any number of the wonderful agro-hotels across the island, you may even spot a gecko in your doorway out to feed on insects.

Sea Life

Cyprus' warm, clear waters are home to over 260 different kinds of fish, and the coves and underwater reefs along its coasts are teeming with

Birding Resources

Birdlife Cyprus (www.birdlife cyprus.org; South Cyprus)

North Cyprus Birdwatching (www.kibrisbirds.net)

The Birds of Cyprus (Jane Stylianou)

Where to Watch Birds in Northern Cyprus (Steve Cale)

WHERE TO WATCH

Birds travelling between Africa and Europe use Cyprus as a stepping stone on their migratory path. Birdwatchers have an excellent window into both more exotic migratory species and local birds. Here are some of the best birdwatching locations on the island:

Larnaka Salt Lake An important migratory habitat that fills with flamingos and water fowl from February to May. There are lookout posts (with seats) at various intervals along the airport road to Larnaka. You can also walk the nature trails around the lakes past the Hala Sultan Tekke.

Troödos Mountains The ranges offer excellent vantage points along the many nature trails in the region. Take binoculars to catch the likes of griffon vultures, falcons and kestrels. One of the best birdwatching spots is the Kaledonia Trail, which showcases large amounts of Cyprus and Sardinian warblers and nightingales.

Cape Greco Peninsula In addition to being the home of wonderful sea caves, the cape, with its scrubland and rocky outcrops, is one of the prime migration zones for birds from across the seas. Expect to see a range of birds, from chukars and spectacled warblers to pallid harriers and red-rumped swallows.

Kyrenia Mountains Bonelli's Eagles nest amid the rugged rock faces and Cyprus warblers and wheatears are easy to spot. Sightings of black-headed bunting, spectacled warblers and blue rock thrush are common.

Famagusta Wetlands Like Larnaka salt lake in the South, the Famagusta wetlands in the North are home to a host of migratory birds. Likely sightings include pelicans, flamingos, Demoiselle cranes and spoonbills.

Top Gulls flying over salt marshes near Lemesos (Limassol; p48)
Bottom Wild donkey grazing

Cypriot mouflon

sea-life such as corals, sponges, mussels and sea anemones, making it a haven for diving and snorkelling.

Schools of grouper, jack, tuna, barracuda, rays and parrot fish are commonly seen by divers here, while the seas surrounding the island are also home to moray eels, octopus, and green and loggerhead turtles.

Endangered Species

Mouflon, the native wild mountain sheep, are timid, nimble and skilled at climbing. The males have enormous curved horns and were hunted for sport by the nobles in Lusignan times. By the early 20th century widespread shooting by farmers and hunters had nearly reduced them to extinction. However, awareness of the plight of the island's national emblem increased, and now they are protected at sites such as Stavros tis Psokas forest station, in Pafos, which shelters a small herd. In the wild, mouflon are only found in remote parts of the mountain ranges and are rarely spotted.

The island's national symbol is the Cypriot mouflon (wild sheep). Once endangered, it's now only found in the remote mountain ranges of Troödos and Pafos, with subspecies reportedly roaming parts of the uninhabited buffer zone between North and South.

Green and loggerhead turtles have bred and lived on Cypriot beaches for centuries, but tourism and beach development has encroached on vital nesting areas. They nest in the soft sands of the northern beaches in particular, which are now signed and closed at night (hatching times). Look out for conservation programs in coastal areas. Follow the rules, stick to allocated swimming times, and plant your umbrellas as close to the water's edge as possible to avoid crushing eggs.

Monk seals are rarely spotted off the coast and had been considered extinct as recently as 10 years ago. However, sightings off the eastern coast and at Cape Greco's sea caves have revived hope. Now it's believed a very small number still survive in remote locations around the island's shores.

The Arts

Cyprus' heritage reflects a rich and diverse love of the arts. Ranging from dazzling icons painted in punchy primary colours to delicate embroidery with minute intricate stitchery, Cypriots have an aesthetic deep-rooted artistic sensibility towards both visual and creative arts. Music is also an important facet of life here and tradition still strikes a resounding chord, particularly in the continuing popularity of the urban Greek folk music, *rebetiko*.

Visual Arts

The art of Cyprus has long reflected both Eastern and Western influences. Political turmoil and the division of the island have similarly had an inevitable impact.

Above Fresco in Agios Ioannis Lambadistis Monastery (p72)

From Frescos to Folk Painters

During the neolithic age, decorative ceramics and mosaics reflected a desire for ornamentation, which continued with the conversion of the island to Christianity in AD 45 and the emergence of Byzantine art. This religious expression was represented most vividly in frescos, mosaics and icons, many of which are still in evidence today in the monasteries and churches. For the most comprehensive collection of stunning artwork from this period, visit the Byzantine Museums and at the Makarios Cultural Foundation in Nicosia (Lefkosia), home to the largest collection of icons relating to Cyprus, and the Kykkos Monastery near Pedoulas in the Troödos Mountains. Kykkos is just one of several monasteries where you can also see richly coloured and complex mosaics. Other recommended monasteries and churches, particularly for Byzantine frescos, include Agios Nikolaos tis Stegis, Panagia tis Podythou, Panagia Forviotissa and Timios Stavros.

Little remains of the Frankish (1192–1489) and Venetian (1489–1571) periods, due to the looting and plundering of numerous invaders. This sorry situation continued after the conquest of the Ottomans in 1570, when physical survival took precedence over art.

The 19th century saw the emergence of folk painters and sculptors who were the forerunners of contemporary Cypriot art. They painted friezes in coffee shops and decorated glass and furniture, particularly traditional iron beds, which were adorned with plant motifs or similar.

20th- to 21st-Century Painting & Sculpture

In the 1950s artists began to return to Cyprus after studying abroad. Important artists who emerged during this period include Christofors Savva (1924–68), who was strongly influenced by the cubist and expressionist movements, and abstract artists Costas Joachim (1936–), Nicos Kouroussis (1937–) and Andreas Ladommatos (1940–).

The 1974 division of the island had a significant influence on trends in art, with a rise in symbolism and subject matter that reflected the spiritual anguish of the time. Important artists from this period include Angelos Makrides (1942–), who represented Cyprus in the 1988 Venice Biennale, and Emin Chizenel (1949–), a Fulbright scholar and Turkish Cypriot who has exhibited on both sides of the divide.

Female artist Haris Epaminonda was born in Nicosia in 1980 and is known for her collages, installations and videos, while Turkish Mustafa Hulusi had a solo show at London's Tate Modern in 2010 and contributed to the *Terra Mediterranea in Crisis* exhibition at the Nicosia Municipal Arts Centre in Nicosia in 2012.

In 2014 the AG Leventis Gallery opened in Nicosia with a collection that includes some of the island's most iconic contemporary artworks. At its heart is the monumental work by the famous late Cypriot painter Adamantios Diamanis, *The World of Cyprus,* based on 75 drawings depicting the landscape and people of the island. Another art museum that provides an excellent insight into Cypriot art is the State Gallery of Cypriot Contemporary Art, also located in Nicosia.

Icons

Although some Cypriot churches and several museums still house magnificent Byzantine icons, many have been looted and their treasures sold on the open market. These are often unwittingly bought by collectors and, occasionally, celebrities. Singer Boy George had an icon hung proudly over his fireplace for decades before it was spotted by an expert during a televised interview. The icon was duly returned to the Church of St Charalambos in Chorio Kythrea in 2011, from where it had been stolen in 1974.

Icons are still being produced in many monasteries today. The most justifiably famous of the contemporary icon painters is Father Kallinikos

Top
Cypriot
Sculptors
....
Demetris
Constantinou
(1924–)
....
Andreas Savvides
(1930–)
....
George Sfikas
(1943–)
....
Nicos Dymiotis
(1930–90)
....
Kypros Perdios
(1942–)
....
Leonidas Spanos
(1955–)

Top Fresco in Panagia tou Araka (p80)
Bottom Roman mosaic, Ancient Kourion (p59)

Traditional lace making in Lefkara (p116)

Stavrovounis, the aged priest of Stavrovouni Monastery (p116), situated between the cities of Nicosia and Lemesos. The money he receives is used for the upkeep of Stavrovouni and other monasteries.

Traditional Crafts

Cyprus continues its healthy tradition of folk arts, ranging from basket making to lacework. Head for a branch of the Cyprus Handicrafts Centre in Nicosia (p142), Lemesos (p54) or Pafos to guarantee authenticity and a fair price.

Pottery

Decorative pottery is worth seeking out. You can't miss the enormous *pitharia* (earthenware storage jars), often used as stylish plant pots. Originally used for storing water, oil or wine, their sheer size renders them impossible to transport home. One of the best places to learn about the history of the *pitharia* is at the Folk Art Museum in Foini (p70) in the Troödos Mountains. Curator Theophanis Pilavakis, now in his 90s, is famed for making an enormous *pitharia* (on display here) that holds 2000 litres and made the *Guinness Book of Records*. The village of Kornos, between Lemesos and Larnaka, is also famous for its pottery, as is Pafos and the southwest region of the Republic.

Basket Making

One of the oldest handicrafts, basket making was traditionally learned by everyone in the family. Baskets are still usually made from reeds found growing next to streams, though in the Akamas Peninsula villages like Kritou Terra are famous for their intricately woven twig baskets. Palm leaves and straw are used for creating distinctive brightly coloured *tsestos* (decorative 'platters' with geometric designs). These are more prevalent

Dance festival, Ancient Salamis (p188)

Theatre throughout Cyprus is an important art form with a long history. Productions range from traditional Greek plays in the South to Ottoman-inspired shadow-puppet theatres (p155) in the North.

in Northern Cyprus, especially in the Karpasia and Mesaoria (Mesarya) regions. Be wary of copies made from plastic, which are easy to spot.

Lacework

One of the most famous folk-art exports is the exquisite Lefkara lacework, from Lefkara village in the southern Troödos foothills. Be wary of cheap Chinese imports. Fyti village in the Pafos region is also famous for needlework, particularly woven and embroidered silk and cotton, and is, to date, not on the coach-tour trail. Check out the Museum for the Preservation of Lace at Timiou Stavrou (Holy Cross) Monastery in Omodos.

Music & Dance

Cypriot music and dance is diverse and reflects Greek, Turkish and Arabic influences. Traditional music has an enduring appeal as evidenced by the distinctive bouzouki twanging out from all those open car windows.

Music

Greek Cypriots have tended to follow the musical preferences of mainland Greece. Conversely, Cyprus has also produced some of its own musicians who have made successful careers in Greece as well as in their homeland. Names to look out for include Larnaka native Anna Vissi who, in 2014, was voted the best female artist by Cyprus' popular radio station, Super FM. Alknoös Ionnides is a young Lefkosian who sings emotional ballads of his own composition, which occasionally verge on rock and rap. He has attracted big audiences in venues like the Opera House in Toronto.

The bouzouki, which you will hear all over Cyprus, is a mandolin-like instrument similar to the Turkish *saz* and *baglama*. It's one of the main instruments of *rebetiko* music – the Greek equivalent of American blues. The name *rebetiko* may come from the Turkish word *rembet,* which means 'outlaw'. Opinions differ as to the origins of *rebetiko,* but it is probably a hybrid of several different types of music. One source was the music that emerged in the 1870s in the 'low-life' cafes called *tekedes* (hashish dens) in urban areas and ports. Today's music scene in Cyprus is a mix of old and new, traditional and modern. Young Greek Cypriots are as happy with *rebetiko* as they are with contemporary Greek rock music.

Cypriot singer and lyricist Evagoras Karageorgis has produced some excellent music including *Topi se Hroma Loulaki* (Places Painted in Violet); a nostalgic and painful look at the lost villages of Northern Cyprus sung in a mixture of Cypriot dialect and standard Greek, accompanied by traditional and contemporary instruments.

In the North, musical trends tend to mirror those of mainland Turkey. However, Greek music is still admired, and both cultures share a remarkable overlap in sounds and instrumentation.

Dance

Traditional Cypriot dances are commonly 'confronted pair' dances of two couples, or vigorous solo men's dances in which the dancer holds an object such as a sickle, knife, sieve or tumbler. Shows at popular tourist restaurants frequently feature a dance called *datsia* where the dancer balances a stack of glasses full of wine on a sieve.

Dances in the North share very similar patterns of development and execution to those in the South, the only real difference being the names. Thus the *tsifteteli* (a style of belly dancing) is the *ciftetelli* in the North. In addition there is the *testi* and the *kozan,* both wedding dances, and the *kaşikli oyunlari,* a dance performed with wooden spoons. Restaurants with floor shows are most likely your best opportunity to sample some of the northern variants of Cypriot dancing.

Dancecyprus (www.dancecyprus.org) is Cyprus' ballet company. It produces inspiring modern and classical works to a European standard with a distinctive Cypriot influence. Venues include the prestigious Rialto Theatre in Lemesos.

Literature

Cyprus has produced a sprinkling of literary illuminati, and the literature scene is actively promoted and encouraged in both the Republic and Northern Cyprus. Home-grown literary talent of the 20th century includes Loukis Akritas (1932–65), who made his mark mainly in Greece as a journalist and writer, and later championed the cause of Cypriot independence through letters rather than violence. His works include novels, plays, short stories and essays.

Theodosis Pierides (1908–67), who wrote actively from 1928 onwards, is one of Cyprus' national and most respected poets. His *Cypriot Symphony* is considered to be the 'finest, most powerful epic written by a Greek poet about Cyprus', according to contemporary and fellow poet Tefkros Anthias (1903–68). Anthias himself was excommunicated by the Orthodox Church and internally exiled by the British administration in 1931 for his poetry collection *The Second Coming.* He was arrested during the liberation struggle of 1955–59 and imprisoned. While in prison he wrote a collection of poems called *The Diary of the CDP,* which was published in 1956.

The North supports a small but healthy literary scene with more than 30 'name' personages. Nese Yasin (1959–) is a writer, journalist and poet, and a founding member of a movement known as the '74 Generation Poetry Movement. This was a post-division literary wave of writers that sought inspiration from the climate generated after Cyprus was divided. Yasin's poems have been translated and published in magazines, newspapers, anthologies and books in Cyprus, Turkey, Greece, Yugoslavia, Hungary, the Netherlands, Germany and the UK.

Top Music Festivals

Bellapais Music Festival (www.bellapaisfestival.com), Bellapais, Northern Cyprus (May)

International Famagusta Art & Culture Festival (www.magusa.org), Famagusta, Northern Cyprus (July)

Berengaria International Music Festival (www.festivalberengaria.com) Lemesos, Republic of Cyprus (March)

Pafos Aphrodite Festival (www.pafc.com.cy) Pafos, Republic of Cyprus (September)

Survival Guide

Directory A–Z

Customs Regulations

Republic of Cyprus

General EU customs rules apply. You are allowed to bring in or out an unrestricted amount of (legal) goods, as long as they are for your own consumption.

Northern Cyprus

Limits for entering or leaving Northern Cyprus:

➡ 200 cigarettes

➡ 1L of spirits or wine

➡ €100 worth of other goods

The importation of agricultural products is subject to strict quarantine control and requires prior approval by the Ministry of Agriculture & Natural Resources.

When travelling, be aware that you become subject to both British and the Republic of Cyprus customs regulations when crossing the border at Pergamos (Larnaka) and Agios Nikolaos (Famagusta), as those two checkpoints are in the Dekelia Sovereign Base Area (Great Britain). The regulations are the same, but it might take a bit more time.

Discount Cards

Senior Discounts

There are reduced prices available for people over 60 or 65 (depending on the location) at various museums in Cyprus.

Student Cards

Students usually receive discounts of half the normal admission fee. You will need some kind of identification (eg an International Student Identity Card; www.isic.org) to prove student status. These are not accepted everywhere.

Electricity

240V/50Hz

Embassies & Consulates

Republic of Cyprus

Countries with diplomatic representation in the Republic of Cyprus are listed below. All missions are in Nicosia (Lefkosia).

Australian High Commission (☑2275 3001; www.cyprus.embassy.gov.au; Pindarou St 27)

French Embassy (☑2258 5353; www.ambafrance-cy.org; Saktouri St 14-16)

German Embassy (☑2245 1145; www.nikosia.diplo.de; Nikitara 10)

Greek Embassy (☑2268 0649; www.mfa.gr/nicosia; Leoforos Lordou Vyronos 8-10)

Irish Embassy (☑2281 8183; www.embassyofireland.com.cy; Aiantas 7)

Netherlands Embassy (☑2287 3666; http://cyprus.nlembassy.org; Dimosthenis Severis 34)

UK High Commission (☑2286 1100; www.gov.uk/government/world/cyprus; Alexandrou Palli)

US Embassy (☑2277 6400; http://cyprus.usembassy.gov; cnr Metohiou & Agiou Ploutarhou, Engomi)

Northern Cyprus

Countries with diplomatic representation in Northern Cyprus are all located in North Nicosia (Lefkoşa).

Australian High Commission (☎227 7332; www.dfat.gov.au/missions/countries/cy.html; Güner Türkmen Sokak 20, Köşklüçiftlik)

Canadian Consulate (☎227 7508; Themistocles Dervis St, 4th fl)

Turkish Embassy (☎600 3100; www.nicosia.emb.mfa.gov.tr; Bedrettin Demirel Caddesi)

UK High Commission (☎228 3861; www.gov.uk/government/world/organisations/british-high-commission-nicosia; Mehmet Akif Caddesi 29, Köşklüçiftlik)

US Embassy (☎227 8295; www.cyprus.usembassy.gov; Güner Türkmen Sokak 20, Köşklüçiftlik)

Food

See the Eat & Drink Like a Local chapter for more information on food and drink in Cyprus.

Gay & Lesbian Travellers

Homosexuality is legal in the Republic. You will find interesting discussions, tips and contacts on anything gay in Cyprus at www.gay-cyprus.com.

In Northern Cyprus, homosexuality, which had long been officially banned, was decriminalised in 2010. However, you may still find an overall conservative attitude, and overt public displays of affection may be frowned upon. To date there are no organised support groups in the North, though there is a handful of gay forums, including www.turkeygay.net/cyprus.html.

Health

Availability & Cost of Health Care

➡ If you need an ambulance, call ☎119 in the Republic of Cyprus or ☎112 in Northern Cyprus.

➡ Pharmacies can dispense basic medicines without a prescription. You can consult a pharmacist for minor ailments.

➡ Emergency medical treatment and assistance is provided free of charge at government hospitals or medical institutions. However, payment of the prescribed fees is required for outpatient and inpatient treatment.

Drinking Water

The tap water is perfectly safe to drink in the South, although most locals drink bottled water, as tap water is very hard. However, the glass of water you automatically receive with your Cypriot coffee will undoubtedly be tap water. It is advisable to drink bottled water in the North.

Health Insurance

➡ Citizens of EU countries are entitled to free or cheaper medical care in the Republic, but not in Northern Cyprus.

➡ EU citizens must carry proof of their entitlement in the form of the European Health Insurance Card (EHIC).

➡ Citizens from other countries should find out if there is a reciprocal arrangement for free medical care between their country and Cyprus, though travel insurance is always recommended.

Recommended Vaccinations

No jabs are required to travel to Cyprus, but the World Health Organization (WHO) recommends that all travellers should be covered for diphtheria, measles, mumps, rubella and polio.

EATING PRICE RANGES

The following price ranges refer to a standard main course.

	REPUBLIC OF CYPRUS	NORTHERN CYPRUS
€	less than €7	less than €5
€€	€7–12	€5–10
€€€	more than €12	more than €10

Insurance

➡ A travel-insurance policy to cover theft, loss and medical problems as well as cancellation or delays to your travel arrangements is a good idea.

➡ Worldwide travel insurance is available at www. lonelyplanet.com/travel_ services. You can buy, extend and claim online anytime – even if you're already on the road.

Internet Access

➡ Wi-fi is increasingly available at most hotels and in many cafes, restaurants and airports, particularly in the Republic.

➡ Wi-fi is generally, but not always, free. Connection speed often varies from room to room in hotels, so always ask when you check in.

➡ Internet cafes are fairly common, particularly in the North, but they do tend to come and go, so check at the local tourist office. Prices per hour range from €1.50 to €3.

➡ Hotels offering wi-fi are indicated throughout this guide with an icon 🛜. If they have a public-access computer terminal instead, the icon is @.

Legal Matters

Drinking & Driving

Driving while under the influence of alcohol is strictly controlled, and being over the limit can result in a stiff fine and a night behind bars.

Drugs

The Cypriot authorities in both Northern Cyprus and the Republic show zero tolerance towards drugs. Although, strictly speaking, a small amount of cannabis for personal use should be permissible (under EU law) in the South, it is just not worth the risk.

Money

The unit of currency in Northern Cyprus is the Turkish lira (Turkye Lira; TL). Exchange rates for the Turkish lira are subject to fluctuations due to a high inflation

rate and will most likely have changed by the time you read this. All prices for Northern Cyprus in this guide are either in euros for accommodation and excursions, or Turkish lira for restaurants, museum admissions and other sundry fees.

Since January 2008, the Republic's unit of currency has been the euro (€), when one Cypriot pound (CY£) was exchanged at a frozen rate of €1.68.

Banks in Cyprus exchange all major currencies in cash (travellers cheques are becoming increasingly rare). Most shops and hotels in Northern Cyprus accept hard currencies such as UK pounds, US dollars and euros.

ATMs

You will find ATMs in most towns and larger villages throughout the island.

Cash

In the Republic, you can get a cash advance on Visa, MasterCard, Diners Club, Eurocard and American Express at a number of banks, and there are plenty of ATMs. In the North, cash advances

---

PRACTICALITIES

Local newspapers & magazines The Republic of Cyprus' English-language newspapers are the *Cyprus Mail* (www.cyprus-mail.com) and the *Cyprus Weekly* (www.incyprus.com. cy). In Northern Cyprus, look for the *Turkish Daily News, Hurriyet Daily News* (www.hur riyetdailynews.com) and *Cyprus Today* (www.cyprustoday.net). UK dailies and German and French newspapers are widely available in the South and North.

Radio Cyprus Broadcasting Corporation (CyBC) has programs and news bulletins in English on Radio 2 (91.1FM). British Forces Broadcasting Services (BFBS) 1 broadcasts 24 hours a day in English on 89.7FM (Nicosia), 92.1FM (west Cyprus) and 99.6FM (east Cyprus). BFBS 2 broadcasts on 89.9FM (Nicosia), 91.7FM (Lemesos) and 95.3FM (Larnaka). BBC World Service is picked up 24 hours a day on 1323AM. Bayrak FM is the voice of the North and has a lively English-language program on 87.8FM and 105FM.

TV CyBC TV has news in English at 8pm on Channel 2. Midrange to top-end hotels will probably have satellite TV.

Weights & measures Cyprus uses the metric system.

Smoking Prohibited in all bars and restaurants, though some owners turn a blind eye and Cyprus hasn't adopted the anti-smoking mentality as strongly as the UK or US. Hotels always have non-smoking rooms.

are given on Visa cards at the Vakıflar and Kooperatif banks in North Nicosia and Kyrenia; major banks (such as İş Bankası) in large towns will have ATMs, while there is an increasing number of petrol stations with ATMs attached. Do carry some cash with you though, especially if you're travelling up to the Karpas (Kırpaşa) Peninsula.

Foreign-currency notes may be all right to use in major tourist centres in Cyprus, but are not much use in villages in the Troödos Mountains. In the North, foreign currency is more likely to be widely accepted in lieu of Turkish lira.

Currency-exchange bureaus in tourist centres operate over extended hours and most weekends.

Credit Cards

Just as popular as ATMs, credit cards can be used in stores, restaurants, supermarkets and petrol stations. In the latter, you can even buy petrol after hours with your credit card from automatic dispensers.

The Republic of Cyprus is more credit-card friendly than Northern Cyprus, though the main restaurants, hotels and car-hire companies in the North will happily take plastic.

International Transfers

If you need to access your funds, international transfers are possible from your home bank to any of Cyprus' major banks. While this method is reliable, it is usually slow – taking a week or more – and not helpful if you need a cash infusion quickly. Telegraphic transfers are nominally quicker (and cost more) but can still take up to three working days to come through.

Private financial agencies such as Western Union are usually the best bet, as you can often obtain your transferred money the same day.

Tipping

➡ In the North and South, a 10% service charge is sometimes added to a restaurant bill; if not, then a tip of a similar percentage is expected.

➡ Taxi drivers and hotel porters always appreciate a small tip.

➡ Bargaining is not normally part of the shopping scene in Cyprus, either North or South.

Travellers Cheques

Increasingly overlooked by card-wielding travellers, travellers cheques are a dying breed. They should not, however, be written off entirely as they're an excellent form of backup.

Amex, Visa and Travelex cheques are the easiest to cash, particularly if in US dollars, British pounds or euros. Banks can charge hefty commissions, though, even on cheques denominated in euros. Whatever currency they are in, travellers cheques can be difficult to exchange in smaller towns. Always take your passport as identification when cashing travellers cheques.

Photography

You can buy a range of memory cards from camera stores. Film is still available, but it can be expensive. You'll find all the gear you need in the photography shops of Nicosia (Lefkosia) and major towns.

For tips on taking great travel photos, take a look at Lonely Planet's *Guide to Travel Photography*.

Photographing People

Cypriots are often very willing subjects for photos. However, it is bad form simply to point a camera at someone without at least acknowledging your subject.

A simple greeting of *'kalimera'* (in the South) or *'merhaba'* (in the North) or just a smile may be all that is required to break the ice and set up a potential portrait scene.

It is not culturally appropriate to take photographs in mosques when people are praying or when a service is in progress. However, outside of these restrictions, it is usually OK.

Restrictions

In general, you can photograph anywhere in Cyprus, with the following fairly obvious exceptions:

➡ You cannot normally photograph anywhere near the Green Line. In practice, this is rarely monitored other than on both sides of the Green Line in Nicosia (Lefkosia), where sensitivities run high. Warning signs, usually a camera with a line through it, are normally displayed prominently, so heed them.

➡ Military camps are another no-go area, and while there are military installations in both parts of Cyprus, you will be more aware of them in the North. Do not even get a camera out if you see a warning sign.

➡ Airports, ports and other government installations are normally touchy photo subjects, so you are advised to keep your camera out of sight near these places too.

➡ Museums do not normally allow you to photograph exhibits unless you have written permission.

➡ Churches with icons do not allow the use of a flash and, depending on the commercial value of the pictures you take, may not allow photos at all.

Opening Hours

The following hours are for high season only and tend to decrease outside that time.

They apply to both the North and South, unless otherwise specified.

Banks Republic of Cyprus 8.30am-12.30pm Monday to Friday; some also open 3.15-4.45pm Monday. Northern Cyprus 8am-noon and 2-5pm Monday to Friday, 8am-noon Saturday and Sunday.

Entertainment 9pm-3am Thursday to Saturday

Restaurants 11am-2pm and 7.30-11pm daily

Shops 9am-7pm weekdays, closing 2pm Wednesday, 9am-2pm Saturday

Tourist offices 8.30am-2.30pm and 3-6.30pm Monday to Friday, 8.30am-2.30pm Saturday and Sunday.

Post

Postal services on both sides of the island are generally very efficient. Post offices are located in all major towns and villages. Services are normally only related to selling stamps and some packing materials. Stamps can also be bought at newsagents and street kiosks. Post boxes are everywhere (in the South, they are yellow, and in the North, red).

If you're sending mail to any address in Northern Cyprus, ensure that you use the suffix 'Mersin 10, Turkey', not 'Northern Cyprus'.

Public Holidays

Republic of Cyprus

Holidays in the Republic of Cyprus are the same as in Greece, with the addition of Greek Cypriot Day (1 April) and Cyprus Independence Day (1 October). Kids are on holiday in August and over the New Year.

New Year's Day 1 January

Epiphany 6 January

First Sunday in Lent February

Greek Independence Day 25 March

(Orthodox) Good Friday March/April

(Orthodox) Easter Sunday March/April

Greek Cypriot Day 1 April

Spring Festival/Labour Day 1 May

Kataklysmos June

Feast of the Assumption 15 August

Cyprus Independence Day 1 October

Ohi Day 28 October

Christmas Day 25 December

St Stephen's Day 26 December

Northern Cyprus

Northern Cyprus observes Muslim religious holidays. These holidays change each year, since they are calculated by the lunar system. The two major holidays are Kurban Bayramı and Şeker Bayramı, both coming at the end of the month-long Ramadan (Ramazan in Turkish) fast. The fast itself is not strictly observed in the North, and restaurants and cafes are open as normal. As in the South, children are on holiday in August and over the New Year. Other holidays:

New Year's Day 1 January

Peace & Freedom Day 20 July

Victory Day 30 August

Turkish National Day 29 October

Proclamation of the TRNC 15 November

Safe Travel

Scams

You may well come across time-share touts if you hang around the main resorts in Cyprus and, in particular, Pafos. If you like the island enough, a time-share may be worth considering, but be careful about how and what you choose. You need to have all your rights and obligations in writing, especially where management companies promise to sell your time-share for you if you decide to buy a new one. A number of 'free' sightseeing tours are little more than a quick trip to a theme park and then a solid round of the hard sell, as touts pressure you to buy time in a property. If you're not into this, say so up front and save yourself the hassle and always allow yourself a 'cooling off' period to consider. In other words, leave the credit cards safely at home.

Telephone

There are no area codes as such in Cyprus; they are an integral part of the telephone number.

In both the North and the South, mobile phones are popular. If you have an international GSM-equipped phone, check with your local service provider if global roaming is available.

You can make overseas calls from any public telephone box. However, calling from your computer using an internet-based service such as Skype is generally the cheapest option of all.

Mobile Phones

REPUBLIC OF CYPRUS

In the South, mobile-phone numbers begin with ☑95/96/97. If you plan to spend any time in the South, you may want to buy a SIM card for your (unlocked) mobile phone. With CYTA's SoEasy pay-as-you-go, for just €7.50 you get a Tourist SIM pack preloaded with €5 free airtime. You can then top up with cards or vouchers of €5, €10, €20 or €35 with a validity period and any top up required to take place within 30 days. Visit www.cyta.comcy/soeasy for details. MTN pay-as-you-go (www.mtn.com.cy) and Prime Tel Pay As You Go (www.primetel.com.cy) offer similar mobile phone services.

NORTHERN CYPRUS

In the North, mobile numbers start with either ☎0542 (Telsim) or ☎0533 (Turkcell). To call a local number, dial the full 11-digit number, ie including the Northern Cyprus code of ☎0392.

Turkcell has good coverage and it costs about 20TL for a pay-as-you-go SIM with enough credit to start you off.

Pay Phones
REPUBLIC OF CYPRUS

In the South, there are two types of public phones: those that accept prepaid phonecards and those that accept coins. Phonecard-operated phones have explanations in English and Greek. Cards to the value of €5, €10 and €15 can be purchased from banks, post offices, souvenir shops and street kiosks, and from Cyprus Telecommunications Authority (CYTA) offices in all towns.

NORTHERN CYPRUS

Public telephone boxes take phonecards (5TL for a 100-unit card), bought at a Turkish Telecom administration office or post office.

Time
Time Zone

Cyprus is normally two hours ahead of GMT and seven hours ahead of EST.

Daylight Saving

Cyprus uses daylight saving time during the summer months. Clocks go forward one hour on the last weekend in March and back one hour on the last weekend in October.

Current Time

A recorded time message can be heard by dialling ☎193 in the Republic of Cyprus.

TELEPHONING BETWEEN NORTHERN CYPRUS & THE REPUBLIC

Despite the ease of crossing the border from South to North and vice versa, telephoning the other side of the island is still done via half of Europe and Asia.

→ Phone calls to Northern Cyprus are usually routed through Turkey. So you first dial Turkey (international access code ☎90), then the regional code for Northern Cyprus (☎392) and finally the local number.

→ Note that these phone calls are billed at international rates.

→ If you have a mobile phone from outside Cyprus with global roaming activated, it's possible to tune into the GSM networks of either side.

→ If you have bought a pay-as-you-go Cypriot card from either side, it will only pick up its own network in Nicosia/North Nicosia. Go any further away from the Green Line and you will have to revert to your international card, as roaming is not supported between the two local mobile networks.

→ Text messaging between the North and the South is not possible.

→ Making a direct mobile phone call (with no international phone code prefix) between North Cyprus and the Republic (and vice versa) was set to become a reality in 2014.

Toilets

Most toilets will display a sign requesting that you do not flush toilet paper as, due to poor island-wide plumbing, this can easily cause a blockage. Wastepaper baskets are provided for this purpose. It is also a wise idea to carry a small packet of tissues with you when you are out and about.

The majority of public toilets are free, while some charge a small fee. You can also use the public facilities in a bar or cafe, although it is standard to offer a small sum or buy a drink in return.

Tourist Information
Republic of Cyprus

Cyprus Tourism Organisation (CTO; ☎2233 7715; www.visitcyprus.org.cy; Aristokyprou 11, Nicosia) The main tourist organisation in the South is the Cyprus Tourism Organisation, known in Greek as Kypriakos Organismos Tourismou (KOT). Its leaflets and free maps are adequate for getting around. The CTO's headquarters are in Nicosia with branch offices in the major towns in Cyprus (Agia Napa, Lemesos, Larnaka, Pafos, Polis and Platres), where brochures and assistance can be found easily. Contact numbers for CTO branches are given in the regional chapters. The CTO has branches in most European countries.

Northern Cyprus

North Cyprus Tourism Organisation (NCTO; ☎228 1057; www.tourism.trnc.net; Bedrettin Demirel Caddesi) The main office of the North Cyprus Tourism Organisation is located in North Nicosia at Kyrenia (Girne) Gate with another branch at the Ledra Palace Hotel crossing point. It also maintains tourist offices in Famagusta, Kyrenia and Yenierenköy (Yialloussa), which have free country and town maps, plus an increasing number of brochures. The NCTO can be found in the UK, Belgium, the US, Pakistan and Turkey; otherwise inquiries are handled by Turkish tourist offices.

Travellers with Disabilities

Overall Cyprus is not geared towards smooth travel for people with disabilities. Most restaurants, shops and tourist sights are not equipped to handle wheelchairs, though midrange and top-end accommodation options generally always have wheelchair ramps, plus rooms with appropriate facilities.

Transport is tricky, but you should be able to organise a specially modified hire car from one of the international car rental companies with advance warning. In fact, advance warning is always a good idea; start with your travel agent and see what they can offer in terms of information and assistance.

Accessible Cyprus (www.accessible-cyprus.com) is overseen by the CTO and lists hotels with facilities for people with disabilities. For mobility equipment hire, visit Disability Cyprus (www.disability-cyprus.com) or Para-Quip (www.paraquip.com.cy).

Visas

➡ In both the Republic of Cyprus and Northern Cyprus, nationals of the US, Canada, Australia, New Zealand and Singapore can enter and stay for up to three months without a visa.

➡ Citizens of South Africa may enter for up to 30 days without a visa.

➡ When you enter the North (whether from the South or at the airport), you must fill in a visa paper that requires

your personal details and passport number. Your entry stamp will also be stamped on this paper rather than in your passport.

➡ You can use the same visa paper for several entries and exits, and it gets stamped each time you cross.

➡ You must have your passport to cross from one side to the other.

➡ The same border-crossing rules apply for Greek and Turkish travellers as for everyone else.

Volunteering

Possibilities for volunteering in projects in Cyprus include:

Transitions Abroad (www.transitionsabroad.com) A good website to start your research.

Earthwatch Institute (www.earthwatch.org) Check to see if there are any Cypriot conservation projects on its program.

Go Abroad (www.goabroad.com) Generally has several volunteering opportunities in Cyprus.

Any Work Anywhere (www.anyworkanywhere.com) Often has volunteer openings in turtle conservation programs, both in Northern Cyprus and the Republic.

Women Travellers

Women travellers will encounter little sexual harassment, though you'll get more or less constant verbal 'approaches' from Cypriot men. This is common for both foreign and Cypriot women, but foreign women merit particular attention from these verbal Romeos. This can get rather tiresome, if not outright offensive. It is best to ignore the advances.

Solo women travellers should take reasonable care at rowdy nightclub resorts,

such as in Agia Napa, where inebriated foreign males may be a nuisance.

Work

Nationals of EU countries, Switzerland, Norway and Iceland may work freely in the Republic of Cyprus. If you are offered a contract, your employer will normally steer you through any bureaucracy.

Virtually everyone else is supposed to obtain a work permit, and if they plan to stay more than 90 days, a residence visa. These procedures are well-nigh impossible unless you have a job contract lined up before you begin.

Language Teaching

This type of work is a more obvious option in Northern Cyprus, where English is not as widely spoken. There is competition, however, and language teaching qualifications are a big help, namely a TEFL qualification.

Information on possible teaching work – in a school or as a private tutor – can be found in universities, foreign-language bookshops and language schools. Many have noticeboards listing opportunities or where you can place your own advert.

Tourist Resorts

Summer work at the main coastal resorts is a possibility, especially if you arrive early in the season and are prepared to stay awhile. Check any local press in foreign languages, which will normally list ads for waiters, nannies, chefs, babysitters, cleaners and the like.

Yacht Crewing

It is possible to stumble upon work on yachts and cruisers, though it will usually be unpaid. Ask around at the various harbours.

Transport

GETTING THERE & AWAY

Most visitors to Cyprus arrive by air. Many of them come on charter flights or inexpensive flights operated by budget airlines, particularly from the UK.

Crossing the Border

Travelling between the Republic and Northern Cyprus is easy nowadays, since the restrictions on crossing the border have been eased; however, you are only allowed to cross at designated checkpoints.

Entering the Country

Citizens of EU member states and Switzerland can travel to the Republic with just their national identity card. Nationals of the UK have to carry a full passport (UK visitor passports are not acceptable), and all other nationalities must have a full valid passport. In Northern Cyprus, EU citizens can stay for up to three months.

You will need a valid passport to cross between the North and South. You'll need to produce your passport or ID card every time you check into a hotel in Cyprus, and when you conduct banking transactions.

Air

There are scheduled flights and an ever-increasing number of charter and budget flights to Cyprus from most European cities and the Middle East. Flights are heavily booked in the high season (mid-summer). Tickets on scheduled flights tend to be expensive, but Europe-based travellers may be able to pick up cheaper tickets with budget companies. If you're in Greece, you can usually find reasonably priced one-way or return tickets to the Republic from travel agents in Athens, Thessaloniki or Iraklio.

Airports & Airlines

THE SOUTH

Two airports handle international flights in the Republic. Note that on most airline schedules, Larnaka is listed as 'Larnaca' and Pafos as 'Paphos'. This is particularly important to know when making online bookings. Cyprus Airways is the national carrier of the Republic of Cyprus.

Larnaka Airport (☑2481 6130; www.cyprusairports. com.cy)

Pafos Airport (☑2624 0506; www.cyprusairports. com.cy)

THE NORTH

Ercan airport (ECN; ☑231 4806), located 14km east

CLIMATE CHANGE & TRAVEL

Every form of transport that relies on carbon-based fuel generates CO_2, the main cause of human-induced climate change. Modern travel is dependent on aeroplanes, which might use less fuel per kilometre per person than most cars but travel much greater distances. The altitude at which aircraft emit gases (including CO_2) and particles also contributes to their climate change impact. Many websites offer 'carbon calculators' that allow people to estimate the carbon emissions generated by their journey and, for those who wish to do so, to offset the impact of the greenhouse gases emitted with contributions to portfolios of climate-friendly initiatives throughout the world. Lonely Planet offsets the carbon footprint of all staff and author travel.

THE ELUSIVE INSURANCE

Since the 2003 border-crossing changes, there has been a lot of talk of the North's car insurance, issued upon entry from the Republic. And after all this talk, things are still as clear as mud. If you ask about the insurance, you are likely to get numerous reactions and conflicting information. This is because the insurance 'law' concerning vehicles and drivers from the South is full of holes and open to interpretation (mainly by the North's police force).

When you enter the North by car (privately owned or rented) at any checkpoint, your own car insurance will no longer be valid, and you will have to purchase Turkish car insurance. It is third-party cover insurance only, so do check exactly (and the cost) that is covered should you be unfortunate enough to be involved in an accident and whatever you do, do not move your car until a police report has been made.

If you're driving a rented car, keep in mind that, while the Republic's car-rental agencies have no objections to you taking rented cars to the North (although they don't condone it), it's up to you to decide whether this risk is worth taking. Establishing who is at fault in an accident can sometimes take a lot longer than you may think and be subject to many twists and turns.

Turkish-owned cars crossing into the South have to get the standard insurance, similar to that in other EU countries. At the time of research, the North's car-rental agencies did not allow taking rented cars into the Republic.

---

of North Nicosia (Lefkoşa) in Northern Cyprus, is not recognised by the international airline authorities, so you can't fly there direct. Airlines must touch down first in Turkey and then fly on to Northern Cyprus. Ercan is smaller than Pafos airport and facilities are simple, but its arrivals and departure halls both have a bank of ATMs and a couple of cafes. Car hire must be arranged beforehand.

The Kibhas airport shuttle (www.kibhas.org) has regular departures to Kyrenia, Farmagusta and North Nicosia from the airport, timed so that they meet most flights.

Northern Cyprus is served primarily by Turkish Airlines, Pegasus Airlines and Onur Air.

AIRLINES FLYING TO & FROM CYPRUS

Aegean Airlines (www.aegeanair.com; hub Athens International Airport, Athens)

Air Malta (www.airmalta.com; hub Malta Airport, Valetta)

Alitalia (www.alitalia.com; hub Rome Fiumicino Airport, Rome)

Austrian Airlines (www.aua.com; hub Vienna International Airport, Vienna)

British Airways (www.britishairways.com; hub Heathrow Airport, London)

Cyprus Airways (www.cyprusairways.com; hub Larnaka Airport, Larnaka)

Easyjet (www.easyjet.com; hub Stansted & Gatwick Airports, London)

Jet2 (www.jet2.com; hub Leeds Bradford Airport, England)

Lufthansa (www.lufthansa.com; hub Frankfurt Airport, Frankfurt)

Monarch (www.monarch.co.uk; hub Luton & Gatwick Airports, London)

Olympic Air (www.olympicair.com; hub Athens International Airport, Athens)

Pegasus Airlines (www.flypgs.com)

Turkish Airlines (www.thy.com; hub Istanbul Ataturk Airport, Istanbul)

Tickets

Tickets to Cyprus are most expensive in August. Try picking up flight-only deals with package-holiday companies during this time or scour the budget airlines (though these are hardly budget in the summer months). Prices depend on the season, and to a lesser degree on the day of the week or even the time you fly.

CHARTER FLIGHTS

Vacant seats on charter flights block-booked to Cyprus by package-tour companies are cheap, but conditions apply. First, you can rarely get more than two weeks for your itinerary and, second, the departure and arrival times are quite inflexible once booked. That said, a percentage of all package-tour seats is given over to flight-only travellers, so consider giving it a go.

INTERCONTINENTAL (RTW) TICKETS

Neither Cyprus Airways nor Turkish Airlines are signatories to any round-the-world (RTW) ticket agreement.

Africa

Olympic Air (www.olympicair.com) Has regular flights to the Republic from several airports, including Johannesburg and Cape Town, via Athens.

Asia

STA Travel (☎6737 7188; www.statravel.com.sg; 534a North Bridge Rd, Singapore, 188749) Reliable throughout Asia, STA Travel has branches in Hong Kong, Tokyo, Singapore, Bangkok and Kuala Lumpur and can advise on the best route and price from cities of departure throughout Asia.

Australia & New Zealand

There are no direct services from Australia or New Zealand to Cyprus, but several airlines fly with just one change of aircraft.

Emirates Airlines (www.emirates.com) Flies more or less directly from Melbourne or Perth via Singapore, with a change of aircraft in Dubai.

Olympic Air (www.olympicair.com) Flies to Athens from Melbourne and Sydney, and can usually offer good-value add-on Cyprus legs.

Singapore Airlines (www.singaporeair.com) Flies into Athens from Adelaide, Brisbane, Melbourne, Perth and Sydney three times a week, and there are daily connections with Cyprus Airways.

Canada

Olympic Air (www.olympicair.com) Has two flights a week from Toronto to Athens via Montreal. From Athens, you can connect with a Cyprus Airways flight to Larnaka.

Continental Europe

Many European carriers and budget airlines fly into Larnaka airport, and some also stop in Pafos, though the bulk of the traffic is made up of charter flights.

FRANCE

Several airlines operate regular services between France and the Republic of Cyprus:

Air France (www.airfrance.fr) Flies to Larnaka from Paris.

Cyprus Airways (www.cyprusairways.com) Flies to Larnaka and Pafos from Paris.

Turkish Airlines (www.thy.com) Links Paris with Ercan airport in Northern Cyprus daily via Istanbul.

GERMANY

Several airlines operate regular services between Germany and the Republic of Cyprus:

Air Berlin (www.airberlin.com) Flies to Pafos and Larnaka from Berlin, Dusseldorf, Hanover and Hamburg.

Condor (www.condor.com) Flies to Larnaka from Berlin, Stuttgart, Dusseldorf and Hamburg.

KLM (www.klm.com) Flies to Larnaka and Pafos from Frankfurt.

Lufthansa (www.lufthansa.com) Flies to Larnaka from several airports, including Frankfurt, Berlin and Munich.

TUI Fly (www.tuifly.com) Flies to Larnaka from Nuremberg.

GREECE

Not surprisingly, Greece is well connected to both Larnaka and Pafos in the Republic of Cyprus with a comprehensive network of flights. Check the websites of the following main airlines for specific routes:

Cyprus Airways (www.cyprusairways.com)

German Wings (www.germanwings.com)

Lufthansa (www.lufthansa.com)

Olympic Air (www.olympicair.com)

It's possible to fly to Northern Cyprus from Greece. Daily flights with Turkish Airlines (www.thy.com) from Athens to Istanbul connect with a daily evening flight to Ercan.

NETHERLANDS

You can fly to Cyprus from the Netherlands daily:

KLM (www.klm.com) Flies to Larnaka and Pafos from Amsterdam.

Middle East

With Cyprus so close to the Middle East, transport links between the countries of the Levant and Larnaka are good, but tickets are rarely discounted. Cyprus Airways is represented in several countries, including Lebanon, Jordan and Syria.

UK & Ireland

Discount air travel is big business in London. Check the weekend broadsheet papers for special deals, many of which include a hotel or apartment with half-board and even car rental in the final price. The following airlines have regular and relatively inexpensive flights to the Republic.

British Airways (www.ba.com) Flies to Larnaka and Pafos (summer only) from London Heathrow and Gatwick.

Easyjet (www.easyjet.com) Flies to Larnaka and Pafos from London (all airports) and several UK airports, including Manchester and Birmingham.

Monarch (www.monarch.co.uk) Flies to Larnaka and Pafos from London (Gatwick and Luton airports), Manchester and Birmingham.

Ryanair (www.ryanair.com) Budget airline with a hub at Pafos. Regular flights from London (Stansted) and several UK airports to Larnaka and Pafos.

Thomson Fly (www.thomson.co.uk) Flies to Larnaka and Pafos from London (all airports) and other UK airports, including Bristol, Glasgow and Manchester.

Turkish Airlines (www.thy.com) Flies to Ercan airport from London Heathrow.

USA

You can fly to Cyprus from the USA with a number of airlines, but all involve a stop and possibly a change of airline in Europe.

Sea

The only way to arrive in the Republic by sea is aboard a cruise boat; there are no longer any passenger ferries. Lemesos is the South's main arrival and departure port, and the port, complete with new marina, is 3km southwest of the town centre.

The Turkish mainland is linked to Kyrenia (Girne) in Northern Cyprus by a car and passenger ferry service that operates year-round, and during summer there is also sometimes a faster passenger ferry service.

GETTING AROUND

Cyprus is small enough for you to get around easily. Roads are good and well signposted, and traffic moves smoothly.

Public transport is limited to buses and service taxis (stretch taxis that run on predetermined routes). There is no train network and no domestic air services in either the North or the South. Four-lane motorways link Nicosia (Lefkosia) with Lemesos and Larnaka, expanding west to Pafos and east to Agia Napa. In Northern Cyprus there is only one motorway, which runs between North Nicosia and Famagusta (Mağusa).

Bicycle

Cycling is a cheap, convenient, healthy, environmentally sound and, above all, fun way of travelling. However, it's advisable to limit long-distance cycling trips to winter, spring or autumn, as high summer temperatures will make the going tough. In the Republic of Cyprus, the Cyprus Tourism Organisation (CTO) produces a very helpful brochure entitled *Cyprus for Cycling*, which lists 19 recommended mountain-bike rides around the South. These range from 2.5km to 19km from the Akamas Peninsula in the west to Cape Greco in the east.

Prospective cyclists are advised to consider the following:

➡ It's best to stick to cycling on ordinary roads, many of which parallel motorways, where cycling is not allowed. The roads are generally good, but there is rarely extra roadside room for cyclists, so you will have to cycle with care.

➡ You will need a bicycle with good gears to negotiate the long hauls up and around the Troödos Mountains and Kyrenia (Girne) Range.

➡ Towns and cities in general are much more cyclist-friendly than their counterparts in other parts of the Mediterranean. In some tourist centres, such as Protaras and Agia Napa, there are urban bicycle paths, as well as beachside boulevards that incorporate space for bike riding.

➡ You cannot take bicycles on all buses.

Hire

Bicycles can be hired in most areas. Rates start from around €15 a day and local tourist offices can provide you with a list of reputable local operators.

Bus

Buses in the South are frequent and run from Monday to Saturday, with limited services on Sunday. Five companies cover their respective districts and all have comprehensive websites:

Emel (www.limassolbuses.com) Lemesos district.

Osea Buses (www.oseabuses.com) Larnaca district.

Osel Buses (www.oseabuses.com) Nicosia district.

Pafos Buses (Map p85; www.pafosbuses.com; Pafos Harbour) Pafos district.

Zinonas Buses (www.zinonasbuses.com) Famagusta district.

A useful website that does a good job of endeavouring to pull together all the routes of the five companies is www.cyprusbybus.com. In addition, buses that connect the cities are run by the **Inter-City Bus Company** (www.intercity-buses.com), which

---

THE BUS SYSTEM

In mid-2010 there was been a major shake-up of the former, reputedly unreliable, bus system in the Republic of Cyprus. Simply put, each of the five districts now operates its own bus company. Fares are government subsidised and have been pegged at €1.50 per ride, €5 per day, €15 per week and €40 for a month of unlimited journeys within the respective districts, which includes rural villages.

In addition, buses that connect the cities are run by the appropriately named **Inter-City Buses** (www.intercity-buses.com), which is also government subsidised and, therefore, very reasonable, given the distances involved. Each route also offers discounted fares on multiple journeys over a day/week/month or year. You can buy your tickets on the bus.

offers discounted fares on multiple journeys.

Buses in the North are a varied mix of old and newer privately owned buses too numerous to list here. See the regional chapters for more details.

Costs

Fares cost €1.50 per ride, €5 per day, €15 per week and €40 for a month of unlimited journeys within a district, which includes rural villages. InterCity Buses are also government subsidised and are surprisingly reasonable, given the distances involved.

Bus prices in the North generally cost between 4TL to 8TL.

See individual city and town entries for bus frequency and departure times.

Reservations

Bus reservations are not normally required in either the South or the North.

Car & Motorcycle

Automobile Associations

In the South, there is a **Cyprus Automobile Association** (☑2231 3233; www.caa.com.cy; Hrysostomou Mylona 12, Nicosia). The 24-hour emergency road assistance number is ☑2231 3131. There is no equivalent organisation in Northern Cyprus.

Bringing Your Own Car

Unless you intend to settle in Cyprus, there is no advantage whatsoever in bringing your own vehicle. For a stay of more than three weeks, the high cost of bringing your own vehicle to Cyprus will be outweighed by the cost of hiring a vehicle locally. You will need to send your car by ferry and take a plane for yourself, unless you are arriving in Kyrenia or Famagusta from Turkey. If you're one of

---

TRAVEL IN THE LOW SEASON

All of the bus transport times in this guide are for the peak season (June to October). You'll find that public transport frequency decreases, together with tourist demand, during off-peak times. This is particularly problematic with mountain destinations, where the buses sometimes don't run at all. So before departure in the quieter months be sure to check all transport times via the respective bus company's website.

---

the very rare visitors to bring your own vehicle, you will need registration papers and an International Insurance Certificate.

Driving Licence

Requirements for renting a car in Cyprus:

➡ Driver's licence. Note that a licence is required for any vehicle over 50cc.

➡ Be aged 21 or over (Republic); 18 or over (Northern Cyprus).

➡ For the major companies at least, have a credit or debit card.

Fuel & Spare Parts

Being a nation that loves its motors, Cyprus is well equipped for all driving needs, with an abundance of petrol stations, spare parts and repairs, and usually a friendly local happy to give you a hand if your car breaks down.

Normally, if you've rented a car, the rental agency will be responsible for any repairs.

Hire

➡ Cars and 4WDs are widely available for hire, and cost around €20 per day for a week's rental.

➡ In some towns, you can also rent motorcycles (from €10) or mopeds (€10).

➡ Rental cars are usually in good condition, but inspect your vehicle before you set off.

➡ Open-top 4WDs are popular options (the Troödos Mountains literally swarms with them on hot weekends). If you hire a 2WD, make sure it has air-conditioning and enough power to get you up hills.

➡ If you rent a car before going to Cyprus, you'll find that it is common practice for the rental agency to leave your vehicle at the airport, unlocked, with the key waiting for you under the floor mat. Don't be surprised: with the obvious red hire-car plates and a nonexistent car theft record, the car is as safe as can be.

Insurance

The Republic of Cyprus issues full car insurance when you rent a car. The North also issues full insurance to cars rented in the North, but has a special third-party insurance for cars coming in from the South.

Road Rules

Blood-alcohol limit The legal limit is 0.009mg of alcohol per 100mL of blood. Random breath testing is carried out. If you are found to be over the limit you can be fined and deprived of your licence.

Front seat belts Compulsory. Children under five years of age must not sit in the front seat.

Legal driving age for cars 21 (Republic), 18 (Northern Cyprus).

Legal driving age for motorcycles and scooters 18 (80cc and

CROSSING THE GREEN LINE

Crossing freely between the North and the South has become pretty straightforward since the easing of border restrictions in 2003. It is now possible to cross at seven points on the island, and there are ongoing negotiations between the two sides about opening more. You can cross at Ledra Palace Hotel and Ledra St (both pedestrians only), Agios Dometios, Pergamos, Agios Nikolaos, Limnitis-Yeşilirmak and Zodhia (vehicles). If you don't have your own transport, a taxi will take you across the border and on to anywhere you want to go.

When you cross from the South into the North, you will have to fill in a visa paper, giving your name, date of birth and passport number. You will then be issued with a 'visa' (the small piece of paper will be stamped) and you'll be allowed to stay for up to three months in Northern Cyprus. It is important to look after this piece of paper, since you will be required to show it when you leave. There are no restrictions on how many times you can cross back and forth. The visa paper is enforced only in the North.

You are now also allowed to cross into the Republic of Cyprus if your point of entry into the country is in the North. All borders are open 24 hours a day, and many people cross in the middle of the night, after a night's clubbing or gambling at the casinos in the North. There are no requirements for crossing from the North into the South, apart from a valid passport.

over) or 17 (50cc and under). A licence is required.

Motorcyclists Must use headlights at all times and wear a helmet if riding a bike of 125cc or more.

Road distances Posted in kilometres only. Road signs are in Greek and Latin script in the Republic of Cyprus; in Northern Cyprus, destinations are given in Turkish only.

Roundabouts (traffic circles) Vehicles already in the circle have the right of way.

Side of the road Drive on the left.

Speed limits In built-up areas, 50km/h, which increases to 80km/h on major roads and up to 100km/h on motorways. Speed limits in the North are 100km/h on open roads and 50km/h in towns.

Hitching

Hitchhiking is never entirely safe in any country in the world, and we don't recommend it. Travellers who decide to hitch should understand that they are taking a small but potentially serious risk. People who do choose to hitch will be safer if they travel in pairs and let someone know where they are planning to go.

Hitching in Cyprus is relatively easy but not very common. In rural areas, where bus transport is poor, many locals hitch between their village and the city. If you do decide to hitch, stand in a prominent position with an obvious space for a ride-giver to pull in, keep your luggage to a minimum, look clean, smart and, above all, happy. A smile goes a long way.

Hitching in the North is likely to be hampered by a lack of long-distance traffic and, in any case, public transport costs are low enough to obviate the need to hitch.

Local Transport

Bus

While urban bus services exist in Nicosia, Lemesos, Larnaka and Famagusta, about the only two places where they are of any practical use are Larnaka (to get to and from the airport); Lemesos, where frequent local buses trundle between the tourist area and old harbour, and

there are also regular services to Kourion and Kolossi from the local bus station; and Ayia Napa, where there are regular services to Paralimni and Protaras.

Taxi

In the South, taxis are extensive and available on a 24-hour basis; they can either be hailed from the street or a taxi rank, or booked over the phone. Taxis are generally modern, air-conditioned vehicles (usually comfortable Mercedes) and, apart from outside the major centres, are equipped with meters that the taxi drivers are obliged to use.

The two tariff periods are from 6am to 8.30pm (tariff 1), and from 8.30pm to 6am (tariff 2). Tariff 1 charges are €3.42 flag fall and €0.73 per kilometre. Tariff 2 charges are €4.36 flag fall and €0.85 per kilometre. Luggage is charged at the rate of €0.75 for every piece weighing more than 12kg. Extra charges of €1 per fare apply during most public holidays.

'Taxi sharing', which is common in Greek cities such as Athens, is not permitted in Cyprus. Taxi drivers are normally courteous and helpful.

In the North, taxis do not sport meters, so agree on the fare with the driver beforehand. As a rough guide, expect to pay around 5.50TL for a ride around any of the towns. A taxi ride from North Nicosia to Kyrenia will cost around 35TL, and from North Nicosia to Famagusta, 70TL.

SERVICE TAXI

Taking up to eight people, service taxis are a useful transport option in the South. They are run by an amalgamation of private companies called **Travel & Express** (☑07 77 477; www. travelexpress.com.cy), with one national phone number. The individual offices can also be contacted directly:
Nicosia (☑2273 0888)
Lemesos (Map p49; Thessalonikis 21; ☺6am-7.30pm Mon-Sat, to 3pm Sun)
Larnaka (Map p107; ☑2466 1010)
Pafos (Map p88; Leoforos Evagora Pallikaridi 9, Ktima).

You can get to and from Nicosia, Lemesos and Larnaka by service taxi, but usually not directly to or from Pafos;

a change in Lemesos is often required.

The fixed fares are competitive with bus travel. Either go to the service taxi office or phone to be picked up at your hotel. Note that pick-ups can often be up to 30 minutes later than booked, so build this into your plans if time is tight. Similarly, if you're departing from a service-taxi depot, expect to spend up to 30 minutes picking up other passengers before you actually get under way.

The North has minibuses (sometimes referred to as *dolmuş*) between Kyrenia, North Nicosia and Famagusta only, which cost about 6TL per person.

TOURIST TAXI

The 'tourist' taxis that await you near the Turkish Cypriot checkpoint at the Ledra Palace Hotel in North Nicosia will take you anywhere you want to go around Northern Cyprus. A round-trip day tour to Kyrenia, Famagusta, Bellapais (Beylerbeyi), Buffavento Castle and St Hilarion Castle costs around €30 to €50. (Although euros are not in general use in the North,

most people will accept them if you have no other currency; Turkish taxis at crossing points will always quote their prices in British pounds.)

Tours

Travel agencies around Cyprus offer a wide variety of pre-packaged excursions. Two reputable tour agencies in the South:

Amathus (☑2536 9122; www.amathus.com; Plateia Syntagmatos, Lemesos)

Salamis Tours Excursions (☑2535 5555; www.salamisinternational.com; Salamis House, 28 Oktovriou, Lemesos)

Land tours in the South usually run from the main tourist centres. They include full-day tours to Troödos and the Kykkos Monastery from Pafos (from €30); day trips to Nicosia from Agia Napa or Larnaka (from €30); boat trips to Protaras from Agia Napa (from €25); and half-day tours of Lemesos, a winery and Ancient Kourion (from €25). These kinds of tours are not available in the North.

Language

Visitors to Cyprus are unlikely to encounter any serious language difficulties since many people in both the North and the South speak English. Neither Greek nor Turkish Cypriots will expect a visitor to be able to speak their respective languages – let alone the Cypriot variants. However, trying a few of the words in the local lingo will go a long way to breaking the ice. The Greek and Turkish spoken in Cyprus differs somewhat from that spoken in Greece and Turkey. However, if you use the mainland varieties – which is what we've included below – you'll be understood just fine.

GREEK

Greek is the official language of Greece and co-official language of Cyprus (alongside Turkish).

The Greek alphabet is explained on the next page, but if you read the blue pronunciation guides given with each phrase in this chapter as if they were English, you'll be understood. Note that dh is pronounced as the 'th' in 'there', gh is a softer, slightly throaty version of 'g', and kh is a throaty sound like the 'ch' in the Scottish 'loch'. All Greek words of two or more syllables have an acute accent (´), which indicates where the stress falls. In our pronunciation guides, stressed syllables are in italics.

In Greek, all nouns, articles and adjectives are either masculine, feminine or neuter – in this chapter these forms are included where necessary, separated with a slash and indicated with 'm/f/n'.

Basics

Hello.	Γειά σας.	ya·sas (polite)
	Γειά σου.	ya·su (informal)
Good morning.	Καλή μέρα.	ka·li me·ra
Good evening.	Καλή σπέρα.	ka·li spe·ra
Goodbye.	Αντίο.	an·di·o

Yes./No.	Ναι./Οχι.	ne/o·hi
Please.	Παρακαλώ.	pa·ra·ka·lo
Thank you.	Ευχαριστώ.	ef·ha·ri·sto
That's fine./	Παρακαλώ.	pa·ra·ka·lo
You're welcome.		
Sorry.	Συγγνώμη.	sigh·no·mi

What's your name?
Πώς σας λένε; — pos sas le·ne

My name is ...
Με λένε ... — me le·ne ...

Do you speak English?
Μιλάτε αγγλικά; — mi·la·te an·gli·ka

I (don't) understand
(Δεν) καταλαβαίνω. — (dhen) ka·ta·la·ve·no

Accommodation

campsite	χώρος για κάμπινγκ	kho·ros yia kam·ping
hotel	ξενοδοχείο	kse·no·dho·khi·o
youth hostel	γιουθ χόστελ	yuth kho·stel
a ... room	ένα ... δωμάτιο	e·na ... dho·ma·ti·o
single	μονόκλινο	mo·no·kli·no
double	δίκλινο	dhi·kli·no
How much is it ...?	Πόσο κάνει ...;	po·so ka·ni ...
per night	τη βραδυά	ti·vra·dhya
per person	το άτομο	to a·to·mo
air-con	έρκοντίσιον	er·kon·di·si·on
bathroom	μπάνιο	ba·nio
fan	ανεμιστήρας	a·ne·mi·sti·ras
TV	τηλεόραση	ti·le·o·ra·si
window	παράθυρο	pa·ra·thi·ro

Directions

Where is ...?
Πού είναι ...; pu *i*·ne ...

Turn left.
Στρίψτε αριστερά. *strips*·te a·ri·ste·*ra*

Turn right.
Στρίψτε δεξιά. *strips*·te dhe·*ksia*

at the next corner
στην επόμενη γωνία stin e·*po*·me·ni gho·*ni*·a

at the traffic lights
στα φώτα sta *fo*·ta

behind	πίσω	*pi*·so
in front of	μπροστά	bro·*sta*
far	μακριά	ma·kri·*a*
near (to)	κοντά	kon·*da*
next to	δίπλα	*dhi*·pla
opposite	απέναντι	a·*pe*·nan·di
straight ahead	ολο ευθεία	*o*·lo ef·*thi*·a

Eating & Drinking

What would you recommend?
Τι θα συνιστούσες; ti tha si·ni·*stu*·ses

What's in that dish?
Τι περιέχει αυτό το φαγητό; ti pe·ri·e·hi af·*to* to fa·ghi·*to*

I'm a vegatarian.
Είμαι χορτοφάγος. *i*·me khor·to·*fa*·ghos

That was delicious.
Ήταν νοστιμότατο! *i*·tan no·sti·*mo*·ta·to

Cheers!
Εις υγείαν! is i·*yi*·an

Please bring the bill.
Το λογαριασμό, παρακαλώ. to lo·ghar·ya·*zmo* pa·ra·ka·*lo*

a table for ...	Ενα τραπέζι για ...	*e*·na tra·*pe*·zi ya ...
(two) people	(δύο) άτομα	(*dhi*·o) a·to·ma
(eight) o'clock	τις (οχτώ)	stis (okh·*to*)
I don't eat ...	Δεν τρώγω ...	dhen *tro*·gho ...
fish	ψάρι	*psa*·ri
(red) meat	(κόκκινο) κρέας	(*ko*·ki·no) *kre*·as
peanuts	φυστίκια	fi·*sti*·kia
poultry	πουλερικά	pu·le·ri·*ka*

GREEK ALPHABET

The Greek alphabet has 24 letters, shown below in their upper- and lower-case forms. Be aware that some letters look like English letters but are pronounced very differently, such as B, which is pronounced 'v'; and P, pronounced like an 'r'. As in English, how letters are pronounced is also influenced by how they are combined, for example the ou combination is pronounced 'u' as in 'put', and οι is pronounced 'ee' as in 'feet'.

Α α	a	as in 'father'	**Ξ ξ**	x	as in 'ox'	
Β β	v	as in 'vine'	**O o**	o	as in 'hot'	
Γ γ	gh	a softer, throaty 'g'	**Π π**	p	as in 'pup'	
	y	as in 'yes'	**P ρ**	r	as in 'road',	
Δ δ	dh	as in 'there'			slightly trilled	
E ε	e	as in 'egg'	**Σ σ, ς**	s	as in 'sand'	
Z ζ	z	as in 'zoo'	**T τ**	t	as in 'tap'	
H η	i	as in 'feet'	**Y υ**	i	as in 'feet'	
Θ θ	th	as in 'throw'	**Φ φ**	f	as in 'find'	
I ι	i	as in 'feet'	**X χ**	kh	as the 'ch' in the	
K κ	k	as in 'kite'			Scottish 'loch', or	
Λ λ	l	as in 'leg'		h	like a rough 'h'	
M μ	m	as in 'man'	**Ψ ψ**	ps	as in 'lapse'	
N ν	n	as in 'net'	**Ω ω**	o	as in 'hot'	

Note that the letter **Σ** has two forms for the lower case – **σ** and **ς**. The second one is used at the end of words. The Greek question mark is represented with the English equivalent of a semicolon (;).

KEY PATTERNS

To get by in Greek, mix and match these simple patterns with words of your choice:

When's (the next bus)?
Πότε είναι   *po*·te *i*·ne
(το επόμενο   (to e·*po*·me·no
λεωφορείο);   le·o·fo·*ri*·o)

Where's (the station)?
Πού είναι (ο σταθμός); pu *i*·ne (o stath·*mos*)

I'm looking for (...).
Ψάχνω για (...).   *psakh*·no yia (...)

Do you have (a local map)?
Έχετε οδικό   e·*he*·te o·dhi·*ko*
(τοπικό χάρτη);   (to·pi·*ko* khar·ti)

Is there a (lift)?
Υπάρχει (ασανσέρ);   i·*par*·hi (a·san·*ser*)

Can I (try it on)?
Μπορώ να   bo·*ro* na
(το προβάρω);   (to pro·*va*·ro)

I have (a reservation).
Έχω (κλείσει   e·kho (*kli*·si
δωμάτιο).   dho·*ma*·ti·o)

I'd like (to hire a car).
Θα ήθελα (να   tha *i*·the·la (na
ενοικιάσω ένα   e·ni·ki·*a*·so e·na
αυτοκίνητο).   af·to·*ki*·ni·to)

Key Words

appetisers	ορεκτικά	o·rek·ti·*ka*
bar	μπαρ	bar
beef	βοδινό	vo·dhi·*no*
bottle	μπουκάλι	bu·*ka*·li
bowl	μπωλ	bol
bread	ψωμί	pso·*mi*
breakfast	πρόγευμα	*pro*·yev·ma
cafe	καφετέρια	ka·fe·*te*·ri·a
cheese	τυρί	ti·*ri*
chicken	κοτόπουλο	ko·*to*·pu·lo
cold	κρυωμένος	kri·o·*me*·nos
cream	κρέμα	*kre*·ma
delicatessen	ντελικατέσεν	de·li·ka·*te*·sen
desserts	επιδόρπια	e·pi·*dhor*·pi·a
dinner	δείπνο	*dhip*·no
egg	αβγό	av·*gho*
fish	ψάρι	*psa*·ri
food	φαγητό	fa·yi·*to*
fork	πιρούνι	pi·*ru*·ni
fruit	φρούτα	*fru*·ta
glass	ποτήρι	po·*ti*·ri

grocery store	οπωροπωλείο	o·po·ro·po·*li*·o
herb	βότανο	*vo*·ta·no
high chair	καρέκλα για μωρά	ka·*re*·kla yia mo·*ro*
hot	ζεστός	ze·*stos*
knife	μαχαίρι	ma·*he*·ri
lamb	αρνί	ar·*ni*
lunch	μεσημεριανό φαγητό	me·si·me·ria·*no* fa·yi·*to*
main courses	κύρια φαγητά	*ki*·ri·a fa·yi·*ta*
market	αγορά	a·gho·*ra*
menu	μενού	me·*nu*
nut	καρύδι	ka·*ri*·dhi
oil	λάδι	*la*·dhi
pepper	πιπέρι	pi·*pe*·ri
plate	πιάτο	*pia*·to
pork	χοιρινό	hi·ri·*no*
restaurant	εστιατόριο	e·sti·a·*to*·ri·o
salt	αλάτι	a·*la*·ti
souvlaki	σουβλάκι	suv·*la*·ki
spoon	κουτάλι	ku·*ta*·li
sugar	ζάχαρη	*za*·kha·ri
vegetable	λαχανικά	la·kha·ni·*ka*
vegetarian	χορτοφάγος	khor·to·*fa*·ghos
vinegar	ξύδι	*ksi*·dhi
with	με	me
without	χωρίς	kho·*ris*

Drinks

beer	μπύρα	*bi*·ra
coffee	καφές	ka·*fes*
juice	χυμός	hi·*mos*
milk	γάλα	*gha*·la
soft drink	αναψυκτικό	a·nap·sik·ti·*ko*
tea	τσάι	*tsa*·i
water	νερό	ne·*ro*
(red) wine	(κόκκινο) κρασί	(*ko*·ki·no) kra·*si*
(white) wine	(άσπρο) κρασί	(*a*·spro) kra·*si*

Emergencies

Help!	Βοήθεια!	vo·*i*·thya
Go away!	Φύγε!	*fi*·ye
I'm lost	Έχω χαθεί.	e·kho kha·*thi*
I'm ill.	Είμαι άρρωστος.	*i*·me a·ro·stos
There's been an accident.	Έγινε ατύχημα.	*ey*·i·ne a·*ti*·hi·ma
Call ...!	Φωνάξτε ...!	fo·*nak*·ste ...
a doctor	ένα γιατρό	e·na yi·a·*tro*
the police	την αστυνομία	tin a·sti·no·*mi*·a

mobile phone	κινητό	ki·ni·*to*
post office	ταχυδρομείο	ta·hi·dhro·*mi*·o
toilet	τουαλέτα	tu·a·*le*·ta
tourist office	τουριστικό γραφείο	tu·ri·sti·*ko* ghra·*fi*·o

Numbers

1	ένας/μία	e·nas/*mi*·a (m/f)
	ένα	e·na (n)
2	δύο	*dhi*·o
3	τρεις	tris (m&f)
	τρία	*tri*·a (n)
4	τέσσερεις	te·se·ris (m&f)
	τέσσερα	te·se·ra (n)
5	πέντε	*pen*·de
6	έξη	e·xi
7	επτά	ep·*ta*
8	οχτώ	oh·*to*
9	εννέα	e·*ne*·a
10	δέκα	*dhe*·ka
20	είκοσι	*ik*·o·si
30	τριάντα	tri·*an*·da
40	σαράντα	sa·*ran*·da
50	πενήντα	pe·*nin*·da
60	εξήντα	ek·sin·da
70	εβδομήντα	ev·dho·*min*·da
80	ογδόντα	ogh·*dhon*·da
90	ενενήντα	e·ne·*nin*·da
100	εκατό	e·ka·*to*
1000	χίλιοι/χίλιες	*hi*·li·i/*hi*·li·ez (m/f)
	χίλια	*hi*·li·a (n)

Shopping & Services

I'd like to buy ...
Θέλω ν' αγοράσω ...   *the*·lo na·gho·*ra*·so ...

I'm just looking.
Απλώς κοιτάζω.   ap·*los* ki·*ta*·zo

I don't like it.
Δεν μου αρέσει.   dhen mu a·*re*·si

How much is it?
Πόσο κάνει;   *po*·so *ka*·ni

It's too expensive.
Είναι πολύ ακριβό.   *i*·ne po·*li* a·kri·*vo*

Can you lower the price?
Μπορείς να κατεβάσεις   bo·*ris* na ka·te·*va*·sis
την τιμή;   tin ti·*mi*

ATM	αυτόματη μηχανή χρημάτων	af·*to*·ma·ti mi·kha·*ni* khri·*ma*·ton
bank	τράπεζα	*tra*·pe·za
credit card	πιστωτική κάρτα	pi·sto·ti·*ki* *kar*·ta
internet cafe	καφενείο διαδικτύου	ka·fe·*ni*·o dhi·a·dhik·*ti*·u

Time & Dates

What time is it?	Τι ώρα είναι;	ti o·*ra* i·ne
It's (2 o'clock).	είναι (δύο η ώρα).	*i*·ne (*dhi*·o i o·ra)
It's half past (10).	(Δέκα) και μισή.	(*dhe*·ka) ke mi·*si*
today	σήμερα	*si*·me·ra
tomorrow	αύριο	*av*·ri·o
yesterday	χθες	hthes
morning	πρωί	pro·*i*
(this) afternoon	(αυτό το) απόγευμα	(af·*to* to) a·*po*·yev·ma
evening	βράδυ	*vra*·dhi
Monday	Δευτέρα	dhef·*te*·ra
Tuesday	Τρίτη	*tri*·ti
Wednesday	Τετάρτη	te·*tar*·ti
Thursday	Πέμπτη	*pemp*·ti
Friday	Παρασκευή	pa·ras·ke·*vi*
Saturday	Σάββατο	*sa*·va·to
Sunday	Κυριακή	ky·ri·a·*ki*
January	Ιανουάριος	ia·nu·*ar*·i·os
February	Φεβρουάριος	fev·ru·*ar*·i·os
March	Μάρτιος	*mar*·ti·os
April	Απρίλιοςα	a·*pri*·li·os
May	Μάιος	*mai*·os

SIGNS

ΕΙΣΟΔΟΣ	Entry
ΕΞΟΔΟΣ	Exit
ΠΛΗΡΟΦΟΡΙΕΣ	Information
ΑΝΟΙΧΤΟ	Open
ΚΛΕΙΣΤΟ	Closed
ΑΠΑΓΟΡΕΥΕΤΑΙ	Prohibited
ΑΣΤΥΝΟΜΙΑ	Police
ΑΣΤΥΝΟΜΙΚΟΣ ΣΤΑΘΜΟΣ	Police Station
ΓΥΝΑΙΚΩΝ	Toilets (women)
ΑΝΔΡΩΝ	Toilets (men)

QUESTION WORDS

How?	Πώς;	pos
What?	Τι;	ti
When?	Πότε;	po·te
Where?	Πού;	pu
Who?	Ποιος;/Ποια;	pi·os/pi·a (m/f)
	Ποιο;	pi·o (n)
Why?	Γιατί;	yi·a·ti

June	Ιούνιος	i·u·ni·os
July	Ιούλιος	i·u·li·os
August	Αύγουστος	av·ghus·tos
September	Σεπτέμβριος	sep·tem·vri·os
October	Οκτώβριος	ok·to·vri·os
November	Νοέμβριος	no·em·vri·os
December	Δεκέμβριος	dhe·kem·vri·os

Transport

Public Transport

boat	πλοίο	pli·o
(city) bus	αστικό	a·sti·ko
(intercity) bus	λεωφορείο	le·o·fo·ri·o
plane	αεροπλάνο	ae·ro·pla·no
train	τραίνο	tre·no

Where do I buy a ticket?
Πού αγοράζω εισιτήριο;   pu a·gho·ra·zo i·si·ti·ri·o

I want to go to ...
Θέλω να πάω στο/στη ...   the·lo na pao sto/sti...

What time does it leave?
Τι ώρα φεύγει;   ti o·ra fev·yi

Do I need to change?
Χειάζεται να αλλάξω;   khri·a·ze·te na a·lak·so

Is it direct/express?
Είναι κατ'ευθείαν/   i·ne ka·tef·thi·an/
εξπρές;   eks·pres

Does it stop at (...)?
Σταματάει στο (...);   sta·ma·ta·i sto (...)

I'd like to get off at (...).
Θα ήθελα να κατεβώ   tha i·the·la na ka·te·vo
στο (...).   sto (...)

I'd like (a) ...	Θα ήθελα (ένα) ...	tha i·the·la (e·na) ...
one-way ticket	απλό εισιτήριο	a·plo i·si·ti·ri·o
return ticket	εισιτήριο με επιστροφή	i·si·ti·ri·o me e·pi·stro·fi
1st class	πρώτη θέση	pro·ti the·si
2nd class	δεύτερη θέση	def·te·ri the·si

cancelled	ακυρώθηκε	a·ki·ro·thi·ke
delayed	καθυστέρησε	ka·thi·ste·ri·se
platform	πλατφόρμα f	plat·for·ma
ticket office	εκδοτήριο εισιτηρίων	ek·dho·ti·ri·o i·si·ti·ri·on
timetable	δρομολόγιο	dhro·mo·lo·gio
train station	σταθμός τρένου	stath·mos tre·nu

Driving & Cycling

I'd like to hire a ...	Θα ήθελα να νοικιάσω ...	tha i·the·la na ni·ki·a·so ...
car	ένα αυτοκίνητο	e·na af·ti·ki·ni·to
4WD	ένα τέσσερα επί τέσσερα	e·na tes·se·ra e·pi tes·se·ra
jeep	ένα τζιπ	e·na tzip
motorbike	μια μοτοσυκλέττα	mya mo·to·si·klet·ta
bicycle	ένα ποδήλατο	e·na po·dhi·la·to

Do I need a helmet?
Χρειάζομαι κράνος;   khri·a·zo·me kra·nos

Do you have a road map?
Έχετε οδικό χάρτη;   e·he·te o·thi·ko khar·ti

Is this the road to ...?
Αυτός είναι ο   af·tos i·ne o
δρόμος για ...   dhro·mos ya ...

Can I park here?
Μπορώ να παρκάρω   bo·ro na par·ka·ro
εδώ;   e·dho

The car/motorbike has broken down (at ...).
Το αυτοκίνητο/   to af·to·ki·ni·to/
η μοτοσυκλέττα   i mo·to·si·klet·ta
χάλασε στο ...   kha·la·se sto ...

I have a flat tyre.
Έπαθα λάστιχο.   e·pa·tha la·sti·cho

I've run out of petrol.
Έμεινα από βενζίνη.   e·mi·na a·po ven·zi·ni

Where's a petrol station?
Πού είναι ένα πρατήριο   pu i·ne e·na pra·ti·ri·o
βενζίνας;   ven·zi·nas

TURKISH

Turkish is the official language of Turkey and co-official language of Cyprus (alongside Greek).

Turkish pronunciation is not difficult as most sounds are also found in English. There are just a few simple things to watch out for.

The Turkish letter ı – undotted in both lower and upper case (eg Isparta *uhs·par·ta*) – is pronounced as uh (a sound similar to the 'i' in 'habit'), while the i – with dots in both cases (eg İzmir *eez·meer*) – is pronounced as ee . Similarly, o is pronounced o as in 'go', ö as er in 'her' (without 'r' sound), u as oo in 'moon' and ü as ew in 'few'. Also note that ğ is a silent letter which extends the vowel before it – it acts as the 'gh' combination in 'weigh', and is never pronounced. The letter h is always pronounced h as in 'house'. The letter j is pronounced zh (as the 's' in 'pleasure'), ç as ch in 'church', and ş as in the sh in 'ship'.

Don't worry about these spelling and pronuniation idiosyncracies – if you read the blue pronunciation guides given with each phrase in this chapter as if they were English, you'll be understood.

Basics

Hello.	*Merhaba.*	*mer·ha·ba*
Hi.	*Selam.*	*se·lam*
Good morning.	*İyi sabahlar.*	*ee·yee sa·bah·lar*
Good evening.	*İyi akşamlar.*	*ee·yee ak·sham·lar*
Goodbye. (when leaving)	*Hoşçakal.* (inf) *Hoşçakalın.* (pol)	*hosh·cha·kal* *hosh·cha·ka·luhn*
Goodbye. (when staying)	*Güle güle.*	*gew·le gew·le*
Yes./No.	*Evet./Hayır.*	*e·vet/ha·yuhr*
Please.	*Lütfen.*	*lewt·fen*
Thank you (very much).	*(Çok) Teşekkür ederim.*	*(chok) te·shek·kewr e·de·reem*
Thanks.	*Teşekkürler.*	*te·shek·kewr·ler*
You're welcome.	*Birşey değil.*	*beer·shay de·eel*
Sorry.	*Özür dilerim.*	*er·zewr dee·le·reem*

What's your name?
Adınız ne? (inf) a·duh·*nuhz* ne
Adınız nedir? (pol) a·duh·*nuhz* ne·deer

My name is ...
Benim adım ... be·*neem* a·*duhm* ...

Do you speak English?
(İngilizce) (een·gee·*leez*·je)
konuşuyor ko·noo·*shoo*·yor
musunuz? moo·soo·*nooz*

I understand.
Anlıyorum. an·*luh*·yo·room

I don't understand.
Anlamıyorum. an·*la*·muh·yo·room

Accommodation

campsite	*kamp yeri*	kamp ye·*ree*
hotel	*otel*	o·*tel*
youth hostel	*gençlik hosteli*	gench·*leek* hos·te·*lee*

Do you have a ... room?	*... odanız var mı?*	*... o·da·nuhz var muh*
single	*Tek kişilik*	*tek kee·shee·leek*
double	*İki kişilik*	*ee·kee kee·shee·leek*

How much is it per ...?	*... ne kadar?*	*... ne ka·dar*
night	*Geceliği*	*ge·je·lee·ee*
person	*Kişi başına*	*kee·shee ba·shuh·na*

air-con	*klima*	*klee·ma*
bathroom	*banyo*	*ban·yo*
fan	*fan*	*fan*
TV	*TV*	*te·ve*
window	*pencere*	*pen·je·re*

Directions

Where is ...?	*... nerede?*	*... ne·re·de*
Turn left.	*Sola dön.*	*so·la dern*

KEY PATTERNS

To get by in Turkish, mix and match these simple patterns with words of your choice:

When's (the next bus)?
(Sonraki otobüs) (son·ra·*kee* o·to·*bews*)
ne zaman? ne za·*man*

Where's (the market)?
(Pazar yeri) nerede? (pa·*zar* ye·*ree*) ne·re·de

Do you have (a map)?
(Haritanız) var mı? (ha·ree·ta·*nuhz*) var muh

Is there (a toilet)?
(Tuvalet) var mı? (too·va·*let*) var muh

I have (a reservation).
(Rezervasyonum) (re·zer·vas·yo·*noom*)
var. var

I'd like (the menu).
(Menüyü) (me·new·*yew*)
istiyorum. ees·*tee*·yo·room

I need (assistance).
(Yardıma) (yar·duh·*ma*)
ihtiyacım var. eeh·tee·ya·*juhm* var

QUESTION WORDS

How?	Nasıl?	na·suhl
What?	Ne?	ne
When?	Ne zaman?	ne za·man
Where?	Nerede?	ne·re·de
Who?	Kim?	keem
Why?	Neden?	ne·den

Turn right.	Sağa dön.	sa·a dern

It's ...

behind ...	... arkasında.	... ar·ka·suhn·da
in front of ...	... önünde.	... er·newn·de
near ...	... yakınında.	ya·kuh·nuhn·da
next to ...	... yanında.	... ya·nuhn·da
opposite ...	... karşısında.	... kar·shuh·suhn·da

It's ...

at the traffic lights	Trafik ışıklarından.	tra·feek uh·shuhk·la·ruhn·dan
close	Yakın.	ya·kuhn
here	Burada.	boo·ra·da
on the corner	Köşede.	ker·she·de
straight ahead	Tam karşıda.	tam kar·shuh·da
there	Şurada.	shoo·ra·da

Eating & Drinking

What would you recommend?
Ne tavsiye edersiniz?	ne tav·see·ye e·der·see·neez

What's in that dish?
Bu yemekte neler var?	boo ye·mek·te ne·ler var

I'm a vegetarian.
Ben vejeteryanım.	ben ve·zhe·ter·ya·nuhm

That was delicious.
Nefisti!	ne·fees·tee

Cheers!
Şerefe!	she·re·fe

Could I have the bill, please?
Lütfen hesabı getirir misiniz?	lewt·fen he·sa·buh ge·tee·reer mee·see·neez

I'd like to reserve a table for ...	... bir masa ayırtmak istiyorum.	... beer ma·sa a·yuhrt·mak ees·tee·yo·room
(two) people	(İki) kişilik	(ee·kee) kee·shee·leek
(eight) o'clock	Saat (sekiz) için	sa·at (se·keez) ee·cheen

I don't eat ...	... yemiyorum.	... ye·mee·yo·room
fish	Balık	ba·luhk
(red) meat	(Kırmızı) Et	kuhr·muh·zuh et
peanuts	Fıstığa	fuhs·tuh·a
poultry	Tavuk eti	ta·vook e·tee

Key Words

appetisers	mezeler	me·ze·ler
bar	bar	bar
beef	sığır eti	suh·uhr e·tee
bottle	şişe	shee·she
bowl	kase	ka·se
bread	ekmek	ek·mek
breakfast	kahvaltı	kah·val·tuh
cafe	kafe	ka·fe
cheese	peynir	pay·neer
chicken	tavuk	ta·vook
cold	soğuk	so·ook
cream	krema	kre·ma
delicatessen	şarküteri	shar·kew·te·ree
desserts	tatlılar	tat·luh·lar
dinner	akşam yemeği	ak·sham ye·me·ee
drinks	İçecekler	ee·che·jek·ler
egg	yumurta	yoo·moor·ta
fish	balık	ba·luhk
food	yiyecek	yee·ye·jek
fork	çatal	cha·tal
fruit	meyve	may·ve
glass	bardak	bar·dak
greengrocer	manav	ma·nav
herb	bitki	beet·kee
high chair	mama sandalyesi	ma·ma san·dal·ye·see
hot	sıcak	suh·jak
ice cream	dondurma	don·door·ma
kebab	kebab	ke·bab
knife	bıçak	buh·chak
lamb	kuzu	koo·zoo
lunch	öğle yemeği	er·le ye·me·ee
main courses	ana yemekler	a·na ye·mek·ler
market	pazar	pa·zar
menu	yemek listesi	ye·mek lees·te·see
nut	çerez	che·rez
oil	yağ	ya
pepper	kara biber	ka·ra bee·ber
plate	tabak	ta·bak
pork	domuz eti	do·mooz e·tee

restaurant	restoran	res·to·ran
salad	salata	sa·la·ta
salt	tuz	tooz
soup	çorba	chor·ba
spoon	kaşık	ka·shuhk
sugar	şeker	she·ker
vegetable	sebze	seb·ze
vegetarian	vejeteryan	ve·zhe·ter·yan
vinegar	sirke	seer·ke
with	ile	ee·le
without	-sız/-siz/	·suhz/·seez/
	-suz/-süz	·sooz/·sewz

Drinks

beer	bira	bee·ra
coffee	kahve	kah·ve
juice	suyu	soo·yoo
milk	süt	sewt
soft drink	meşrubat	mesh·roo·bat
tea	çay	chai
water	su	soo
wine	şarap	sha·rap
white	beyaz	be·yaz
red	kırmızı	kuhr·muh·zuh

Emergencies

Help!	İmdat!	eem·dat
Go away!	Git burdan!	geet boor·dan
I'm lost	Kayboldum.	kai·bol·doom
I'm ill.	Hastayım.	has·ta·yuhm
There's been an accident.	Bir kaza oldu.	beer ka·za ol·doo

Call ...!	... çağırın!	... cha·uh·ruhn
a doctor	Doktor	dok·tor
the police	Polis	po·lees

Numbers

0	sıfır	suh·fuhr
1	bir	beer
2	iki	ee·kee
3	üç	ewch
4	dört	dert
5	beş	besh
6	altı	al·tuh
7	yedi	ye·dee
8	sekiz	se·keez
9	dokuz	do·kooz

10	on	on
20	yirmi	yeer·mee
30	otuz	o·tooz
40	kırk	kuhrk
50	elli	el·lee
60	altmış	alt·muhsh
70	yetmiş	yet·meesh
80	seksen	sek·sen
90	doksan	dok·san
100	yüz	yewz
1000	bin	been

Shopping & Services

I'd like to buy ...	... almak istiyorum.	... al·mak ees·tee·yo·room
How much is it?	Ne kadar?	ne ka·dar
It's too expensive.	Bu çok pahalı.	boo chok pa·ha·luh
Do you have something cheaper?	Daha ucuz birşey var mı?	da·ha oo·jooz beer·shay var muh

ATM	bankamatik	ban·ka·ma·teek
bank	banka	ban·ka
credit card	kredi kartı	kre·dee kar·tuh
internet cafe	internet kafe	een·ter·net ka·fe
mobile phone	cep telefonu	jep te·le·fo·noo
post office	postane	pos·ta·ne
toilet	tuvalet	too·va·let
tourist office	turizm bürosu	too·reezm bew·ro·soo

SIGNS

Giriş	gee·reesh	Entrance
Çıkış	chuh·kuhsh	Exit
Açık	a·chuhk	Open
Kapalı	ka·pa·luh	Closed
Danışma	da·nuhsh·ma	Information
Yasak	ya·sak	Prohibited
Tuvaletler	too·va·let·ler	Toilets
Erkek	er·kek	Men
Kadın	ka·duhn	Women

Time & Dates

What time is it?	*Saat kaç?*	sa·at kach
It's (ten) o'clock.	*Saat (on).*	sa·at (on)
It's half past (ten).	*(On) buçuk.*	(on) boo·chook

today	*bugün*	boo·gewn
tomorrow	*yarın*	ya·ruhn
yesterday	*dün*	dewn
morning	*sabah*	sa·bah
(this)	*(bu)*	(boo)
afternoon	*öğleden sonra*	er·le·den son·ra
evening	*akşam*	ak·sham
Monday	*Pazartesi*	pa·zar·te·see
Tuesday	*Salı*	sa·luh
Wednesday	*Çarşamba*	char·sham·ba
Thursday	*Perşembe*	per·shem·be
Friday	*Cuma*	joo·ma
Saturday	*Cumartesi*	joo·mar·te·see
Sunday	*Pazar*	pa·zar

January	*Ocak*	o·jak
February	*Şubat*	shoo·bat
March	*Mart*	mart
April	*Nisan*	nee·san
May	*Mayıs*	ma·yuhs
June	*Haziran*	ha·zee·ran
July	*Temmuz*	tem·mooz
August	*Ağustos*	a·oos·tos
September	*Eylül*	ay·lewl
October	*Ekim*	e·keem
November	*Kasım*	ka·suhm
December	*Aralık*	a·ra·luhk

Transport

Public Transport

boat	*vapur*	va·poor
(city) bus	*şehir otobüsü*	she·heer o·to·bew·sew
(intercity) bus	*şehirlerarası otobüs*	she·heer·ler·a·ra·suh o·to·bews
plane	*uçak*	oo·chak
train	*tren*	tren

Where do I buy a ticket?		
Nereden bilet alabilirim?	ne·re·den bee·let a·la·bee·lee·reem	
What time does it leave?		
Ne zaman kalkacak?	ne za·man kal·ka·jak	
Do I need to change?		
Aktarma yapmam gerekli mi?	ak·tar·ma yap·mam ge·rek·lee mee	
Does it stop at ...?		
... durur mu?	... doo·roor moo	
What's the next stop?		
Sonraki durak hangisi?	son·ra·kee doo·rak han·gee·see	
I'd like to get off at ...		
... inmek istiyorum.	... een·mek ees·tee·yo·room	
A one-way ticket, please.		
Gidiş bileti lütfen.	gee·deesh bee·le·tee lewt·fen	

A ... ticket, please.	*... bilet lütfen.*	... bee·let lewt·fen
1st-class	*Birinci mevki*	bee·reen·jee mev·kee
2nd-class	*İkinci mevki*	ee·keen·jee mev·kee
return	*Gidiş-dönüş*	gee·deesh·der·newsh

cancel v	*iptal etmek*	eep·tal et·mek
delay n	*gecikme*	ge·jeek·me
platform	*peron*	pe·ron
ticket office	*bilet gişesi*	bee·let gee·she·see
timetable	*tarife*	ta·ree·fe
train station	*tren istasyonu*	tren ees·tas·yo·noo

Driving & Cycling

I'd like to hire a/an ...	*Bir ... kiralamak istiyorum.*	beer ... kee·ra·la·mak ees·tee·yo·room
4WD	*dört çeker*	dert che·ker
car	*araba*	a·ra·ba
motorbike	*motosiklet*	mo·to·seek·let
bicycle	*bisiklet*	bee·seek·let

Do I need a helmet?		
Kask takmam gerekli mi?	kask tak·mam ge·rek·lee mee	
Is this the road to ...?		
... giden yol bu mu?	... gee·den yol boo moo	

How long can I park here?

Buraya ne kadar	boo·ra·ya ne ka·dar
süre park	sew·re park
edebilirim?	e·de·bee·lee·reem

The car/motorbike has broken down (at ...).

Arabam/	a·ra·bam/
motosikletim	mo·to·seek·le·teem
... bozuldu.	... bo·zool·doo

I have a flat tyre.

| Lastiğim patladı. | las·tee·eem pat·la·duh |

I've run out of petrol.

| Benzinim bitti. | ben·zee·neem beet·tee |

GLOSSARY

For words dealing with Cypriot cuisine, see p32.
Abbreviations
(Fr) = French
(Gr) = Greek
(Tr) = Turkish
(m) = masculine
(f) = feminine
(n) = neutral

agios (m), **agia** (f; Gr) – saint

bedesten (Tr) – covered market

belediye (Tr) – town hall

bulvarı (Tr) – boulevard, avenue

burnu (Tr) – cape

Byzantine Empire – Hellenistic, Christian empire lasting from AD 395 to 1453, centred on Constantinople (Istanbul)

caddesi (Tr) – road

camii (Tr) – mosque

commandery – a district under the control of a commander of an order of knights

CTO – Cyprus Tourism Organisation, the Republic of Cyprus' official tourism promotion body

dolmuş (Tr) – minibus, shared taxi (literally 'stuffed')

enosis (Gr) – union (with Greece); the frequent demand made by many Greek Cypriots before 1974

entrepôt (Fr) – commercial centre for import and export

EOKA – Ethniki Organosi tou Kypriakou Agona (National Organisation for the Cypriot Struggle); nationalist guerrilla movement that fought for independence from Britain

EOKA-B – post-independence reincarnation of *EOKA*, which mostly fought Turkish Cypriots

ethnarch (Gr) – leader of a nation

garigue (Fr) – low, open scrub-land with evergreen shrubs, low trees, aromatic herbs and grasses, found in poor or dry soil in the Mediterranean region

Green Line – the border that divides Greek Cypriot Nicosia (Lefkosia) from Turkish Cypriot North Nicosia (Lefkoşa); also the whole border between North and South

hammam (Tr) – public bath-house

kafeneio (Gr) – coffee shop

kalesi (Tr) – castle

kato (Gr) – lower, eg Kato Pafos (Lower Pafos)

KKTC (Tr) – Kuzey Kıbrıs Türk Cumhuriyeti (Turkish Republic of Northern Cyprus)

KOT (Gr) – Kypriakos Organismos Tourismou; the official tourist organisation of the Republic of Cyprus; see *CTO*

leoforos (Gr) – avenue

Lusignan – Cypriot dynasty founded by French nobleman Guy de Lusignan in 1187, which lasted until 1489

maquis (Fr) – thick, scrubby underbrush of Mediterranean shores, particularly of the islands of Corsica and Cyprus

Maronites – ancient Christian sect from the Middle East

Mesaoria (Gr), **Mesarya** (Tr) – the large plain between the Kyrenia (Girne) Range and the Troödos Mountains

meydanı (Tr) – square

meze (s), **mezedes** (pl) – literally 'appetiser'; used in Cyprus to mean dining on lots of small plates of appetisers

mouflon (Fr) – endangered indigenous wild sheep of Cyprus

narthex (Gr) – railed-off western porch in early Christian churches used by women and penitents

NCTO – North Cyprus Tourism Organisation; Northern Cyprus' tourism-promotion body

neos (m), **nea** (f), **neo** (n; Gr) – new; common prefix to place names

Ottoman Empire – Turkish empire founded in the 11th century AD, which ruled Cyprus from 1571 to 1878; it was abolished in 1922

panagia (Gr) – church

panigyri (Gr) – feast or festival

Pantokrator (Gr) – the 'Almighty'; traditional fresco of Christ, painted in the dome of Orthodox churches

paşa (Tr) – Ottoman title roughly equivalent to 'lord'

pitta (Gr) – flat, unleavened bread

plateia (Gr) – square

Ptolemies – Graeco-Macedonian rulers of Egypt in the 4th century BC

rembetika (Gr) – Greek equivalent of American blues music, believed to have emerged from 'low-life' cafes in the 1870s

sokak (Tr) – street

Sufi (Tr) – adherent of the Sufi variant of Islam

taksim (Tr) – partition (of Cyprus); demanded by Turkish Cypriots in response to Greek Cypriots' calls for *enosis*

taverna (Gr) – traditional restaurant that serves food and wine

tekkesi (Tr) – gathering place of the Sufi; mosque

tholos (Gr) – the dome of an Orthodox church

TRNC (Tr) – Turkish Republic of Northern Cyprus; see KKTC

Unesco – United Nations Educational, Scientific and Cultural Organization

Behind the Scenes

SEND US YOUR FEEDBACK

We love to hear from travellers – your comments keep us on our toes and help make our books better. Our well-travelled team reads every word on what you loved or loathed about this book. Although we cannot reply individually to your submissions, we always guarantee that your feedback goes straight to the appropriate authors, in time for the next edition. Each person who sends us information is thanked in the next edition – the most useful submissions are rewarded with a selection of digital PDF chapters.

Visit **lonelyplanet.com/contact** to submit your updates and suggestions or to ask for help. Our award-winning website also features inspirational travel stories, news and discussions.

Note: We may edit, reproduce and incorporate your comments in Lonely Planet products such as guidebooks, websites and digital products, so let us know if you don't want your comments reproduced or your name acknowledged. For a copy of our privacy policy visit lonelyplanet.com/privacy.

OUR READERS

Many thanks to the travellers who used the last edition and wrote to us with helpful hints, useful advice and interesting anecdotes:

A Jakub Adamowicz, Sain Alizada, Audrey Audhoe **B** Filip Barac, Renate Breithecker **C** Dan & Sharron Clatworthy, Jon Cook **D** Laura Demetris, Steve Dixon, Greg Dodd **F** Kingsley Flint **G** Glen Green, Simon Godfrey, Cath Greig **K** John Karayiannis, Brian Kelly, Marina von Koenig **L** Hindrek Lootus **M** Lea Mayer, Samantha Mckenna, Narayan & Mallika Moorthy **O** Mübeccel Orsel **P** Mark Pearson, Stefan Puiu **R** Martin Risse **S** Kerry Shields, David Smallwood, Nick Speller, Andreas Stylianou, Sarah Sumner **T** Chrystalla Thoma **V** Dirk Vanhoecke, Katrien Vertonghen **W** Debby Willems

AUTHOR THANKS

Josephine Quintero

I would like to thank all the helpful folk at the various CTO tourist offices, in particular Kiki Avgoustidou at the Lefkosia Information Office. Thanks also to Yiannis Hadjiloizou, Marios Kolios, Chris Kikas and all the other folk who I met on the road. Thanks too to fellow author Jessica Lee and to all those involved in the title from the Lonely Planet offices, as well as to Robin Chapman for looking after Marilyn (the cat).

Jessica Lee

Huge thanks to Gülay Yinal, Özbek Dedekorkut, Engin Şah, Kutlay Keço, Robin Snape and Angela Charlton-Gokasan for taking the time to answer my many questions. Also, a major thank you to the exceedingly helpful staff at both the Lemesos and Agia Napa tourist information offices in the South.

ACKNOWLEDGMENTS

Climate map data adapted from Peel MC, Finlayson BL & McMahon TA (2007) 'Updated World Map of the Köppen-Geiger Climate Classification', Hydrology and Earth System Sciences, 11, 1633-44.
Cover photograph: Bellapais Abbey (p171), Ken Gibson/Alamy.

THIS BOOK

This 6th edition of Lonely Planet's *Cyprus* guidebook was researched and written by Josephine Quintero and Jessica Lee. The previous edition was written by Josephine Quintero and Matthew Charles. This guidebook was commissioned in Lonely Planet's London office, and produced by the following:

Commissioning Editor James Smart

Destination Editor Brana Vladisavljevic

Coordinating Editor Gabrielle Innes

Product Editor Kate James

Senior Cartographer Valentina Kremenchutskaya

Book Designer Katherine Marsh

Assisting Editors Pete Cruttenden, Jeanette Wall

Assisting Cartographers Laura Bailey, Hunor Csutoros, Julie Dodkins

Cover Research Naomi Parker

Thanks to Sasha Baskett, Indra Kilfoyle, Claire Naylor, Karyn Noble, Dianne Schallmeiner, Luna Soo, John Taufa, Angela Tinson, Tony Wheeler

Index

Map Legend

Sights

- Beach
- Bird Sanctuary
- Buddhist
- Castle/Palace
- Christian
- Confucian
- Hindu
- Islamic
- Jain
- Jewish
- Monument
- Museum/Gallery/Historic Building
- Ruin
- Shinto
- Sikh
- Taoist
- Winery/Vineyard
- Zoo/Wildlife Sanctuary
- Other Sight

Activities, Courses & Tours

- Bodysurfing
- Diving
- Canoeing/Kayaking
- Course/Tour
- Sento Hot Baths/Onsen
- Skiing
- Snorkelling
- Surfing
- Swimming/Pool
- Walking
- Windsurfing
- Other Activity

Sleeping

- Sleeping
- Camping

Eating

- Eating

Drinking & Nightlife

- Drinking & Nightlife
- Cafe

Entertainment

- Entertainment

Shopping

- Shopping

Information

- Bank
- Embassy/Consulate
- Hospital/Medical
- Internet
- Police
- Post Office
- Telephone
- Toilet
- Tourist Information
- Other Information

Geographic

- Beach
- Hut/Shelter
- Lighthouse
- Lookout
- Mountain/Volcano
- Oasis
- Park
- Pass
- Picnic Area
- Waterfall

Population

- Capital (National)
- Capital (State/Province)
- City/Large Town
- Town/Village

Transport

- Airport
- Border crossing
- Bus
- Cable car/Funicular
- Cycling
- Ferry
- Metro station
- Monorail
- Parking
- Petrol station
- Subway station
- Taxi
- Train station/Railway
- Tram
- Underground station
- Other Transport

Note: Not all symbols displayed above appear on the maps in this book

Routes

- Tollway
- Freeway
- Primary
- Secondary
- Tertiary
- Lane
- Unsealed road
- Road under construction
- Plaza/Mall
- Steps
- Tunnel
- Pedestrian overpass
- Walking Tour
- Walking Tour detour
- Path/Walking Trail

Boundaries

- International
- State/Province
- Disputed
- Regional/Suburb
- Marine Park
- Cliff
- Wall

Hydrography

- River, Creek
- Intermittent River
- Canal
- Water
- Dry/Salt/Intermittent Lake
- Reef

Areas

- Airport/Runway
- Beach/Desert
- Cemetery (Christian)
- Cemetery (Other)
- Glacier
- Mudflat
- Park/Forest
- Sight (Building)
- Sportsground
- Swamp/Mangrove

OUR STORY

A beat-up old car, a few dollars in the pocket and a sense of adventure. In 1972 that's all Tony and Maureen Wheeler needed for the trip of a lifetime – across Europe and Asia overland to Australia. It took several months, and at the end – broke but inspired – they sat at their kitchen table writing and stapling together their first travel guide, *Across Asia on the Cheap*. Within a week they'd sold 1500 copies. Lonely Planet was born.

Today, Lonely Planet has offices in Franklin, London, Melbourne, Oakland, Beijing and Delhi, with more than 600 staff and writers. We share Tony's belief that 'a great guidebook should do three things: inform, educate and amuse'.

OUR WRITERS

Josephine Quintero

Coordinating Author; Pafos & the West, Nicosia (Lefkosia), North Nicosia (Lefkoşa), Troödos Mountains Josephine has visited Cyprus many times and finds that the island continually throws up surprises, although there is one constant: the genuine friendliness of the locals, on both sides of the Green Line. Highlights during this trip included sipping coffee and chatting to locals in simple village tavernas in the Akamas Heights, scuffing sand and avoiding turtle eggs at Lara Beach and gazing at the soul-stirring art in Lefkosia galleries and Byzantine churches. She also happily increased her knowledge (and her waist measurement) by sampling endless meze, washed down with local Cypriot wine from one of the growing number of wineries in the Troödos.

Read more about Josephine at:
lonelyplanet.com/members/josephinequintero

Jessica Lee

Lemesos & the South, Larnaka & the East, Kyrenia (Girne) & the North, Famagusta (Mağusa) & the Karpas (Kırpaşa) Peninsula Jessica Lee fell head-over-heels for the rugged beauty of Cyprus' mountains the first time she visited over 10 years ago. This trip took her from the bustling resorts of Lemesos and Larnaka out into the wilderness of the Karpas and up to the craggy castle-topped peaks of the Kyrenia Range. Her favourite place on the island, though, will always be Famagusta. When there, she is usually found sitting atop the old Venetian walls, eating *dondurma* (ice cream) while reimagining the Gothic splendour. Jessica also wrote the Life Outdoors, The Cyprus Way of Life and Landscapes & Wildlife chapters, and cowrote the Accommodation chapter.

Read more about Jessica at:
lonelyplanet.com/thorntree/profiles/jessicalee1

Published by Lonely Planet Publications Pty Ltd
ABN 36 005 607 983
6th edition – Feb 2015
ISBN 978 1 74220 756 8
© Lonely Planet 2015   Photographs © as indicated 2015
10 9 8 7 6 5 4 3 2
Printed in China

Although the authors and Lonely Planet have taken all reasonable care in preparing this book, we make no warranty about the accuracy or completeness of its content and, to the maximum extent permitted, disclaim all liability arising from its use.